CRUCIAL

ISSUES

in

Education

CRUCIAL ISSUES in Education

seventh edition

Henry Ehlers

HOLT, RINEHART and WINSTON

New York   Chicago   San Francisco   Philadelphia
Montreal   Toronto   London   Sydney
Tokyo   Mexico City   Rio de Janeiro   Madrid

Library of Congress Cataloging in Publication Data

Ehlers, Henry J   comp.
    Crucial issues in education.

    Includes bibliographical references and indexes.
    1. Education — Addresses, essays, lectures. I. Title.
LB7.E45   1981   370   80-27924
ISBN 0-03-058089-7

CBS COLLEGE PUBLISHING
Holt, Rinehart and Winston
The Dryden Press
Saunders College Publishing

PREFACE

This anthology does not presume to provide clear-cut answers to the problems raised, nor to decide the "right side" or the "wrong side" of a disputed area. Rather the book presents claims and counterclaims, assertions and denials, proofs and disproofs, conflicting values and rival hypotheses. The anthology is an attempt, within the limits permitted by a single book, to provide a forum for some of the outstanding educators of our time, to allow them to speak on the important issues of our day. To gain the most from this book, the readers should strive not merely to understand the opposing points of view but also to clarify their own attitudes and beliefs.

Why should we read *both* (or several) sides of a disputed issue? The reason is clear. We are so comfortable with ourselves, and with the prejudices which make us what we are, that we are loath to read anything that might upset these cherished beliefs. As scholars, however, we must abide by the Socratic maxim, "The unexamined life is not worth human living." This may also be translated, "The unexamined belief is not worth human holding." A careful study of opposing viewpoints will generally help to clarify an issue and to replace emotional outbursts by rational understanding. The upshot is a restructuring of our original beliefs which have now become more comprehensive and more precise. The net result should be an increase in personal esteem and self-confidence because our beliefs, and the personality they reflect, are now maintained with understanding and integrity.

An open society is progressive and dynamic precisely because different individuals and organizations are permitted to defend their opposing viewpoints with passionate intensity before the court of public opinion. It is hoped that these controversial issues may some day be resolved in a manner reasonably satisfactory to all, but the process of arriving at a viable position is one of tension, not rest. As Ralph Waldo Emerson wrote in his essay *Intellect*:

> God offers to every mind its choice between truth and repose. Take what you please — you can never have both. Between them, as a pendulum, man oscillates. He in whom the love of repose predominates will accept the first creed, the first philosphy, the first political party he meets — most likely his father's. He gets rest, commodity and reputation: but he shuts the door of truth. He in whom the love of truth predominates will keep himself aloof from all moorings, and afloat. He will abstain from dogmatism, and recognize all the opposite negations between which, as walls, his being is swung. He submits to the inconveniences of suspense and imperfect opinion, but he is a candidate for truth, as the other is not, and respects the highest law of his being.

As a candidate for truth, the reader should enter into a lively mental dialogue with at least some of the hundred or so writers whose ideas appear in this anthology. In the words of the late Robert Maynard Hutchins, "Education is a kind of continuing dialogue, and a dialogue assumes, in the nature of the case, different points of view."

Not every issue in this anthology will seem of equal importance to you, the reader. Accordingly, ask yourself at the very start, "What issues are most crucial to *me*?" Peruse the book hurriedly, study the general contents carefully, and decide which topics you would like to study in greatest detail. What issues would you add to — or drop from — this anthology? If you would like to reach out in different directions, the Quotations for Further Thought and Discussion at the end of each chapter may provide helpful clues to other books and magazine articles which you should study at greater length for topics of especial interest to you. The Subject Index includes some topics that are treated in more than one chapter.

About 70 percent of the articles in this anthology have been written within the past five years, and most of the remaining 30 percent within the past fifteen years. So in a very real sense this seventh edition of *Crucial Issues in Education* is a *new* book. On the other hand, although the articles and the authors keep changing, and although the perspective of the 1980s differs from the perspective of the 1960s and 1970s, most of the *issues* remain fairly constant — for example, racial equality; the use and abuse of educational technologies, including those used in measurement; ways to deal with individual differences in a society that is becoming increasingly pluralistic; and religion and/or moral values in public education.

To better understand the book's overall structure, review the *Contents*. Observe that the book is structured into three parts: (1) Liberty, (2) Equality, and (3) Fraternity. Like the three legs of a stool, these three values stand or fall together as the basic support for democratic education.

Do not expect clear-cut answers to these problems. We live in a sea of unverified beliefs, and life is too short for any of us to check them all. In seeking a system of beliefs that seem most reasonable, we must learn neither to believe everything nor to doubt everything. But we should strive to recognize the difference betwen fact and fancy, between history and myth, betwen truth and prejudice, between science and superstition, and — most of all — between enduring values and transitory values.

The task is a difficult one. In the *Odyssey*, Homer describes the dangers Ulysses faced as he steered his ship through a narrow passageway. On the one side was the huge rock Scylla. On the other side was the whirlpool Charybdis. Scylla the rock may be taken to symbolize the danger of fixed, unchanging laws, customs, traditions, and beliefs. Charybdis stands for the equally great danger of losing oneself in a whirlpool of doubt, scepticism, cynicism, moral relativism, and intellectual chaos. In times of rapid change it is difficult to avoid one or the other of these two extremes.

There are periods in history when iconoclasts perform a necessary function. For when icons litter and cramp the place, there is little room for either thought or action. But the iconoclasts have had their day, and what we need most in the 1980s are constructive plans and programs, new ways to adapt to changing times, and dedicated teachers who face the future, not in despair but with hope and enthusiasm.

Hope for the future is inspired by the past, including the great ideals of the American and French revolutions: Liberty, Equality, and Fraternity. Indeed, at a time in history when we are all obsessed by the *new*, it may be worth noting that stimulation for writing this book came from such ancient wisdom as the following:

Say not, What is the cause that former days were better than these? — Ecclesiastes 7:10

Look to this day, for it is life. In its brief course lie all the verities and realities of your existence: the bliss of growth, the glory of action, the splendor of beauty. For yesterday is but a dream, and tomorrow is only a vision; but today, well-lived, makes every yesterday a dream of happiness and every tomorrow a vision of hope. Look well, therefore, to this day.
—from the Sanscrit

All men are equally men; but some are great men,
   and some are little men. How is this?
Those who follow that part of themselves which is great are great men.
Those who follow that part of themselves which is little are
   little men. — Mencius

In putting this book together, the joy of learning far exceeded the labor of writing. I wish to express thanks to the many authors whose words are used, and to the many others whose ideas helped formulate my own thinking, and to the publishers who granted permission to quote from their publications. I fully realize that most of the brief excerpts do not do full justice to the original book or article, not to mention the additional references and footnotes found in most of those books and articles and omitted in the excerpts.

For their many helpful suggestions and criticisms made after reading one or more of three manuscript versions, I am much indebted to my University of Minnesota (Duluth Campus) colleagues Philip C. Campbell, Dean A. Crawford, Francis A. Guldbrandsen, and Rudolph Johnson; to two teacher-administrators with the Duluth Public Schools, Mr. Larry Annett and Mr. Sydney Kundson; and to several members of the Philosophy of Education Society, especially Professors Walter Feinberg (University of Illinois, Urbana), Michael J. B. Jackson (Memorial University of Newfoundland, St. John's), David J. Void and Charles Estes (University of Alabama), and Betty Sichel (Long Island University, Greenvale, New York). For their ever-willing services in helping me keep abreast with the rapidly changing educational scene these past thirty years — and seven editions — I am especially indebted to librarians too numerous to mention by name. Finally, for her constant patience with an absent-minded husband, I thank my wife.

Henry Ehlers
Emeritus Professor of Philosophy
University of Minnesota, Duluth
January 1981

CONTENTS

Part 1.   LIBERTY

1.   Educational Freedom in an Age of Television and the Computer

2.   Freedom — and Responsibility — in the Classroom

3.   Freedom, Self-Determination, and Human Dignity

Part 2.   EQUALITY

4.   Race, Ethnicity, Pluralism

5. Measurement and Evaluation

6. Education for Work and for Leisure

Part 3.   FRATERNITY

7. Some Nonacademic Aspects of Education

8. Adapting Traditional Values to Modern Education

9. Changing Values in an Emerging World Community

PART ONE

LIBERTY

Proclaim liberty.
The hound pursues the hare; the hare pursues freedom.
A plowman on his legs is higher than a gentleman on his knees.
He who loses his freedom has nothing else to lose. — German

No bird soars too high if it soars with its own wings.
Liberty is always dangerous, but it is the safest thing we have. — Harry
   Emerson Fosdick

Eternal vigilance is the price of liberty. — Wendell Phillips

Lean liberty is better than fat slavery. — Thomas Fuller

Where the spirit of the Lord is, there is liberty. — II Corinthians 3:17

Freedom in this sick and melancholy time of ours has become not a thing
   to use but a thing to defend. . . . The test of freedom is in its *use*.
   It has no other test. — Archibald MacLeish

In America we are committed to the proposition that out of freedom come
   questioning and criticism, out of criticism comes creativity, out of creativity come some highly constructive discoveries and contributions and
   adjustments which make for progress and which give our free society, in
   competition with unfree societies, a distinct advantage in the struggle for
   survival. —William G. Carleton

EDITOR'S NOTE   In a free society, liberty is education's primary value. But liberty takes on different shades
of meaning as new technologies come into being. Chapter 1 illustrates this point with a case study: the
impact of television.
   Chapter 2 calls attention to the fact that, although "freedom" and "anarchy" are both seven-letter words,
their similarity ends there. Chapter 2 may also be viewed as an introduction to Part 2 (Equality) and, to
reduce the number of cross references, Chapter 2 might well be made the first of a group of four chapters
relating liberty and equality: Chapters 2, 4, 5, and 6.
   Even as Chapter 2 provides a brief historical introduction to Part 2, so Chapter 3 provides a psychological
and philosophical background for Part 3. Accordingly, Chapter 3 may be made the first of a group of four
chapters (3, 7, 8, and 9) showing the intimate relation between liberty and fraternity.
   In brief, liberty should not be viewed as an end in itself. To be meaningful, liberty must be conjoined with
equality and with fraternity.

Chapter 1. EDUCATIONAL FREEDOM IN AN AGE OF TELEVISION AND THE COMPUTER

1.1 Using Scientific Technology to Enhance Humanistic Values
INTRODUCTION

In primitive societies the cultural heritage was passed on from generation to generation by word of mouth, with medicine men and poets assuming the role of teachers. Thus in ancient Greece, Homer, the blind poet, moved from one Greek community to another reciting from memory what we have come to know as the *Iliad* and the *Odyssey*.

Then came parchment and scrolls — which only a few priests and scribes were able to decipher. But compared to man's unaided memory, these recorded writings — the Vedas of ancient India, the five great Classics of China, the fables, histories, dramas and philosophies of ancient Greece, the Biblical and Talmudic scrolls of the Hebrews — such writings distinguished civilized from barbaric peoples; and we should not wonder that many of them were viewed as divinely inspired.

The modern world was ushered in by another great advance in technology: the printing press; and it represents the single, most important element in the growth of universal education and of democracy. The teacher now assumed roles formerly taken by medicine men or scribes; John Locke rightly noted: "The school that has good teachers needs little else, and the school that is without good teachers will be little better with anything else."

Now in the twentieth century we enter a new epoch, centered around radio, television, and vast international communication networks based on a host of new electronic, computerized inventions. When we consider that widespread use of television has come about only since World War II, we can understand why we cannot yet understand what it is doing to us. Is TV destroying the things we hold most sacred?

EDITOR'S NOTE   In this chapter, selections 1.2 — 1.5 deal with television. Selections 1.6 and 1.7 open up some of the broader questions concerning the impact of new technologies on education. For other recent innovations (not covered in this anthology) read Christopher Evans, *The Micro Millennium*, New York: Viking, 1979.

Or it is elevating us to new levels of achievement? The answer to *both* of these questions is *"Yes!"* So perhaps the most crucial issue of all the issues facing contemporary thinkers is this: How can we employ the new *means* which science and technology have given us, without becoming so absorbed in them that we lose sight of the great humanizing values — the great *ends* — that characterize civilized peoples?

The unique, yet interrelated, qualities of science and humanism have been well expressed by John Duncan Spaeth:

> Science is organized knowledge of the law for things. Efficiency is the result of the use of this knowledge. Humanism is insight into the law for man; enrichment of life, enlargement of spirit is the fruit of this insight. Science advances by experiment; humanism builds on experience. We experiment with what happens outside ourselves; we experience what happens within. Science through controlled experiment builds the knowledge that is power; humanism through controlled experience creates the power that is character. Science as opposed to empiricism is controlled experiment; humanism as opposed to temperamentalism is controlled experience. Humanism builds up personality by enriching it with the experience of the past. This enrichment of personality by vicarious experience is culture.
>
> The conflict between the so-called cultural and the scientific type of higher education cuts to the very core of human nature, because man belongs to two worlds — the world of things and the world of experience, the world of fact and the world of faith, the world of matter and the world of mind, the world of sense and the world of spirit. The primary business of education is the unification of the two worlds in each individual.[1]

[1]John Duncan Spaeth, "Science and Humanism in University Education," an address delivered at the 69th Commencement of Washington University, June 10, 1930, St. Louis, Mo.: Washington University Studies, m.s., 1950. By permission. Mr. Spaeth was Murray Professor of English Literature at Princeton University and, from 1956 to 1958, served as president of the University of Kansas City.

1.2 Two Competing Learning Systems: The Schools and TV
NEIL POSTMAN

The first point to be made about television and school is to observe that each of them is a curriculum. . . . [We may] define a curriculum as a specially constructed information system whose purpose, *in its totality*, is to influence, teach, train, or cultivate the mind and character of our youth. By this definition, television and school not only *have* curricula but *are* curricula; that is, they are total learning systems. Each has a special way of organizing time and space; their messages are encoded in special forms and moved at different rates of speed; each has its special way of defining knowledge, its special assumptions about the learning process, and its own special requirements concerning how one must attend to what is happening. Moreover, each has a

Excerpts from Neil Postman, "The First Curriculum: Comparing School and Television," *Phi Delta Kappan* 61: 163-168, November 1979. This *Phi Delta Kappan* article, in turn, was taken from *Teaching as a Conserving Activity*, by Neil Postman, Copyright © 1979 by Neil Postman. Used by permission of Delacorte Press, *Phi Delta Kappan*, and the author. All rights reserved.

Neil Postman is Professor of Education, New York University.

Read also "Television Entertainment: Taking It Seriously," by George Comstock and others, *Character* 1: 1-8f., October—November 1980.

characteristic subject matter, ambience, and style, all of which reflect the unique context within which one experiences what is going on. And, though their effects are strikingly different, each has as its purpose the control of our young. Viewed in this way, television is not only a curriculum but constitutes the major educational enterprise now being undertaken in the United States. That is why I call it the First Curriculum. School is the second.

The first task of a curriculum is to engage the attention of its students for a certain period of time. Thus there are two questions to be addressed: How much time? How to get their attention? If we assume a child will go to school for 13 years — say, starting in kindergarten and ending with high school — a typical American child will be in the presence of a school curriculum 2,340 days, or about 11,500 hours. There are only two activities that occupy more of a youngster's time during those years: sleeping and attending to television.

Studies of TV viewing are far from definitive, but a fair estimate is that from ages 5 to 18 an American child watches TV for approximately 15,000 hours. That is 30% more time than he is engaged at school, a very significant difference. If we add to the 15,000 hours of TV viewing the time occupied by radio and record listening, as well as movie-going, we come up with a figure very close to 20,000 hours of exposure to an electronic media curriculum — almost double the amount of time spent in school.

And so the television curriculum is first in the time given to it by students, and it is also first in their hearts, primarily because of the manner in which the two curricula command attention. Both the school and the TV curricula use compulsion: the school directly through legal means, television indirectly through psychological means. If we ask what the roots of these different types of compulsions are, we arrive at some interesting answers. For instance, the school curriculum includes a content or subject matter selected, in principle, for its significant cultural or intellectual value. But its content may or may not be of interest to the student — in fact, traditionally is not — thus requiring legal force to compel attendance to it. . . .

The television curriculum is based on an entirely different principle of compulsion. Whereas the school curriculum compels attention through law and even occupational necessity, the TV curriculum requires no such external controls. *Television is an attention-centered curriculum.* In one sense it has no goal other than keeping the attention of its students. Unlike the school, which selects its subject matter first and then tries to devise methods to attract interest in it, television first selects ways to attract interest and allows content to be shaped accordingly. This is not to say that the content of the school curriculum is alway significant or that the content of television is always trival; only that, in the first instance, attention is subservient to content, and, in the second, content is wholly subservient to attention.

In the school curriculum, if the student repeatedly does not pay attention, the teacher may remove him from class. In the TV curriculum, if the student repeatedly does not pay attention, the teacher is removed from class.

This exceedingly important fact means that the television curriculum need not concern itself with penalties. Most children, at least beyond a certain age, attend school largely to avoid the penalties for not doing so, whether the source be their parents, the law, or the future. School is, to a considerable extent, a penalty-laden curriculum. Not television. There is no penalty for not attending to one's TV lessons and none is needed. This fact surrounds the experience of television attendance with a benign psychological ambience that the school can never achieve.

In addition, the information in each curriculum is codified in different fashions.

School is essentially language-centered. All language is a digital form of information. (By digital, I mean that meanings are arbitrary, abstract, and segmented. Analogic forms of information, on the other hand — photographs, for instance — have an intrinsic relationship to what they signify and are not decomposable into small units of meaning.) In addition to its being arbitrary, abstract, and segmented, language has several other characteristics that distinguish it from analogues, two of which are especially important. The first is that words do not call to mind specific referents. A word does not refer to a specific thing so much as it refers to a category of things: that is, words are concepts. When I say or write the word *man*, you do not know which man. I have brought to your mind a concept of a man, a composite of possibilities. To be sure, I could use more words to give you a more specific idea. But it is not possible, through language, to achieve a level of specificity that would make it unnecessary for you to have an *idea* about the words. Descriptive words such as the adjectives in "a tall, dark, handsome man" merely limit the concept of "man" by introducing additional concepts. As long as words are being used, we are always at a considerable remove from reality, for words are not representations of reality. They are representations of ideas about reality.

That is why (and this is the second point) all language is paraphrasable. By using different words, one can always approximate what someone else has said. If this were not so, there could be no such thing as translation. Translation can occur because an idea, unlike a picture, can be represented in various ways. Words have synonyms. Pictures do not. Analogic forms, such as pictures, are not ideas; nor are they paraphrasable. A picture must be experienced to be experienced. This is what people mean when they say, "You have to see it," or "You should have been there." They mean that the symbolic event must be directly apprehended in the form in which it exists. There is no translation of it. There is no idea of it. If you attempt to use a different form to convey the meaning, you will change the meaning. Ten thousand words or a million will not translate into the picture. Words are of a different order of abstraction, requiring an entirely different mode of intellectual activity.

The image — concrete, unique, nonparaphrasable — versus the word — abstract, conceptual, translatable. This is one of the several conflicts between TV and school, and perhaps the most important. Obviously, the curriculum of television is essentially imagistic, that is, picture-centered. Its teaching style is therefore almost wholly narrative. To put it simply, the content of the TV curriculum consists of picture stories. The school curriculum, on the other hand, tends to be word- or concept-centered, and its teaching style is exposition. The school curriculum — at least in its content — consists of abstract propositions: linguistic statements of which we may say they are true or false, verifiable or not, logical or confused.

This is another way of saying that the TV curriculum does its work in analogic symbols that appeal directly to emotional and largely unreflective response, while the school curriculum, relying heavily on digital symbolism, requires sophisticated cognitive processing. It is not true, as so many have insisted, that watching TV is a passive experience. Anyone who has observed children watching television will know how foolish that statement is. In watching TV, children have their emotions fully engaged. It is their capacity for abstraction that is quiescent. In school the situation is apt to be reversed: Children are required, in principle, to understand and consider what is *said*, expected to be able to paraphrase, translate, and reformulate what is said, which is why tests are so easy to give in school. In experiencing TV you are required to *feel* what is *seen*, which is why there can be no paraphrase and no meaningful test.

This difference between symbols that demand conceptualization and reflection and symbols that evoke feeling has many implications, one of the most important being that the content of the TV curriculum is irrefutable. You can dislike it but you cannot disagree with it. There is no way to refute Donny and Marie, or an Ajax commercial . . . Propositions are true or false; pictures are not.

I am not ridiculing television but merely describing an important bias of the form of the medium. Television is not to be faulted because it consists of pictures. To do so would be like faulting an English sentence for having a subject and predicate. Nor can the television curriculum be faulted for its moralistic and value-laden bias. That is its nature. Narratives of any kind — in this case, picture stories — are inevitably aphoristic and metaphorical. Exposition, on the other hand, works through definition, assertion, explication, and analysis — an ensemble which by contrast with the form of narration is relatively value-neutral. . . .

It comes down to this: Because the school curriculum's primary form of information is language, its style of teaching is expository. And because its style of teaching is expository, it concerns itself with facts and arguments. And because of that, it cannot help (even when its teaching is done badly) promoting concepts of knowledge and ways of knowing that stress the importance of detachment, objectivity, analysis, and criticism. In a sentence, the school curriculum is both rationalistic and secular in its outlook.

Television is both aesthetic and (at least) quasi-religious. Because its primary form of information is the image, its style of teaching is narration. And because of that, it is concerned with showing concrete people and situations toward which one responds by either accepting or rejecting them on emotional grounds. Television teaches you to know through what you see and feel. Its epistemology begins and largely ends in the viscera.

In the TV curriculum, there is no such thing as "falling behind." All lessons are on the same plane. There is nothing to be retarded and nothing to be developed.

This fact is one of the sources of TV's enormous capacity to satisfy. Within the TV curriculum there is no deferred gratification. Perhaps the most powerful bias of television is its emphasis on immediate gratification, for television has no need to put its learners on "hold" with a view toward later intellectual or emotional satisfaction. TV does not require you to remember or anticipate anything. In fact, the TV curriculum has achieved, in an unexpected and upside-down way, what so many educators have always hoped for: learning for its own sake. Whereas the school curriculum promises future intellectual rewards for learning its lessons, the TV curriculum promises no rewards whatsoever. *Attending to it is its own reward.* In a nonhierarchical, analogic information system based on immediate emotional response, there is no future, or sense of continuity, or need for preparation. The pleasure of total comprehension and involvement is immediately accessible.

This dimension of immediacy is reinforced in many ways on television, particularly in the length of its lessons. The learning modules of the TV curriculum are extremely short and compact: Commercials run anywhere from 10 to 60 seconds; what are called "programs" run from 30 to 60 minutes but are always sequenced in eight- to 10-minute modules.

The commercials are an especially important component of the TV curriculum because between the ages of 5 and 18 a youngster will see approximately 675,000 commercials, at the rate of about 1,000 per week. This makes the television commercial the most voluminous information source in the education of youth. And this means that we can assume that our youth are being conditioned to intense concentration for short periods of time and deconditioned, so to speak, to sustained concentration.

Moreover (and this is important), television commercials, which are subject to easy ridicule by those who know little about information environments, are almost never about anything trivial, especially from the point of view of youth. Mouthwash commercials are not about bad breath. They are about the need for social acceptance and, frequently, about the need to be sexually attractive. Beer commercials are almost always about the need to share the values of a peer group. An automobile commerical may be about one's need for autonomy or social status, a toilet paper commercial about one's fear of nature.

Television commercials are about products only in the sense that the story of Jonah is about the anatomy of whales. To miss this point is to miss much of what the television curriculum sets out to do, for, especially in commercials, it teaches, by parable, that serious human worries are resolvable through relatively simple means and that, therefore, the resolution of anything problematic is never far away. The lesson is almost the exact opposite of what schools are accustomed to assume about the nature and resolution of human problems.

In fact, the TV curriculum contradicts in another, hardly subtle way what traditional schools have always assumed. It is an axiomatic part of scholarship that all things have consequences and that our history is never irrelevant to our present or future. Even our traditional theology teaches that. We may overcome or reproach our history but we cannot deny its existence. But TV's imagistic, present-oriented, time-compressed curriculum is nonsequential: that is, discontinuous. Hardly anything on television, however high its quality, has anything to do with anything else on television.

There is an almost overwhelming sense of incoherence to the TV curriculum. A school curriculum, even one that has not been well thought out, always tries to proceed from some organizing principle. It may be based on a hierarchy of concepts, as in mathematics. Or it may move chronologically from one point to another, as in history. Or it may be held together by some theme, as in literature. In television, however, there is no organizing principle. There is no chronology, or theme, or logical sequence. The world to which television is the window is presented as fragmented, unorganizable, without structure of any kind. . . .

Perhaps the most coherent content of the entire TV curriculum is a five-day weather forecast in which one is shown what a rainstorm in Texas on Monday has to do with a snowstorm in New York on Friday. The rest of the content consists of discrete and isolated events, images, and stories that have no implications very far beyond themselves and that certainly have no continuity. Whereas the content of school may be likened at least in principle to a play in which there is a beginning, middle, and end, the content of TV is like a vaudeville show in which there are only acts. They are replaceable and reversible, having no relationship to each other. But it is a vaudeville show without an end, for the TV curriculum runs almost continuously. You are not excused from it for summer vacations, illness, weekends, or Christmas holiday. And in some places it operates around the clock. Thus it is able to integrate itself into the student's life in a way that the school curriculum can never approach. . . .

Two other characteristics of the TV curriculum bear mentioning because they are in sharp contrast with the school curriculum. They are also in sharp contrast with each other, which makes them especially interesting. The first is that the TV curriculum is largely authoritarian; that is, its information moves in one direction. There is no way that television students can modify or control the speed, pace, form, quantity, content, or anything else of their lessons. No questions may be addressed to their instructor. No complaint may be lodged. No special arrangements can be requested. Even the "elective" nature of the TV curriculum, alluded to before, does not mitigate the absence of any feedback possiblities. To be sure, a student can turn off a lesson —let us say, "Happy Days" — and turn to another more to his liking — say, "Baretta" —but he remains entirely impotent to affect either the structure or the content of the lesson.

School, of course, is not famous for its democratic structure. But even the harshest school critic will concede that the classroom is by no means a unidirectional system. If nothing else, misbehavior itself is a form of feedback, and no teacher can be indifferent to it. But except in the rarest instances (and I have never seen one), a teacher will permit questions, will ask for and even demand responses, will repeat and review according to need, will encourage students to exert influence on their lessons. Even when a teacher is asking "what-am-I-thinking" types of questions, the point is to produce *output* from students.

Output is not possible in the TV curriculum, at least not in the sense I mean it here. The TV curriculum provides only input, and this, incidentally, may have something to do with the increase in student misbehavior in school. When people are denied access to routes of response in one information system, they will frequently be outrageously expressive when they find themselves in a situation where response is both possible and permissible. The school curriculum, then, for all of its legendary demands for obedience and passivity, is far less authoritarian than the TV curriculum. It has, at least, an audience, meaning people who are capable of acting on the environment. TV, in this sense, has no audience.

At the same time, while the school curriculum tries to distribute knowledge in an orderly and authoritative way, the TV curriculum continuously undermines authority. Television is both authoritarian and contemptuous of authority at the same time.

As Harold Innis points out, every new medium has the capability of breaking up "knowledge monopolies." The phonetic alphabet broke the knowledge monopoly of the priests whose secrets were codified in complex ideographs. The printing press broke the knowledge monopoly of those few writers and readers who controlled the manuscript culture. Television attacks the monopoly of the printed word.

In fact, by distributing information, albeit in pictures, to everyone in the culture simultaneously, TV threatens all systems that have a hierarchical structure. A hierarchy is a drama played by superiors, inferiors, and equals. Information is the means by which we assign people their role in the drama and, indeed, justify that role. In principle, those at the top have more information and more access to information than those at the bottom. That is essentially why they are at the top and the others at the bottom. Moreover, every hierarchy has a certain pattern of distributing information. For example, you cannot get into medical school until you have been to college, and to college until you have been to high school. This is what is called "prerequisites," to which I alluded earlier. The concept of a prerequisite is based on the metaphor of constructing a building. The earliest information you get will provide the foundation. Then, in an orderly, sequential way, you will, by acquiring a measured and predetermined amount of information, move toward the top floor. This is an entirely rational way of proceeding — it is certainly the way of the school — except when there is a television antenna on the roof.

Television is the enemy of foundations and prerequisites, and is therefore hostile to the basis of traditional authority. TV turns hierarchies on their sides. By conveying information in nonhierarchical distribution patterns, it creates a deeply felt impression that there is no rational reason for tops and bottoms, or for secrets, or for knowledge monopolies. In such a situation, everyone goes into business for himself. Or believes that he ought to. We move toward a culture of political, spiritual, and social entrepreneurs. It could be very dangerous, especially when the means by which traditional authority is undermined is, itself, exceedingly authoritarian.

Now, you may have the impression that I strongly disapprove of the TV curriculum. But this is not the case, and it is also beside the point. TV will not go away. In all likelihood, it will continue to increase its influence and prestige in our information environment. It is pointless to spend time or energy deploring television, or even making proposals to "improve" it. Of course, the seriousness, maturity, and general quality of the content of its programs certainly can be improved. But the characteristics I am talking about are deeply embedded in the structure of television. They are an integral part of the *environment* that television creates. From this point of view, television cannot be improved. As I have described it, the TV curriculum has the following characteristics. It is:

- attention-centered
- nonpunitive
- affect-centered
- present-centered
- image-centered
- narration-centered
- moralistic
- nonanalytical
- nonhierarchical
- authoritarian
- contemptuous of authority
- continuous in time
- isolating in space
- discontinuous in content
- immediately and intrinsically gratifying

No amount of academic complaints or "responsible" calls for TV reform can change any of the above. TV is not a school, or a book, or any curriculum other than itself. It does what its structure makes it do, and it teaches as it must. The real pragmatic issue is not TV but its relationship to other systematic teachings in the information environment. The question is, To what extent can the biases of TV be balanced by the biases of other information systems, particularly the school? But before we get to that, we must first consider, in some careful way, what are likely to be the consequences of an unchallenged television education. What will its biases lead to? Without considering that, we cannot know what sorts of defenses to prepare.

1.3 Educational Television: Tapping the Potential
EDITORIAL ESSAY

The Children's Television Workshop (CTW) was created about twelve years ago to explore new ways of using television to help preschool children, particularly those from the lower-income groups, to gain specific skills and concepts that would help them to succeed in school when they entered kindergarten or first grade. The result was "Sesame Street," which went on the air in 1969.

With grants from the Carnegie Corporation, the Ford Foundation, and the United States Office of Education, "Sesame Street" was designed to combine entertainment with education. Without the entertainment feature, the program could not cope with its commercial competitors. Without the educational aspect, its basic purpose would not be met. Hence, although these programs use Big Bird and his friends, the Muppets, animated cartoons, music, actors, and other attention-holding features, the central purpose is to teach such basics as letters and numbers.

Although this essay was not written by Joan Ganz Cooney, it credits her as the founder of the Children's Television Workshop and the guiding spirit behind "Sesame Street," "The Electric Company," and (since January 1980) "3-2-1 Contact."

The concluding portion dealing with "3-2-1 Contact" is from "Teaching the Scientific ABCs," *Time* 115: 79, January 21, 1980. Reprinted by permission from *Time*, The Weekly Newsmagazine, Copyright Time Inc. 1980.

In reading Chapter 1, it is well to remember that with the exception of Marconi's invention of wireless telegraphy in 1896, almost everything related to radio, television, computers, and space travel are innovations of the twentieth century, many of them since 1950. Many of these new developments in rockets, satellites, guided missiles, and computers were used by the military, and were classified. So we can hardly blame our schools for not keeping abreast of the new science and technology.

But commercial interests could not be held in check, and this in itself explains why radio and television have been largely directed toward financial profit from entertainment, rather than toward the dissemination of knowledge. It was only in the 1970s that major steps were taken to employ radio, television, and the stored information of computers for educational use.

So the situation today is this: There is a yawning gap between the tens of millions of us who sit in front of boob tubes and the few thousand who have genuine understanding of these new technologies. The next time you use a telephone, consider the fact that the air waves (which carry the sound of our voices) are transformed into electrical impulses (which are then transmitted by wire or by air to distant places); and then, at the other end of the telephone, these electrical impulses are, within a fraction of a second, transformed back into sound waves. In America today, only about one college graduate in ten, and perhaps one high school graduate in a hundred, has even an elementary understanding of the Fourier analysis, which makes such transformations possible.

This selection calls attention to one small step recently taken to help rectify this imbalance.

The effectiveness of carefully planned balance of content, appeal, and motivation is attested by the fact that an estimated eight million American youngsters are now watching "Sesame Street"; and millions of other children also watch it in a dozen foreign nations.

A sequel to "Sesame Street" is "The Electric Company," which is designed not only for home use but also for classroom use in grades one to five. "The Electric Company" has been seen in more American classrooms than any program in the medium. Today, nearly three million children in grades one to six watch "The Electric Company." Many teachers report that gains are being made in the the reading skills of children who watch the show, and, although it is too early to know for sure, their reports are fairly well confirmed by independent impact studies.

3-2-1 Contact

How do you pet a bee?
Very care-ful-ly.

That sort of whimsical patter is a specialty of the Children's Television Workshop [which on January 21, 1980,] began applying its zingy production style to a more complex and elusive subject: science. The series of 30-min. shows, with the space-age title "3-2-1 Contact," provides glimpses of everything from leaping lizards and killer whales to computers that talk and roller coasters that whip their riders upside down.

Big Bird, Ernie and other "Sesame Street" favorites are gone from CTW's newest undertaking, which aims at a somewhat older and presumably savvier audience, ages eight to twelve. The show's hosts are three young people, Lisa, Marc, and Trini, who are forever leaving their Tinkertoy clubhouse for short, filmed sorties to labs, beaches and races — a total of 100 trips in 65 shows. At the start of each episode, Marc announces, "Science is fun," and then tries to prove it. Cartoons are shown to explain how things work, and celebrity guests occasionally drop by to take part in the action: Tennis Pro Arthur Ashe, for example, hits a serve timed by radar, and Actor Gene Wilder illustrates communication by talking to a dog. The episodes end with a minimystery film starring three young detectives, known as the Bloodhound Gang, who reason their way to the solution of a crime.

CTW President Joan Ganz Cooney explains that her team wants "to build an appetite for science, not force feed it." Elementary-school teachers, responding to CTW's announcement of the show, have requested 100,000 copies of a free classroom guide. Though the show will generally be aired after school, the Friday program, which reviews the week's material, will also be broadcast during morning hours for classroom use.

"3-2-1 Contact" was developed at a cost of $11.7 million, using grants from the U.S. Office of Education and National Science Foundation, as well as the Corporation for Public Broadcasting and the United Technologies Corp. The sponsors hope that the show can help close a gap in science education in the early grades. Says CTW Research Director Milton Chen: "In surveys of science achievement, you see a pattern of declining interest in science around junior high. We're trying to intervene earlier to try to encourage kids to stay tuned in to science." Another goal: stimulating interest in scientific careers among minorities, who now make up only 4.4% of scientists and engineers, and among women, who constitute just 9.7% of the total. Host Marc is a young black; Trini, one of his two girl companions, occasionally speaks Spanish on the show.

For each week of the 13-week series, the shows stick to a general theme, such as hot and cold, near and far, big and little. "These are dimensions that eight- to twelve-year-olds use themselves in organizing their own experience," says Chen. For example, to demonstrate that sound consists of vibrations, Marc and Lisa play with a toy telephone made by stretching a string between two tin cans. Then the scene shifts to two cartoon characters who joke about dialing wrong numbers. To introduce gravity, "3-2-1 Contact" skips the traditional account of Sir Isaac Newton and the falling apple and shows a Hollywood stunt man plummeting from a four-story building; sensibly, Marc refuses to follow him.

CTW surveyed 10,000 youngsters to help develop the series. The surveys found that students were quick to grasp pictures, but yawned at lengthy explanations. "3-2-1 Contact" thus keeps the film rolling and dialogue fast paced. The inevitable result: few detailed discussions of scientific theories or principles. National Frisbee Champion Krae Van Sickle, for instance, likens the spinning disc to a gyroscope, but fails to explain what a gyroscope is or how it works. The show rushes on to a glider sailing through the Colorado skies. It is all pleasant viewing, but does it really teach science? Probably not, in any systematic sense, as CTW admits. Says Research Director Chen: "This is a show focused on attitudes, on encouraging positive feelings toward science." Adds Joan Duea, past president of the Council for Elementary Science International: "The show doesn't replace teaching. The teacher still has a job to do."

1.4   The TV Cartoonists Who Own Saturday Morning
JOHN MARIANI

One hour out of every 24, a Hanna-Barbera cartoon entertains some segment of the world's population, capturing an international audience Walt Disney never even dreamed of. Yogi Bear, Fred Flintstone, Huckleberry Hound, and Scooby-Doo are embraced by 500 million people in 80 countries. Hanna-Barbera's parent company, Taft Broadcasting Company, manages the largest merchandising operation of its kind in the world, with more than 1,500 licensed manufacturers turning out some 4,500 different products based on Hanna-Barbera characters, including everything from Fred Flintstone window shades to Banana Splits bubble bath.

Were you to turn on the tube on a Saturday morning this winter, you would be

John Mariani is a free-lance writer and frequent contributor to the *Saturday Review*.

hard put to escape the "Funtastic World of Hanna-Barbera," created by the studio that this season has sold the networks seven hours of children's programming over a four-and-a-half-hour schedule. Hanna-Barbera cartoons run the gamut of children's fare, from lovable dopey animal characters like Scooby-Doo and his "rascal side-kick" Scrappy-Doo to classic epic heroes like Superman and Wonder Woman. There are black characters (the Super Globetrotters), and monster characters (Godzilla), and supernatural characters aided by liberated females (Casper and the Angels). Most of these shows are interrupted by drop-in safety tips and educational admonishments, and for those children who are too dumb to know when to respond to a joke, there are laugh tracks. The CBS network bought Hanna-Barbera's *The Popeye Hour*, while ABC has *The World's Greatest Superfriends* and *Scooby and Scooby-Do*. NBC is filling out its entire 7:30 to noon slot with Hanna-Barberisms: *Casper and the Angels, Fred and Barney Meet the Thing, The Super Globetrotters, The New Shmoo, Godzilla, Johnny Quest*, and *The Jetsons*.

Every Saturday, Bill Hanna and Joe Barbera babysit for an audience of 25 million American children, a situation some would call a stranglehold. As babysitters Hanna and Barbera would claim a benign influence on the children who sit mesmerized by their cartoons from dawn to noon, but the total command Hanna-Barbera has over the networks at those impressionable hours troubles the people who see themselves as guardians of the children during that four-and-a-half hour period. Peggy Charren, president of Action for Children's Television (ACT), argues, "Our organization has always been against censorship of any kind and for all kinds of diversity in children's programming. But if you want diversity you don't hire Hanna-Barbera to produce 77 percent of your children's schedule, as NBC has done. The networks have all that money and they could be making the finest children's programs in the world, yet they come up with a schedule that in its entirety — not in any individual show — is an insult to children."

Joe Barbera, who is generally credited with being the creative member of the Hanna-Barbera team, responds to such citizens' group criticism by saying, "The networks themselves have killed all the creativity in Saturday morning animation. They won't make a decision on the fall schedule until late in the spring, and then they send down directives that force us to alter the characters we've created, even down to their voices. Bill Hanna and I were the first to do Tom and Jerry back at MGM in the Forties — we won seven Academy Awards for those cartoons. Now we're told those Tom and Jerry shorts are too violent, even though in syndication on local channels they've scored very high ratings. We can't do slapstick anymore. Every year the network tells us what we can and can't do. This year Popeye can't hit Bluto with his fist. Characters may not use guns, but they may use lasers. It's crazy — you simply can't plan a character that way. We haven't had real violence in our cartoons for a decade, but the networks still find something to complain about." . . .

The storm over the effects of TV violence on children has raged for more than a decade ("Ever since Bobby Kennedy was shot," says Barbera), but none of the numerous studies on the subject has come up with anything approaching hard evidence against it, especially with regard to animated cartoons . . . [The reason:] the statistical tally of violent acts made no distinction between Fred Flintstone tripping over a dinosaur bone and Superman blowing up an alien spaceship. . . .

[It was in the 1930s at the Walt Disney Studios that animation was] burgeoning into a remarkable art form at a thousand drawings per minute. Disney's hallmarks were pefection and experimentation. The studio drew the finest talent and most dedicated animators in the world and plowed its profits back into new animation techniques. Joe Barbera never even got an interview, but found work at Metro-Goldwyn-Mayer, where he met Bill Hanna, an engineer from New Mexico, in 1937. At MGM the two animators developed the *Tom and Jerry* cartoon series that usually played with the studio's double-feature programs at a time when the big studios owned the theaters.

The *Tom and Jerry* cartoons were based on the theme of cat meets mouse, cat chases mouse, cat gets blown to smithereens. But the animation was excellent, the characters were well delineated, and the slapstick was inventive, if sometimes a bit grizzly, as when the cat was sliced into salami sections after hitting a wire fence. No matter. He was back together in the next scene, ready to be hit by a truck. . . .

[By the early 1950s, using] the newly developed technique of "limited animation" —(invented by United Productions of America, a cartoon factory) in which only certain simplified movements are animated, thereby giving the characters a more stilted, less lifelike action — Hanna and Barbera could cut down the number of drawings shot per minute from 1,000 to about 300 or less. By 1959 Disney animator Ub Iwerks had also developed a more practical method of turning out cartoons: a Xerox process for copying animators' original drawings onto transparencies called "cels." Although this technique compromised the line and modeling of the figures, it eliminated a costly, laborious, separate inking process.

These two techniques allowed Hanna and Barbera to produce animated television series on a weekly basis, first for children's shows, then for prime-time television. "Our first prime-time series, *The Flintstones*," says Barbera, "was about a cave man, his family, and friends. We had all this clever stuff with dinosaurs and everyday objects made out of stone, and it wasn't violent either. . . . The show was a smash. It won an Emmy."

The Flintstones was innovative insofar as the characters were human beings rather than animals; in fact, they were modeled on the Jackie Gleason — Art Carney series, *The Honeymooners* (which had gone off the air in 1957), and plots involved Fred Flintstone's struggle to make ends meet in the Stone Age town of Bedrock. What started out as an adult show was certainly enjoyed by children, and subsequently *The Flintstones* was tailored for Saturday morning, where it now appears on NBC. . . .

[Other new series were] based on Laurel and Hardy, *The Three Musketeers*, and *Moby Dick*. The studio now also produces live-action shows and movie features, including the Emmy Award-winning *The Gathering*, which starred Maureen Stapleton and Edward Asner. Currently in production, are *Jesus at XVI*, about Christ as an adolescent, and, the project dearest to Hanna-Barbera's heart, *Heidi's Song* — a full-length animated feature that will depend on animation techniques more reminiscent of the Golden Age of cartoons than of the dreary Saturday mornings of children's programming.

"We're so proud of *Heidi's Song*," says Barbera from behind his sunglasses. "We're really spending our own money on this one — $8 million — to make it truly special and wondrous. The animation will be the finest we can make, sometimes better than the old Disney days because we know so much more about special effects now. It's the kind of project I'd like to do more of, but the economics are just too rough." . . .

"Y'know," [said Joe Barbera's partner, Harry Lowe,] "Disney spends $8 million on an animated feature and takes two-and-a-half years to make it. That's 90 minutes of animation. For the Saturday morning cartoons Hanna-Barbera turns out *seven* hours of animation every single week. You can't get real quality. But, if the networks said to us, 'Make good cartoons,' we would. We can do it; it just takes time and money. That's why we're all excited about *Heidi's Song*, which won't be ready until 1981. And Disney's making *The Black Hole* — an outer space film combining live action with animation. These things will be beautiful to see" . . .

We walked through the hallways flanked by small offices full of idea men, story men, master animators, producers, and directors. Then into the cavernous rooms full of background artists, layout artists, inkers, painters, paint checkers, camera operators, Xerox operators, film editors, sound scorers, music scorers and arrangers, dubbing engineers, special-effects people, and then on and on through the labyrinth. . . .

Later on, I was encouraged to learn that the truly harmful aspect of cartoons — their mass, and unimaginative, production — is perhaps not so bad as I'd thought. Despite Hanna-Barbera's domination of the Saturday morning schedule, despite their ability to churn out seven hours of animation a week, despite all the wringing of hands over citizens' group pressure, the most popular of all the Saturday morning cartoons is still *The Bugs Bunny — Road Runner Hour* — for reasons, I suspect, that have little to do with cannons, pistols, dynamite, and other instruments of animated destruction. Those characters never condescend to children; indeed, Bugs Bunny and Daffy Duck are closer to the Marx Brothers than to Captain Kangaroo.

Children realize at once that Bugs, Daffy, and Wile E. Coyote are playing out their own fantasies of revenge, aggression, and fair play, as opposed to the current crop of cartoons wherein characters like Casper the Friendly Ghost and Scooby-Doo are reflections of all the imbecilic human characters on prime-time situation comedies. The characters on *The Bugs Bunny — Road Runner Hour* series are sophisticated, but, beyond that, the drawing, the backgrounds, the way a character lifts his foot and casts a shadow still have the ability to rivet the attention of the child and adult because of the stretch and elasticity invested in the flesh of wisecracking rabbits, daffy ducks, and lisping cats.

Joe Barbera remembers how he used to draw Tom and Jerry back at MGM. "The cat would rig up an anvil over the mouse," he says, "and somehow the cat would get in the way and he'd get hit with the anvil — a 10,000-pound anvil! — and the mouse would peel him off the ground, and you'd hear it like a Band-Aid, right? But the cat was in perfect condition in the next sequence. We can't do that stuff anymore. They tell me it's not good for kids to see. I don't understand what they're talking about!"

It occurred to me that the men who *own* Saturday morning have become too successful at what they once loved best — drawing characters who seem not only lifelike but true to life's complications — and now there's little heart left in them or the characters they create. Which is the definition of television itself: success at the expense of the ineffable quality of true fantasy. For true fantasy, especially in animated terms, gives us the world as it should be, a place where witches get thrown in ovens, and cats, just scraped off the sidewalk, bounce back to rounded life again and again and again.

1.5 "The Ascent of Humanity": A Coherent Curriculum
NEIL POSTMAN

[As] I view it, the teachings of the media are hostile to language and language development, hostile to vigorous intellectual activity, hostile to both science and history, hostile to social order, and hostile in a general way to conceptualization. The teachings of the media stress instancy, not constancy; discontinuity, not coherence; immediate, not deferred, gratification; and emotional, not analytical, response. The thermostatic function of education would suggest that the schooling of our youth at all levels must provide the opposite of, or at least an alternative to, these biases. If the schools do not do it, there is no institution in the culture that will.

COHERENT CURRICULUM NEEDED

From this perspective, perhaps the most important contribution we can make to the education of our youth is to provide them with a sense of coherence in their studies. At present, the typical high school or college curriculum reflects the fragmentation one finds in television's weekly schedule. Each subject, like each program, has nothing to do with any other. We must say this for television, however; it offers what it does in the hope of winning the student's attention. Its major theme is psychological gratification of the viewer. Schools, on the other hand, offer what they do either because they have always done so, or because the colleges or professional schools require it. There is no longer any principle that unifies the school program and furnishes it with meaning, unless it is simply that education is to provide jobs, which is hardly a moral or intellectual theme.

While one obviously treads on shaky ground in suggesting a plausible theme, with all due apprehension I would propose as a possibility the theme that animates Jacob Bronowski's *The Ascent of Man*. This book and its philosophy are filled with optimism and suffused with the transcendent belief that humanity's destiny is the discovery of knowledge. Moreover, although Bronowski's emphasis is on science, he finds ample warrant to include the arts and humanities as part of the quest to gain an understanding of nature and of our place in it. Thus, to chart the ascent of humanity, we would

Brief excerpt from Neil Postman, " 'The Ascent of Humanity': A Coherent Curriculum," *Educational Leadership* 37: 300-303, January 1980. Reprinted with permission of the Association for Supervision and Curriculum Development and Neil Postman. Copyright © 1980 by the Association for Supervision and Curriculum Development. All rights reserved.
This selection may be viewed as a continuation of Selection 1.2.

join art and science, but we would also join the past and present, for the ascent of humanity is above all a continuous story.

"THE ASCENT OF HUMANITY" AS CURRICULUM

The virtues of adopting the ascent of humanity as a scaffolding on which to build a school curriculum are many and various. For one thing, it does not require that we invent new subjects or discard old ones. The structure of the curriculum that presently exists in most schools is entirely usable. For another, it provides students with a point of view from which to understand the meaning of subjects. For each subject can be seen as a battleground of sorts, an area in which a fierce intellectual struggle has taken place and continues to take place. Each idea within a subject marks the place where someone fell and where someone rose. From this point of view, the curriculum may be seen as a celebration of human intelligence and creativity, not a meaningless collection of academic requirements.

But best of all, the theme of the ascent of humanity provides us with a nontechnical, noncommercial definition of education. It is a definition drawn from an honorable humanistic tradition, and it reflects a concept of the purposes of academic life that goes counter to the biases of the media. I am referring to the idea that to become educated means to become aware of the origins and growth of knowledge and knowledge systems; to be familiar with the intellectual and creative processes by which the best that has been thought and said has been produced; and to learn how to participate, even if as a listener, in what Robert Maynard Hutchins once called The Great Conversation.

You'll note that such a definition of education is not student-centered; it is not training-centered; it is not skill-centered; it is not even problem-centered. It is idea-centered and coherence-centered. It is also other-worldly, in the sense that it does not assume that what one learns in school must be directly and urgently related to a problem of today. In other words, this is a definition of education that stresses history, the scientific mode of thinking, the disciplined use of language, a wide-ranging knowledge of the arts and religion, and the continuity of human enterprise.

To give this conception of education somewhat more specificity, let me mention briefly five areas of inquiry on which a curriculum centered on the ascent of humanity would build.

1. *History.* History is not merely one subject among many that may be taught in school. Every subject has a history. To teach what we know today without also teaching what we once knew, or thought we knew, is to reduce knowledge to a mere consumer product. I would recommend, therefore, that every subject be taught as history. In this way our students can begin to understand, as they presently do not, that knowledge is not a fixed thing but a stage in human development, with a past and a future.

If every subject were taught with a historical dimension, the history teacher would be free to teach what histories are, which is to say, theories about why change occurs. This task of the history teacher, then, would be to become a histories teacher, to show

how histories are themselves theories, and how and why they differ. To teach the past simply as a chronicle of indisputable, fragmented, concrete events is to replicate the biases of the media that largely deny our youth access to concepts and theories, and provide them only with a stream of meaningless events. In other words, the idea is to raise the level of abstraction at which "history" is taught. This would apply to all subjects, including science.

2. *Science*. Just as every science course should include a serious historical dimension, I would propose that every school offer and require courses in the philosphy of science. Such courses should include a consideration of the language of science, the nature of scientific proof, the sources of scientific hypotheses, the role of imagination, the conditions of experimentation, and especially the value of error and disproof. Such courses would get at the notion that science is not pharmacy, technology, or magic tricks, but a special way of employing human intelligence. It is important that students learn one does not become scientific by donning a white coat, which is what television teaches, but by practicing a set of canons of thought, many of which have to do with the disciplined use of language.

3. *Language*. I should like to propose that every school offer a course in semantics —that is, in the processes by which people make meaning. It would be extremely useful to the growth of our youth's intelligence if special courses were available in which fundamental principles of language were identified and explained. Such courses would deal not only with the various uses of language, but with the relationship between things and words, symbols and signs, factual statements and judgments, and even grammar and thought. These courses should also emphasize the kinds of semantic errors that are common to all of us and which are avoidable through awareness and discipline.

4. *The Arts*. In using the ascent of humanity as a theme, we would of necessity elevate such subjects as literature, music, and art to prominence. The most obvious reason is that their subject matter contains the best evidence we have of the unity and continuity of human experience and feeling. And that is why I would propose that in the teaching of the humanities, we should emphasize the enduring creations of the past. Because of the nature of the communications industry, our students have continuous access to the popular arts of their own times. Their knowledge of the form and content of this art is by no means satisfactory, but their ignorance of the form and content of the art of the past is cavernous.

School must make available the products of classical art forms, precisely because they are not so available, and because they demand a different order of sensibility and response.

5. *Religion*. Finally, I want to propose that high school and college curriculums include a course or courses in comparative religion. Such courses would deal with religion as an expression of humanity's creativeness, as a total integrated response to fundamental questions about the meaning of existence. The courses would be descriptive, promoting no particular religion, but illuminating the metaphors, the literature, the art, the ritual of religious expression itself. I'm not unaware of the difficulties such courses would face. But I do not see how we can claim to be educating our youth

if we do not ask them to consider how different people, of different times and places, have tried to achieve a sense of transcendence.

A CONSERVATIVE EDUCATION

To summarize, I am proposing a curriculum in which all subjects are presented as a stage in humanity's historical development, in which the philosophy of science, of history, of language, and of religion are taught, and in which there is strong emphasis on classical forms of artistic expression. Such an education might be considered conservative. But I believe it is justified by the fact that we are surrounded by a culture that is volatile, experimental, and very nearly monolithic in its technological biases. Without the schools to teach the values and intellectual predispositions that our media ignore, and even despise, our students will be disarmed and their future exceedingly bleak. . . . [In short,] *education should keep things in balance by providing students with alternatives to current biases of society.**

---

*EDITOR'S NOTE   As we approach the end of Chapter 1, a word is in order concerning the overall structure of this anthology. There is a sense, of course, in which each of the book's nine chapters deals with a separate issue. But these issues are not altogether separate and distinct. Nor are Parts 1, 2, and 3. Because man is a social being, Liberty (Part 1) necessarily involves Equality (Part 2); and neither freedom nor equality can thrive except in an atmosphere of social harmony and fraternity (Part 3).

It will be noted that the curriculum proposed by Neil Postman is one which emphasises liberal education. The aim of liberal education has always been to liberate students from unwitting dependence on their immediate social environment. Further discussion of this topic may be found by consulting the following topics listed in the Subject Index:

1.6   Important Achievements — and Unanticipated Consequences
WILLIS HARMAN

"Successes"	Resulting Problems
Prolonging the life span	Regional overpopulation; problems of the aged
Highly developed science and technology	Hazard of mass destruction through nuclear and biological weapons
Machine replacement of manual and routine labor	Exacerbated unemployment, urbanization
Advances in communication and transportation	Increasing air, noise, and land pollution; information overload; vulnerability of a complex society to breakdown
Efficient production systems	Dehumanization of ordinary work
Affluence	Increased per capita consumption of energy and goods, leading to pollution and depletion of the earth's resources
Satisfaction of basic needs	Worldwide revolutions of "rising expectations"; rebellion against non-meaningful work
Expanded power of human choice	Unanticipated consequences of techno-logical applicants
Expanded wealth of developed nations	Increasing gap between "have" and "have-not" nations; frustration of the "revolutions of rising expectations"*

Brief excerpt from Willis Harman (Stanford Research Institute), "The Coming Transformation of Our View of Knowledge," *The Futurist* 8: 126-128, June 1974.

This brief selection calls attention to an age-old truth, namely, that life is a complex mixture of good and evil, that every godlike Faust within us is accompanied by a diabolical Mephistopheles, and that "progress" is not a simple movement from bad to good because gains in one dimension of life are, almost without exception, accompanied by losses in some other dimension.

---

*EDITOR'S NOTES   The reader will find it instructive to ponder other examples, on the personal or on the social level, in which success or progress in one dimension of life gives rise to unintended side-effects.

This is not to deny or to belittle the importance of success or of progress. It is simply to take note of the fact that changes in one aspect of our lives (for example, the widespread use of television) involves other changes as well.

Here we make a distinction between a problem and an issue. A problem is an undesirable state of affairs. An issue is an attempt to focus on competing, viable solutions to that problem. One "solution," for example, would be to get rid of television. In the early nineteenth century, the Luddites sought a solution to their problem by destroying the laborsaving machines that were causing them to lose their jobs. But the Luddites lost their case: in general it is easier and better to adapt new inventions and technologies to humane and worthy ends.

1.7 Quotations for Further Thought and Discussion

(A)   The fact is, that civilization requires slaves. The Greeks were quite right there. Unless there are slaves to do the ugly, horrible, uninteresting work, culture and contemplation become almost impossible. Human slavery is wrong, insecure, and demoralizing. On mechanical slavery, on the slavery of the machine, the future of the world depends.

— Oscar Wilde.

(B)   Manual labor, though an unavoidable duty, though designed as a blessing, and naturally both a pleasure and a dignity, is often abused, till, by its terrific excess, it becomes really a punishment and a curse. It is only a proper amount of work that is a blessing. Too much of it wears out the body before its time, cripples the mind, debases the soul, blunts the senses, and chills the affections. It makes a man a spinning jenny, or a ploughing-machine, and not "a being of large discourse that looks before and after." He ceases to be a man, and becomes a thing.

— Theodore Parker, 1810-1860

(C)   Changes between 1880 and 1980 may be summarized by grouping them into three phases:

Phase I 19th c. to WW II	Phase II Post WW II to 1970s	Phase III 1970s and beyond
Industrial revolution	World perceived as a	Worldwide political and
Rapid growth of	single ecosystem [with	economic planning
machine technology	attendant] technological	Increased cooperation
Laissez-faire	growth	among big powers
capitalism	Rise of planned	Limits to natural
Democratization of	economics	resources
political process	Spread of social	Limits to economic
Rise of commercialism	welfare programs	growth
Rationalism and	Big power political,	Population decline
secularization	economic dominance	
	Countercultures	
	Population planning	

— John J. Poggie, Jr., and Robert W. Lynch, *Rethinking Modernization: Anthropological Perspectives* (London: Greenwood Press, 1971), Table 1.

(D)   An expert is someone who knows some of the worst mistakes that can be made in his subject, and how to avoid them.

— Werner Heisenberg

(E)   . . . the foreseeable future may be the first time since the dawn of civilization when

These brief quotations are intended to serve three purposes: (1) to call the reader's attention to other articles which would have been included in this anthology if space had permitted, (2) to suggest other issues not covered in this book — issues, however, which might well serve as topics for individual written reports or for class panels, and (3) to present, as the title indicates, quotations for further thought and discussion.

appreciable cultural advantages could be conferred on a substantial proportion of the whole population.

— Lawrence Cremin, *The Genius of American Education* (University of Pittsburgh Press, 1965), p. 48.

(F)   Youth culture is both a product and a target of the media. . . . The mass media did not invent the notion of youth as an objectively distinct period of anyone's life, but it has specified and popularized some aspects of it. . . . Thus the youth of America . . . see themselves as a distinct group with their own problems and solutions. . . .

[Today, most people view] youth as a distinct period of life, with associated traumas and behavior, including widespread deviance. . . . [What is more important,] young people today can obtain a sense of what it is to be 16 years old when they are 10. Not surprisingly, many do not wait until they are 16 to "act 16." The upshot is that the problems of youth will appear earlier, last longer, and are likely to take newer forms.

— David L. Altheide (Arizona State University), "The Mass Media and Youth Culture," *Urban Education* 14: 236–253, July 1979.

(G)   How many highly educated people today understand the inner workings of their televisions, their calculators, their microwave ovens, or even their automobiles and telephones? Behind such a question is an awareness of alienation from indispensable ingredients of everyday life that raises a host of other troubling questions. If we are daily so alienated from the fruits of science, will we long respect science? If this alienation means ignorant dependence, are we not subjects rather than masters of technology? Can one expect self-confident individualism from persons ever more dependent in their daily lives on tools which they comprehend only in their uses and can neither explain nor repair? Can human reason continue to flourish in a society whose most widely used artifacts, even though derived from applied reason in the form of science, seem to their users to be mysteries that to them — the users — defy analysis, understanding and, to a perceivable extent, control?

— Steven Muller in *Daedalus* 107:31–45, Winter 1978.

(H)   It would be a shame if we were to regress to the methodologies of the 30s —memorize and drill — in the name of "back to basics" when there are so many excellent manipulatives, games, activities, and materials available for classroom use. . . . Computation skills must be developed thoroughly. But mathematics must also be taught in a way that will enhance thinking skills and problem solving in an enjoyable atmosphere.

— Ann M. Wilderman and Verena Sharkey, in *The Instructor* 89: 34, January 1980.

(I)   The New Humanism . . . is a fight on many fronts: . . . against the pseudohumanists who would kick science out of the humanities; . . . against the bigoted Westerners who reject Oriental ideas and Oriental religions; . . . against the narrow-minded technicians who do not appreciate spiritual values.

— George Sarton, "The Old World and the New Humanism," in *Man's Right to Knowledge, First Series: Tradition and Change* (New York: Muschel, 1954), p. 66.

(J)   It is the achievement of a lofty and very strong soul to know how to come down to the childish gait and guide it. . . . If, as is our custom, the teachers undertake to regulate many minds of such different capacities and forms with the same lessons and a similar measure of guidance, it is no wonder if in a whole race of children they find barely two or three who reap any proper fruit from their teaching.

—Montaigne, *On the Education of Children* (1580).

(K)   Despite the existence of sophisticated technology in schools, classrooms remain as "labor-intensive" as ever. Often, educators are embarrassed by the fact and promise hard effort to change things [so each teacher can handle more students]. I hope these efforts don't succeed. "Labor-intensity," after all, only means a low ratio of children to adults. In view of all the needs that children have for love, compassion, and just plain attention, it seems to me that a labor intensive school is likely to be a good school.

— William E. Gardner, Dean, College of Education, University of Minnesota, Minneapolis (July 9, 1980).

(L)   The choice is ours. We may choose to commit ourselves to a lifetime of learning, secure in the knowledge that life and learning are one and the same. Or we may choose to commit ourselves to a lifetime of defending the fruitless attitudes and efforts in which we have engaged. . . .

Several decades ago, we left an era when simple and essentially good people had simple and good goals they understood, sacrificed for and, in sacrificing, experienced deprivation as a privilege. Then we entered an era of self-indulgence with no standards, full of temper tantrums and tragic contempt for old and new learning. Now, for the sake of survival as well as growth, we must create an era of teaching and learning that has no plateau.

— Robert R. Carkhuff and Bernard G. Berenson (Carkhuff Institute of Human Technology) in *Teaching as Treatment* (Amherst, MA: Human Resources Development Press, 1976) pp. 270, 272.

(M)   A powerful tide is surging across much of the world today creating a new, often bizarre, environment in which to work, play, marry, raise children, or retire. In this bewildering context, businessmen swim against highly erratic economic currents; politicians see their ratings bob wildly up and down; universities, hospitals, and other institutions battle desperately against inflation. Value systems splinter and crash, while the lifeboats of family, church, and state are hurled madly about.

— Alvin Toffler, *The Third Wave* (New York: William Morrow, 1980), p. 18.

(N)   "It is provided in the very nature of things," said Walt Whitman, "that from any fruition of success, no matter what, shall come forth something to make a greater struggle necessary." John Ciardi puts it this way: "There is no success. There is only engagement. Any man who believes he has succeeded has settled for a limited engagement. At any time in one's life there is only the prospect of engaging more fully. If there is achievement, it is to be put by. Achievement is only what brings into view the next thing to be engaged."

Chapter 2. FREEDOM — AND RESPONSIBILITY — IN THE CLASSROOM

2.1 School Discipline in an Age of Social Unrest
INTRODUCTION

A major problem in any school is to balance orderliness and direction in the instructional program against the realities of human diversity and curriculum variety. Curriculum variety is required in order that schools keep abreast of the times, for example, mathematics in an age of hand computers, geography in an age when news deals not only with the local community but also with events from all parts of the world. Although human diversity is a fact of life even in the most isolated cultures, it becomes immeasurably greater when classrooms contain students from varied social, racial, religious, and ethnic backgrounds.[1]

In their 1977 book on *Problem Behavior and Psycho-Social Development*, Richard and Shirley Jessor came to these conclusions:

> The adolescent who is likely to engage in problem behavior is one who does not value academic achievement, does not expect to do well academically, is much concerned with independence, regards society as problematic and deserving criticism and reshaping, has a tolerant attitude toward transgressions, and lacks interest in conventional institutions such as church and school. The Jessors note, however, that this set of correlates of problem behavior is synonymous with a set of developmental trends that characterize most youth: growth of independence, decline of support for traditional ideology, increase in relativistic morality, increase in peer orientation, and increase in modeling of problem behavior. Thus,

---

Throughout this Seventh Edition of *Crucial Issues in Education*, a central belief is dominant: While the primary task of the school may be to teach basic skills and subject matter, a second goal must be to help young people develop responsible and effective social behavior. This second goal is probably the most fundamental goal of all, because it is a necessary prerequisite to the first goal. In short, a sense of *fraternity* is needed if we are to enjoy either *liberty* or *equality*.

But teachers cannot operate schools on the basis of such generalities. So Chapter 2 focuses on problems of discipline and classroom management. Selections 2.2–2.9 provide some social and historical backgrounds to the problem. Selections 2.10–2.18 deal with down-to-earth classroom procedures.

[1]This variety of social, racial, religious, and ethnic backgrounds is the reason why *equality* has become the central issue in American education in recent decades. It is also the reason why Chapter 2 may be viewed as an introduction to Part 2 (Chapters 4, 5, and 6).

they conclude that "the normal course of developmental change in adolesence is in the direction of greater problem-proneness."

In the 1975 nationwide survey on discipline conducted by the National Education Association, teachers cited irresponsible parents and poor home conditions as the two major causes of disciplinary problems and violence in schools. The teachers also listed overcrowded classes, an irrelevant curriculum, lack of service for exceptional children, and lack of authority for teachers as other major contributing causes. An ad hoc committee on school discipline of the National School Boards Association surveyed a variety of schools regarding discipline and violence. The committee concluded that among the contributing factors to the problem are large classes, influence of peers, lax enforcement of rules, incompetent and indifferent teachers, poor communication between home and parents, poor home conditions, weak controls in the schools, emergence of student rights, integration that has brought diverse cultures together, weak administrative support and an irrelevant curriculum.[2]

Although school discipline is usually rated as the Number 1 Problem in today's secondary schools, we are inclined to believe that it is a problem caused by other problems — by other social, economic and personal factors about which educators should be concerned. Indeed, it may be that the problem arises from the very nature of our dynamic society based on the premise that people should learn to govern themselves. On this point, a statement by Israel Scheffler seems appropriate [italics added].

To choose the democratic ideal for society is wholly to *reject* the conception of education as an instrument of rule; it is to *surrender* the idea of shaping or molding the mind of the pupil.

The function of education in a democracy is rather to *liberate* the mind, *strengthen* its critical powers, *inform* it with knowledge and the capacity for independent inquiry, engage its human sympathies, and *illuminate* its moral and practical choices. . . .[3]

It is our belief that too many educators have overemphasized the negative words *reject* and *surrender*, and have underemphasized the positive words *liberate, strengthen, inform, illuminate.*

It is hoped that the anthology you are reading will help to restore a balance between the negative and the positive aspects of moral education.

A statement by Robert Maynard Hutchins may further emphasize the problems educators face in contemporary America.

[When we remember] that it is only a little more than fifty years ago that the 'average man' began to have the chance to get an education, we must recognize that it is too early to despair of him. . . . we shall find that he will respond to the demands of education for freedom if we will give him the opportunity.[4]

---

[2] The paragraphs from the Jessor book are taken from an article by John Feldhusen (Purdue University), in *Classroom Management: The 78th Yearbook of the National Society for the Study of Education* [NSSE], edited by Daniel L. Duke, (Stanford University) (University of Chicago Press, 1979), pp. 222, 228–229. By permission.

[3] Israel Scheffler (Harvard University), in *Moral Education . . . It Comes With the Territory,* edited by David Purpel and Keven Ryan, Berkeley, CA.: McCutchan, 1978.

[4] *School and Society* 54: 260–261, 1941.

2.2 Our Disjointed Culture
WILLIAM DOLL, JR., (AND DANIEL BELL)

Past cultures, argues Bell, have had some sort of "unifying inner principle," some thread which ran through all the realms and made the realms into a "structural whole." In Western society it has been "the bourgeois idea . . . which has molded the modern era for the past 200 years." In America the union of the Puritan temper and the Protestant ethic, with its emphasis on "work, sobriety, frugality, sexual restraint, and a forbidding attitude towards life," has given a common meaning to the social, the political, the cultural. But now this bourgeois era has come to an end, and without something to replace it there is left only a disjunction of realms and a rampant hedonism:

> When the Protestant ethic was sundered from bourgeois society, only hedonism remained, and the capitalist system lost its transcendental ethic.

The advent of industrialism, in the late 18th and early 19th century, brought with it, in the form of laissez-faire capitalism, a "radical experimental individualism." The "laws" of the market place were to solve all economic and social problems. While each individual was to strive for personal gain the conflict among individuals and between sellers and buyers would "naturally" produce the best for the individual and for the community. This "unrestrained economic impulse," a feature built into the very nature of capitalism, "was held in check by Puritan restraint and the Protestant ethic." The Puritans "because they had founded their community as a covenant in which all individuals were in compact with each other" did not let individualism, in either the economic or social realm, go to far. Their polity was clearly a communal one. The Protestants, with their emphasis on frugality, industry and delayed gratification, encouraged a sense of self that was anti-hedonist. The combination of these forces formed what Bell calls the "bourgeois world-view," which itself served both to coalesce society and to restrain the radical individuality of capitalism. This structure outlived the Puritan and Protestant movements actually dominating American society until after World War II. After this war many forces conspired to bring about a disjunction: social and geographic mobility, the decline of religious absolutism, the transformation of the cities, the rise of national and multinational corporations. Bell singles out two factors as contributing most to the demise of the bourgeois world-view: the "victory" of the avant-garde in culture, and the economic rise of liberal capitalism. Quoting Irving Howe, Bell declares that the role of the avant-garde, the modern, the new is "to struggle with an unyielding rage, but never quite to triumph against the established order." . . .

[Devoid of respect for tradition, and lacking in feeling for historical continuity, the avant-garde relishes novelty for novelty's sake:]

Brief excerpts from William E. Doll, Jr. (State University of New York at Oswego), "Schooling in a Post-Industrial Society," from the *High School Journal*, Volume 61, Number I, May 1978 (pp. 333–352). Copyright 1978 The University of North Carolina Press. Reprinted by permission of the publisher. (Footnote references are omitted.)
The full selection may be viewed as an educator's summary and intepretation of the writings of Daniel Bell.

Everything is to be explored, anything is to be permitted, including lust, murder, and other themes which have dominated the modernist sur-real.

The other factor contributing most to the demise of the bourgeois culture has been the advent of liberal capitalism:

The greatest single engine in the destruction of the Protestant ethic was the invention of the installment plan, or instant credit. Previously one had to save in order to buy. But with credit cards one could indulge in instant gratification. The system was transformed by mass production and mass consumption, by the creation of new wants and new means of gratifying those wants.

For Bell this creation of a debt economy combined with a desire to experience the new has overthrown the traditional restraints of Protestant frugality and delayed gratification. Add to this the loss of a Puritan covenant with its insistence on a sense of community and what is left is nothing but hedonism. The public household is an attempt not to recapture the lost ethic of bourgeois Protestantism but to establish a new transcendent ethic which will bind together the realms of the social, the political, and the cultural.

The Public Household . . .

The public household is, to go back to Aristotle, 'a concern more with the good condition of human beings than with the good condition of property.' It is the centrality of conscious decisions, publicly debated and philosophically justified. . . .

To accomplish this there must be a willingness on the part of individuals to balance their wants against the needs of others. This will not be easy to accomplish, for over the past two hundred years western society has given precedence to the individual, and the community has been considered, as Jeremy Bentham said, as nothing but an abstraction of the "sum of the interests of the several members who compose it." . . .

[Bell, like Aristotle, places his ultimate hope] in the rationality of humans to use their intellectual powers to solve social problems. But Bell realizes this will not happen automatically. It is a "question of whether there is a common will." . . . The development of such a will is a mammoth task, but then the alternative of a hedonistic society given over to the exploration of all sensations is one that "leads to debauchery, lust, degradation, murder," and ultimately chaos and tyranny. If this alternative is to be avoided, the vehicle for the development of a common will and a sense of public household lies in education, for it is through education that a self-conscious maturity might just possibly arise. . . .

[It is more likely to arise to the extent that schools place] greater emphasis on cooperation, internal motivation, group interaction: and . . . pay more attention to the qualitative, the personal, the intentional.

2.3   American Education Today: Success or Failure? Two Viewpoints

The Tragedy of Contemporary American Youth: Some Factual Data
EDWARD A. WYNNE

- Between 1950 and 1977, the rate of death by suicide for white males, ages 15 through 19, increased 337%. The suicide rate for older adults remained relatively stable during this period.
- Between 1959 and 1977, the rate of death by homicide for white males, ages 15 through 19, increased 207%. Most of the assailants were other white male adolescents. This was the highest rate of increase for any group of white males.
- Between 1950 and 1977, the estimated number of illegitimate births for unmarried white females, ages 15 through 19, increased 166%. The rate of increase among these young persons far exceeded any increases among older females. . . .
- The level of white adolescent illegitimacy is at the highest rate in this century; the levels of homicide and suicide are about 10% below the century's maximums, attained in 1975.
- In an affluent suburban community, the number of seventh grade boys who began drinking during the previous year increased from 52% in 1969 to 72% in 1973. A 1974 national survey disclosed that 24.1% of the respondents of both sexes between 13 and 19 reported being drunk four or more times during the previous year.
- Between 1957 and 1974, the number of delinquency cases disposed of by U.S. juvenile courts increased 96%.
- Two careful surveys of school crime and violence both concluded that the level of school crime has increased gradually since (about) 1955, and that, if the increase has leveled off, there has been no sign of any decrease. Students are in more risk of being criminally victimized in school than in any other environment where they ordinarily spend their time.
- In two surveys of national samples of students in American research universities, the proportion of students who admitted engaging in some form of cheating rose from 5.4% in 1969 to 9.8% in 1976 — an 87% increase.
- Between 1960 and 1973, throughout the country, arrests of males under 18 for narcotics violations increased 1,288%.
- National surveys report no significant declines in levels of youth drug use, and surveys of high school graduating classes of 1975 and 1977 found that the percentage of males who had used marijuana before tenth grade had increased from 18.2% to 30.6%.
- A variety of surveys of youth attitudes and conduct between 1948 and 1973 have disclosed a steady increase in attitudes evincing withdrawal, cynicism, loneliness, and hostility to authority. Two national surveys of adult attitudes found that the level of tension and worry among young adults (ages 21 through 39) increased from about 30% (in 1957) to 50% (in 1976). These developing attitudes are clearly inconsistent

From Edward A. Wynne, "Facts about the Character of Young Americans," *Character,* Volume I, Number 1, (November 1979). By permission. Sources of these factual data may be obtained from Edward A. Wynne, editor of *Character,* 1245 West Westgate Terrace, Chicago, Ill. 60607.
Edward A. Wynne teaches at the Chicago Circle, University of Illinois.

with a serious acceptance of social responsiblity and with a sense of wholesome self-respect.

What's Right with Education
HAROLD HODGKINSON

Of all the issues involving the knowledge base in education, none is as explosive as the issue of testing — minimum competency testing, SAT score declines, and truth-in-testing legislation. Yet data on the issue are often presented in a one-sided or ridiculous way, exemplified in many newspaper stories suggesting that as many as 50% of American students are reading "below average." Any adequate review of the literature would report the following:

1. Reading scores on both comprehension and vocabulary have increased steadily over the past decade for the first three grades of schooling. (We've worked very hard on the techniques of early reading, and here is the result: In nearly every school, students can sound out words and read simple sentences.) Reading scores begin to decline in grade 7, when the task is to handle larger units of material — paragraphs and chapters. We need to work on these later cognitive reading skills.

2. National Assessment of Educational Progress data suggest that students aged 9, 13, and 17 know basic skills rather well, but they have trouble applying them in new situations. Students know *how* to add and subtract but not *when*. They can read a 10-page report and retain facts but have trouble writing a tight precis in one or two paragraphs of their own prose. "Basics" in the sense of reading print, performing math operations, are well learned; the problem is in critical thinking. We need to know more about these skills and their acquisition.

3. American students at age 14 do very well in comparison with students of other nations in reading. In science they do better than their counterparts in Britain, the Netherlands, and Italy but not as well as those in Japan and Germany. They do as well in math as Swedish youngsters but not as well as those in Japan or France . . . [Moreover], in terms of *those who go on to college*, preparation for college by the public schools has not declined in quality. (The only areas in which college faculty members report declines of significance are in math *reasoning* — not operational skills — and in writing, particularly precis and summary writing.) Given the fact that over 50% of high school graduates (and remember that 70% to 85% now graduate from high school) now try for further education, compared to the 10% to 20% in 1950 who entered postsecondary education, it is a remarkable achievement that American public schools are now doing for half of the school population what they used to do for only the top 10%. . . . No other nation has carried such a high percentage of its citizens so far.*

Brief excerpts from *Phi Delta Kappan* 61: 159–162, November 1979. (Footnote references are omitted.)
© 1979, Phi Delta Kappa, Inc. By permission.
    Harold Hodgkinson is president of National Training Laboratories, Arlington, VA.
    Read also "Do Schools Stink? Why Not Quote the Sweet Facts?" *American School Board Journal* 167: 20–21, June 1980. Condensed in *Education Digest* 46: 20–21, November 1980.

*EDITOR'S NOTE   This topic is pursued in greater detail in Chapter 5 on *Measurement and Evaluation*.

2.4   The Growing Federal Influence Over Public Schools
TYLL VAN GEEL

Thirty years ago, a treatise on the law of the school curriculum would [merely have explained] how the state legislatures carried out their constitutional duties and powers in specifying the content of the school program and in allocating administrative authority over the schools. . . .

[This article describes some of the many ways in which the federal government has assumed control over many aspects of school curricula which previously had been completely under local control.]

FORMULA GRANTS

Title I of ESEA

Historically, the most significant congressional effort to reform the American public schools is in Title I of the Elementary and Secondary Education Act of 1964. . . . Congress adopted a formula that implied that, while states and districts were entitled to a certain amount of money, they had first to file applications and proposals in order to receive the money. . . .

Title I, as interpreted by the commissioner, has had and continues to have the potential for dramatically changing educational programs at the local level. Briefly, Title I requires local districts to spend more money on the educationally disadvantaged than on other children. It requires local districts to design programs suitable to the needs of the disadvantaged and not merely to offer them the same programs that make sense for middle-class, high-achieving children. . . .

Title VI [1964]

[In] Title VI, Congress has given HEW [Department of Health, Education and Welfare] and OCR [Office of Civil Rights] a powerful base which . . . can be used to reshape such other aspects of the educational program as classification practices, testing procedures, guidance and counseling programs, extracurricular activities, disciplinary procedures, special education, instructional methodologies, and the curriculum in general. The notion of racial and ethnic discrimination is an expandable concept that can, with a little diligence, be found in every aspect of school operations. . . .

Brief excerpts from Tyll van Geel (University of Rochester), "The New Law of the Curriculum," reprinted from *School Review* 86:4(78) 594–563, August 1978, by permission of The University of Chicago Press. Copyright 1978.

These brief excerpts cannot do justice to this 31-page article with its 125 footnotes. Furthermore, it deals only with the growth of Federal influence, and omits all mention of the growing state control and the diminishing local control of public schools.

Read also Francis Keppel (Harvard University), "Education in the Eighties," *Harvard Educational Review* 50: 149–155, May 1980.

After stating why he believes the 1980s will witness greater state and local control, Keppel writes: "Many of the current social and educational issues will continue: equal opportunity, equity, fairness in teachers' salaries and benefits, the need for encouraging research, the diffusion of new knowlege, and many others. Of these, the most important may be desegregation and bilingual and bicultural education."

Title IX

What Title VI does to racial discrimination, Title IX does to sexual discrimination. . . . [Briefly,]

Title IX prohibits discrimination with regard to course offerings and requirements, counseling and guidance programs, admission to special schools and programs and to school organizations such as social and service clubs, extracurricular activities, hair and dress codes, rules with regard to pregnancy and parenthood, and athletics. The regulations thus foreshadow significant federal involvement in the school program. . . .

CONCLUSIONS

Congress, like the courts, has shown a concern with meeting the special educational needs of minority, handicapped, and non-English-speaking students. And like the courts, Congress has evinced a desire to end both racial and sexual discrimination in the public schools. But Congress has gone beyond the courts in several respects by affirmatively promoting vocational education and instruction in science, mathematics, foreign languages, and environmental education. That is, Congress, unlike the courts, is in a position to encourage the study of particular subjects, disciplines, skills, and bodies of knowledge. . . . [For example, a recent Report by a House Congressional Committee affirms:]

> The Committee believes that a start must be made now in fostering in our youth an awareness of the value of these different ethnic heritages and of the role which they have played and continue to play in forming our country.

In this example we have an expression of intent on the part of Congress to reform one of the most sensitive aspects of the school program — and it is a reform effort that is not tied to any felt need to bolster our national defense in the face of a Russian threat or to a general "war on poverty." This purely and simply represents congressional dissatisfaction with the traditional curriculum of the public schools. It represents how far we have come in our thinking with regard to federal influence over the public schools.*

---

*EDITOR'S NOTE   Cities, no less than schools, are feeling the impact of federal controls. *Washington Post* columnist Neal R. Peirce (February 17, 1980) tells the story of Edward Koch, now Mayor of New York City. For nine years, as a member of the United States Congress, Koch voted in favor of laws that he now discovers are crippling his city.

Leading Koch's list of mandate horrors is the now-notorious Section 504 of the Rehabilitation Act of 1973, a single and ambiguous sentence of law which federal departments have interpreted to require total accessibility of the handicapped to all buses and subway cars.

It would be cheaper, says Koch, to provide every seriously disabled person in New York with taxi service rather than make all the city's 225 subway stations wheelchair-accessible at a cost of $1.3 billion. But it was easy to vote for the 1973 bill: "When you are a member of Congress and you are voting a mandate and not providing the funds for it, the sky's the limit."

Federal law requires the city to provide special education for handicapped children. But Congress, notes Koch, has

2.5   Why Autonomy Must Be Restored to School Principals
NASSP BULLETIN SURVEY

The NASSP 1979 survey revealed that, in a single year (1979) almost 10% of the 5000 principals responding to the survey had decided to leave their principalships that year. Their reasons for leaving, followed by the percent of respondents listing each specific reason, are these:

excessive time demands (56.5)
heavy work load (50.4)
fatigue (37.0)
constraints caused by courts/legislation (35.7)
emotional health (stress) (52.5)

Brief excerpts from "Why Principals Quit — and What Can Be Done About It," by Nancy DeLeonibus (McLean, Virginia) and Scott D. Thomson (Reston, Virginia), *NASSP Bulletin* 63: 1–10, December 1979. This article is a summary of an NASSP (National Association of Secondary School Principles) survey questionnaire. Reprinted by permission.

---

reneged on the costs of paying the bill so that this year New York will get $8.5 million in federal aid for a program costing the city $221 million.

New York, under another federal statute, must stop dumping its sewage sludge at sea by 1982. But because the sludge's heavy metal contents would contaminate the water table in ordinary dumping on land, New York must build a $150 million treatment plant — which will be obsolete within a decade. The only other way he can see to get rid of the sludge, quips Koch, is "to take it to my apartment."

State mandates, Koch observes, can be equally onerous. One of the nation's most egregious is New York's "heart law" which forces disability boards to classify any heart ailment of a retiring fireman or policeman as a work-related "accident" — thus entitling him to a tax-free disability pension at three-quarters pay. The city must pay the millions of additional pension payments, without compensating state aid.

The tragedy of mandates, says Koch, is that they divert funds desperately required for other urban programs. He has a set of possible cures. Cities could get waivers if they could meet the mandate's objective in a different way. Federal mandates wouldn't be imposed until the Congressional Budget and Technology Assessment Offices gauge their impact. No federal or state mandate would be imposed unless the higher government paid all the cost.

Throughout American history, a basic principle has been that there should be a balance of power between the legislative, executive and judicial branches; a balance between federal, state and local agencies; and a balance between the public and the private sectors of society.

Today, if the Youngstown (Ohio) plant of U.S. Steel is no longer efficient, the company can abandon the plant, even though the decision means the loss of thousands of jobs. Yet no president, regardless of campaign promises, has ever been able to abolish or abandon a major federal regulatory agency. Even if he did, the job security of that agency's personnel would not be threatened. Thus we have created a federal bureaucracy that is out of control.

(More will be said on this point in the concluding footnote to Selection 9.13)

Speaking in broader terms, Robert A. Nisbit (*Community and Power*, New York: Oxford University Press, 1962, page 54) analyzes our present situation as follows:

Our present crisis lies in the fact that whereas the small traditional associations, founded upon kinship, faith, or locality, are still expected to communicate to individuals the principal moral ends and psychological gratifications of society, they have manifestly become detached from positions of functional relevance to the larger economic and political decisions of our society. Family, local community, church, and the whole network of informal interpersonal relationships have ceased to play a determining role in our institutional systems of mutual aid, welfare, education, recreation, and economic production and distribution. Yet despite the loss of these manifest institutional functions, we continue to expect them to perform adequately the implicit psychological or symbolic functions in the life of the individual.

---

desire for change (40.8)
lack of support from superiors (35.9)
lack of teacher professionalism (35.2)
student discipline (29.6)
student apathy (28.9) . . .

At least five major changes in the past 20 years have diminished principals' power and authority. Each is reflected in the data from this survey.

1. *New federal and state laws and court decisions*, particularly those concerning student rights and special groups. Part of the excessive time demands cited by many exiting principals is directly caused by federal or state mandates for implementation of laws. This constraint was evident in the fact that 35.7 percent of respondents listed concern over these laws as a factor related to their leaving.

2. *The formal teacher contract.* Some teacher contracts restrict the amount of time teachers can commit to their schools; thus, the principal is hindered in planning and organizing school programs. While lack of teacher cooperation was cited by only 14 percent of respondents, lack of teacher professionalism was mentioned by 35 percent. Related to this perceived lack of teacher professionalism in many instances is the negotiated contract which places constraints on the assignment and work day of teachers.

3. *Erosion of public commitment to education* is evident. Community factors, while lower in frequency and intensity than job factors as reasons for leaving principalships, reflect the decline of public confidence. Lack of parental support for programs was cited by 25 percent of respondents, lack of tax funds by 22 percent, and insufficient budget/resources by 27 percent. This withdrawal of strong public support is ironic in the face of greater public demands on schools.

4. *The family as a social unit and changing social values* also have an impact on the principalship. Neither parent in many two-paycheck homes has sufficient time to devote to school/home relationships. When parental concern and support in matters of student guidance are lacking, part of the burden falls on principals.

5. *Loss of autonomy.* Not only has the power base of principals been usurped by others; they have also lost job autonomy. The principalship role is experiencing a steady attrition in its scope of influence, organizational power, authority base, and latitude for decision-making. Respondents report that loss of autonomy (28 percent) and lack of input for policies affecting the school (22 percent) affected their decisions to leave. . . *

---

*EDITOR'S NOTE   George Neill, in *Phi Delta Kappan* 61: 517-518, April 1980, made the following "Washington Report":

A bright decade lies ahead for the nation's high school principals if they are permitted once again to lead their schools.
"I think it's beginning to happen," Scott Thomson, the new executive director of the Washington-based National Association of Secondary School Principals (NASSP), told "Washington Report" in a recent interview. . . .
[Principals] "don't like being trapped between a rising volume of demands at the same time having less and less authority to respond."
Asked to identify the reasons for this loss of authority, Thomson blamed federal programs, categorical programs, court decisions, community pressure groups, and boards of education that are uncertain of their conflicting priorities.

2.6   Twenty-Five Years of Curriculum Change
ROBERT J. HAVIGHURST

[This article briefly surveys the past two decades, 1955-1965 and 1965-1975, and then] examines what kind of curriculum is needed for the next century . . .

THE 1955–1965 PERIOD

The decade following 1955 was one of constructive change and improvement in American education. The American economy was prosperous, and the public school system was generally approved by parents and community leaders. The National Science Foundation became interested in supporting collaboration of research scholars and school teachers to improve the curriculum. . . . [and] the following curriculum projects were carried through:

- Biological Sciences Curriculum Study (BSCS)
- School Mathematics Study Group (SMSG)
- Chemical Bond Approach (CBA)
- Chemical Education Material Study (CEMS)

[Near the end of the 1950s, James B. Conant, former president of Harvard University, accepted a $350,000 grant from the Carnegie Corporation to conduct a study of the American high school. Conant's *The American High School Today* summarized this study. It recommended the four courses mentioned above for talented students, conjoined with somewhat less rigorous general education courses for all students.]

Excerpts from Robert J. Havighurst, "Twenty-Five Years of Curriculum Change," *Educational Leadership* 36: 118–121, November 1978. (Footnote references are omitted.) Reprinted with permission of the Association for Supervision and Curriculum Development and Robert J. Havighurst. Copyright © 1978 by the Association for Supervision and Curriculum Development. All rights reserved.
Author of numerous books and articles, Robert J. Havighurst spent most of his career at the University of Chicago.

"How can a principal spend the needed time on educational leadership when he's filling out reports, holding hearings, and doing other quasi-legal procedures?" Thomson asked.

In Thomson's opinion, the elimination of these many activities that distract a principal from instruction and learning is essential for what he calls a "modernization" of the nation's high schools.

Asked to expand on his recommendations for "modernization" of secondary schools during the 1980s, Thomson listed the following as important "evolutionary" reforms to improve instruction and learning:

- Regain a balance in the comprehensive high school that supports the talented as well as the marginal student, the college-bound as well as the job-bound.
- Increase emphasis on reading comprehension and reading speed.
- Increase emphasis on written expression.
- Teach students by using the learning style most effective for them.
- Limit high school enrollment, when possible, to 1,200-1,500 students and junior high schools to 800 students.
- Consider the entire community in the high school's scope of learning.
- Include job opportunities and job placement as part of the school's role.

Bruner and The Process of Education

During this same fruitful 1955-65 period, the psychologists who were interested in education produced a synthesis of learning theory and social psychology that laid the basis for a new approach to the structure of the curriculum. By this time Piaget's major work on the development of intelligence from infancy to maturity had been translated into English and was being studied by curriculum-makers.

In the summer of 1959, the Harvard psychologist Jerome Bruner secured funds from the National Academy of Science to pay for a ten-day conference at Woods Hole, Massachusetts, which brought a dozen psychologists together with the directors of several curriculum groups. Out of this conference came the book by Bruner entitled *The Process of Education*. The human mind was conceived in this conference not as a storehouse of information, but as an instrument for learning. This led to Bruner's famous dictum that "any subject can be taught usefully to any child at any stage of development." This foreshadows the general idea that runs through present-day curriculum making: pupils should be taught the "structure" of a subject, rather than a summary of its content. They should learn certain habits of mind, ways of looking at the world, and ways of asking questions and organizing facts that will make their factual knowledge intelligible. Also at this time, J. Richard Suchman, then teaching at the University of Illinois, came out with his inquiry method of teaching elementary school pupils.

THE SHAKE-UP: 1965-1975

There was a marked change in the tone and content of curriculum discussion and writing beginning about 1965. Reasons for this include:

1. Passage of the Civil Rights Act of 1964 and the Elementary and Secondary Education Act of 1965. These called attention to the poor educational achievement of low socioeconomic and some minority groups in the public schools and brought out proposals for compensatory education of disadvantaged students.

2. The vigorous writings of a group of philosophical anarchists, disciples of Jean-Jacques Rousseau, who opposed rules and institutions set up by society to regulate the conduct and development of its members. The ablest spokesmen of the anarchist group were Paul Goodman, John Holt, and Ivan Illich. Paul Goodman wrote: "We can, I believe, educate the young entirely in terms of their free choice, with no processing whatsoever."

John Holt, in a 1971 book, answered a question directed to him by an educational journal: If America's schools were to take one giant step forward this year toward a better tomorrow, what should it be? His answer:

> It would be to let every child be the planner, director and assessor of his own education, to allow and encourage him, with the inspiration and guidance of more experienced and expert people, and as much help as he asked for, to decide what he is to learn, when he is to learn it, how he is to learn it, and how well he is learning it.
> It would be to make our schools, instead of what they are, which is jails for children, into a

resource for free and independent learning, which everyone in the community, of whatever age, could use as much or as little as he wanted.

Of course, there were many criticisms of the anarchist writers. For instance, B.F. Skinner. . . .

True personal freedom can only be gained by disciplined study of the real world, he argued, and this requires the assistance of a teacher. "The natural, logical outcome of the struggle for personal freedom in education is that the teacher should improve control of the student rather than abandon it."

3. Leaders of disadvantaged minority groups wanted schools with curricula that would be most useful to their particular cultural groups. They were opposed to de-schooling; they wanted schooling that would accomplish two quite different objectives: (a) improve the basic mental skills of the pupils, and (b) help them become aware of and appreciative of their identity as members of a minority racial, language, or religious group. They want a pluralistic society, with schools helping to maintain such a society. Their position was strengthened by the passage of Title VII of the Elementary and Secondary Education Act of 1967, known as the Bilingual Education Act. This provides federal government money for programs of bilingual-bicultural education.

CURRICULUM FOR A POST-INDUSTRIAL SOCIETY

Out of the present perplexity and complexity of the curriculum, and looking ahead to the nature of our post-industrial society, we may state three basic propositions:

1. The curriculum should stress the *structure* of the subjects that are studied, rather than the student storing up discrete bits of information. This will make use of much of what was done in the productive 1955-1965 period.

2. The curriculum should support a constructive and democratic cultural pluralism. This will contribute to:
   a. Mutual appreciation and understanding of every subculture by the other ones.
   b. Freedom for each subculture to practice its culture and socialize its chidren.
   c. Sharing by each group in the economic and civic life of the society.
   d. Peaceful coexistence of diverse life styles, folkways, manners, language patterns, religious beliefs and practices, and family structures.

This policy will support the efforts of certain subcultural groups to maintain their separation from the economic and civic mainstream of American life — for example, the Amish and the Hutterites, and some Alaskan Eskimos and native Americans. However, their youth will have the option of getting an education to help them move into the mainstream, if they wish to place less stress on their subcultural identity.

3. The curriculum should convey to all youth a body of shared knowledge and experience that helps them to grow up and live successfully in the post-industrial society. This applies especially to the area of the social sciences, with the middle school and the high school teaching what is appropriate to the maturity of the student on the following topics:

- Technology of post-industrial society, including energy policy and problems
- Population problems
- The civics and economics of metropolitan areas, including renewal of the central city
- Monetary problems and issues — inflation
- World interdependency of nations.

Finally, there must be a concern for a curriculum that teaches a cohesive civic unity, with full opportunity for diversity of life styles. This has been stated cogently by R. Freeman Butts of Columbia University:

> Achieving a sense of community is the essential purpose of public education. This work cannot be left to the vagaries of individual parents, or small groups of like-minded parents, or particular interest groups, or religious sects, or private enterprisers or cultural specialists. . . .
> I believe that there must be a mobilization to insist that the public schools concentrate as they never have before on the task of building a sense of civic cohesion among all the people of the country.

2.7 Formal Versus Informal Classrooms
NEVILLE BENNETT AND OTHERS

[Formal education is here contrasted to informal education, or to what was once called progressive education, and in recent years is called open education.]

Open education is an approach to education that is open to change, to new ideas, to curriculum, to scheduling, to use of space, to honest expressions of feeling between teacher and pupil and between pupil and pupil, and open to children's participation in significant decision-making in the classroom.

Open education is characterised by a classroom environment in which there is a minimum of teaching to the class as a whole, in which provision is made for children to pursue individual interests and to be actively involved with materials, and in which children are trusted to direct many aspects of their own learning. . . .

[In our 1974-76 study, a] strong relationship was found between teacher aims and opinions and the way teachers actually teach. . . .

Formal teachers lay much greater stress on the promotion of a high level of academic attainment, preparation for academic work in the secondary school, and the acquisition of basic skills in reading and number work. Informal teachers on the other hand value social and emotional aims, preferring to stress the importance of self-expression, enjoyment of school and the development of creativity.

Brief excerpts from Neville Bennett, with a foreword by Jerome Bruner (Harvard University) and with research assistance by Joyce Jordan, George Long, and Barbara Wade — all British educators. *Teaching Styles and Pupil Progress*, (Cambridge, MA: Harvard University Press, 1976), pp. 2-4, 5, 8, 151, 152, 158, 160-161, 162-163. (Footnote references are omitted). Reprinted by permission.
On the back cover of the book, Noel Entwistle (Professor of Educational Research, University of Lancaster), states that all four members of the research team had previously written articles which, if they showed prejudice at all, were prejudiced in favor of "progressive" or "open" or "informal" classroom procedures. Yet this study provides strong evidence that "formal" or "traditional" procedures are more effective for most students and for most teachers.

These differences in emphasis were again demonstrated in the marked disagreements in opinions about teaching methods. The results . . . illustrate how wide the opinion gap is. Formal teachers defend their methods in entirety and disagree with all the arguments made against them by informal teachers. This is also true of informal teachers, who defend the efficacy of their methods except on the question of discipline, where two-thirds agree that their methods could create discipline problems. On the other hand informal teachers are prepared to concede certain points to formal methods, e.g. that they teach basic skills and concepts effectively, and provide an environment in which pupils are aware of what to do, and minimise time wasting and daydreaming. Formal teachers for their part concede that informal methods are likely to encourage responsibility and self-discipline, and to teach pupils to think for themselves. Mixed teachers, although generally aligning themselves more with formal teachers, agree and disagree with a number of opinions expressed by both. . . .

The results [documentation of which is not included in these brief excerpts] form a coherent pattern. The effect of teaching style is statistically and educationally significant in all attainment areas tested. In reading, pupils of formal and mixed teachers progress more than those of informal teachers, the difference being equivalent to some three to five months' difference in performance. In mathematics formal pupils are superior to both mixed and informal pupils, the difference in progress being some four to five months. In English formal pupils again out-perform both mixed and informal pupils, the discrepancy in progress between formal and informal being approximately three to five months. It is interesting to note that these differences are very similar to those which have been found in the most recent American research. . . .

This is not to deny that the quality of the environment in which children work is important, but merely to suggest that its effect may be relatively marginal in fostering learning. And learning, as Pluckrose (1975), a teacher dedicated to informal teaching, recently pointed out, is still 'the teacher's prime function.' . . .

It seems generally accepted that to teach well informally is more difficult than to teach well formally. It requires a special sort of teacher to use informal methods effectively — one who is dedicated, highly organized, able to work flexibly, able to plan ahead and willing to spend a great deal of extra time in preparatory work. How many teachers do we have who could meet these specifications? . . . Burt (1969) . . . [was] concerned with this question [when he wrote:]

> With younger children, particularly those drawn from overcrowded homes in drab surroundings, they [informal methods] have at times undoubtedly achieved a conspicuous success: the duller pupils are surprisingly happy, and the brighter make remarkable progress. But these results are exceptional: they are the work of exceptional teachers provided with an exceptional amount of space and equipment — usually able and ingenious enthusiasts who have themselves devised the techniques they practise. . . .

[Here we may recall] the fate of the American progressive education movement when informal methods spread from the hands of the exceptional teacher in the university laboratory schools to the average teacher in the state system. It would be a pity if this extreme reaction were to happen in Britain. . . .

It is difficult to know what specific outcomes informal teachers intend in developing self-expression. Informal pupils certainly interact more, but the benefits derived from this are not clear from the evidence gathered. Improvements in sociability and self-esteem are no different from those in formal schools, time wasting tends to be manifested more often and there is no academic payoff, providing some support for the doubtful efficacy of 'learning by talking' commented on by Froome (1975).

In summary, formal teaching fulfils its aims in the academic area without detriment to the social and emotional development of pupils, whereas informal teaching only partially fulfils its aims in the latter area as well as engendering comparatively poorer outcomes in academic development.

The central factor emerging from this study is that a degree of teacher direction is necessary, and this direction needs to be carefully planned, and the learning experiences provided need to be clearly sequenced and structured.

2.8   The Pupil-Centered School
A. S. NEILL, JOHN HOLT, AND WILLARD J. CONGREVE AND GEORGE J. RINEHART

A. S. NEILL

The function of the child is to live his own life — not the life that his anxious parents think he should live, nor a life according to the purpose of the educator who thinks he knows what is best. All this interference and guidance on the part of adults only produces a generation of robots. . . .

In all countries, capitalist, socialist or communist, elaborate schools are built to educate the young. But all the wonderful labs and workshops do nothing to help John or Peter or Ivan surmount the emotional damage and the social evils bred by the pressure on him from his parents, his schoolteachers, and the pressure of the coercive quality of our civilization.[1]

JOHN HOLT

Nobody starts off stupid. You have only to watch babies and infants, and think seriously about what all of them learn and do, to see that, except for the most grossly retarded, they show a style of life, and desire and ability to learn that in an older person we might well call genius. Hardly an adult in a thousand, or ten thousand, could in any three years of his life learn as much, grow as much in his understanding of the world around him, as every infant learns and grows in his first three years. But what happens, as we get older, to this extraordinary capacity for learning and intellectual growth?

This selection consists of brief excerpts from books by A. S. Neill, by John Holt, and by Willard J. Congreve and George J. Rinehart. This and the remaining selections in Chapter 2 are closely related to Chapters 4, 5, 6, and 7.

[1] From *Summerhill* New York: Pocket Books, Simon and Schuster, 1970.

What happens is that it is destroyed, and more than by any other one thing, by the process that we misname education — a process that goes on in most homes and schools. We adults destroy most of the intellectual and creative capacity of children by the things we do to them or make them do. We destroy this capacity above all by making them afraid, afraid of not doing what other people want, of not pleasing, of making mistakes, of failing, or being *wrong*. Thus we make them afraid to gamble, afraid to experiment, afraid to try the difficult and the unknown. . . .

For we like children who are a little afraid of us, docile, deferential children, though not, of course, if they are so obviously afraid that they threaten our image of ourselves as kind, lovable people whom there is no reason to fear. We find ideal the kind of "good" children who are just enough afraid of us to do everything we want, without making us feel that fear of us is what is making them do it.

We destroy the disinterested (I do *not* mean *uninterested*) love of learning in children, which is so strong when they are small, by encouraging and compelling them to work for petty and contemptible rewards — gold stars, or papers marked 100 and tacked to the wall, or *A*'s on report cards, or honor rolls, or dean's lists, or Phi Beta Kappa keys — in short, for the ignoble satisfaction of feeling that they are better than someone else. We encourage them to feel that the end and aim of all they do in school is nothing more than to get a good mark on a test, or to impress someone with what they seem to know. We kill, not only their curiosity, but their feeling that it is a good and admirable thing to be curious, so that by the age of ten most of them will not ask questions, and will show a good deal of scorn for the few who do. . . .

We cannot have real learning in school if we think it is our duty and our right to tell children what they must learn. We cannot know, at any moment, what particular bit of knowledge or understanding a child needs most, will most strengthen and best fit his model of reality. Only he can do this. He may not do it very well, but he can do it a hundred times better than we can. The most we can do is try to help, by letting him know roughly what is available and where he can look for it. Choosing what he wants to learn and what he does not is something he must do for himself. . . .

When we better understand the ways, conditions, and spirit in which children do their best learning, and are able to make school into a place where they can use and improve the style of thinking and learning natural to them, we may be able to prevent much of this failure. School may then become a place in which *all* children grow, not just in size, not even in knowlege, but in curiosity, courage, confidence, independence, resourcefulness, resilience, patience, competence, and understanding. To find how best to do this will take us a long time.[2]

WILLIAM J. CONGREVE AND GEORGE J. RINEHART

[Here are five common misconceptions about individualized instruction:]

[2] From *How Children Fail* by John Holt. Copyright © 1964 by Pitman Publishing Corporation. Excerpts are from pp. 167, 168, and 179. The final paragraph is excerpted from *How Children Learn*, by John Holt, pp. vii–viii. Copyright © 1964 by Pitman Publishing Corporation. Reprinted by permission of Pitman Learning, Inc., Belmont, California.

1. It involves students accepting responsibility for their own learning and when they do not accept this responsibility, the program is not working.

    Not so. Independence in learning is different from individualized instruction. Both the independent and the dependent learner progress under individualized instruction. Each is given the proper amount of guidance and direction needed to cause him to learn. The child who needs to be told exactly what to do, when, and how, will be told in an individualized instruction setting. An additional goal might be to make the dependent learner independent, self-directing and responsible. If that is the case, the kinds of guidance and direction given him will be tailored to help him learn how to reach this additional goal.

2. All children must be doing something differently.

    Not true. If what is to be learned is appropriate for ten, twenty, or 100 children at one time, there is no reason why they cannot learn it as a group. As long as they all need it and are ready for the same level learning experience, the teacher is providing for their individual learning needs even though all are doing it together.

3. The teacher must personally explain the same thing thirty different times.

    Not true. Readiness is a flexible concept. Johnny may be ready right now, but this could be delayed a few moments or a day or so until three or four others were also ready, and the explanation could be made to more students. Although there is what Havighurst has called the "teachable moment," that moment is not a specific second in a child's life, but rather is a fairly lengthy time span when motivation and readiness are high.

4. Children should always be working by themselves.

    Not true. Nothing can be more boring than to have to work alone all the time. Excellent learning takes place under pleasant conditions for people who enjoy working together. More and more adults are doing this all the time.

5. Packets and contracts are essential to providing for the learning needs of individual children.

    Not true. They can be helpful, but they can also be an interference. The important thing is the cooperative diagnosis involving student and teacher, the identification of what should be learned next, and the determining of the materials, equipment and process needed for learning. It is the availability of a variety of materials and techniques which is important.

We could go on. The key to the issue is our definition — doing the best possible job of giving each child what he needs at a particular time to cause his learning to go forward.[3]

[3] From *Flexibility in School Programs*, by William J. Congreve and George J. Rinehart, © 1972 by Wadsworth Publishing Company, Inc., Belmont, California 94002. Reprinted by permission of the publisher, Charles A. Jones Publishing Company.

2.9   Three Reasons Why Children Fail
KENNETH KENISTON

[Let us begin with some embarrassing facts. Consider] how scandalously high is our infant mortality rate: The U.S. stands fifteenth among the 42 nations ranked by the United Nations, just below East Germany and just above Hong Kong. We are among the very few modern nations that do not guarantee adequate health care to mothers and children.

Or consider malnutrition. Between 1955 and 1965, the percentage of diets deficient in one or more essential nutrients actually increased. Millions of American children today remain hungry and malnourished. One-sixth of them live below the officially defined poverty line. *One-third* live below that level defined by the government as minimum but adequate.

Why are such things so? I suggest that the answer is to be found in the forces of our economic system. Let me examine this suggestion in the context of three problems, which I will call the depopulation of the family, the intellectualization of the child, and the perpetuation of exclusion.

Depopulation of the Family

For the first time in our national history, most children now have mothers who work outside the home and most of these mothers work full time. A particularly depopulated set of families are those with only one parent. In 1973, one out of seven children was in a single-parent family. Another trend is the disappearance of nonparental relatives from families. In less than 25 years, the number of other relatives in the single-parent family has dropped from 50 percent to 20 percent. Brothers and sisters are also increasingly scarce; today, the average child has less than one sibling.

Thus, millions of American children today are being raised for larger and larger portions of time by nonrelatives, often completely outside of their family. And, finally, increasing numbers of children are simply growing up with no one to care for them. They stay alone in empty houses while their parents work. Such are some effects of the depopulation of the family.

The entry of mothers and other women into the occupational system seems irreversible. In many cases it is desirable. Our effort is not to condemn but to try to understand.

Certainly one thing that we have come to understand is that the economic forces at play on us are sharply at odds with our sentiments that children should receive consistent care and nurturance in and from the family. If families in America become little more than dormitories and quick-service restaurants we must look not to the negligence of American parents but to the pressures of the economy for the main explanation. . . . [We return to this topic in Chapters 4–7.]

Excerpts from Kenneth Keniston, "Do Americans *Really* Like Children?" *Childhood Education* 52: 4–13, October 1974; reprinted in reduced form in *Education Digest* 41: 10–13. February 1975. Reprinted by permission of Kenneth Keniston and the Association for Childhood Education International, 3615 Wisconsin Ave., N.W., Washington, D.C. Copyright © 1974 by the Association.
     Kenneth Keniston is Chairman and Executive Director, Carnegie Council on Children, New York City.

Intellectualization of the Child

While we have been depriving our children of what they might obtain from a complete and vital family, what have we been doing to them at school? I believe that we are witnessing the creation, through our preschools and schools, of a breed of children whose value and progress are judged primarily by their capacity to do well on tests. Although children are whole people full of imagination, physical grace, social relationships, initiative, love, and joy, the overt and above all the covert structure of our system of schooling largely ignores these other human potentials to concentrate on the cultivation of a narrow form of intellect.

We measure the effectiveness of education by whether or not it produces income increments, not by whether it improves the quality of life of those who are educated. And we measure the success of schools not by the human beings they promote, but by increases in reading scores. We have allowed quantitative standards, so central to our economic system and our way of thinking about it, to become the central yardstick for our definition of our children's worth. [We return to this topic in Chapter 5.]

CHILDREN BROUGHT UP TO FAIL

The Perpetuation of Exclusion

The two problems I have so far mentioned affect *all* American children. Now I turn to the problem of the excluded — children born in the cellar of our society and systematically brought up to remain there. Our excluded include one-quarter of all American children, and the tragic truth is that this *one-quarter of all American children today are being brought up to fail*.

I am talking about children who are being deprived of the opportunity to realize a significant portion of their human potential, who are being actively injured, hurt, deprived at times even of the right to live. This is happening to them for four reasons: race, poverty, handicap, and being born of parents too overwhelmed by life to be able to care responsively and lovingly for them.

One out of every five children in America is nonwhite, and must somehow cope with the persistent racism of our society. One out of three children lives below the minimum adequate budget established by the Department of Labor and must face the multiple scars of poverty. One out of every 12 children is born with a major or minor handicap. One out of every 10 children has a learning disability. Approximately one-quarter of all American children do not receive anything approaching adequate health care. Millions of children live in substandard housing. Millions attend deplorable schools.

What makes these facts even more disturbing is the frequency with which they occur together. The single-parent family is likely to be poor — and vice versa. Poverty is irrevocably linked to inadequate medical care. To speak of the poor and the hungry is almost redundant — and a hungry child can rarely do well in school. But the most powerful forms of exclusion are not physical but social and psychological.

Excluded children are systematically trained for failure. As people they are defined as no good, inadequate, dirty, incompetent, ugly, dumb, and clumsy. They learn that the best strategy for coping is never to venture out, to take no risks, or constantly to be on the attack. This pathetic sense of self and this view of the world is in fact an accurate perception of the messages our society gives these children. It is also the perception that condemns them to lives of failure in social if not in human terms.

The themes that dominate our social and political history sing with our commitment to equality and fair play. How, then, can we understand the perpetuation of exclusion? One answer, put forward for almost two centuries in America, is that those at the bottom belong there because they lack virtue, merit, industriousness, or talent. Or because they are immoral — lazy, dependent, profligate, or licentious.

But no thoughtful person can accept such an unjust explanation. And here I suggest, once again, that the excluded are among us not because of their individual inadequacy or immorality, but rather because of the way our society has worked for more than a century.

Let me point to one cold and significant fact: The distribution of wealth and income in this nation has not changed materially in 150 years. But exclusion persists not because of the evil motives of robber barons or the wicked intentions of industrialists. It persists because we all live in a system driven by the relentless quest for innovation, growth, and profit. That system has made us the most prosperous and technologically advanced nation in world history. Most Americans have shared in the profit.

But I think it is indispensable to appreciate that the profit has been reaped at costs that do not appear on corporate ledger sheets — the misery and despair and neglect and hunger of that vast fraction of us whom I have called the excluded. Such costs cannot be quantified in IQ points or dollars and cents. And maybe that is one reason we have yet as a nation to take them into account.

Some prices we should not be willing to pay. In the long run, the price of exclusion is enormous — not only in dollars laid out for remedial services, for prisons, for mental hospitals, but in the anguish and pain exacted by social tension, unrest, and discontent. And finally, this nation pays a continuing price far more serious: the moral and human price we pay simply by tolerating a system that wastes a significant portion of the potential of the next generation, wherein the advantage of some rests on the systematic deprivation of others. . . .

I think it is now indispensable for us to see that millions of American children who suffer unmet needs for care and opportunity should not be blamed, nor should their parents, for crippling situations that are in fact wrought by us all within this system. No doubt individualism can and should continue to be a cherished value of this society. But it is time for us to behave not like a collection of competing individuals but like a family of related people. It is time for old-style individualism to give way to some old-style sense of community.*

---

*EDITOR'S NOTE   Although we all yearn for "some old-style sense of community," we are not likely to recover the *old* style. Why not? Because we are living at a time when some very fundamental changes are occurring in the way people live. Consider the following:

The second most fundamental revolution in the affairs of mankind on earth is now occurring. The first came when

2.10   The Modern Students' Struggle for Freedom
B. F. SKINNER

What we may call the struggle for freedom in the Western world can be analyzed as a struggle to escape from or avoid punitive or coercive treatment. It is characteristic of the human species to act in such a way as to reduce or terminate irritating, painful, or dangerous stimuli, and the struggle for freedom has been directed toward those who would control others with stimuli of that sort. Education has had a long and shameful part in the history of that struggle. The Egyptians, Greeks, Romans all whipped their students. Medieval sculpture showed the carpenter with his hammer and the school-master with the tool of his trade too, and it was the cane or rod. We are not yet in the clear. Corporal punishment is still used in many schools, and there are calls for its return where it has been abandoned.

A system in which students study primarily to avoid the consequences of not studying is neither humane nor very productive. Its by-products include truancy, vandalism, and apathy. Any effort to eliminate punishment in education is certainly commendable. We ourselves act to escape from aversive control, and our students should escape from it too. They should study because they want to, because they like to, because they are interested in what they are doing . . .

[To resolve this problem, some educators seem to recommend] a total commitment to the present moment, or at least to an immediate future. . . . But it has always been the task of formal education to set up behavior which would prove useful or enjoyable *later* in the student's life. Punitive methods had at least the merit of providing current reasons for learning things that should be rewarding in the future. We object to the

From B. F. Skinner, "The Free and Happy Student." Reprinted with permission from *New York University Education Quarterly* IV, 2 (Winter, 1973): 2–6. © New York University. This article was reprinted in *Phi Delta Kappan* 55: 13–16, September, 1973.

Burrhus Frederick Skinner is Edgar Pierce Professor Emeritus of Psychology, Harvard University.

man settled down from hunting, fishing, herding, and gathering to sedentary agricultural and village life. The second is now occurring as women, no longer so concentrated and sheltered for their childbearing and childrearing functions, are demanding equality of treatment in all aspects of life, are demanding a new sense of purpose. — from the Carnegie Commission on Higher Education, *Opportunities for Women in Higher Education*, New York: McGraw-Hill, 1973.

Although this anthology does not include a special chapter to Women's Liberation, and does not treat it as a special issue, it is a fact of modern life and might well be the topic of a class panel or of special reports for students who would like to focus attention on this topic.

A related topic is that of the adolescent *peer group*. Lawrence Cremin calls our attention to the fact that, during the past century, the influence of parents has weakened as that of schools has increased. Thus, children of the same age were grouped together in school classrooms. But in recent years, continues Cremin, these peer groups

. . . became the target of special films, special radio programs, and special advertising campaigns for special products; put otherwise, that group became a special market clientele, which was systematically taught styles of dress, entertainment, and . . . consumption. The household mediated this educative influence to some extent, but the influence was powerful nontheless and in many ways competed with the purposeful efforts of parents, pastors, and school teachers. —Lawrence Cremin, *Traditions in American Education*. (New York: Basic Books, 1977), p. 111.

See also "Women's liberation" in the Subject Index. Careful study of the Subject Index reveals numerous other such cross references and shows the interrelatedness of ideas in the nine chapters of this anthology.

punitive reasons, but we should not forget their function in making the future important. . . .

The teacher can often make the change from punishment to positive reinforcement in a surprisingly simple way — by responding to the student's success rather than his failures. Teachers have too often supposed that their role is to point out what students are doing wrong, but pointing to what they are doing *right* will often make an enormous difference in the atmosphere of a classroom and in the efficiency of instruction. Programmed materials are helpful in bringing about these changes, because they increase the frequency with which the student enjoys the satisfaction of being right, and they supply a valuable intrinsic reward in providing a clear indication of progress. A good program makes a step in the direction of competence almost as conspicuous as a token.

Programmed instruction is perhaps most successful in attacking punitive methods by allowing the student to move at his own pace. The slow student is released from the punishment which inevitably follows when he is forced to move on to material for which he is not ready, and the fast student escapes the boredom of being forced to go too slow. . . . [Well-planned programmed instruction provides] nonpunitive reasons for acquiring behavior that will become useful or otherwise reinforcing at some later date.*

2.11   10 Steps to Good Discipline
WILLIAM GLASSER

School discipline is a big problem. The 10-step approach to it discussed here will work only in a school where people would normally choose to be — in the school which is continually striving to a a "good" place. A good place is one where people are courteous, where one often hears laughter that springs from genuine joy brought about by involvement with caring people engaged in relevant work, where communication is practiced, not just preached. A good place is one that has reasonable, democratically determined rules which everyone agrees on because they are beneficial to the individual and the group. A good place is one where administrators support and actively participate in an approach to discipline that teaches self-responsibility.

The approach I advocate is based on the following concepts of Reality Therapy:

Condensed from *Today's Education* 46: 60–63, November–December, 1977; and from *The Education Digest* 43: 2–5, February 1978.

---

*EDITOR'S NOTE   For models of ways to implement three methods of nonpunitive teaching, read Thomas R. McDonald (Converse College, Spartansburg, S.C.) "Exploring Alternatives to Punishment: The Keys to Effective Discipline," *Phi Delta Kappan* 61: 456-458, March 1980. McDonald outlines three models: (1) *The Behavioral Model*, based on B. F. Skinner's theories of positive reinforcement, (2) *The Human Relations Model*, based on theories of Carl Rogers, Haim Ginott, Thomas Gordon, and William Purkey, and (3) *The Pedagogical Model*, based on the ideas of such men as Rudolph Dreikurs, Don Dunkmeyer, Frederick Jones, and William Glasser.

- Be personal. Use personal pronouns: "I care enough about you to be involved, to be your friend."
- Refer to present behavior. Awareness of behavior is the first step. Avoid references to the past. Emphasize behavior, not feelings.
- Stress value judgments. Ask students to evaluate their own behavior. The decision to do something better than what they are now doing must be theirs.
- Plan. Work with students to formulate alternatives. Keep the plan simple with short spans of time. Build success into the plan.
- Be committed. Build in a way to check back, follow up. Give positive reinforcement. Students need to accept some responsibility for this. A written form may be helpful.
- Don't accept excuses. Eliminate discussion of excuses to show you know students can succeed. Replan with them. Don't give up.
- Do not punish. Punishment lifts responsibility from students. Set rules and sanctions with them. They have to understand that they are responsible for themselves. This takes time and consistency.
- Never give up. Each of us must define "never," but hang in there longer than the student thinks you will. With the 10-step approach, this means at least a month. Firm results often take two months or more.

The 10-step approach will work well if a majority of the school staff studies, practices, and continually reinforces Reality Therapy. Here are the 10 steps.

Step One. Set aside some quiet thinking time for yourself, and choose a student who is an ongoing discipline problem to work with. Choose someone you think you can succeed in helping. List what you now do when this child is disruptive. Be honest.

Step Two. Analyze the list and then ask yourself, "Are these techniques working?" If not, make a commitment not to use any of these responses the next time a problem develops unless they correspond to the procedures in Steps Three through Seven.

Step Three. Plan a better tomorrow for your student. Send him on a special errand or do something that says, "You're special. I care about you." Continue these activities, but don't expect immediate improvements. In extreme cases, the student may reject you even more strongly than before. But stay calm and be persistent. Treating your most difficult students well will eventually lead them to improve their behavior.

Step Four. When a problem occurs, ask the student, "What are you doing?" Such a question often causes the student to stop what he is doing and think about it, which can sometimes help him to own the behavior. Being responsible for it is not far behind. If you persist, the student will tell you what he is doing. The answer will probably contain some embellishment or distraction ("I pushed him, but he pushed me first."). When you get an answer that contains the behavior, simply say, "Please stop it."

Step Five. In spite of persistent use of Steps Three and Four, the problem is continuing. This calls for a short conference. Start it by again asking, "What are you doing?" Now ask, "Is it against the rules?" And then, "What should you be doing?" Explicit in the third question is the idea that you expect the unacceptable behavior to be replaced by the answer to this last question. When asking these questions, try to convey warmth, support, and firmness.

A POSITIVE ACTION PLAN

Step Six. The short conferences are not working. Repeat all of Step Five except the last question. Substitute, "We have to work this out. What kind of plan can you make to follow our rules?" The plan has to be more than just, "I'll stop." It has to be a plan of positive action that helps the student move toward responsible behavior. In order to work, the plan should be short-term, specific, and simple. In the beginning, you may have to put many of your ideas into the plan because the process will be unusual to the student. Gradually, however, he will make more contributions to the plan. The more the student considers the plan his own, the better it will work.

Step Seven. The problem student disrupts again, and because of repeated use of all the previous steps, you are sure that their further use won't work. Now is the time to isolate or "time out" the student. This may be your decision or else it may be a natural consequence agreed on at the conclusion of your planning conference from Step Six. . . . Either way, students know they cannot participate in class activities until they have devised a plan for following the rules, gotten your approval of the plan, and made a commitment to follow the plan. A student who disrupts while in isolation must be excluded from the classroom or quiet area.

Step Eight. In-school suspension is the next step. There are no questions to be asked. Make this statement: "Things are not working out here for you. You and I have worked hard on the problem, but now you're going to have to spend some time outside of the class and perhaps talk with some other people. Please report to the principal's office."

The in-school suspension place should be set up along the same lines as the in-class "time out" place. It should be a comfortable, nonpunitive place staffed by someone who communicates these basic ideas to students: "We want you to be in class, but we expect you to follow our reasonable rules. As soon as you have a plan for returning to class and following the rules, let me know, and I'll help you." . . .

If the student says, "But I'm getting behind in my work," the response should be, "Yes, I see that, and that does present a problem for you. Please feel free to do your schoolwork right here. But you cannot go back to class until you have a plan." The staff person has to help the student understand that there are really only two alternatives: return to class and follow reasonable rules or continue to sit there and be outside of class.

If more than one day is required, parents should be notified that their child is not in class. Sometimes a week or more is required.

Step Nine. If any student is totally out of control and cannot be contained in an in-school suspension room or office, parents must be notified and asked to take the child home. Further, they should be told that tomorrow is a new day. This can be done by saying, "We would like your son to return and stay with us as long as his behavior is reasonable. When it goes beyond reasonableness, he will again be asked to go home." If behavior is reasonable, then it's back to Step Eight. . . .

Step Ten. Any student who continually is unsuccessful in Step Nine must stay home permanently or be referred to some other community agency. As a last resort, even juvenile hall is a possibility. Though this sounds harsh, sometimes it will finally jolt the student awake, and he will then be ready to plan a way to return to school.

The student should always be welcome to return to school, but only after having made a specific plan and commitment to follow reasonable rules. . . .

Some variations in the 10-step approach . . . are to be anticipated because it is impossible to have a generic "blueprint" applicable to every school. The program succeeds in part because the staff cooperates to design the one that will work best in their school. They own the program and feel responsible for maintaining it.

This approach works. A survey of 17 schools using it found office referrals down 20-80 percent in the 10 elementary schools and 5-75 percent in the five junior high schools. All 17 schools reported fighting reduced — by 10-80 percent in elementary schools and by 25-95 percent in junior high schools. Both senior high schools saw suspensions reduced — one by 50 percent, the other by 75.*

2.12   Compulsory School Attendance: A Second Look
DAVID L. MOBERLY, EDWARD C. BANFIELD, AND ROBERT L. EBEL

DAVID L. MOBERLY (Superintendent, Seattle Public Schools):

In 1973 the National Commission on the Reform of Secondary Education made 32 specific recommendations for a new set of national goals in secondary education. Recommendation 28 of that report reads: "If the high school is not to be a custodial institution, the state must not force adolescents to attend. Earlier maturity — physical, sexual, and intellectual — requires an option of earlier departure from the restraints of formal schools. The formal school-leaving age should be dropped to age

This selection consists of brief excerpts from three sources:

David L. Moberly, "Compulsory School Attendance: A Second Look," *The High School Journal* Volume 63, Number 5, (195–199), February 1980. Copyright 1980 The University of North Carolina Press. Reprinted by permission of the publisher. (Condensed in *Education Digest* 45: 6–9, May 1980).

Edward C. Banfield, *The Unheavenly City Revisited* (Boston: Little, Brown, 1975), pp. 170–171. Copyright © 1968, 1970, 1974 by Edward C. Banfield. By permission of Little, Brown and Company.

Robert L. Ebel, "The Failure of Schools without Failure," *Phi Delta Kappan* 61: 386–388, February 1980. © 1980 by Phi Delta Kappa, Inc. Used by permission.

*EDITOR'S NOTE   When William Glasser enumerates these Ten Steps to Good Discipline, he is in no way embracing the notion that schools should not maintain discipline. Glasser's nonpunitive approach to teaching is quite different from that of the "romantic critics" of the 1960s and 1970s, whose views were summarized by Henry J. Perkinson in 1976 as follows:

> [The romantic critics] reject imposition and advocate a child-oriented or learner-centered education. The smorgasbord curriculum of John Holt, the inquiry method of Postman and Weingartner, the open classroom of Herbert Kohl, the free school of George Dennison, the learning web of Ivan Illich — all point to an educational process where people learn what, how, and when they like. — Henry J. Perkinson, cited in R. Freeman Butts in *Public Education in the United States* (New York: Holt, Rinehart and Winston, 1978), pp. 373–375.

14. Other programs should accommodate those who wish to leave school, and employment laws should be rewritten to assure on-the-job training in full-time service and work." . . .

[The 1970s provided a growing body of] evidence that, for at least some youth, school is an exercise in frustration. A recent investigation in Philadelphia found that 52 percent of the boys dropping out of school had police contacts before leaving school, whereas only 3.8 percent of those dropouts initiated their delinquent careers after leaving school. Of those 52 percent who were delinquent prior to leaving school, only 14 percent continued to violate the law. This is in keeping with the "pressure on, pressure off" phenomena reported by a number of juvenile courts. Many communities report an increase in the delinquency rate around examination time and a decrease during the summer months.

It is clear that in this day of individual rights, attacks on the concept of *in loco parentis*, increased permissiveness, increased violence and disruption in schools, changing lifestyles, the public calling for accountability based on traditional measuring instruments, and the inability of school to provide alternatives in learning, it is necessary that we *challenge* the concept of forced schooling for teenagers. Secondary education cannot meet the needs of all of society nor the needs of all of America's youth. There is little doubt that many of our youth could find more appropriate or more immediately useful educational experiences outside the typical high school.

Whether compulsory schooling is to remain legal or not, it is urgent that teachers, school administrators, and boards of education give attention to increasing the number of alternatives available to young people within our school systems. Compulsory schooling has not created the incentive to provide such alternative programs. Rather, it has fostered a population of bitter youth who see no point to, or cannot succeed in, a narrow, college-oriented curriculum. Perhaps educators should be forced to compete with on-the-job training programs in business and industry or with other types of training that could be offered by local, state, and national agencies.

Three Options

Barring another serious international military involvement, the problems associated with forcing reluctant students to stay in school are not going to go away. If the profession is serious about moving toward solutions, at least three options are worth considering:

1. Policymakers could make the school program offer educational preparation for the world of work at least comparable in quality to that provided for the college-bound student. Admittedly, this would be costly, but if it is cheaper to expand the services of an existing institution than it is to create a new one, this approach should be given serious consideration.

2. School districts could attempt to form a consortium of institutions, schools, trade schools, and business and industry, and — through the coordination of a variety of sites and establishments — deliver the experiences required. This approach is appealing in that it requires a minimum of new programs and support facilities, but the coordination problems appear formidable.

3. Federal policymakers could opt for a form of national public service of two years for *all* youth at the transition stage. The model of the Depression-era Civilian Conservation Corps could be expanded to address our present problems. Universal public service has a long and successful history in Switzerland and, more recently, in Israel.

Whether or not society elects one of these alternatives or some other course of action, there must first of all be a clearly stated policy with strong national commitment. The cost will be high whatever approach is chosen, but the ultimate cost of neglecting this problem will be incalculable.

EDWARD C. BANFIELD (Harvard University)

Boys, especially working-class ones, frequently want to leave school for the very practical reason that changing their status from "schoolboy" to "worker" will give them independence and even a certain prestige at home. If not permitted to leave, the boy who finds the "schoolboy" role intolerable may replace it with membership in a youth gang or other delinquent subculture. Indirectly, then, the school may be a factor generating delinquency.

The frustration, anger, and contempt for authority engendered by the school may possibly enter into the personality of the individual, coloring his attitudes in adulthood and leading him to take a cynical and resentful view of the society and all its works. Conceivably, the practice of forcing the incapable and unwilling to waste their adolescent years in schoolrooms further weakens the already tenuous attachment of the lower classes to social institutions. The discovery that the school consists largely of cant and pretense may prepare the way for the discovery that the police and the courts, for example, do too. . . .

A second reason for getting nonlearners out of the school is — paradoxical though it may seem — to give them opportunities and incentives to learn. Not everything worth learning must be (or indeed can be) learned from books and teachers, and not everyone — not even everyone with a first-rate mind — learns better from books and teachers than from other sources. . . . To be sure, some of the boys and girls here in question are not likely to learn much from *any* source. . . . [Nevertheless] on a job a worker is usually rewarded at once if he learns something that improves his performance; the job, that is, gives incentives to present-oriented people, whereas the school gives them only to the future-oriented.

ROBERT L. EBEL (Michigan State University)

If we intend to hold teachers accountable for the achievement of their pupils in learning, we must allow them to hold their pupils accountable for reasonable efforts to learn. Let them shape up or ship out. Faced with this alternative, most pupils will shape up. Those who ship out will gain the freedom they seek. Some of these may use the freedom to grow. Others will use it to decay. Either way, the responsibility for what happens to them is ultimately theirs. The only way to free them from that responsibility is to take away all of their other freedoms.

Schools without failure have failed. When lack of learning no longer made any obvious differences in progress through school, deficiencies in learning became more numerous and more serious. Let us stop pretending that pupils never fail to learn satisfactorily. Let us shirk neither the hard task of identifying it nor the disagreeable task of reporting it when it occurs. Most serious deficiencies in school learning result not from want of ability but from want of effort. Let us reward the effort by promotion and penalize lack of effort by retention. When learning succeeds, our pupils deserve much of the credit. When it fails, let us ask them to accept a substantial part of the responsibility. Our responsibility as teachers is to arrange and conduct classroom activities that will stimulate and facilitate pupil efforts to learn.

2.13 Some Problems of Mainstreaming
DAVID A. POWERS

Educators concerned with mainstreaming have moved from an initial concern with maximizing the regular classroom participation of educable mentally retarded (EMR) students at the elementary level toward efforts to implement mainstreaming strategies at the secondary school level. The seven statements listed below, reflecting a number of frequently voiced concerns regarding mainstreaming of EMR students at the secondary level, would appear to represent substantial support for a case *against* the practice. A closer examination of each issue, however, suggests a case *for* the modifiability of the secondary school program.

1. *There is inadequate empirical support for the efficacy of mainstreaming at the secondary level.* . . .

2. *The curriculum offered in regular classrooms at the secondary level is inconsistent with the needs of EMR students.* . . .

The high school of today is an organization of multiple curricula, manifesting a vast range of goals. It is inaccurate to assume that EMR pupils can be successfully involved in all regular classes. It is equally unproductive, however, to assume that all regular classes are inappropriate. Personalization of course selection is a requirement for effective mainstreaming.

3. *The availability of personnel necessary to support mainstreaming is currently too limited to assure its success.*

Without additional teacher personnel mainstreaming is not likely to be successful. . . .

4. *Teachers at the secondary level are subject-matter-orientated rather than person-centered, and*

Slightly adapted from David A. Powers (East Carolina University, Greensville, N.C.), "Secondary School Mainstreaming of the Educable Mentally Retarded," from *The High School Journal*, Volume 62, Number 3: (102–108), December 1979. Copyright 1979 The University of North Carolina Press. Reprinted by permission of the publisher. Condensed in *Education Digest* 45: 46–48, March 1980. By permission.

Read also Barry Guinagh (University of Florida, Gainesville), "The Social Integration of Handicapped Children," *Phi Delta Kappan*, 62: 27–29, September 1980; Rachel M. Lauer, "Handicapped—According to Whom?" *The Humanist* 41: 16–17, November/December 1980; and Louis Rubin, editor, *Critical Issues in Educational Policy* (Boston: Allyn and Bacon, 1980), pp. 291–298 (by Gordon Hoke), pp. 314–325 (by Colin Hook), pp. 429–432 and 450–452 (by Louis Rubin).

possess neither the expertise nor the motivation to deal with the significant learning problems EMR students may possess. . . .

Insofar as this is true, teachers must be carefully selected, and, in most cases, given special training. . . .

5. *Policies and operational procedures at the secondary level are inflexible, resulting in a system that is resistant to change and innovation.*

Policies and procedures must *reflect* rather than dictate the purpose of any institution. To suggest that mainstreaming cannot work because it is in conflict with existing operational procedures is to allow purposes to be established by historical policy. Such an environment is unhealthy for *any* new idea; schools must be the place where new ideas are nurtured.

6. *The large number of teachers with whom each student must deal renders meaningful communication and cooperation impossible and reduces each teacher's sense of individual responsibility for the student and his growth.*

There must be a single person who holds responsibility for coordination of the mainstreamed student's program. Only in exceptional cases should a regular subject matter teacher be asked to assume such responsibilities. . . .

7. *Individualized instruction is impossible in the regular secondary level classroom due to limitations in time available to design, implement, and monitor individualized programs, inadequate preparation of secondary level teachers for this task, the large number of students contacts, and administrative demands for time-controlled rather than response-controlled progression through course-prescribed material.*

The process of fully individualizing instruction is rarely accomplished outside of clinical and other very controlled, precise environments. A more practical concept and a more accurate term is *personalization of instruction.* . . .

[Even with "normal" students, to "personalize" instruction requires great skill, ingenuity, and patience. There are some exceptional teachers who can personalize instruction to reach EMR students as well. But we should realize that only a few teachers possess such talents.]

2.14   New Forms of Educational Decision and Choice
EVANS CLINCHY and ELISABETH ALLEN CODY

It was only about 125 years ago that this country decided to provide both the opportunity and, if possible, the reality of formal schooling to every child and young person, including eventually all the children who had always been benignly ignored by everyone — the poor, the foreign born, the physically and mentally handicapped. As recently as 1921 there were only 334,000 young people graduating from high school, or 17.1% of all the country's 17-year-olds. By 1975 the number had jumped to 3,140,000, or 74.4% of the nation's 17-year-olds.

Excerpts from Evans Clinchy and Elisabeth Allen Cody (Educational Planning Associates, Inc., 584 Chestnut St., Newton, MA.) "If not Public Choice, Then Private Escape," *Phi Delta Kappan* 60: 270–273, December 1978. © 1978, Phi Delta Kappa, Inc. Used by permission of publisher and authors.

Read also "Restoring School Efficacy by Giving Parents a Choice," by Mary Anne Raywid, *Educational Leadership* 38: 134–137, November 1980 (bibliography).

Despite all the criticisms that have been both justly and unjustly leveled against it, the American system of public education between 1850 and the present has undertaken and largely succeeded in accomplishing the most massive formal schooling effort in the history of humankind. The system has produced — or has been instrumental in producing — the most literate and well-informed people on earth.

In order to achieve this miracle, in order to provide schooling for so many people in so short a time at the lowest possible cost, the public education establishment borrowed — or had forced upon it — the organizational structure and many of the managerial techniques of the mass-production, assembly-line industrial corporation. The typical American school system became a vertically organized, hierarchical bureaucracy with all basic decisions made at the top and then passed down through the ranks to the workers and clients at the bottom.

As part of this structure, and in an effort to make sure that every child is treated both equally and efficiently, public educators have felt compelled to search for and impose a single, standardized, and largely uniform type of schooling throughout most school districts.

Having adopted this structure and performed the miracle of mass education, the public education establishment now finds itself confronted with the results of its labors. It is faced with an adult population of parents who are knowledgeable, questioning, and restive. Increasingly, they reject the autocratic operations of the system as being impossibly rigid, thoroughly undemocratic, and quite unable to respond to the diverse but legitimate demands that parents are making on behalf of themselves and their children.

What this new, highly informed breed of parents — and perhaps especially the young parents of the postwar baby boom generation — is in the midst of discovering is that there is no single, uniform, widely agreed-upon, indisputably "right" way to educate all children. They are discovering that the so-called experts, from academic theoreticians to practicing school administrators, simply do not agree on any one approach.

Many parents as well as teachers and other educators believe that children — or at least some children — will benefit most from a highly structured, traditional, or back-to-basics type of schooling. Still other parents and educators believe that children will benefit from a less structured or "continuous progress" type of schooling in which each child moves through the prescribed course of study at his own most appropriate speed. Still other parents and educators believe that children will benefit from a developmental type of schooling that sees children as the primary agents in their own intellectual growth and therefore gives children a role in deciding what the day-to-day activities of schooling will be.

What these parents are discovering is that they are asking for something — educational diversity and choice — that the present educational structure is simply not designed to provide. . . .

[More and more educators are also recognizing the need for greater educational diversity and choice. Indeed, future historians may credit the 1960s and 1970s as the decades when this discovery was made, and the 1980s and 1990s as the decades when this discovery was implemented.]

Instead of an industrial, mass-production corporate structure, we will have developed what economist Peter Drucker describes as a model based upon "socialist competition." Under this arrangement the schools remain public and are therefore owned by and open to everyone. But within that public structure the individual schools are responsive to the marketplace and reflect what the clientele wants. This does not mean that every parent is compelled to choose or must make decisions without the advice and assistance of educators in the system. One of the options offered would be the opportunity of not choosing, of having a child assigned to whatever school the professional educators believe is best for that child. A system of diversity and choice, however, does empower every parent who wishes to control his child's education with the right to do so. . . .

In the few places where a system of diversity and choice has been tried within a public school system, the results have been impressive. In 1971 the Minneapolis, Minnesota, school system launched a pioneering effort in educational options called the Southeast Alternatives project. Using a small part of the city (the southeast section, including 29,000 people), the school system offered parents and teachers a choice among four different kinds of elementary schools: traditional, continuous progress, British primary/integrated day, and a K-12 free school.

Before this experiment was put into effect, a poll of the parents indicated that only about 35% of them were "satisfied" with what the school system was then offering them. After four years of diversity and choice, the parent satisfaction level reached 85%. . . .

What is perhaps even more impressive is that the offering of educational options is being used to desegregate the schools in that city. Each optional school has racial quotas guaranteeing that at no time can the minority enrollment in an option exceed that of the school system as a whole. Since this approach to desegregation appears to be working without all the furor and turmoil that normally accompanies desegregation, the parents in Minneapolis, even if they have to put their children on buses, evidently feel that the educational benefit their children receive at the end of the bus ride is well worth the rigors of the trip. . . .

[Indianapolis seems to be enjoying equal success as it offers] six district educational options: a back-to-basics or fundamental school; a traditional school; a continuous progress school; a continuous progress school operating in open space (a building without interior walls or regular classroom spaces); a Montessori school; and a developmental or integrated-day school.

2.15   A New Concept of Discipline
KENNETH HENSON

. . . As our students change, so must we teachers change our roles. Therefore, few set answers are to be found to the teacher's plea, "What should I do when confronted with a certain situation?" By examining some of the recent changes in adolescents and in school environment, some insights into desirable methods for coping with prob-

From Kenneth Henson (University of Miami at Coral Gables), "A New Concept of Discipline," *The Clearing House* 51: 89–90, October 1977. (Footnote references are omitted.) By permission.

lems may be gained. The following are some facts about discipline which consider the nature of the contemporary adolescent and the environment in the contemporary school.

Discipline is different than before. Students are louder and more active. A brief visit to many of our classes will remind us how fast the pace of American life has increased. Students are busier than ever before. They have more responsibilities and less time to attend to each. So we see students running to classrooms, learning centers, and extracurricular functions during the school day and even extending into the afternoon or evening hours. As the curriculum expands, the length of each period diminishes. These added responsibilities and the resulting increase in the pace throughout the school force the student to be much more active — and naturally noisier, which makes the once desirable image of student passiveness and quietness obsolete. Therefore, good discipline is no longer considered synonymous with quietness, stillness, and obedience. How quiet should a teacher expect students to be? How still? How obedient? Just enough to allow him and others to pursue the objectives of the class (objectives which may be selected cooperatively by the teacher and the class, a group, or an individual).

Students are more outspoken. With the increase of adolescent responsibilities, many of which have placed the student in a leadership role forcing him to make suggestions and decisions, is it not surprising that the contemporary student has more opinions which he not only wishes to share but which he feels responsible to share? Therefore, we teachers must adjust our style so as to begin seriously listening to students and considering their opinions. . . .

Today's students know their rights. The many court cases in the past decade which found that students' rights have been violated by the schools have made all students more aware of their rights. The resulting condition is that since today's student is more aware of his rights, he actually *has* more rights. This is important because students are less submissive to those teacher demands or requests which are questionable and seem unfair or without purpose. . . . [This means that, when faced with a troublesome student, today's teacher should . . .]

Always ask "why?" Whenever a rule is broken, we should want to know why the student chose to violate it. Only then can we hope to find a permanent solution to the problem. Anytime a person misbehaves, the type of behavior he chooses is that which seems best to him in the particular situation. There is some reason(s) why the student could not follow the rules. The best approach to finding this reason is through a private discussion between the teacher and student. According to one source, the private talk is "by far the most effective way of dealing with disciplinary and other types of problems."

In private discussions, we should never take an opposing (you-against-me) stand. Rather, we should explain that both we and the student have a problem. We must find out why the student cannot abide by the rule, and then decide whether the rule or the student must change. We then should ask the student for his suggestions. Until a satisfactory answer can be found and agreed upon by both parties, the student who is disrupting the class must not be permitted to return to the class.

Confrontations are best avoided. To many teachers, any discussion on classroom discipline would be incomplete if it failed to address the inevitable question, "What should I do when confronted by an irate student?" While each situation is unique, one fact withstands. Whenever possible, we should avoid confrontations in the classroom. The student who has become emotionally upset has temporarily lost his ability to use good judgment. Often students create a scene to secure peer attention. Whatever the reason, we teachers stand to gain nothing from an emotional dispute, and much to lose. Our yielding to this temptation reveals poor judgment and lack of self control, qualities essential for good leadership. Students who witness such teacher behavior will be led to doubt that the teacher possesses other essential teaching qualities such as his expertise in his own subject area. . . .

Misbehavior in our schools today is common and serious enough to deserve time in the curriculum for discussions by faculty and students. Our approach to coping with it should be coherent with our desire to produce citizens who are self-disciplined and who obey our laws, not as a result of fear but out of their desire to do what they believe is right, and because of their desire to live harmoniously with others. Any procedures that are worthy of our consideration must be consistent with this goal.

2.16   Control, Conflict and Collaboration in the Classroom
DEAN TJOSVOLD

[Students, no less than teachers,] want to be the cause or origin of their own behavior and resent attempts by others to control them. Research on influence strategies indicates that people resist control influence attempts. . . .

The use of controlled, directive teaching, in other words, appears to induce (1) students to resist the influence and resent the teacher, (2) the teacher to undervalue the students, and (3) the teacher and the students to perceive their relationship as competitive. Furthermore, though control orientation of the school has been defended as helping students develop self-discipline, it is unlikely to do so.

Control orientation also may increase the incidence of conflict, generating hostility

Brief excerpts from Dean Tjosvold (Simon Fraser University, Burnaby, B.C., Canada), "Control, Conflict and Collaboration in the Classroom," *The Educational Forum* 44: 195–203, January 1980; and condensed in *The Educational Digest* 45: 17–20, April 1980.
    Compare the following statements from *Education for Critical Consciousness* by Paulo Freire (New York: Seabury Press, 1973), pp. 68–69; 125.

No philosophers, no scientists, develop their thought or systematize their scientific knowledge without being challenged and confronted by problems. While this does not mean that a person who is challenged automatically or necessarily becomes a philospher or a scientist, it does mean that challenge is basic to the constitution of knowledge. . . .
    Students, as they are posed with problems relating to themselves in the world and with the world, will feel increasingly challenged and obliged to respond to that challenge. . . . Their response to the challenge evokes new challenges, followed by new understandings, and gradually, the students come to regard themselves as committed [to learning].

A follower of Paulo Freire, Alfred S. Alschuler in *School Discipline: A Socially Literate Solution* (New York: McGraw-Hill, 1980, pp. 260-261) writes:

Students need to feel that their courses are relevant and that they have some control over what happens to them. Otherwise, their feelings of frustration can erupt in violence. . . . The violent students are more likely to be those who have given up on school, do not care about grades, find courses irrelevant and feel that nothing they do makes any difference.

toward the teacher and causing teachers pressured to control students to be punitive toward unwilling students. A minority of students have protested in various ways against their dependent position in schools.

Control orientation also appears to interfere with effective methods of resolving conflicts. A control-oriented teacher may blame students for any conflict because they have not behaved as required. The students are unlikely to accept full responsibility and may even be willing to continue or escalate the conflict rather than accept responsibility.

Educators committed to control may freely express their dissatisfaction with students, refusing to encourage student expression or viewing students as "discipline problems"; their preferred course of action is to reestablish discipline by silencing the students and regaining control. To the extent that teachers (and their colleagues) define their goal in the conflict as maintaining control, they are unlikely to make concessions. They may seek to "win" the conflict by inducing the student to do as commanded. . . .

Educators may be committed to the control of students because they believe the only alternative is a *laissez-faire* orientation which sanctions refraining from attempts to influence or control students. But, as research suggests, collaboration is a more effective alternative. Collaborative orientation recognizes that educators and students should influence students and in turn be influenced by them; it encourages joint decision-making among educators and students. . . .

In collaborative classrooms, teachers learned to treat students as origins (i.e., as students who could follow their own ideas and interests); they did not simply indulge them. The teachers provided opportunities for the students to make and implement decisions as a classroom and as individuals. Furthermore, they helped the students to develop cooperative groups that encouraged self-examination.*

2.17 Why Not Retain the Best of Both Worlds: Progressive and Traditional?
JOHN LORDON

In this era of public and teacher cynicism about public education we are in danger of losing sight of some important educational philosophies and principles that held so much promise a few years ago. The back-to-basics movement and its minimum competency testing baggage have given the conservative camp considerable cause to rejoice; a shift to the right has gathered alarming impetus. In my view, much of the impetus for the back-to-basics bandwagon arose from misunderstanding of the practices that noted educators espoused during the 1960s.

From John Lordon (Chatham, New Brunswick, Canada), "Continuous Progress Revisited: A Plea for Educators to Adopt the Best of Both Worlds: Progressive and Traditional," *Phi Delta Kappan* 61: 198–200, November 1979. © 1979, Phi Delta Kappa, Inc. By permission of publisher and author.

*EDITOR'S NOTE. Compare "A Theory of Liberal Education" by Elizabeth Steiner (Selection 6.10).

The following "dialogue" is an attempt to draw together many issues that are currently being debated in our school systems. In essence, it is a plea for educators to adopt the best of both worlds. There is logic in both the progressive and traditional positions.

Does teaching in a continuous progress system mean that teachers and students are free to "do their own thing"?

Let's deal with the teacher and the student separately. If by "doing his own thing" you mean the teacher is free to make necessary adaptations of curriculum materials, to use supplementary materials, to use wider resources than those prescribed, and to base his selection of materials and activities on the needs of the children he is teaching, then by all means yes, he should be encouraged to do his own thing. If, on the other hand, you are talking about doing only those things perceived as fun by the children, or paying no attention to planning for sequential skill and concept development, or abandoning sound evaluation practices, then no, the teacher should not be permitted to do his thing.

What about the student? If you mean that the student is allowed to progress at a rate compatible with his abilities, that *his* best is accepted and credited, that he is encouraged to develop *his* special skills and talents, then yes, let him do his own thing. If it means that he works when he wants to, at what he wants to, up to a standard of his own choice rather than a tougher one he is capable of meeting, then of course he should not be allowed to do his own thing.

How can teachers in a department or at the same grade level communicate effectively unless they are all teaching the same unit at the same time to all the students?

Of course there will be some advantage in describing a basic core of skills and concepts to be covered by the majority of students at a given grade level. Serious problems immediately surface, however, if teachers expect every child to be *capable* of mastering all the work prescribed for a certain grade level. The problem is that we have not made a serious enough effort to determine what each child is capable of and then to insist that he work to his capacity. We have, it seems, been forcing some children to work at frustration levels while allowing some, successful on the surface, to drift along basically unchallenged. We must find out the level of achievement and mastery each child has attained when he reaches us. Then we must determine as objectively as possible what the child's abilities are. Then we can plan our teaching approach for the class as a whole, for groups within the class, and even for individual students. It should not concern us unduly if we have to abandon "grade-level work" for *some* students. If we believe the results of empirical research, we know that we shall have to accommodate children of widely differing abilities and levels of achievement. We have several options: We can teach the "course" and ignore differences, we can blame the teachers "below us" for sending "unprepared students," or we can make an honest effort to discover student needs and abilities.*

---

*EDITOR'S NOTE   This topic is considered in greater detail in Selection 5.8.

Does continuous progress mean continuous "pushing on," whether the child achieves or not?

Unfortunately, it has come to mean just that for some teachers. Ideally, it should mean that the child, while working with students of approximately his own age, will be instructed at his own level of comprehension, skill development, and achievement. Even with careful assessment — and attempts to individualize — motivation, attendance, and discipline will still present problems. Some teachers have adopted the attitude that they can ignore such problems and "push them on" to the next teacher. This is not continuous progress; it is neglect of responsibility. These children should be identified and every resource at our disposal should be focused on solving their problems.

We still have an obligation to insist on correct conduct and to develop good work habits in our students. Where there is evidence of misbehavior, poor motivation, and poor attendance, we should undertake a serious search for the reasons. Admittedly, we shall have our failures. One factor that is under our control, however, is instruction. We must challenge, but not frustrate, our students.

An afterthought on this issue: In a continuous progress system, fully developed, grade designations would disappear. The question of grade level would be secondary to the question of achievement level. It is important that evaluation be used as a diagnostic tool and that prescriptive teaching for groups of children be planned.

It is hard to argue against the logic of the principle that a child should be instructed at a level with which he can cope. Our job is to find that level and encourage the child to do his best without excessive pressure. It is a delicate problem.

It is equally hard to see the logic of those who talk of "pushing kids on." This is simply a misinterpretation of the intent and practice of continuous progress.

Is there any "failure" in a continuous progress system?

Of course there is failure. The purpose of a continuous progress system is to *minimize the impact of failure.* Failure will come on smaller units of instruction. The necessity for remedial work should be recognized and attended to much sooner than it generally is. Failure in a full year's work should never occur. Repetition of large blocks of work should be discouraged. Such a concept, of course, soon demands real differentiation of instruction for groups and individuals. Moreover, it demands greater attention to evaluation, and it requires much more dialogue and communication between teachers at various levels. It demands increased attention to good record keeping.

We can talk of failure in another sense. Some children will fail to try, especially if they are frustrated. Some will fail to attend school regularly. Many will fail to have the tools they need to work with. These are very real human problems and they will continue to plague us. It is *our failure* if we ignore them, blaming their existence on an instructional philosophy. A commitment to an instructional philosphy of any kind will not eliminate human foibles. Some kinds of failure will always be present.

Does the concept of continuous progress—and the many new programs of the past few years—not imply taking a "fun and games" approach to teaching rather than the "scholarly discipline" approach? . . .

It seems that this is another area where serious misinterpretations have been creeping into our thinking. Surely we can find an appropriate balance of the cognitive and the affective, between role learning tasks and creative ones, between mental and physical activity.*

Given that the human spirit is subject to highs and lows, we must realize that learning will sometimes be drudgery and sometimes be exciting. We must adopt the best of modern motivational approaches, and we must put into practice what we know about the ways people learn. We must, on the other hand, reject the concept that all school experience should be "entertaining" for children.

Is it not a fact that some modern approaches have led to a decline of discipline in our schools?

Discipline continues to emerge as the number one concern of teachers and parents. Witness the results of the last several Gallup polls on education in the U.S.

My own view is that educational practices have had a minimum impact on growth of the malaise that seems to be afflicting us today. Other social forces are overwhelming. I believe that, fundamentally, there are four causes for the decline of discipline: 1) the growth of "irresponsible individualism" characterized by the "do your own thing" syndrome, 2) the corrosion of human values and the decline of morality in the modern world, 3) the breakdown of family life and the erosion of the authority of the home, and 4) the emphasis of the modern world on materialism. Any one of these points could be developed at great length, of course, and who knows where the beginnings of each phenomenon lie?

Nevertheless, I believe it is the duty of the school to combat these trends with vigor. A sound instructional program and philosophy will help. It is not the only answer, nor should it bear the whole blame when kids misbehave.

What are the implications of continuous progress for teacher planning?

It is the responsibility of the teacher to plan, as much as is humanly possible, for what the student is to learn, at what level, in what sequence, and in what style. The importance of evaluation and assessment of each student's strengths and weaknesses is central to such planning.

What about the back-to-basics movement?

Some who favor a return to "basics" advocate revival of a rigid lock-step curriculum, with failure and repetition of a grade's work. They advocate abandonment of attempts to differentiate instruction. They would continue the use of corporal punishment. They would reestablish matriculation of external exams. They would eliminate so-called frills in education.

The danger of the movement, as I see it, is that it would return us to practices we all regarded as inhumane a short time ago.

The kind of back-to-basics movement I advocate emphasizes greater teacher participation in formulating a sound educational philosophy, with intense efforts to understand and adhere to that philosophy.

To reject the back-to-basics movement in its current form does not imply rejection of certain basic values:

---

*EDITOR'S NOTE.   Chapter 7 is devoted to this topic.

- that discipline is important;
- that work and study are essential;
- that respect for life and property are of paramount importance;
- that essential language and math skills must be learned;
- that development of a social conscience must be emphasized.

These kinds of traditional values can be developed in the context of a humane, concerned school. There's a great danger in abandoning these values, but there's an equally great danger in an indiscriminate rejection of all the reforms of the Sixties and Seventies or an indiscriminate return to all the practices of the past.

2.18 Quotations for Further Thought and Discussion

(A)   The trend toward individualization in the schools — with a true respect for individual differences in skills, needs and learning styles — requires that teachers take a closer look at their use of homework assignments . . . [Because unless carefully handled,] homework frequently compounds learning problems and becomes the focus of family friction rather than serving as the aid intended by the teacher.
— Lillie Pope, "A New Look at Homework," *Teacher* 96: 94–95,
October 1978.

(B)   [A great] many alternative schools begin as "do your own thing" schools, face a crisis, and then (a) fall apart, (b) revert to conventional patterns, or (c) become hybrids.
— Terrence E. Deal and Robert R. Nolan, "Alternative Schools: A
Conceptual Map," *School Review* 87: 29–49, November 1978. Read also
Lester B. Ball's review of the *1977–78 National Directory of Public Alternative Schools* in *The High School Journal* 62: 40–41, October 1978.

(C) (1)   [Many of us teachers] are leaving because we are casualties of professional "burnout" and no longer have the energy and enthusiasm necessary for effective teaching . . . [Although halfway to retirement I finally decided] I had to leave teaching for my own sake and for the benefit of my students.
— Pamela Bardo, "The Pain of Teacher Burnout," *Phi Delta Kappan*
61:252–256, December 1979.

(2)   Yes, the children are different from children 16 years ago. They are more insecure, more inattentive, more openly rebellious [in the underprivileged area where I teach]. Their home life is different, their modes of entertainment are different, their attention spans are different. But fundamentally they are still kids. Still curious, still touchingly vulnerable, still in need of knowing about the complex world they will enter as adults. For me at least, the challenge and the delight of teaching remain as valid and fulfilling as I found them in 1963.
— Jayne Freeman, "The Joy of Teaching," *Phi Delta Kappan* 61: 252–256,
December 1979. Read also Barbara Hendrickson, "Teacher Burnout:
How to Recognize It; What to Do About It," *Learning,* 7: 37–39, January
1979.

(D)   Classroom control depends in large measure on the teacher's ability to plan interesting, student-centered, multi-activity lessons to promote a high degree of student involvement and participation. If students are actively and meaningfully involved in their own learning, the problem of classroom control is less likely to arise. While this observation is, no doubt, little more than a glimpse into the obvious, its truth can not be over-estimated. The old chestnut about "an ounce of prevention" has no clearer or better application anywhere. Meaningful learning is the best prevention of discipline problems in the classroom.

> — Concluding sentences from Thomas R. McDaniel (Converse College), "Principles of Classroom Discipline" *The Clearing House*, 51: 149–152, December 1977.

(E)   The test of a first rate intelligence is the ability to hold two opposed ideas in the mind at the same time, and still retain the ability to function. One should, for example, be able to see that things are hopeless and yet be determined to make them otherwise.

> — F. Scott Fitzgerald, in *The Crack Up* (1956)

(F)   A man [or woman] who is to educate really well and is to make the young grow and develop into their full stature, must be filled through and through with the spirit of reverence. . . . The child is weak and superficially foolish; the teacher is strong, and in an every-day sense wiser than the child. The teacher without reverence, or the bureaucrat without reverence, easily despises the child for these outward inferiorities. . . .

The man who has reverence . . . feels in all that lives, but especially in human beings, and most of all in children, something shared, indefinable, unlimited, something individual and strangely precious, the growing principle of life, and embodied fragment of the dumb striving of the world. In the presence of a child he feels an unaccountable humility — a humility not easily defensible on any rational ground, and yet somehow nearer to wisdom than the easy self-confidence of many parents and teachers. The outward helplessness of the child and the appeal of dependence make him conscious of the responsibility of a trust. His imagination shows him what the child may become, for good or evil, how its impulses may be developed or thwarted, how its hopes must be dimmed [or animated]. . . .

All this gives him a longing to help the child in its own battle; he would equip and strengthen it, not for some outside end proposed by the State or by any other impersonal authority, but for the ends which the child's own spirit is obscurely seeking. The man who feels this can wield the authority of an educator without infringing the principle of liberty.

> — Bertrand Russell, *Principles of Social Reconstruction* (London: Unwin, 1960), pp. 102–104.

(G)   Public education was not built solely by idealistic reformers, nor solely by calculating schemers who used their rhetoric to hide their real intentions to exploit or control the lower classes. The history of education in the United States should not glorify crusaders of the past as persons who bequeathed us an untouchable heritage, nor should it impeach them as perpetrators of dirty educational tricks upon the American people. . . .

[We look upon] public education as an essential ingredient of the persistent tensions created by three basic themes in American civilization: the cohesive value claims of a democratic political community summed up in the constituional ideals of liberty, equality, justice, and obligation for the public good; the pluralistic loyalties that give particular identity and coherence to the different segments of society that arise from diversities of religion, language, culture, ethnicity, race, and locality; and the long-term worldwide modernization process that has been pushing all Western societies for more than 200 years toward national centralization, popular participation, industrialization, urbanization, and secularization.

> — R. Freeman Butts, *Public Education in the United States*, New York: Holt, Rinehart and Winston, 1978.

(H)   *Let's celebrate "our season of the rising sap"*

We are in America's Elizabethan period and don't know it.

We have been told so often that capitalism and the West are in their twilight and the best we can hope for is to make the remaining years as comfortable as possible. In fact, this is our season of the rising sap.

This is the century in which the United States became the most powerful country on earth militarily, the wealthiest country on earth, the country that developed the capacity to exterminate mankind with the atomic bomb but then went ahead and developed an escape route to the stars through the space program.

This is the country that started the phenomenon — which Europe is beginning to catch up with — of wealth at every class level except the class that doesn't work at all. This is our Bourbon Louis period. It's been a time of tremendous exuberance, tremendous energy, tremendous growth. Yet people of influence in this country so often act as if it were the opposite.

Because of these achievements, it's hard for me to be terribly pessimistic about the rest of this century.

— Tom Wolfe, quoted in an interview, *U.S. News & World Report* 88:
68–69, November 5, 1979.*

---

*EDITOR'S NOTE   For many other optimistic views about the 1980s, read *Next*, Vol. 1, No. 5, December 1980. For longer, more comprehensive but equally optimistic statements concerning excellence in education, read *Fifteen Thousand Hours: Secondary Schools and Their Effects on Children*, by Michael Rutter and others (Cambridge, MA: Harvard University Press, 1979), reviewed in *Educational Leadership* 35: 90–91, October 1980.

Chapter 3. FREEDOM, SELF-DETERMINATION, AND HUMAN DIGNITY

3.1 Freedom and Determinism: Two Facets of Human Nature
INTRODUCTION

In the age-old debate between determinists and free willers, those of us who believe in freedom should realize that some of the world's greatest thinkers — St. Augustine, Calvin, Loyola, Spinoza, Leibniz, Newton, LaPlace, Mendel, Marx, to name only a few — were determinists. Indeed, we might characterize the determinism of B. F. Skinner as a secular-scientific naturalistic leaf from the Puritan twig of the Calvinistic branch of the Augustinian limb of Christian theology.

But with all due respect to determinism, most of us believe that a universe without freedom is not one in which we wish to dwell. We wish to believe that human beings, in some ways at least, can transcend the determinism espoused by natural science. We are not troubled by the fact that rocks are completely determined by physical or chemical laws. And we may also go along with sociobiologists when they declare that plants and lower animals are determined by their genetic heritage, even though their theory of genetic *mutations* seems to be an admission that in biology Nature has a way of breaking its own laws.

But humans are different. Granting that each of us is very largely determined by cause-and-effect relations (that is, by past-to-present relations), are we not also "determined" by our hopes and aspirations toward the future, that is, by present-to-future "causes"? The human mind is not completely restricted by the here and now of sense experience or by memories of past events. The human mind can reach beyond the world of space-time-matter into what Teilhard de Chardin called the *noosphere* (as contrasted with the *geosphere* and the *biosphere*) — into the world of language, thought, imagination, and meaning. This world of meanings contains an immense domain of **supermen and bionic women**, of angels and demons, of gods and devils, of Peter Pans and Donald Ducks, of imps, trolls, gnomes, and a thousand and one other types of imaginative creatures. They are "creatures," that is, part of the "created world" (according to a major theistic ideology); but (according to contemporary psychology) they are creatures of a special type, because they have been created by men, women, and children. This *noosphere* also includes the world views of philosophers and theologians, and the competing hypotheses of scientists, economists, and political theorists.

In this chapter, the first several selections approach freedom from the viewpoint of history, philosophy, and psychology. The remaining selections approach freedom from the viewpoint of economics and political theory. The chapter as a whole may be viewed as a confirmation of Whitehead's dictum that all Western philosophy is but a series of footnotes to Plato. It may also be viewed as an introduction to Part 3 (Chapters 7, 8, and 9).

3.2 Finding Identity and Selfhood Through Meaning Systems
MAX LERNER

Man is a growing animal, a security- and identity-seeking animal, a belonging animal, a meaning-seeking animal, a feeling/interacting animal, a believing animal. Each of these phases of his being and striving is the source of his search for values related to that phase. And each cluster of these values searchings — and all of them together — becomes the central concern and indeed the substance of the curiously fumbling, painful, joyful developmental Pilgrim's Progress that we call an education. . . .

A life without values is an empty life, a life with unformed or distorted values is a warped one. Education is not meant to lead to empty or warped lives but to lives as full as we can make them. Hence the fiery centrality of values in education. . . .

How then has it happened that values teaching has been neglected in American public education? An answer may lie in [six] . . . historical directions.

First, the churches tainted values teaching as parochial. . . .

Second, politics tainted values teaching as partisan. . . .

Third, the home and other institutions preempted much of the values task [at the very time when public schools were asked to assume more and more responsibility for education]. . . .

Fourth, the dominant pragmatism interfered. With the the triumph of industrialism the practical men who ran the school districts found little that was usable in values education. . . .

Fifth, the dominant educational establishment bungled it.* Under the pressure of rebel educators, reacting against the dry as dust tradition, the movement for the teaching of values came to be associated with "life adjustment" concepts of "progressive" education. This pleased neither the conservatives, who placed their stress on "basics" and "essentials" and derided the new trend, nor the intellectual sophisticates,

From Max Lerner, *Values in Education* (Bloomington, Ind.: Phi Delta Kappa, 1976), pp. 9–10, 14–20, 31, 32, 35. © 1976 Phi Delta Kappan Educational Foundation, 1976. By permission.
   Author of numerous books and authors, Max Lerner is perhaps best known for his book *America as a Civilization*.

*EDITOR'S NOTE   Like the six preceding editions of *Crucial Issues in Education*, this Seventh Edition presents numerous — and contradictory — explanations of ways in which educators "have bungled it."

who felt that it would lead to consensus and conformity rather than to the "new social order" they aimed at. . . .*

[Finally, although we fully recognize the importance of] the press, TV, film, sports, music, the arts, holiday experience, and travel . . . in the formation of values . . . [we have often allowed our new machines and technologies to become ends in themselves; and we have ignored the age-old truth that values deal with inward, personal experiences.] Because the inward journeys form part of what is for each person, however inchoately or stumblingly, the nub of meaning, they form a setting for values shaping and consolidation, whether as religion, faith, commitment, mystique or belief system. Without this [inward, autonomous] value setting it would be hard to understand any of the core experiences that give education its dimension and meaning and to which in turn education tries to give definition. To call them, as Maslow does, peak-experiences is to overstress the sensory and the conscious in them. I prefer the term core experiences or—from another standpoint—*meaning systems* . . . [Meaning systems are a vital part of our moral heritage. They] not only express values but also furnish a setting for shaping values. . . .

[This shaping of values is an expression of our] need for *selfhood* or *identity* . . . The quest for identity — the search for the authentic self — is not a one-time episode, over with as soon as it is achieved. It is a continuing process in the course of the life cycle, which becomes a kind of stations-of-the-cross journey: at each stage selfhood needs to be reestablished, uniqueness needs to be reaffirmed, the boundaries dividing oneself from others need to be redefined. . . .

[This process of moral and intellectual] growth does not flourish in a situation of formlessness and anarchy. For healthy growth an organism needs not only freedom but a sense of limits. Adaptability means little unless there is a given to adapt to. Flexible change would mean chaos unless there were also continuities. Choices and decisions would also lose meaning if the options were limitless; it is the fact of limits that makes the choices growth-producing. An organism without limits would go berserk. . . .

[In sum] selfhood must have limits; carried all the way it becomes solipsism. Individualism has its corruptions, always tending toward the sterility and the swollen pride of the "imperial I." In the long history of biological evolution the selection process, operating through genetic competition, has stressed selfhood — a kind of biological selfishness. But the history of social and cultural evolution produced a counter-tendency, toward altruism, a concern about what happens to others. Human beings need not only to feel cared *for*; they need also to *care*. The isolated individual, unloving, unable to receive love, dries up and withers. He needs to feel that he is one with others.

---

*EDITOR'S NOTE   It was opposition to such tendencies toward social conformity which prompted Lionel Trilling in *Beyond Culture* (1965) to affirm that human nature, and especially the human mind, contains

> . . . a hard, irreducible, stubborn core of biological urgency, and biological necessity, and biological *reason*, that culture cannot reach and that reserves the right, which sooner or later it will exercise, to judge the culture and resist and revise it.

3.3   Toward a Psychology of Being — and of Education
ABRAHAM H. MASLOW

Psychology is in part a branch of biology, in part a branch of sociology. But it is not *only* that. It has its own unique jurisdiction as well, that portion of the psyche which is *not* a reflection of the outer world or a molding to it. . . . (PB)

[Psychology may be viewed as a study of] the free choices or preferences of various kinds of human beings, sick or healthy, old or young, and under various circumstances. . . . (PB)

Freud has supplied us with . . . our best system of psychotherapy . . . [Even today, his system, in its varied modified forms,] is useful for the therapist trying to cure psychological illness. (MV)

However, it is quite unsatisfactory as a general psychology of the whole human being, especially in his healthier and more admirable aspects. The picture of man it presents is a lopsided, distorted puffing up of his weaknesses and shortcomings that purports then to describe him fully. This it clearly fails to do. Practically all the activities that man prides himself on, and that give meaning, richness, and value to his life, are either omitted or pathologized by Freud. Work, play, love, art, creativeness, religion in the good sense, ethics, philosophhy, science, learning, parenthood, self-sacrifice, heroism, saintliness, goodness — these are all weakly handled, if at all. . . . [MV]

Human life will never be understood unless its highest aspirations are taken into account. Growth, self-actualization, the striving toward health, the quest for identity and autonomy, the yearning for excellence (and other ways of phrasing the striving "upward") must now be accepted beyond question as a widespread and perhaps universal human tendency. (MP)

And yet there are also other regressive, fearful, self-diminishing tendencies as well, and it is very easy to forget them in our intoxications with "personal growth," especially for inexperienced youngsters. I consider that a necessary prophylactic against such illusions is a thorough knowledge of psychopathology and of depth psychology. We must appreciate that many people choose the worse rather than the better, that growth is often a painful process and may for this reason be shunned, that we are afraid of our own best possibilities in addition to loving them, and that we are all of us profoundly ambivalent about truth, beauty, virtue, loving them and fearing them too. . . . (MP)

This point of view in no way denies the usual Freudian picture. But it does add to it and supplement it. To oversimplify the matter somewhat, it is as if Freud supplied to us the sick half of psychology and we must now fill it out with the healthy half. Perhaps this health psychology will give us more possibility for controlling and improving our lives and for making ourselves better people. Perhaps this will be more fruitful than asking "how to get *unsick*." (PB)

These excerpts are mainly from *Toward a Psychology of Being* (PB), 2nd edition, by Abraham H. Maslow (pp. 5, 167, 185, and 212–213.) © 1968 by Litton Educational Publishing Inc. Reprinted by permission of D. Van Nostrand Company. Brief excerpts are from Maslow's *Motivation and Personality* (MP) revised edition, (New York: Harper & Row, 1980), by permission; and from *Abraham H. Maslow: A Memorial Volume* (MV) (Monterey, CA.: Brooks/Cole, 1972), pp. 12–13, 71; by permission.

[Freud concentrated on sickness and on "neuroses." In contrast, Maslow emphasizes] peak-experiences.*

[Man's inner core, or self, is more than the end result of a series of cause-and-effect antecedents. Why? Because, to some extent at least, it is *future-oriented*, it is autonomous, and it is able to transcend the past. Hence, says Maslow, two principles follow:]

1. [The] autonomous self or pure psyche . . . must not be treated as *only* an adaptational instrument. . . .
2. Even when we deal with our relations with environment, we must make a theoretical place for a receptive relation to the environment as well as a masterful one. . . .

[Granting that each individual's "inner being" or self is unique and singular, and that, in some respects at least, it transcends the worlds of biology and sociology, it must be recognized nevertheless that no individual exists by himself alone, but is a part of an intricate network of social and biological relationships. Maslow expresses this idea as follows:]

---

*EDITOR'S NOTE   In *The Farther Reaches of Human Nature* (New York: Viking Press, 1971, Chapter 21) Maslow describes many types of peak experience. In a peak experience, one transcends or lifts oneself above, or disentangles one's higher self from, the lower self's immediate physiological demands. Such transcendence occurs, for example, when people concentrate on what they are reading, and shut off noise, hot or cold temperature, and other sensations from their consciousness. When people perform their duty, they transcend immediate desires and the lower needs of the self for some "higher" duty, cause, or mission. One may even transcend one's own will in favor of the spirit of "not my will be done but Thine," and, indeed, it is ability to transcend dangers and tragedies, whether by humor or by heroic suffering, which enables people, in extreme suffering, to maintain their sanity. In short, says Maslow, "Transcendence refers to the very highest and most inclusive or holistic levels of human consciousness, behaving and relating, as ends rather than as means, to oneself, to significant others, to human beings in general, to other species, to nature, and to the cosmos . . . [A saint's 'being at one with God' or the Taoist or naturalist's] 'being in harmony with nature' implies this ability to yield, to be receptive to, to respond to, to live with extrapsychic reality as if one belonged with it. . . . [Transcendence enables us to hold firm against the opinions of others, to be] a self-determining Self. It means to be able to be unpopular when this is the right thing to be, to become an autonomous, self-deciding Self; to write one's own lines, to be one's own man, to be not manipulatable or seduceable. . . . [It also means the ability to transcend the Freudian superego by] coming up to the level of intrinsic conscience, and intrinsic guilt, deserved and suitable remorse, regret, shame." In the second edition of *Motivation and Personality*, which was published the year of his death (1970), Maslow listed his hierarchy of needs, namely:

1. *Safety*: physiological needs; self-preservation.
2. *Security*: need for stability in life, freedom from fear, anxiety, or chaos; need for structure, order, law, protection, limits.
3. *Love*: belongingness; affectionate relationships with mate, family friends, identification group.
4. *Esteem*: need for self-respect and for the esteem of others. Self-esteem is based on strength, achievement, competence. Esteem of others—less important than self-esteem—means reputation or recognition by others of one's worth and importance.
5. *Self-actualization*: the desire to become everything one is capable of becoming, and to maximize one's special talents and abilities.

These needs are hierarchical; and, in general, unless needs 1, 2, and 3 are satisfied, 4 and 5 tend to recede from one's consciousness.

An important existential problem is posed by the fact that self-actualizing persons (and *all* people in their peak experiences) occasionally live out-of-time and out-of-the-world (atemporal and aspatial) even though mostly they *must* live in the outer world. Living in the inner psychic world (which is ruled by psychic laws and not by the laws of outer-reality), i.e., the world of experience, of emotion, of wishes and fears and hopes, of love, of poetry, art, and fantasy, is different from living in and adapting to the non-psychic reality which runs by laws [man] never made and which are not essential to his nature even though he has to live by them. (He *could*, after all, live in other kinds of worlds, as any science fiction fan knows.) The person who is not afraid of this inner, psychic world, can enjoy it to such an extent that it may be called Heaven by contrast with the more effortful, fatiguing, externally responsible world of "reality," of striving and coping, of right and wrong, of truth and falsehood. This is true even though the healthier person can also adapt more easily and enjoyably to the "real" world, and has better "reality testing," i.e., doesn't confuse it with his inner psychic world. (PB)

It seems clear now that confusing these inner and outer realities, or having either closed off from experience, is highly pathological. The healthy person is able to integrate them both into his life and therefore has to give up neither, being able to go back and forth voluntarily. The difference is the same as the one between the person who can *visit* the slums and the one who is forced to live there always. (*Either* world is a slum if one can't leave it.) Then, paradoxically, that which was sick and pathological and the "lowest" becomes part of the healthiest and "highest" aspect of human nature. Slipping into "craziness" is frightening only for those who are not fully confident of their sanity. Education must help the person to live in both worlds. . . . (PB)

The human being needs a framework of values, a philosophy of life, a religion or religion-surrogate to live by and understand by, in about the same sense that he needs sunlight, calcium or love. This I have called the "cognitive need to understand." The value-illnesses which result from valuelessness are called variously anhedonia, anomie, apathy, amorality, hopelessness, cynicism, etc., and can become somatic illness as well. Historically, we are in a value interregnum in which all externally given value systems have proven to be failures (political, economic, religious, etc.) e.g., nothing is worth dying for. What man needs but doesn't have, he seeks for unceasingly, and he becomes dangerously ready to jump at *any* hope, good or bad. The cure for this disease is obvious. We need a validated, usable system of human values that we can believe in and devote ourselves to (be willing to die for), because they are true rather than because we are exhorted to "believe and have faith." Such an empirically based Weltanschauung seems now to be a real possibility, at least in theoretical outline. (PB)

Much disturbance in children and adolescents can be understood as a consequence of the uncertainty of adults about their values. As a consequence, many youngsters in the United States live not by adult values but by adolescent values, which of course are immature, ignorant and heavily determined by confused adolescent needs. (PB)

3.4   On Human Nature
EDWARD O. WILSON

Human nature is not just the array of outcomes attained in existing societies. It is also the potential array that might be achieved through conscious design by future societies. By looking over the realized social systems of hundreds of animal species and deriving the principles by which these systems have evolved, we can be certain that all human choices represent only a tiny subset of those theoretically possible. Human nature is, moreover, a hodgepodge of special genetic adaptations to an environment largely vanished, the world of the Ice-Age hunter-gatherer. Modern life, as rich and rapidly changing as it appears to those caught in it, is nevertheless only a mosaic of . . . elements created in an evolutionary age now long vanished. . . .

It is a misconception among many of the more traditional Marxists, some learning theorists, and a still surprising proportion of anthropologists and sociologists that social behavior can be shaped into virtually any form. Ultra-environmentalists start with the premise that man is the creation of his own culture: "culture makes man," the formula might go, "makes culture makes man." Theirs is only a half truth. Each person is molded by an interaction of his environment, especially his cultural environment, with the genes that affect social behavior. Although the hundreds of the world's cultures seem enormously variable to those of us who stand in their midst, all versions of human social behavior together form only a tiny fraction of the realized organizations of social species on this planet and a still smaller fraction of those that can be readily imagined. . . .

[This book is an attempt] to study human nature as part of the natural sciences, in an attempt to integrate the natural sciences with the social sciences and humanities. . . .

In my opinion the key to the emergence of civilization is *hypertrophy*, the extreme growth of pre-existing structures. Like the teeth of the baby elephant that lengthen into tusks, and the cranial bones of the male elk that sprout into astonishing great antlers, the basic social responses of the hunter-gatherers have metamorphosed from relatively modest environmental adaptations into unexpectedly elaborate, even monstrous forms in more advanced societies. Yet the directions this change can take and its final products are constrained by the genetically influenced behavioral predispositions that constituted the earlier, simpler adaptations of preliterate human beings. . . .

Although the evidence suggests that the biological nature of humankind launched the evolution of organized aggression and roughly directed its early history across many societies, the eventual outcome of that evolution will be determined by cultural processes brought incresingly under the control of rational thought . . . [And surely *reason* (foresight, intelligence) is the supreme example of *hypertrophy* in man.]

[The sharing of responsibilities by the two sexes is another example of *hypertrophy*; in the cooperative rearing of children there gradually developed feelings of *loyalty* — first of all, to the family; but also, loyalty to the gens, the tribe, the clan, the nation, and today, even to the welfare of the international community.]

Brief excerpts from Edward O. Wilson (Sociobiologist, Harvard University), *On Human Nature* (Cambridge, MA and London, Eng.: Harvard University Press, 1978; paperback edition, New York: Bantam Books, 1979), pp. 6, 18–19, 89, 116, 150, 165–166, 167, 190, 191, 192, 196, 206, 209. Reprinted by permission.
Read also *Godel, Escher, Bach: An Eternal Golden Braid* by Douglas R. Hofstadter (New York: 1979).

[But the supreme example of *hypertrophy* is *altruism*, the feeling of human-heartedness and the willingness to sacrifice oneself in behalf of one's fellow humans.] The annihilating mixture of reason and passion, which has been described often in first-hand accounts of the battlefield, is only the extreme phenomenon that lies beyond the innumerable smaller impulses of courage and generosity that bind society together. . . .

[Equally potent is a trait quite the opposite of altruism — *aggression*. Countless millennia of struggle for sheer survival, and later for dominance over other species, led to built-in genetic traits of *aggressiveness*. The combination of *aggressiveness* with *altruism* in the theories of sociobiologists is thus quite parallel to the religious beliefs whereby men are both "children of God" and "sinners" (who were driven out of the Garden of Eden because of the "fall of man.") The Chinese parallel to this *aggression-altruism* duality of human nature is found in the next selection (3.5) by Mencius. Selection 3.6 deals with the same duality.]

"If only it were all so simple," Aleksandr Solzhenitsyn wrote in *The Gulag Archipelago*. "If only there were evil people somewhere insidiously committing evil deeds, and it were necessary only to separate them from the rest of us and destroy them. But the line dividing good and evil cuts through the heart of every human being. And who is willing to destroy a piece of his own heart?" . . .

[We come now to a crucial philosophical question:] Can the cultural evolution of higher ethical values gain a direction and momentum of its own and completely replace genetic evolution? I think not. The genes hold culture on a leash. The leash is very long, but inevitably values will be constrained in accordance with their effects on the human gene pool. The brain is a product of evolution. Human behavior — like the deepest capacities for emotional response which drive and guide it — is the circuitous technique by which human genetic material has been and will be kept intact. Morality has no other demonstrable ultimate function. . . .

[In spite of the civilizing influences of philosophy and science, it remains] obvious that human beings are still largely ruled by myth. Furthermore, much of contemporary intellectual and political strife is due to the conflict between three great mythologies: Marxism, traditional religion, and scientific materialism. Marxism is still regarded by purists as a form of scientific materialism, but it is not. . . .

Marxism is sociobiology without biology. . . .

But if Marxism is only an inaccurate product of scientific materialism, a failed satrap so to speak, traditional religion is not. As science proceeds to dismantle the ancient mythic stories one by one, theology retreats to the final redoubt from which it can never be driven. This is the idea of God in the creation myth: God as will, the cause of existence, and the agent who generated all of the energy in the original fireball and set the natural laws by which the universe evolved. So long as the redoubt exists, theology can slip out through its portals and make occasional sallies back into the real world. . . .

The scientist's devotion to parsimony in explanation excludes the divine spirit and other extraneous agents. Most importantly, we have come to the crucial stage in the history of biology when religion itself is subject to the explanations of the natural sciences. . . .

If this interpretation is correct, the final decisive edge enjoyed by scientific naturalism will come from its capacity to explain traditional religion, its chief competitor, as a wholly material phenomenon. Theology is not likely to survive as an independent intellectual discipline. But religion itself will endure for a long time as a vital force in society. Like the mythical giant Antaeus who drew energy from his mother, the earth, religion cannot be defeated by those who merely cast it down. The spiritual weakness of scientific naturalism is due to the fact that it has no such primal source of power. . . .

[Like most humanists, I have great faith] in the power of knowledge and the idea of evolutionary progress over the minds of men. I am suggesting a modification of scientific humanism through the recognition that the mental processes of religious belief — consecration of personal and group identity, attention to charismatic leaders, mythopoeism [i.e., the adaptation of, and the promulgation of, morally inspiring myths], and others — represent. . . . [the results of] thousands of years of genetic evolution. As such they are powerful, ineradicable, and at the center of human social existence. . . .*

[Let us conclude with one of these myths:] Prometheus has gone somewhat out of fashion in recent years as a concession to resource limitation and managerial prudence. But we should not lose faith in him. Come back with me for a moment to the original, Aeschylean Prometheus:

> *Chorus*: Did you perhaps go further than you have told us?
> *Prometheus*: I caused mortals to cease foreseeing doom.
> *Chorus*: What cure did you provide them with against that sickness?
> *Prometheus*: I placed in them blind hopes.

---

*EDITOR'S NOTE   Compare:

Let's consider this question of human uniqueness. Imagine a Martian scientist who studies human beings from the outside, without any prejudice. Suppose that he has a great deal of time at his disposal, say, thousands of years. He notices immediately that there exists on earth a unique organism, whose conditions of life change considerably without corresponding changes in his constitution; that is, modern man. Apes and monkeys live as they lived millions of years ago, while human life changes radically and very rapidly. It is extremely varied, yet there is no corresponding diversity within the human species. Take a child from a Stone Age culture and raise him in New York: he will become a New Yorker. Raise an American baby in New Guinea, and he will become a Papuan "native." The genetic differences one finds are superficial and trivial, but human beings have the extraordinary characteristic of being able to live in very different ways. Human beings have history, cultural evolution, and cultural differentiation. Any objective scientist must be struck by the qualitative differences between human beings and other organisms, as much as by the differences between insects and vertebrates. . . .

If our hypothetical Martian observer searches a bit further, he will find that human beings are unique in many respects, one of these being their ability to acquire a rich and varied linguistic system, which can be used freely and in the most subtle and complicated ways, merely by immersion in a linguistic community in which the system is used. It seems to me that a rational observer would conclude that specific qualities of "intelligence," proper to this species, must be assumed. If he is of an inquiring mind and enterprising, he will seek to determine the genetically fixed mental structures which underlie the unique achievements of this species. — Noam Chomsky (Professor of Linguistics, Massachusetts Institute of Technology) *Language and Responsibility* (New York: Pantheon Books, 1977), pp. 94–96. Translated from the French by John Viertel. Copyright © 1977 by Pantheon Books, a division of Random House, Inc. By permission.

Compare also: "The human psyche is part of the observed data of science. We can retain it and still be good empirical biologists and psychologists. — Harold J. Morowitz (Professor of Biophysics and Biochemistry, Yale University), "Rediscovering the Mind," *Psychology Today* 14: 12-16, August 1980.

The true Promethean spirit of science means to liberate man by giving him knowledge and some measure of dominion over the physical environment. But at another level, and in a new age, it also constructs the mythology of scientific materialism, guided by the corrective devices of the scientific method, addressed with precise and deliberately affective appeal to the deepest needs of human nature, and kept strong by the blind hopes that the journey on which we are now embarked will be farther and better than the one just completed.

3.5 Parable of the Barren Hillside
MENCIUS

Mencius said, "The trees of the Niu Mountain" were once beautiful. But can the mountain be regarded any longer as beautiful since, being in the borders of a big state, the trees have been hewed down with axes and hatchets? Still with the rest given them by the days and nights and the nourishment provided them by the rains and the dew, they were not without buds and sprouts springing forth. But then the cattle and sheep pastured upon them once again. That is why the mountain looks so bald. When people see that it so bald, they think that there was never any timber on the mountain. Is this the true nature of the mountain? Is there not [also] a heart of humanity and righteousness originally existing in man? The way in which he loses his originally good mind is like the way in which the trees are hewed down with axes and hatchets. As trees are cut down day after day, can a mountain retain its beauty? To be sure, the days and nights do the healing, and there is the nourishing air of the calm morning which keeps him normal in his likes and dislikes. But the effect is slight, and is disturbed and destroyed by what he does during the day. When there is repeated disturbance, the restorative influence of the night will not be sufficient to preserve (the proper goodness of the mind). When the influence of the night is not sufficient to preserve it, man becomes not much different from the beast. People see that he acts like an animal, and think that he never had the original endowment (for goodness). But is that his true character? Therefore with proper nourishment and care, everything grows, whereas without proper nourishment and care, everything decays. Confucius said, 'Hold it fast and you preserve it. Let it go and you lose it. It comes in and goes out at no definite time and without anyone's knowing its direction.' He was talking about the human mind."*

From *A Source Book in Chinese Philosphy*, translated and compiled by Wing-Tsit Chan (Princeton, N.J.: Princeton University Press, 1963), pp. 56–57. Reprinted by permission of Princeton University Press.
  Mencius, who lived in the fourth century B.C., was Confucius' most famous interpreter.

---

*EDITOR'S NOTE   Note the parallel between the hillside before and after it became barren (in Mencius' parable) and the joyful condition of Adam and Eve in the Garden of Eden, who were made "in the image of God" (Genesis 1:27), but who soon fell from grace (Genesis, Chapter 3).
  ALthough Mencius and the authors of Genesis approach human nature from a different point of view than does Edward O. Wilson (in Selection 3.4), Wilson's two inherited genetic traits Altruism and Aggres-

3.6   The Pathway from Slavery to Freedom
FREDERICK DOUGLASS

. . . The frequent hearing of my mistress reading the Bible aloud, for she often read aloud when her husband was absent, awakened my curiosity in respect to this mystery of reading, and roused in me the desire to learn. Up to this time I had known nothing whatever of this wonderful art, and my ignorance and inexperience of what it could do for me, as well as my confidence in my mistress, emboldened me to ask her to teach me to read. With an unconscious and inexperience equal to my own, she readily consented, and in an incredibly short time, by her kind assistance, I had mastered the alphabet and could spell words of three or four letters. My mistress seemed almost as proud of my progress as if I had been her own child, and supposing that her husband would be as well pleased, she made no secret of what she was doing for me. . . . Master Hugh was astounded beyond measure and . . . proceeded to unfold to his wife the true philosophy of the slave system, and the peculiar rules necessary in the nature of the case to be observed in the management of human chattels. Of course he forbade her to give me any further instruction, telling her in the first place that to do so was unlawful, as it was also unsafe, "for," said he, "if you give a nigger an inch he will take an ell. Learning will spoil the best nigger in the world. If he learns to read the Bible it will forever unfit him to be a slave. He should know nothing but the will of his master, and learn to obey it. As to himself learning will do him no good, but a great deal of harm, making him disconsolate and unhappy. If you teach him how to read, he'll want to know how to write, and this accomplished, he'll be running away with himself."

. . . His iron sentences, cold and harsh, sunk like heavy weights deep into my heart, and stirred up within me a rebellion not soon to be allayed. . . .

"Very well," thought I. "Knowledge unfits a child to be a slave." I instinctively assented to the proposition and from that moment I understood the direct pathway from slavery to freedom. . . . Wise as Mr. Ault was, he underrated my comprehension, and had little idea of the use to which I was capable of putting the impressive lesson he was giving to his wife. . . . That which he most loved I most hated, and the very determination which he expressed to keep me in ignorance only rendered me the more resolute to seek intelligence. In learning to read, therefore, I am not sure that I do not owe quite as much to the opposition of my master as to the kindly assistance of my amiable mistress.

Excerpt from *The Life and Times of Frederick Douglass*, by Frederick Douglass. (New York: Macmillan/Collier Books, 1962).

siveness are not very different in their ultimate meaning from Grace (built around Love and Humility) and Sin (caused by Pride and Egoism) in traditional Western theology.

Selection 3.6 may be viewed as a case study illustrating the manner in which these two seemingly contradictory character traits — Altruism and Aggressiveness — combined to motivate his desire to learn how to read.

Later in the chapter (Selection 3.11), we see how Adam Smith's theory of "benign selfishness" — a theory which no longer branded "aggressiveness" as merely "sinful pride" — used the same duality of human nature to encourage free trade and private enterprise, two bulwarks of modern civilization.

3.7   Human Nature and Conduct
FREDERICK C. NEFF

. . . Except in a strictly biological sense, human nature is not given at birth; rather, it consists of those specific traits of character that have been deliberately cultivated through the medium of education. Human beings at birth are predisposed to act neither morally nor immorally. Moral conduct is learned rather than innate, and it is socially oriented rather than privately intuited. Nor is that kind of behavior that has been conditioned or indoctrinated in accordance with some set of rules governing "propriety" worthy of being labeled moral, for it lacks the undergirding of reflective accountability. . . .

The power of choice which democracy prizes has always been understood as ability to select freely among alternatives and to act accordingly. Only in situations where no alternative exists is choice denied, as in the drudging life of the slave or the strictured living conditions of the prisoner, for such lives require no more than conformity to rules already laid down. . . .

[Free] will is not an entity or metaphysical substance; nor is it autonomous in the sense that it exists in isolation from contextual circumstances. It is simply an ill-chosen term that needs to be redefined as *the power to choose without unwarranted restraint from among competing alternatives.* Since no choice deserves the name that is not freely undertaken, it carries with it the burden of moral responsibility for the consequences to which it may lead. The fact that nonhuman animals give no indication of acting in any moral sense but behave on the basis of instinct, habituation, or conditioning necessitates the conclusion that morality is a uniquely human construct. Nor can any human act be dignified as moral except as it is an outgrowth of reflection, intention and consideration of the desirability of all its probable consequences. . . .

Preoccupation with behavior manipulation has deflected our concern from the attitudes, values and ideals of the learner. As a result, we have prized not knowledge, responsibility, and understanding but a semblance of them; we have forgotten that to live without purpose is not to live in any human sense at all. If, with Dewey, we hold that "the ideal aim of education is creation of power of self-control" — and, if such aim is taken seriously rather than as platitude — a shift from preoccupation with behavior to concern for conduct is in order. Concern with reflection for its own sake divorces thought from its practical issue in conduct, while exclusive concern with behavior fails to provide for its being a culmination of reflection. Although all behavior may be regarded as in some sense controlled, *that unique kind of behavior over which individuals exercise self-control and that is not exclusively shaped by factors extraneous to themselves is precisely what is meant by conduct.*

Use of the term conduct has the advantage of distinguishing thoughtful, purposive and morally sensitive activities from those that are merely accidental or habituated. Conduct requires acceptance of responsibility for actions deliberately undertaken as over against indifferent and merely responsive kinds of behavior; it represents a

Brief excerpts from Frederick C. Neff (Wayne State University, Detroit), "Generic Behavior and Human Conduct: Reflections on an Educational Dilemma," *Educational Considerations* 6: 2–13, Fall 1978 (published by the College of Education, Kansas State University, Manhattan, Kan. 66508). By permission.

conjoining of reflection with action. In so far as self-control is not inborn, it is a crucial task of education to create, nurture and develop it in individually and socially productive ways. To learn is to grow in powers of responsible decision-making; and to educate is to foster utilization of such powers in the intelligent conduct of life. All skills and knowledge are necessary means to this end.

3.8 What Makes Man Different From Other Animals?
RENÉ DUBOS

A distressing aspect of our times is that so many people of Western civilization have lost their pride in being human, and suffer from a dampening of the spirit that makes them doubt our ability to deal with the future. This common frailty appears the more painful when one compares it with the confident mood of the eighteenth century.

In 1743, Benjamin Franklin offered his follow Americans "A Proposal for Promoting Useful Knowledge Among the British Plantations in America." He had in mind an academy that would, he hoped, "let Light into the Nature of Things, tend to increase the Power of Man over Matter, and multiply the Conveniences or Pleasure of Life." Franklin's concept eventually resulted in the creation of the American Philosophical Society, which finally obtained its charter in 1780. The wording of Franklin's proposal and of the American Philosophical Society's charter reflect pride in being human and confidence that human life can be improved by knowledge. This sense of pride and confidence was characteristic of the eighteenth-century Enlightenment but has become much weaker in our times. I want to discuss here the effect of social attitudes on the development of technological civilization but find it necessary to express first some of my views concerning human nature.

The shape of the modern world has been largely determined by the philosophers of the Enlightenment. Among them, none has been more influential than Voltaire and Jean Jacques Rousseau, both of whom died in Paris two hundred years ago, in 1778.

Voltaire and Rousseau had spent their lives in France and Switzerland, except for a few years in England; both associated with Diderot and the other encyclopedists; both had acquired literary fame early in life and had been lionized in the French salons by men and women of wealth and influence. Despite this commonality of social conditioning, however, they developed in adulthood opposite attitudes concerning ways of life and views of humankind.

Voltaire believed in reason — always. He was convinced that humankind could be enlightened and improved by pure intellectuality and by putting wit at the service of strong logic. Although sickly during most of his life, he derived much pleasure from

From René Dubos, "The Despairing Optimist," reprinted from *The American Scholar*, Volume 47, Number 4; Autumn 1978 (pp. 440–449). Copyright © 1978 by the United Chapters of Phi Beta Kappa. By permission of the publishers.

Now editor of *The American Scholar*, René Dubos is Professor Emeritus (of biology) at the Rockefeller University. This essay was presented as the Phi Beta Kappa oration at Harvard University on June 6, 1979.

his social contacts and from the fortune he accumulated. In contrast, Rousseau had little faith in reason. He trusted instead in feelings and in passionate action dictated by the heart. His vision was in many ways unsophisticated and his social life became increasingly limited. Through choices they made early in life, Voltaire and Rousseau thus came to symbolize two opposite aspects of French civilization and of human life — the cult of reason and the worship of instincts.

Among artists, Thomas Rowlandson and William Blake constitute other examples of similarities and contrasts. Both died in 1827 at seventy years of age. Both were Londoners, respectively the sons of a wool merchant and a hosier. Both studied painting at the Royal Academy, proclaimed the superiority of line over volume, and used watercolor as their preferred medium. Neither artist accepted the world for what it was, and each in his own way used painting as a vehicle for his social ideas. Yet, while having all these things in common, the two men had a very different view of life. Rowlandson, the gambler, depicted society with the cynical art of the caricaturist. William Blake, the poet and idealist, perceived and expressed creation with the bright-eyed innocence of a child.

Reńe Descartes and Blaise Pascal were two scientists of the same period who also presented striking resemblances and contrasts. Both were born in prosperous, highly cultivated families in the legal profession in the French provinces; both exhibited early in life great gifts in the sciences and especially in mathematics; both achieved international fame and were socially feted — yet they developed opposite intellectual attitudes. Descartes became more and more convinced that all aspects of creation, including human nature, would eventually be understood through the use of reason and analytical processes. Pascal, in contrast, appealed increasingly to faith as the only valid approach to knowledge and concluded that the heart has reasons that the rational mind cannot possibly know.

These examples make me skeptical of attempts to explain human behavior by environmental conditioning or other sociobiological processes. Human life is of course influenced by genetic and environmental factors, but the really interesting aspects of life — those that make humans so obviously different from animals — clearly transcend such primitive biological explanations. Behaviorists and sociobiologists can account for the animal aspects of human life but have little of interest to say concerning the choices that make us transcend our animality. Artists and other humanists are skilled in the perception and description of human traits but are no more able than scientists to predict what a particular person would like to become or wants to do at a particular time. All human beings live, as it were, in worlds of their own, never completely accessible to other persons.

Thus, human nature is not so simple that it can be reduced to the knowledge of twentieth-century scholars. Humanists and scientists have contributed much to the understanding of our characteristics, our origins, and our potentialities. As specialists, however, we are prone to suffer from a peculiar kind of infantilism that makes us regard the phenomena studied in our own discipline as the most important for the understanding of human nature. We tend to take a deterministic view of life and history because we overestimate the explanatory power of our knowledge while underestimating the freedom that humans enjoy in making choices and decisions.

Admittedly, free will cannot be proven, let alone explained, but this failure does not weigh much against the countless manifestations of freedom in everyday life. What Samuel Johnson wrote in 1778 is still just as true in 1978: "All theory is against the freedom of the will, all experience for it." The most important aspects of human nature are not necessarily those that can be explained by contemporary knowledge. Human beings — and most likely animals also — constantly choose and decide in a way that makes a mockery of orthodox biological and social determinism.

The deterministic view of human fate has been recently strengthened by the widespread assumption that technology — or rather what Jacques Ellul calls *la technique* — is now entirely governed by objective science and has developed an internal logic of its own which is almost independent of human control. Yet it is obvious that human choices continue to influence all aspects of technological societies, as they have always influenced other human institutions. The rapid changes in architectural fashions during recent decades provide visual evidence of the fact that human caprice plays a dominant role in the use of modern technology for the design of buildings. For example, architects are now advocating a change from "modernism" to "post modernism," not by reason of new technologies or new social concepts, but simply because of a desire for change. "Less is More" was the motto of designers of a generation ago. The phrase "Less is Bore" is now considered sufficient justification for change.

In 1605, at the very beginning of the scientific era, Francis Bacon wrote in *The Advancement of Learning* that "The invention of the mariner's needle which giveth the direction is of no less benefit for navigation than the invention of the sails which giveth the motion." This was a clear warning that technological progress would depend on the formulation of goals as much as on the development of techniques. Admittedly, Bacon's warning did not have much influence until recently because most technologists have been more eager for motion than concerned with direction, but there is evidence that the social mood is beginning to change. While bigness and speed are still the most widely accepted criteria of success, we have come to realize that the word progress means only moving forward, as likely as not on the wrong road.

The change in public attitude can be seen in the light of an event that occurred less than half a century ago. In 1933, the city of Chicago held a World's Fair to celebrate the "Century of Progress" which had elapsed since its birth in 1833 and which had seen the triumph of scientific technology. The organizers of the Fair were so convinced that scientific technology invariably improves human life that they stated in the guidebook, "Science discovers, genius invents, industry applies, and *man adapts himself to* or is *molded by new things.*" One of the subtitles of the guidebook was "Science Finds, Industry Applies, Man *Conforms*" (italics mine). This philosophy was still dominant among the futurologists of the 1950s when they tried to forecast what the world would be like in the year 2000. With dismal uniformity, they envisioned a future shaped by far-out technologies and architectures, without relevance to human needs or to natural conditions.

A fundamental change of attitude occurred during the 1960s and 1970s. No one would dare state today that humans must conform to technological imperatives or that they will be molded by technological forces. We want instead that industrial development be adapted to humankind and to nature — not the other way around, as was advocated by the organizers of the Chicago Fair. This new attitude, based on human and ecological criteria, will determine the role played by knowledge and technology in the future.

Charles Lindbergh's life, as reported in his posthumously published *Autobiography of Values*, symbolizes how the modern world has evolved from fascination with sophisticated technologies to the realization that unwise and excessive dependence on these technologies threatens fundamental human values. While on a camping trip in Kenya during his late adult life, Lindbergh had become intoxicated with the sensate qualities of African life which he perceived "in the dances of the Masai, in the prolificacy of the Kikuyu, in the nakedness of boys and girls. You feel these qualities in the sun on your face and the dust on your feet . . . in the yelling of the hyenas and the bark of zebras." Experiencing these sensate qualities made Lindbergh ask himself, "Can it be that civilization is detrimental to human progress? . . . Does civilization eventually become such an overspecialized development of the intellect, so organized and artificial, so separated from the senses that it will be incapable of continued functioning?"

Lindbergh's doubts concerning civilization were the more surprising to me because, in the 1930s, I had known him as a colleague in the laboratories of the Rockefeller Institute for Medical Research, where he was developing an organ perfusion pump in collaboration with Dr. Alexis Carrel. His dominant interest at that time was, along with aviation, mechanical devices to explore what he calls in his book "the mechanics of life." His *Autobiography of Values* reveals how he eventually moved from an exclusive interest in the mechanical applications of science to a deep concern for its social and philosophical implications. He remained enamored of modern science and was, for example, fascinated by space exploration, but became increasingly distraught at seeing technology used for trivial and destructive ends.

Thus, Bacon at the beginning of the scientific era, and Lindbergh more than two centuries later, expressed in different words a concern which has become central to our form of civilization. Science and technology provide us with the *means* to create almost anything we want, but the development of means without worthwhile *goals* generates at best a dreary life and may at worst lead to tragedy. . . .

Two hundred years ago the act incorporating the American Philosophical Society began with the statement that "the cultivation of useful knowledge, and the advancement of the liberal arts and sciences in any Country, have the most direct tendency towards the improvement of agriculture, the enlargement of trade, the ease and comfort of life, the ornament of society, and the increase and happiness of mankind." We have gone far toward fulfilling the scientific and technological aspects of Franklin's proposal but have not contributed much to the "ornament of society" or to human happiness. We are much better at developing means than at formulating ends, as for example when we create sophisticated means of communication but use them to transmit trivialities or when we increase productivity of certain goods while neglecting the experiences that could be derived from what is being produced. The most difficult and important problems relate to questions of values. As Bacon stated in 1605, direction is at least as important as motion.

The relation between means and ends, however, is far more complex than appears from the contrast between the two words. Exalted ends are often the ultimate expressions of means developed for minor uses or even for their own sake. No one is born with a biological need for writing or reading, and many societies have indeed gotten along well without these skills. But once writing had been invented — probably first in Sumer to keep records of supplies — it generated ends unrelated to its first use and became a creator of new values. To a large extent, the growth of civilization depends upon the possibility of formulating new ends that become attainable because new means are available.

Ends thus evolve with the means created by civilization, in our time particularly by science and technology. But ends are desirable only to the extent that they contribute worthwhile values to life and to the earth. In this light, the difference between means and ends, although often blurred, is nevertheless real. Ends refer to the quality of the experience, means to the techniques that can be used to enlarge and enrich this experience. Ends might be regarded as the domain of the humanities, means as that of the sciences. Western civilization will not be really successful until its humanists and scientists learn to formulate and develop together, as advocated by Franklin in 1743, "philosophical experiments" that enlarge and enrich the interplay between humankind and the rest of creation.

In 1837, Emerson concluded his famous Phi Beta Kappa oration with a plea that the American scholar strive for independence from European models. I would submit that the most important task for the American scholar today is to achieve the integration of the sciences and the humanities.

3.9   Some Famous Maxims and Epigrams (The Search for Truth)

(A)   Everyone is ignorant, only in different ways. — Will Rogers

(B)   It ain't what a man don't know that makes him a fool, but what he does know that ain't so. — Josh Billings

(C)   He may be called a fool who calls himself wise. — Thomas North

(D)   To turn events into ideas is the proper function of literature. — George Santayana

(E)   Form is the Golden Vase wherein Thought, that fleeting essence, is preserved for posterity. — Anatole France

(F)   The proper method for hastening the decay of error is . . . by teaching every man to think for himself. — William Godwin

(G)   The only foes that threaten America are the enemies at home, and these are ignorance, superstition and incompetence. — Elbert Hubbard

(H)   Let us try not to laugh at the acts of man, nor to lament them, nor to detest them, but to understand them. — Spinoza

(I)   Contact with strange civilizations [whether geographically or historically distant] brings new standards of value, with which the native culture is reexamined, and conscious reformation and regeneration are the natural outcome. — Hu Shih

(J)   Time takes no account of great thoughts. They are as fresh today as when they first passed through their author's mind, ages ago. — Samuel Smiles

(K)   True virtue is life under the direction of reason . . . The ultimate end of the state is not to dominate men, nor to restrain them by fear; rather it is to free each man from fear that he may live and act with full security and without injury to himself or to his neighbor. — Henry Thoreau

(L)   The man who is guided by reason is more free in a state where he lives under a general system of law, than in solitude, where he is independent. — Spinoza

(M)   PRO: Reading without thinking gives one a disorderly mind, and thinking without reading makes one flighty and erratic. — Confucius

Every sentence I utter must be understood not as an affirmation, but as a question. — Neils Bohr

CON: A book is like a mirror. If an ass looks in, you can't expect an angel to look out. — Schopenhauer

Aristotle calls man a rational animal. All my life I have been seeking to confirm this. — Bertrand Russell

(N)   Reading that is an avoidance of conversation rather than a prelude to it shrinks the personality more than it expands the mind. — Sydney J. Harris, columnist (July 17, 1980)

3.10   Two Forms of Democracy: Political and Economic

Any realistic assessment of human freedom must recognize that liberty, equality, and fraternity have many dimensions: political, economic, psychological, sociological, religious, and philosophical. The following several selections, although not directly related to our classrooms, are nevertheless related to education because today's education is dependent upon and intimately related to contemporary technology and economics.

Until the early twentieth century, industry — even such industries as U.S. Steel or Standard Oil — was viewed purely as a form of private enterprise, and was thus relatively free from governmental interference. For example, at the turn of the century Andrew Carnegie "earned" several millions of dollars each year, when there was no income tax whatsoever and no inheritance tax. Under such a system, the rich were obviously getting richer and richer, while the poor had little chance to succeed. But "one man, one vote" meant that political power could control economics; and the twentieth century saw the growth of labor unions, child labor laws, workmen's compensation legislation, social security benefits, compulsory education, and other ways to help equalize economic opportunity.

The most significant changes came not from government but from industry itself. The design of products with replaceable parts, begun by Eli Whitney (1765-1825), came into full bloom in the early twentieth century. Perhaps the most notable example was the Model T car of Henry Ford (1863-1947).

But a modern corporation involves more than replaceable parts and repeatable work tasks. It involves the coordinate effort of corporate bodies of managers, financiers, workers, researchers, and salesmen — all joining forces to concentrate their varied abilities on a single problem — and, for the most part, excluding everything else as irrelevant.

Unfortunately what is "irrelevant" to one problem may be extremely relevant to another. For example, when auto makers found ways to roll glass in the same way that steel is rolled, tens of thousands of glass blowers — doing a type of work that had been done for two or three thousand years — lost their jobs. So too did makers of wagons, carriages, and harnesses. And as other industries imitated the automobile industry, thousands of other long-established types of work ceased to exist.

Improved techniques of agriculture dramatize the manner in which increased efficiency of production has resulted in major problems of unemployment:

> Between 1945 and 1965, more than four million people were displaced [by cotton mechanization], most of them blacks in the rural South. Where did these people go? A number of studies indicate that much of the overpopulation and urban blight found in Northern and Eastern cities is directly attributable to this mass migration of unemployed workers and their families because of the mechanization of cotton. Agricultural economists estimate that the benefit to the consumer of cotton, due to mechanization, has been $1.25 per person per year. . . .
>
> Today in the University of California, machines are being developed for mechanizing thirty-four different crops. The Department of Labor estimates that within the next ten years, more than two hundred thousand farm workers will lose their jobs in California alone. Where will these people go? What skills will they have to develop? What are the social costs of this mass displacement?
>
> More important, . . . how are these decisions reached? Who are the people who decide that we shall mechanize thirty-four different crops in California? Are they farm workers? Are they consumers? Are they small farmers? . . .[1]

Other "irrelevant side effects" have to do with the ways in which new industries have changed the entire environment. Thus, the combustion of leaded gas has led to air pollution; the mining of coal has left large areas desolate of foliage and subject to ravishing floods; the absence of birth control information has led to overpopulation; the use of chemical insecticides has caused air and water contamination; the use of charge accounts has resulted in millions of people becoming enslaved by debts.

Such incidental side effects, which were largely ignored by the industries responsible for them, has meant, especially during the past fifty years, that most capitalistic societies — and all communistic countries — have given more and more power to the public sector, as opposed to the private sectors, of the economy. Indeed, the changes wrought by the industrial revolution have been so momentous that Marxists — and many others as well — believe that capitalistic democracy is on the decline and that nothing less than a major revolution can bring about the type of changes needed to establish a just and equitable society suitable for our industrial or postindustrial age. This book is built around the belief that "major revolutions" are needed — and are in

[1] Marian Standish, "Whom Does the University Help?" *The Center Magazine* 13: 42–46, November-December 1980.

process — but that they come about most quickly under our constitutional system, with its free and open discussion and its attempt to help as many people as possible — including students — understand not only the changes that have occurred, but the manner in which they have occurred. The remaining selections of this chapter deal with such topics.

3.11   Adam Smith's "Benign Selfishness" As Seen in Contemporary Enterprise

Last year [1977] 475,388 new companies were incorporated — more than double the number 20 years earlier. Each year since 1960 (except for the recession year 1974), the number of business incorporations has steadily increased. To be sure, about 30 percent of new businesses fail within their first year, and half of them close down within two years. But the proportion has remained relatively steady. The government's index of net new business formation, which subtracts the dropouts from the newcomers, has risen by 42 percent over the past two decades. Recently it has been running at an all-time high. . . .

[In the 1970's] many persons who run their own businesses seem driven by a compulsive desire to succeed. The challenges of overcoming obstacles is more of a goad to their efforts than the prospect that new wealth will let them indulge sybartic fantasies. "The fear of being a failure is what drives me," observes Ken Brown, thirty-three, a college dropout who was recently grossing some 53.5 million a year from various motorcycle ventures. "Money is just a way of keeping secure."

Many entrepreneurs, of course, toil all their lives with no more hope of stiking it rich than the neighborhood laundryman or the proprietor of a mom-and-pop corner grocery. But thousands become millionaires, sometimes almost overnight. In the past 15 years, the number of individuals in the United States with a net worth of $1 million or more has nearly quadrupled, from 54,000 people in 1962 to nearly 200,000 people at the last estimate. In 1975, there were 1,189 U.S. taxpayers who reported annual incomes of $51 million or more, nearly twice as many as in 1970.

Brief excerpt from "The New Entrepreneur: Romantic Hero of American Business" by Gurney Breckenfeld (of *Fortune* magazine), *Saturday Review* 5: 12–15, July 22, 1978. Copyright © 1978 by Saturday Review. All rights reserved.

It should be remembered that Adam Smith's *Wealth of Nations* came off the press in 1776, the same year as the American Declaration of Independence.

The essence of the free enterprise system was expressed by Adam Smith as follows:

> In almost every other race of animals each individual, when it is grown up to maturity, is entirely independent, and in its natural state has occasion for the assistance of no other living creature. But man has almost constant occasion for the help of his brethren, and it is in vain for him to expect it from their benevolence only. He will be more likely to prevail if he can interest their self-love in his favour, and show them that it is for their own advantage to do for him what he requires of them. Whoever offers to another a bargain of any kind, proposes to do this. Give me that which I want, and you shall have this which you want, is the meaning of every such offer . . . It is not from the benevolence of the butcher, the brewer, or the baker that we expect our dinner, but from their regard to their own interest. We address ourselves, not to their humanity but to their self-love, and never talk to them of our own necessities but of their advantages.

Read also Ernest V. Heyn, "Ten Better Mousetraps (Eight of Which Made Money)," *Saturday Review* 5: 20–21, July 22, 1978. We should remember that "better mousetraps" are invented, in part at least, because our society grants patents and copyrights and thus provides rewards to persons with original ideas. In former times, such rewards, if any, came only at the whim of a king.

3.12   The Bold Mixtec
CAMILLA CAMPBELL

[In the beginning, according to this ancient Mixtec legend, Sun ruled everything. But Man desired more power and freedom, and he wanted it so badly that he challenged Sun to a contest. Admiring Man's courage, but realizing Man's weakness, Sun agreed to the contest only if Man could first be made more strong and skillful. To make their contest fair and just, Sun insisted that Man should have a weapon to match Sun's rays.]

So the Sun told the Man to pick up a long twig from the tree that was soft wood and to curve it the way Rainbow curved. Then he was to fit it with a thong as straight as the horizon. This the Man did and made himself the first bow.

The twigs from the other tree were hard and stiff. From these the Man made arrows for his bow.

"I am ready," he warned the Sun.

The immense Sun smiled to see the tiny Man waiting so boldly to fight with him. Laughing, he sent down a weak ray.

The Man didn't move. "You cannot destroy me. I am a Mixtec and therefore very brave," he shouted.

The Sun sent a stronger ray, and then a stronger one, but still the Mixtec withstood them and refused to run away and hide. The Sun stopped laughing. He didn't even smile as he threw against the Man his very strongest ray.

Still the Man held his ground. He began to shoot his arrows at the Sun so straight and fast that the mighty ruler of all the Earth became afraid. He ducked behind a dark thunderous cloud. Soon the Man could hear him moaning and weeping. Thunder and lighting and rain filled the heavens.

By these signs the Man knew that he had won. This was the way, explained the Mixtec chieftain to the Aztecs, they had won their land. And so impressed were the Aztecs with Mixtec strength and courage they left and went toward the northeast to settle.*

For a twentieth-century reader, living in an age of spaceships and intercontinental ballistic missles, a bow and arrow may seem unimportant. But for the Native American Indian living five centuries ago such was not the case. In all ages and cultures of man, people have gained power and have taken great pride in their inventions, from bows and arrows to airplanes and computers.

---

*EDITOR'S NOTE   Compare this myth with the myth of Prometheus (see Selection 3.4). Much of history is a story telling how those societies which have the more advanced technologies of warfare are able to conquer others. Consider how Cortez, with a few hundred men, was able to conquer thousands of Mexicans. As individuals, were the Spaniards that much superior to the native Americans? Hardly. But the natives had no horses, no wheels, no wagons or caissons to carry their supplies and their weapons, no swords or shields of metal, no ships, no writing. . . . And so the Spaniards conquered and hailed themselves as the "bearers of civilization." But in the succeeding centuries of cultural cross-breeding, it became evident that the Mexicans also made many contributions, including such peacetime arts as the growing of corn, potatoes, and many other agricultural products.

3.13   Some Strengths and Weaknesses of Our Business Civilization
ROBERT L. HEILBRONER

[The main] reason for the decline of business civilization is that businessmen persuade people to change their lifeways, not out of any knowledge of, or deeply held convictions about, the "good life," but merely to sell whatever article or service is being pandered. I do not think we pay sufficient heed to the power of advertising in making cynics of us all: at a business forum I was once brash enough to say that I thought the main cultural effect of television advertising was to teach children that grown-ups told lies for money. How strong, deep, or sustaining can be the values generated by a civilization that generates a ceaseless flow of half-truths and careful deceptions, in which it is common knowledge that only a fool is taken in by the charades and messages that supposedly tell us "the facts"?

[This blatant disregard for truth suggests the] crassness of outlook, the self-centeredness of behavior, so inextricably mixed with the idea of a business culture. This attitude is not, of course, peculiar to capitalism, although it may be peculiar to all commercial relationships. But it is in the nature of capitalist society that it has celebrated and made a norm of social values that are at least tolerated in other civilizations. No other civilization has permitted the calculus of selfishness so to dominate its lifeways, nor has any other civilization allowed this narrowest of all motivations to be elevated to the status of a near categorical imperative. [In Part 3 (Chapters 7, 8, and 9) this point is discussed in greater detail.]

[There] is, I think, a second reason why the material achievements of a business civilization fail to generate the satisfactions we expect of it. This is the disregard of business for the value of work. A business civilization regards work as a means to an end, not as an end to itself. The end is profit, income, consumption, economic growth, or whatever, but the act of labor itself is regarded as nothing more than an unfortunate necessity to which we must submit to obtain this end.

Now, of course, labor *is* a necessity on which material survival depends. In an environment of scarcity, even under the most enlightened and democratic government, work must be performed, some of which can be justified only in terms of the end to which it is directed . . . But this subordination of the act of labor to the overriding calculus of technology and efficiency is given a special blessing under a business civilization, where the values of output are celebrated and those of input merely calculated. . . . [More is said about this topic in Chapter 6.]

But it would be wrong to sum up business civilization solely in terms of the philistinism that is its ugliest aspect. Bourgeois culture has also brought into being, and permitted to survive, other aspects of the individualism that is implicit in its economic philosophy. The ideas of political equality and dissent, of intellectual adventure, of social nonconformity, however much hedged about or breached in practice, owe much of their development to bourgeois thought. . . .

[It is possible that capitalism's greatest achievement may be its stimulus to a world society. For some future historian, multinationals may appear] to the nation-state what the nation-state itself was to the disorganized crazy-quilt of feudal autarchy.

Already bigger and more powerful, in financial terms, than any but the largest nations, they suggest that capitalist enterprise, freed from the confines of its cramping national borders, will find in its multinational existence the organizational form required for its survival.*

---

*EDITOR'S NOTE   To these remarks we add a few sentences from the 1975 *Encyclopedia Britannica* article on Capitalism:

> Predictions concerning the survival of capitalism are, in part, a matter of definition. One sees everywhere in capitalist countries a shifting of economic activity from the private to the public sphere. None of the five great events of the first half of the 20th century — World War I, the Russian Revolution, the great depression, World War II, and the Chinese revolution — were favourable to the future of capitalism. By the 1960s the process of transformation had gone so far that capitalist economies bore little resemblance to classical capitalism of the 19th century. . . .
> Whatever its faults, historically the capitalist system led the way from an age of scarcity to an age of potential abundance. Karl Marx, capitalism's most formidable critic, wrote in 1848 that capitalism " . . . in scarce 100 years has created more massive and more colossal productive forces than have all preceding generations together."

3.14   Two Levels of Morality and Justice
MICHAEL POLANYI AND HARRY PROSCH

. . . the distinction between a free and a totalitarian society lies [in this:] . . . a free society . . . does *not* engage, on principle, in attempting to control what people find meaningful, [whereas] a totalitarian society does attempt such control. . . . [Indeed, it should be clearly recognized] that a free society *rests upon a traditional framework* of a certain sort . . . [and should not be viewed purely as an "open society", i.e., as a society lacking in structure or defined meaning.]

[We usually speak of freedom] as though it were something desirable. But "freedom" is an ambiguous term, and in some of its meanings it has sometimes been severely criticized.

One very basic meaning of "freedom" seems to be the "absence of external restraint." The rational limits to freedom, understood in this fashion, are set by the condition that our exercise of a freedom must not interfere with other people's right to the same freedom. These are reasonable limits, because this sort of freedom cannot possibly exist in a social situation (i.e., be accepted as "right" by everyone in a society) without tacking these limits onto it. This sounds very simple, and certain examples can be adduced that are easily understood and acceptable to everyone. Take, for instance, the freedom to go to sleep or to watch TV. I should have that freedom, this principle of limitation says, as long as my exercise of it does not interfere with my neighbor's freedom to choose between the same alternatives. We have inherited this principle governing the use of individualistic freedom from the great Utilitarians of our past. They linked it to the idea that the pursuit of a good society is the same as the pursuit of the greatest happiness of the greatest number and that freedom in the sense we are discussing it here is a necessary condition for the effective existence of this pursuit.

At its base, however, this is an individualistic, self-assertive conception of freedom and, because this is what it is at bottom, it unfortunately can be used — and has been used — to justify all kinds of socially objectionable and even destructive behavior. The worst kinds of exploitation — of the poor, of children, of women, even the keeping of slaves — have been practiced in its name. It also has served as the ground for the Romantic movement, exalting the unique, lawless individual, and for those nations striving for "greatness" at any price.

There is another meaning for freedom that is almost the exact opposite of the one we have just been discussing. It regards "freedom" as "liberation from personal ends by submission to impersonal obligations." When Martin Luther faced the Diet of Worms and declared, "Here I stand and cannot do otherwise," he was not asserting his lack of freedom to do otherwise. He was maintaining that his acknowledgment of a moral demand gave him a freedom from the pursuit of merely personal ends (such as the protection of his own life) as well as, in this case, a freedom from having to obey the authorities in religious matters. This is, of course, a form of liberation, although it is quite different from the self-assertive, individualistic one of the Utilitarians; it is indeed, from their point of view, even foolish.

But such a meaning for freedom can become very much like a theory of totalitarianism. It becomes exactly that by the mere addition of the notion (not Luther's intentions, of course) that the state is the supreme guardian of the public good. Then the dangerous paradox mouthed by all the totalitarians of our century follows: the individual is made free by surrendering completely to the state.

The preservation of freedom in the lives of men is thus gravely imperiled by both these conceptions of freedom; for even if men do not go to the extreme of either anarchy or totalitarianism under the thrust of these meanings, they may well feel, on the one hand, that the individualistic theory of freedom is simply selfish. At least it is uninspiring. Certainly the young men of Europe who were inspired by the totalitarian view of freedom to march to their deaths in World War II had found the individualistic view of freedom to be uninspiring. On the other hand, the theory of freedom as self-surrender to impersonal obligations does not seem to accord with our sympathy for the individual's pursuit of his own happiness in his own personal manner.

If we reflect now upon the structure that freedom was seen to have in the paradigms provided by the scientific community and the legal community, we can see how these existing communities do, in fact, weave into a working whole the two aspects of freedom we have just discussed. The freedom of a scientist or a judge is not one of simple self-assertion. It is freedom to pursue certain obligations and to share in a system of mutual authority. Nevertheless, this freedom implies an absence of external restraint because it also entails a right to make personal judgments (often quite innovative) — judgments that bring whole segments of our person into them.

Let us now also try to use this paradigm of a scientific community to enlighten ourselves on what sort of structural principles a free society as a whole might need.

By a simple and obvious analogy, a free society must exist within the context of a tradition that provides a framework within which members of the society may make free contributions to the tasks involved in the society. The freedom of mere self-assertion can lead only to disintegration of our standards and institutions. It may from time to time result in an equilibration of social forces — interests — that mutually tone one another down to the point where they all can live together in some sort of working balance. This is something like what Madison hoped would be the case in the large society he expected the United States to become. However, no one who holds the view that freedom is mere self-assertion will be devoted to maintaining such a balance; he will rather be devoted to upsetting it, whenever possible, in order to achieve more of his own interests. Thus any balance that happened to exist at any time would always be threatened and almost certainly would, from time to time, be completely destroyed. As Adam Smith foresaw, the chief danger to the optimal balance that could be achieved under institutions of free trade would come from the manufacturers, for none of them would have any interest in maintaining a free system of competition; their interest would rather lie in securing monopolies in order to control their markets. The adjustments that could and should be forced into existence by a free market would then not occur — in their case. Since all industrial producers would be doing the same thing, none of them would be doing what a free market would require. Smith thought, therefore, that only a tremendous effort to educate farmers and workers in their self-interest could ever bring a free market into existence or preserve an existing one. Actually, he seemed to have little hope of its success.

What needs to come into the picture of a viable free society is a traditional devotion to the spiritual objectives, such as truth, justice, and beauty — those that require for their pursuit free, self-determinative communities: of scientists, scholars, laywers and judges, artists of all sorts, and churchmen. For without a general public devotion to these spiritual objectives, free, self-determinative communities could not long continue to exist. The public (or public officials) would most certainly decide at some point to try to control these pursuits in the interest of the "general welfare." Of course a public which succumbed to this temptation would soon have little or nothing to use for increasing the general welfare, for it would have inhibited, if not annihilated, *real* inquiry, *real* spiritual or moral insight, *real* justice, and *real* art. What it would have left, in the caricatures of these activities, would be powerless because meaningless. However, a too explicit and "official" devotion to these ideals (defining them too explicitly and setting up public agencies to promote them) would also destroy them, because it would destroy the freedom of people in these fields to make innovative mutual adjustments relevant to their pursuit. Such a society would to some degree become ossified into a rigid set of meaningless (perhaps mainly verbalized) objectives. Thought police would find an important niche in such a society as much as in the one in which the pursuit of ideal ends is subordinated to something called the "public good." What would have been forgotten is that such ideals as scientific truth, justice under the law, and good art cannot be given concrete definitions. What these really are, *in concreto*, is simply what all members of each relevant group are striving together to delineate. Truth, for instance, is given specific form only as the community of scientists is free to work out what its form is — and this task is never finished. The same thing is true of justice in the practical development of legal systems and of art in the continuing work of artists.

These enclaves of freedom — science, the law, art, and so forth — will have to consist of autonomous circles of men, free from public control to work out their problems through mutual adjustment and authority; in other words, they must be little republics of their own. The public must respect them sufficiently to refrain from trying to direct them in any way toward something called the "public good." Even the economy, since it *is* an industrialized economy, must be allowed its freedom to operate . . . by mutual adjustment of its participating parts through the mechanisms of markets and pricing and profits. Interference with this system of mutual adjustments can and must be made, of course, from time to time for various purposes of great importance to the public or for the preservation of the system of mutual adjustments itself; but attempts to supplant it altogether by central planning would simply bring an industrial society to a halt, as well as place power to control all activities of groups and persons in the hands of public officials, since all working capital (resources) would be controlled and distributed according to their judgments.

It would seem to be clear, under the concept of the free society that we have been outlining, that many of the affairs of the society would be managed through the development of various *spontaneous* orders — ordered wholes that develop freely by means of mutual adjustments rather than *corporate* orders, ordered wholes given their shape from the top down, i.e., centrally controlled. It is our contention that a system that develops from the bottom up, through free interaction of its parts upon one another (subject only to a free, common dedication of its participants to the value of certain standards, principles, and ideal ends), is the only social system that can meaningfully be called free. The alternative is to control social affairs centrally from the top down, and so establish a corporate order — which is the essence of totalitarianism.

Such a system of spontaneous order(s) is, however, [possible only when citizens are fully aware of two levels of morality: (a) the personal selfish level, motivated by a desire for fame, power or wealth, and (b) the impersonal, higher level, motivated by a love and respect for truth, beauty and goodness. For example,] regardless of the *private* motives that move a person to be, for example, a judge — ambition for status, for power, for respect, for money, or whatever — he is *not* a judge unless he performs according to the standard incentives of that profession, and not according to his own private motives for entering it. These standard incentives are: to find the relevant law and the relevant facts and to make a decision that either follows the precedents or creates a new pecedent on grounds that his colleagues can find (or at least *ought* to find) reasonable.

The foregoing observations show us that the individuals in these elites will operate on two levels: one is the lower level of ambition — of power and profit; the other is a higher level of moral obligation. . . . * [But this higher,] moral level can exist only if it

---

*EDITOR'S NOTE   The laboring man no less than the "elite" professional man has such feelings of moral obligation. Eric Hoffer puts it this way:

rests on the lower. The lower provides the private proddings or "kicks" that individuals who are to act morally in various positions must have in order to act at all. But these proddings also put limits to moral attainment. Just as our bodies make possible the intellectual systems within which we dwell (we cannot think without a brain), so also they set limits to our attainments in these systems. This is why we can never be perfect at anything — whether it is science, art, morality, or religion. The notion of perfection in any pursuit is an imaginative projection of what the full and unlimited operation of the principles governing these higher mental levels would look like. But the fact is that the operation of these higher mental levels is rooted in the physiological levels of our bodies. So our minds, in their actual operation, can never achieve independence from our bodies. . . .

[Hence it is that] the moral sphere of man's life is made possible — but also limited — by the systems of power and profit and restricted parochial interests upon which his moral sphere rests. . . .

[We conclude, then, that in a society that is both just and free, the higher,] moral level exists on the foundation of a lower, essentially nonmoral level, and [this lower, nonmoral level] must inevitably place limits on the accomplishments of the higher level.

3.15   Human Freedom and the Sense of Duty
EDITORIAL

The Enlightenment thinker Immanuel Kant (1724–1804) analyzed man's inner moral consciousness as follows:

Duty is action performed out of respect for law; but in order for law to reach a moral level, that law must be *freely* obeyed. In other words, duty is never mere obedience to rules imposed on an individual by outside forces — whether by "outside forces" we mean Church or State. Duty is always the free and responsible action of an autonomous individual. To further emphasize the point that men are free and responsible agents — and that their essential humanity consists in this fact — Kant held that moral laws are universally valid only if they guarantee that no person will be used merely as a means toward ideological ends, but that every man is an end in himself. It is meaningless to speak of a person's *duty* unless that person has some measure of *freedom*. Or — if you are a determinist who insists that everything is determined — there are many things that happen to us that are not determined by

As to the passion for excellence, it may sound highfalutin but it actually concerns common, everyday affairs. I have spent 50 years doing back-breaking work in the fields, in lumber camps and on the waterfront. Many of the people I lived and worked with had courage and, whether they knew it or not, a passion for excellence. The word "job" used to have a magical connotation in this country. It was something you had to do the best way you knew how. A job might be unpleasant, dangerous or trivial, but it still had to be done, and it had a claim on your skill and ingenuity. Even the simplest job had its mysteries; and once you fathomed them, time flew. — Eric Hoffer, "What We Have Lost," *New York Times Magazine*, October 20, 1974, pp. 110–117.

ourselves, and for which we are not responsible, e.g., a tornado or cyclone which causes much damage. But there are at least some things which are *self*-determined, e.g., the reader of this page may be (self-) *determined* to finish it. So, there is a sense in which the distinction between freedom and determinism is nothing more than a distinction between autonomous (self-determined) behavior and behavior which is explainable by extrinsic (external) factors.

We can repeat what was just said by using traditional terminology. If by "conscience" we mean "one's inner conscience" or the "still small voice" within one's own consciousness, then "freedom" is nothing more or less than the ability to "think for oneself" and to make moral decisions without external compulsion. In I *Kings* 19: 11–13, the Bible tells how Elijah was unable to hear the voice of God in the wind, or the earthquake, or the fire; but heard it only through the "still small voice" within. And, as has often been noted, it is this "still small voice" which so often makes us feel *still smaller!* Which is to say, we are morally immature unless we have some inner convictions and beliefs which give meaning and integrity to our lives.

Such inner convictions and beliefs must be in accord with human nature. As noted in Selection 3.4, the contemporary sociobiologist Edward O. Wilson gives special emphasis to two inherited traits: *altruism* and *aggressiveness*. Fifty years earlier, two American anthropologists put the matter this way:

> The key virtues are (1) sympathy or love, and (2) enthusiasm or courage; justice is only sympathy universalized, and temperance is only enthusiasm clarified by intelligence. Promotion of these virtues is rightly regarded as [paramount because] . . . they are permanent and intrinsic sources of happiness.[1]

It should be noted that these *two* virtues are reaffirmations and reformulations of Plato's four cardinal virtues, namely: (1) Prudence (Wisdom), (2) Courage (Fortitude), (3) Temperance (Moderation), and (4) Justice (Social Harmony and Personal Integrity).

We conclude with an ancient Greek adage: "There is only one virtue — knowledge; only one vice — ignorance." This knowledge and ignorance refers to the thing that matters most: the road to human happiness. In 1946 C. I. Lewis restated this ancient Greek adage as follows:

> At least half of the world's avoidable troubles are created by those who do not know what they want and pursue what would not satisfy them if they had it.[2]

---

[1] W. F. Ogburn and A. Goldenweiser, *The Social Sciences* (Boston: Houghton Mifflin, 1927), p. 2.

[2] C. I. Lewis, *An Analysis of Knowledge and Evaluation*, (La Salle, Ind.: Open Court Publishing Co., Inc. 1946), pp. 373–374.

3.16   The Zen Master: A Japanese Parable

In a foolish quarrel, a samurai once murdered a farmer, and then left the area without trial or punishment. Soon afterward the farmer's son also left the village hoping to find his father's murderer and to gain revenge.

Before long the samurai began to feel guilty and decided that he must do a good deed to atone for his sins. As he was traveling along he came to a very steep road over a mountain and discovered that many people had been killed trying to cross it. So he decided to build a tunnel through the mountain.

He had been working for a year when the son of the farmer whom he had killed appeared and threatened to cut off his head.

"You have a right to kill me," said the samurai. "But could you please wait until I finish this tunnel?"

The young man agreed, and after watching for several weeks he began to work with his old enemy. Finally, after several more months, the tunnel was completed and people could walk safely through the mountain.

"Now you may kill me," said the samurai.

"How can I kill you now?" said the young man. "You are my own teacher."*

This Japanese myth, slightly adapted, is from *Rites*, by John Cafferata, p. 361. Copyright © 1975 by McGraw-Hill Book Company. Used with the permission of the McGraw-Hill Book Company.

This story may be viewed as an example of rehabilitation through work, or of enlightenment through selfless service to others, or of atonement resulting from detachment from prejudice and from the cultivation of a sense of duty.

In feudal Japan a samurai was a member of the military aristocracy.

---

*EDITOR'S NOTE   In his book *Whatever Became of Sin?* (New York: Basic Books, 1976, p. 181) Karl Menninger chides some of his colleagues for whom psychoanalysis seems ". . . to be a punitively expensive process for rationalizing and intellectualizing aggressive behavior. . . . [so that the patient is relieved from anxiety] for the wrong reason! This [tendency to eliminate personal responsibility] is bowdlerized in Anna Russell's "Psychiatric Folksong":

At three I had a feeling of	But now I'm happy; I have learned
Ambivalence toward my brothers,	The lesson this has taught;
And so it follows naturally	That everything I do that's wrong
I poisoned all my lovers.	Is someone else's fault.

3.17   Excellence: A Quest for Integrity (Plato)
CONCLUSION

Human integrity is attained when one's body, mind, and will are conjoined in harmony and are guided by a sense of duty and a feeling of commitment to a cause larger than one's self. This concept of integrity goes back at least as far as Plato, (427?–347 B.C.), and, as A. M. Whitehead once remarked, "All Western philosophy is but a series of footnotes to Plato." Without attempting to summarize Plato's philosophy, we may perhaps get the spirit of it by recalling a myth from Plato's *Republic*:

Gyges, a shepherd and servant of the king of Lydia, found a gold ring which had the remarkable property of making its wearer visible when he turned the collet one way, and invisible when he turned it the other way. Perceiving this wonderful power in his ring, the shepherd managed to become a messenger to the court, where he, with the help of his magic ring, was able to kill the king, to seduce the queen, and to take over the kingdom.

Plato asks us what we should do if we had such a ring. If we could do anything we pleased, however unjust and however cruel, without anyone being the wiser, and with no fear whatsoever of punishment, would we follow the example of Gyges? Or would we pursue the path of righteousness?

Plato defends "virtue for virtue's sake" as follows: Our "self" has two components; (1) a lower, animal-like nature, with its personal cravings for food, drink, and sex, and with it social desires for weath, power, and social prestige; and (2) a God-like nature with its aspirations toward truth, beauty, and goodness. Because enduring values give more lasting satisfaction than transitory ones, (2) gives more lasting satisfaction than (1). Moreover, if during our life we concentrate on sensual gratification, wealth, power, social prestige, and other such "externals," our nature becomes more and more like that of an animal or beast. On the other hand, if, in spite of poverty, hardship, and self-sacrifice, we hold firmly to our highest ideals, it is our higher, better self which will grow, and we will enjoy the inner satisfaction of having attained the maximum realization of what is highest, and of what is unique, in man.

Plato's ethics may be summarized in a rhetorical question: "How would a man profit if he gain, fame, wealth, and power if, in doing so, he would subordinate the nobler part of his nature to the baser part?" (Compare Matthew 16:26.)

Emily Dickinson (1830–1886) caught the spirit of Plato in eight short lines:

In this short life	Opinion is a flitting thing,
That only lasts an hour	But Truth outlasts the Sun —
How much — how little — is	If then we cannot own them both —
Within our power.[1]	Possess the oldest one.[2]

[1]"Life" from *The Poems of Emily Dickinson.* Cambridge, MA: The Belknap Press of Harvard University Press, Copyright 1951, 1955, 1979 by the President and Fellows of Harvard University. Reprinted by permission of the publishers and the trustees of Amherst College.

[2]From *Life and Letters of Emily Dickinson* by Martha Dickinson Bianchi, © 1924 by Martha Dickinson Bianchi. By permission of Houghton Mifflin Company, Boston.

EDITOR'S NOTE   Although the eight lines from Dickinson are sometimes joined together, the first four were probably written in 1873, the last four in 1879.

3.18   Quotations for Further Thought and Discussion

(A)   Hitch your wagon to a star. Let us not fag in paltry works which serve our pot and bag alone.

— Ralph Waldo Emerson

(B)   Excellence is the perfect excuse. Do it well, and it matters not what.

— Ralph Waldo Emerson

(C)   That country is richest which nourishes the greatest number of noble human beings.

— John Ruskin

(D)   He is the greatest artist who has embodied, in the sum of his works, the greatest number of the greatest ideas.

— John Ruskin

(E)   I know of no more encouraging fact than the unquestioned ability of man to elevate his life by a conscious endeavor. It is something to be able to paint a picture, or to carve a statue, and so to make a few objects beautiful; but it is far more glorious to carve and paint the very atmosphere through which we look, which morally we can do. To affect the quality of the day, this is the highest of arts. Every man is tasked [i.e., is challenged] to make his life, even in its details, worthy of the contemplation of his most elevated and critical hour.

— Henry Thoreau

(F)   They talk of the dignity of work. Bosh! The dignity is in leisure.

— Herman Melville

(G)   Leisure . . . freedom to do what we like . . . is the most difficult of arts . . . [because it involves] an obligation to be what we are not yet, to become on the creative side of character whatever is possible for us. . . . Mere amusements and diversions [do not satisfy. . . . They] are not sufficiently creative. The true use of leisure is to produce something characteristic of ourselves, to project our personalities, to stretch our souls.

— John Erskine

(H)   Act so as to produce harmonious rather than discordant desires.

— Bertrand Russell's — and Plato's — supreme moral axiom

(I)   Lust for power is the strongest of all passions. . . . The power of a man is his present means to obtain some apparent future good.

— Thomas Hobbes

(J)   Reason is not a force contrary to the passions, but a harmony possible among them. Except in their interests it could have no ardor; except in their world, it could have no point of application, nothing to beautify, nothing to dominate.

— George Santayana

(K)   Where a great proportion of the people are suffered to languish in helpless misery, that country must be ill-policed and wretchedly governed; a decent provision for the poor is the true test of civilization.

— Samuel Johnson

(L)   The notion of structure [hence the notions of justice and of social harmony as well as of personal integrity] is composed of three key ideas: the idea of wholeness, the idea of transformation, and the idea of self-regulation.

— Jean Piaget

(M)   Other things being equal, human beings enjoy the exercise of their realized capacities (their innate or trained abilities), and this enjoyment increases the more the capacity is realized, or the greater its complexity.
— Aristotle's — and John Rawls' — supreme moral axiom

(N)   Most of us would agree that it is unnatural and unwholesome to live in solitude, yet those who live only in the present, drawing no nourishment or sense of continuity from history, are alientated from our common past, and live in a kind of temporal solitude.
— Sydney Harris, (February 28, 1980)

(O)   In each person I catch the fleeting suggestion of something beautiful and swear eternal friendship to it.
— George Santayana

(P)   The best form of civilian defense is to make oneself worth defending.
— Niccolo Tucci

(Q)   A machine can be made to do the work of 50 ordinary men, but not 50 machines can do the work of one extraordinary man.
— Hilaire Belloc

(R)   I celebrate myself, and sing myself
And what I assume you shall assume,
For every atom belonging to me as good belongs to you.
— Walt Whitman, in *Song of Myself*

(S)   The famous lines of Robert Burns

The rank is but a guinea stamp,
A man's a man for a' that

do not mean that *quality* does not matter. On the contrary, it means that every man, woman and child should have a fair chance to attain, not merely equality, but quality.
— Christopher Dawson (1975)

(T)   In heaven, methinks, there is laid up a pattern of the good city which he who desires may behold, and beholding, may set his own house in order. But whether it exists or ever will exist on earth is no matter, for the wise man will live after the manner of it, having nothing to do with any other.
— Plato, *Republic* IX, 592 (Jowett translation)

(U)   [This concluding quotation for Part One is from Lord Acton's *History of Freedom in Antiquity* (1877):
By liberty I mean the assurance that every man shall be protected in doing what he believes [to be] his duty against the influence of authority and majorities, custom and opinion.

PART TWO

EQUALITY

Liberty, Equality, Fraternity — three lines enclosing a space called Civilization.

There are eight letters in the word Equality. Of these, seven are Quality. Without Quality, E[quality] is meaningless.

If two ride on a horse, one must ride behind. — Latin

Democracy is based on the conviction that there are extraordinary possibilities in ordinary people. — Harry Emerson Fosdick

Inequality is as dear to the American heart as liberty itself. — W. D. Howells

There is only one categorical imperative. Act only on that maxim whereby thou canst at the same time will that it should become a universal law. — Immanuel Kant

I'd rather not live at all than live by alms. — Montaigne

He who boasts of his descent is like a potato: the best part of him is underground.

There is no slavery but ignorance. — Robert Ingersoll

The greater the number of dimensions along which excellence is measured, the less the inequality. — Harold R. Bowen

Democratic equality signifies belief in the worth and dignity of every individual, wherever he lives, whatever his station, his color or the degree of his learning; and in the right of every individual to feel that he has an honored voice in the management of his own affairs, whether in the home, his place of work, his community or his world. — Charles W. Ferguson

EDITOR'S NOTE   *Reminder:* Chapter 2 may be conjoined with Chapters 4, 5, and 6.

Chapter 4. RACE, ETHNICITY, PLURALISM

4.1 Introduction to Part 2: Something Happened: Education in the Seventies
BEN BRODINSKY

[If] there was one dominant theme underlying education events of the Seventies, it was the yearning for equality. This was the decade in which Americans battled to bring equal school dollars to all school districts, whether poor or rich. It also brought new hope for equality to the handicapped, to women, to foreign-language-speaking groups.

It was a decade troubled by controversies over busing, prayer in the schools, the rights of students, and the integrity of textbooks. Educators saw their school budgets eroded by inflation and hit by rising fuel costs. Big cities were pinched by one severe financial crisis after another. Classrooms, hallways, and playgrounds were wracked by student violence and crime.

Biggest newsmakers in education were not educators; they were the U.S. Supreme Court, Congress, executive departments. Operating more than 100 federal aid programs, officials in Washington guided, influenced, or sought to control education to an extent that could hardly be measured or comprehended either by educators or the public.

The climate of the 1970s was not healthy for learning, excellence in education, or intellectual daring. There was little time for improvement of the curriculum, which in many instances retrogressed to the traditionalism of an earlier generation. Little was done for the ailing high schools, and reform efforts left secondary education just about where it was in the 1950s. The concepts of early childhood education failed to make much impression upon the nation's schools.

But it was a decade that gave off heat, steam, or smoke about vouchers, performance contracting, "Sesame Street," the role of private schools, Proposition 13, teacher centers, and the fact that the President's daughter enrolled in an inner-city Washington public school for one year.

Out of the welter of such events I select 10 for elaboration.

Ben Brodinsky, "Something Happened: Education in the Seventies," *Phi Delta Kappan* 61: 238–241, December 1979. © 1979, Phi Delta Kappan, Inc. By permission of publisher and author.

Ben Brodinsky is editor of the *Edpress Newsletter*, a monthly advising the staffs of nearly 600 U.S. and Canadian educational journals. His annual analysis has been a feature of Education Press Association of America for more than twenty-five years.

Of the three great democratic ideals — liberty, equality, fraternity — it is *equality* which has dominated the American scene for the past twenty-five years. Hence, even though the main thrust of *Crucial Issues in Education* is toward the future rather than toward the past, it seems appropriate to open Part 2 with this brief historical survey of the recent past.

SERRANO AND SONS

When the California Supreme Court decreed that school districts relying primarily on the local property tax may be depriving children of equal protection under law (*Serrano v. Priest*, 1971), the ruling "shook the foundations of American school finance." Or so it seemed at the decade's beginning. It did not seem so as the decade ended.

But the *Serrano* decision influenced an equally famous case, *Rodriquez*, in which a U.S. district court in Texas agreed that total reliance on property taxes creates sharp differences in the quality of education for children: Rich school districts provide schooling of high quality, poor districts short-change schoolchildren.

With what seemed like bated breath, the nation's educators waited for decisive word from the U.S. Supreme Court. When it came, the word (*Rodriguez*, 1973) was by no means resolute. The Court left the use of property taxes for schools pretty much undisturbed, but urged that states correct any constitutional deficiencies by devising new school taxing and spending plans.

Throughout the Seventies some 25 states labored to equalize educational opportunities between poor and rich school districts. In these efforts only one thing was certain: The task of reforming school finance has been lifted from the talk stage at educational conferences to the action arenas of state legislatures, courts, and state education agencies. That may be the decade's most significant achievement in school finance.

What about results? A 1979 Rand Corporation study found that school finance reforms have somewhat loosened school revenue ties to local property and that state treasuries have assumed larger shares of school expenses. But poor schools remain poor, rich schools remain rich, and equalization is still a long way off.

ON BEHALF OF THE HANDICAPPED

When, in 1971, a U.S. district court ruled that Pennsylvania schools must provide education for all retarded children, ages 4 to 21, regardless of cost, the decision proved momentous. It touched off battles for the handicapped in half the states and provided a *cause célèbre* for many professional organizations.

It was a cause calling for humanity, compassion, and dollars. Knock on 10 doors on any street, ran the argument, and behind at least one of them you will find a handicapped child or youth. His chances of getting an adequate education have been slim — clearly a case of deprivation of equal opportunity.

By the middle of the decade about a score of legislatures had enacted laws requiring "appropriate" programs for the handicapped. Educators groaned — and struggled to meet the new challenges. They complained of a lack of special teachers, instructional materials, and funds to do what the laws (or the courts) required. And they kept calling for help from Washington.

Help seemingly came in 1975. Congress passed the Education for All Handicapped Children Act, which has since become famous as P.L. 94-142. Never before has any people in any land accepted so daring a challenge. It requires a massive effort, the provision of individualized schooling for five to seven million physically, mentally, and emotionally handicapped students. It also calls for expensive changes in school plants and facilities to make them accessible to all.

Federal grants to states were the inducements, and a gradual phasing-in was one of the palliatives. But the pain, struggle, and red tape of meeting federal mandates on behalf of the handicapped promoted a rising volume of complaints and doubts among educators: Can "the boldest, most humane of educational ventures" be carried out effectively?

FOR WOMEN AND THE BILINGUAL

From the decade's beginning to its end, American education was embroiled in struggles to achieve equality for women in schools and colleges — and for students to whom English was a second language.

Title IX was the big legal stick Congress handed to those who wanted to end discrimination against women. It was part of the Educational Amendments of 1972. The big year for Title IX was 1975, when federal regulations took effect — and they touched on scores of aspects of hiring, firing, promotion, benefits; on curriculum and extracurriculum; on sports and physical education; on participation of girls and women in school life and educational administration.

Textbook publishers began reexamining their products to root out sexist attitudes and biased reporting. Writers were urged to purge their prose of sexism.

Discrimination against non-English-speaking children had been troubling the conscience of educators for generations. It was not until the 1970s, however, that something practical was done. A Bilingual Education Act, on the statute books since 1965, began to take effect in the mid-Seventies with a trickle of federal dollars.

The U.S. Supreme Court decision in *Lau v. Nichols* (1974) gave new impetus to the movement. In a case originating on the West Coast, the Court required public schools to "rectify language deficiencies" in order to open up the instructional programs to children who do not speak or understand English.

The initiatives and programs in Washington, state capitals, and local districts on behalf of bilingual students mounted into the hundreds by 1979. Still, advocates charged it was not enough, that funds, teachers, and instructional materials were inadequate to serve the millions of Latinos, Orientals, and American Indians who are entitled to instruction in their native tongues. These advocates had a sound political base; nevertheless, they were challenged by others, educators and laymen, who saw philosophical defects, and even mischief, in bilingual education. The worth and value, the how and why of the movement, will be debated in the next decade, possibly in the next century.

DUE PROCESS FOR STUDENTS

The 1970s gave toughness to the dictum, established in the 1969 *Tinker* case, that "students do not shed their constitutional rights at the schoolhouse gate." Within 60 days in 1975 the U.S. Supreme Court ruled in two cases that students are protected by the due process clause of the Fourteenth Amendement. The decisions created shock waves among educators, or so said the National School Boards Association at the time.

In *Goss v. Lopez*, a case involving student suspensions, the High Court said that a student facing suspension must be given oral or written notice of the charges against him and an opportunity to present his side of the story. The majority opinion stated: "We do not believe we have imposed procedures on school disciplinarians which are inappropriate in a classroom setting. Instead, we have imposed requirements which are less than a fair-minded school principal would impose upon himself in order to avoid unfair suspensions. . . ."

In *Wood v. Strickland*, another suspension case, the Court went further, ruling that a student whose rights have been violated may sue school authorities for damages. Said the court: "While school officials are entitled to a qualified good-faith immunity from liability of damages, they are not immune from such liability if they knew or reasonably should have known that the actions they took violated constitutional rights of students."

Pained cries from administrators that the rulings meant erosion of local school control, a threat to discipline, and a menace to teachers and principals lasted only a short time. State departments of education soon began publishing impressive brochures detailing student rights (usually coupled with responsibilties), and boards of education wrote or rewrote policies and regulations dealing with due process.

Arbitrary and unilateral procedures against students — where and if they existed — were dealt a blow during the years that historians may call the decade of human rights.

BASICS AND COMPETENCY

"Back to the basics" was the decade's best advertising slogan, a theme for mass media editorials and political oration; and an emotional topic for boards of education and PTA meetings.

The popular outcry was for more and better reading, writing, and arithmetic instruction. But at the movement's height, about mid-decade, demands arose for drill, recitation, more homework, stricter discipline, the teaching of patriotism, and an end to social promotions.

A small number of school districts responded by instituting what they called back-to-basics programs, or they set up alternative schools devoted to the three Rs, with history taught by chronology and science by memorization. Other school districts publicized their dedication to fundamental subjects and declaimed: "We've been teaching the basics all along. We've never stopped teaching basics." Still others reexamined their curricular programs and allotted a bit more in time, money, and staff to whatever list of "basics" local communities demanded.

It was not a shining hour for curriculum improvement. Back-to-basics advocates (and they included some educators) gave little, changed little.

More significant were the actions of minimum competency proponents through-out the 1970s. Their arguments ran as follows: Students indeed require a set of basic skills to get along in the world after graduation. These included, over and above the three Rs, skills for citizenship, employment, family life, consumerism, enjoyment of the arts. It's possible to identify these minimum skills, teach them to all (or nearly all) students, and not let anyone move up the educational ladder to graduation until the students pass required tests.

The public liked the idea. States enacted minimum competency laws at a rapid pace throughout the late Seventies. Not a state dared neglect demands for such programs. This bright hope for education began to dim, however, by 1979, as educators confronted the problems and the court actions generated by minimum competency laws. Disturbing also was a finding reported by the Education Commission of the States: "No research evidence is available to show that mandated student competency programs are working."

BAKKE AND AFFIRMATIVE ACTION

"The most anxiously awaited court decision of the century." "The most significant civil rights case of the generation." "The most far-reaching educational dispute since the battles for school desegregation."

So ran the hyperbole on the *Allan Bakke* case for more than a year before the U.S. Supreme Court announced its decision on 28 June 1978. National interest was intense, fanned more by words in the mass media than in the literature of education.

The center of attention was a thirty-fivish Marine Corps veteran of Vietnam who was passionately interested in studying medicine. His applications to the University of California Medical School at Davis were denied. Bakke thought he was rejected because he is white. He saw special places reserved for minority students under a two-track system for applicants. He saw black students admitted who were less well qualified than he when he was rejected.

"Reverse discrimination" was the cry. The lines of legal battle formed, often along racial lines. More briefs, on both sides of the issue, were filed with the Supreme Court than on any other case within the last 20 years. Hanging in the balance, many thought, was the national policy of affirmative action, under which minority groups were given preference in education and employment. Would the U.S. Supreme Court nullify this hard-won right?

When the decision finally came, it read: "Affirmed in part and reversed in part." It meant that the Court affirmed Bakke's right to enter the university but rejected the argument that affirmative actions based on race should be outlawed. Admissions programs favoring minorities, the Court said further, must be kept under "strict judicial scrutiny."

Neither whites not blacks were completely happy with the decision. Few thought that the basic issues of affirmative action or admissions policy were resolved. Most predicted that another generation of court cases would follow the *Bakke* ruling.

CAREER EDUCATION

The average life of an educational reform in the U.S. is about three years. Career education, introduced in 1971 with much fanfare, has outlived most efforts to reform some aspect of schooling. At the end of the decade career education was still alive and doing well, or doing something, in probably a fourth of the nation's school districts.

Credit for the concept goes to Sidney P. Marland, Jr. When he took office as U.S. commissioner of education, he startled the country, and jarred the education community, with a proposal that career education should begin in the first grade and remain a central concept through graduate school.

Was he talking about vocational education? No, but partly yes. Was he talking about occupational information? No, but partly yes. He declined to offer a definition. Career education, he said, should be a bridge between school years and work years; it should stress reality in all classrooms, no matter what subject is taught.

Despite its vagueness, Marland's idea generated enormous public interest, caught the fancy of Congress, and gave rise to a stream of speeches, articles, research studies, and books. Its proponents offered career education as a corrective for problems of dropouts, poor discipline, youth unemployment, apathy in learning. It is a true basic, they said.

In 1975 a research group counted 9,300 school districts where "career education was under way." Even more important, said the research, a fifth of all districts had started inservice programs to help teachers incorporate career concepts into their lessons.

Always a concept in search of a definition, career education was the decade's moderate success story. Countless teachers, for the first time, helped students discover their interests and aptitudes, provided them with the facts about the world of work, and called it career education. When the Dallas school system built and operated a 21-million-dollar facility for the instruction of everything from aeronautics to television, that too went to the credit side of career education.

DECLINING ENROLLMENTS

Few Americans took note when enrollments in the nation's schools dropped by half a million during 1971 and 1972. But when, in 1974, some 700,000 fewer boys and girls entered the elementary grades, both laymen and educators discovered what statisticians had been predicting. The nation's schools had entered a decade-long decline in enrollment. Instead of problems of growth, educators had to meet problems of shrinkage.

What to do with emptying schools and how to reduce the teaching force, with justice, became major challenges for educators during the Seventies.

In some districts school plants went up for sale or rent. In others school boards used freed-up space to expand art, music, science, and library resources and activities. Still others used the new space for adult education or preschool programs.

But efforts to dispose of surplus teaching stations were usually met with community protests and even court actions. The art of closing a public school was new to most administrators and had to be learned slowly. Advice from experts was to plan ahead four to five years. "In closing schools, figure what it takes to get a bond issue passed," said the Educational Facilities Laboratories of New York, "then double or triple the time."

Long-range planning was also required for solution of staff problems created by enrollment declines. The options included reducing class size and teacher/pupil ratios — if budget and school board policy allowed. In most instances, however, districts resorted to reassignments, voluntary early retirement, freezes on hiring, and reduction in force.

No matter what action was proposed or taken, it created staff anxiety or community discord. And invariably administrators became entangled in the laws, regulations, and negotiated contract clauses governing personnel, with lawsuits to follow.

ASSESSMENT, ACHIEVEMENT, SCORES

A daring educational venture of the 1970s was the continual probing into almost impenetrable questions: What are American students learning? What do they know and what can they do? And the puzzle of the decade was, Why aren't they doing better?

First facts about the quality of schooling came from the National Assessment of Educational Progress (NAEP) in 1970. This agency, controversial at first, gained credibility as it got down to work measuring student achievement in art, careers, citizenship, literature, mathematics, music, reading, science, social studies, and writing.

Its 1970 findings dealt with science and citizenship, and the report card for elementary and secondary schools was a mix of Cs and Ds, with a few As or Bs. As year after year NAEP poured out thousands of facts about student progress, valuable clues came here and there for curriculum workers, textbook writers, and teacher educators. America accepted periodic assessment of its students as an instrument of education. Funds from the federal government and other sources kept the tests going.

In the middle of the decade NAEP began to send out ominous clues about declines in achievement in science, math, and language arts skills among the groups tested. But NAEP did not prepare Americans for the 1975 shock. The College Entrance Examination Board reported that scores on its Scholastic Aptitude Tests had dropped 10 points on the verbal section and eight points on the mathematics section from the year before. Moreover, the nation learned that the declines, which had begun in the 1960s, would probably continue.

A panel of educators took two years to search for the reasons. Its findings included a long list of factors — from the debilitating role of television to the increase in numbers of minority students taking the tests.

But critics of the schools were convinced that the responsibility lay with "permissive education," "lack of discipline," and "the retreat from the basics."

STRIKES, BARGAINING, POWER

Organized teachers took power during the 1970s. They did it though collective bargaining, political action, and use of the strike when necessary.

Opposition to unionism within the profession virtually disappeared during the 1970s.[1] Educators looked at labor tactics and saw they were good, especially for classroom teachers.

Labor taught American educators that they must organize, must show militance, must have the right to collective bargaining with their employers, and must work only under contracts negotiated in good faith by both sides. The lessons appealed especially to teacher activists; within the decade labor unionism dominated the NEA as well as the AFT and swept into supervisory and administrative groups.

The collective bargaining contract became the main tool for teacher power. Only 15 years ago fewer than 100,000 public school teachers were serving under written contracts. As the 1970s drew to a close, "most" American teachers were covered by contracts negotiated under state laws. Intense lobbying by teachers in all state capitals brought these laws into being.

American education produced few leaders during the 1970s who could be recognized by the public at large. Teacher unionization produced such a leader. He is Albert Shanker, head of the 520,000-member American Federation of Teachers, who taught the ways of the labor union to schoolpeople. Admired, hated, respected, Shanker emerged as a personality who could charm teachers as well as their bosses. "Power is better than powerlessness," said Shanker.

[1] Although the National Association of Professional Educators, headquartered in Washington, D.C., claims 46,000 members, its impact was not great enough to gain it listing in the U.S. Office of Education's 1977–1978 *Directory of English Associations.*

4.2 New Heirs to an Emerging Civilization
EDITORIAL ESSAY

About ten million children of school age population throughout the United States are non-Anglo and consequently differ from the culturally dominant population.

Some five million of these children come to school speaking a language other than English. Historically, they have been considered "marginal" children — barely worth educating, just as marginal products are barely worth producing. They live in ghettos, on reservations, or barrios; they have drop-out rates as high as 50 or 60 percent.

The remaining four or five million minority children speak English, but they too are culturally and ethnically different from the dominant Anglo population. These children too, because of their differences, are subject to alienation, exclusion, poor grades, and high drop-out rates.

Let us begin with the blacks. In spite of many ups and downs, blacks have been steadily upgrading themselves into better jobs, an effort that should sooner or later get family incomes moving up once again. The proportion of blacks holding white-collar jobs has increased by 50 percent in the past ten years. Blacks have been pouring into the trade unions, where they account for 12 percent of the total membership and a third of all new members.

Perhaps the greatest advance from 1960 to 1980 is the realization that problems are not solved by name-calling or by the use of stereotypes. Just how destitute must a person be to be called "poor"? If children are "culturally deprived," who deprived them of their culture? If they are "underprivilged," what privileges have been taken away? If they are "educationally handicapped," what evidence do we have to support this? If they are "lower class," why won't they admit it? Educators are becoming surer about three things; (1) "they" have poorer health; (2) "they" have lower IQs, achievement, and grades by the testing methods we have been using; and (3) most of them are beset by deficiencies in reading and language. But such deficiencies vary from group to group, and from individual to individual. Hence there are no educational panaceas. There is no single program or method suitable to the varied students who enter our schools.

But although nearly all educators are quite sure about the above three truths, there still persists in our society a tendency to indulge in such circular reasoning as the following:

Blacks are too ignorant to learn, therefore they should not go to school; they do not go to school, therefore they are too ignorant to learn. Blacks are shiftless, therefore they are unable to find jobs; they are unable to find jobs, therefore they are shiftless. Blacks are poor and destitute, therefore they do not respect middle-class moral standards; they do not respect middle-class moral standards, therefore they are poor and destitute.

How can we escape these vicious circles? The answer is that "blacks" and "they" are vague and indefinite terms — terms that refer to "some" but not to "all" members of the group. The solution to the problem will come as we concentrate on the "some," and give special help to those among the destitute and downtrodden who show reasonable promise of rising to higher social, economic, and cultural levels. Although the number of persons in the lowest socioeconomic group who have such potential may not appear to be large at present, with persistent effort we may be confident that this number will gradually increase, until the same proportion of blacks as of whites may realize their full potential.

Already, many are coming close to realizing their full potential:

Between 1970 and 1977, the proportion of black families earning real incomes of $15,000 or more rose by 24 percent, compared with 14 percent for whites; black families earning $25,000 or more increased 50 percent, against 34 percent for whites.

Just as telling, however, are figures that disclose a more baleful story: Since 1964, blacks' median family income has vacillated between 54 and 62 percent of the figure for whites. In 1954, furthermore, only 4 percentage points* separated jobless figures for white and black

---

*EDITOR'S NOTE   This occured at a time when there were no minimum wage laws.

youths; in 1978, the gap was 22 percentage points. . . . [and there are millions] of uneducated blacks, crowded together in the inner cities and seemingly bonded to poverty — with virtually no hope of ever getting worthwhile jobs, winning respect or sharing in the affluence they see on television.

Most in this group are functionally illiterate, unable to compete in an economy that has little place for the unskilled. Many tend in their midteens to drop out of school and into street life, with its defeatism, frustration, drugs and criminal pursuits, which become a way of survival.[1]

But better civil rights, based on the democratic principle of "one man, one vote," has led to surprising advances: From Congress to city halls, blacks now hold about 4,500 elective offices nationwide, 45 times as many as in 1954. Between 1970 and 1979 the number of blacks holding elected offices advanced: in Congress, from 10 to 17; in state and county offices, from 261 to 721; as mayors, from 48 to 170; as city officials, from 575 to 1,989; as judges and other law officers, from 213 to 454; and as school officials, from 362 to 1,139 — making a grand total from 1,469 to 4,489.

Although the number of 20- to 24-year-olds who completed high school has nearly doubled during the past twenty years, the proportion of school dropouts among blacks — and also among Hispanics, native American Indians, and other ethnic minorities — remains extremely high. Part of this is due to the notion that "Black is Beautiful" implies that "White is Ugly." Reporting on such attitudes, two black scholars write:

"No way I'm going to do things The Man's way," says Ben, a black senior who says he is failing most of his courses and doesn't particularly care. Teachers say Ben isn't untypical. "Many of the black kids feel it's just not hip to study and they put pressure on others to conform," notes Lucia Peele, a high school guidance counselor who also is black. . . .

Black academic successes which have run counter to the prevailing ideology have been largely ignored — most notably the success of Dunbar High School, which was brought to national attention by Thomas Sowell, an economist who is black. Dunbar was an all-black high school in Washington, D.C., that for 85 years consistently came in first in citywide tests given in both black and white schools. It produced large numbers of well-educated graduates whose outstanding achievements enriched American society. These graduates included America's first black general, the first black cabinet member, the discoverer of blood plasma, and the first black senator since Reconstruction. Dunbar's success was not the result of its racial segregation (except as it may have contributed to a competitive desire to make a black high school the best), but because students, parents, and faculty, in miserably inadequate facilities, enthusiastically supported and worked for the academic goals of the school. Although at least 88% of the students came from homes of nonprofessionals, they subscribed to an ethic based on work and achievement. There was no self-defeating assumption that high academic performance was a value antithetical to blacks.

Dunbar, for 85 years, proved that blacks can achieve in the public schools. Race, in relation to achievement, was irrelevant. What was important was the motivation, the belief in excellence. . . .

At bottom, learning and achievement are individual matters. As Martin Mayer insists, opportunity does not mean results: "The best that can be given is opportunity; the burden

[1] From "Blacks in America: 25 Years of Radical Change," *U.S. News & World Report* 86: 48–68 (feature article), May 14, 1979.

will continue to rest on the Negro community because there is no way to transfer it. Governments cannot legislate and courts cannot mandate results." Schools can provide the educational technology and committed teachers. The responsibility rests on the black community to lead its young away from the suicidal belief that excellence and achievement somehow involve a disloyal collaboration with a white enemy.[2]

But attitudes are extremely important, particularly self-attitudes; and we should realize that a child's attitude toward himself very often reflects the attitudes of others toward him — the so-called Pygmalian effect. If a child's speech is defective because he lisps or is tongue-tied, most teachers will see that he receives special attention. But if a child speaks defectively because his parents speak broken English, the child may be judged to be not sufficiently "abnormal" to require extra help — and the child may end up with a poor concept of himself.

Such data has led many to conclude, particularly at the elementary levels, that race is less of an intrinsic barrier than many suppose; and that we must give more attention to language.

But we should not despair; we should realize what tremendous gains have been made by blacks and other racial and ethnic groups. To better appreciate these gains, let us first note the attitudes which antedated the Civil War. In 1856, speaking for a majority of the United States Supreme Court, Chief Justice Roger B. Taney described the situation as follows:

> This unfortunate class [the black people] have, with the civilized and enlightened portion of the world, for more than a century, been regarded as an inferior order and unfit associates for the white race, either socially or politically, having no rights which white men are bound to; and [hence] that the Negro might justly and lawfully be reduced to slavery for his benefit.

These attitudes persisted far beyond the Civil War. The opening sentence of the chapter "Racial Segregation in Education" in the first edition of *Crucial Issues in Education* began with these words:

> Within the memory of some people still alive [in 1955], there was a time when human beings were bought and sold as chattel property, when men honestly affirmed that dark-skinned people had neither souls nor intellects, and that Negroes were incapable of rational, moral action or of intellectual achievement.

We conclude with a statement by Kenneth S. Tollett:

> My past has enabled me to understand and sympathize with some aspects of every phase of black protest thought and action. Yet, I have to conclude that, although hatred of whites and glorification of blacks may be mentally liberating in a transitional period, it is not a very useful or productive emotion. A measure of separation may be necessary for blacks to find and accept themselves. A lot of integration is necessary for whites to find and accept blacks. Much pride, some anger, more self-respect and self-reliance, but most of all love and the recognition of the dignity and integrity of all human beings are what is most needed if the American Dream is to become a reality for blacks and whites, Jews and Gentiles, Catholics and Protestants, Democrats and Republicans.[3]

---

[2] Bilione Whiting Young and Grace Billings Bress, "A New Educational Decision: Is Detroit the End of the School Busline?" *Phi Delta Kappan* 56: 515–520, April 1975. By permission.

[3] Kenneth S. Tollett (former dean of Texas Southern University Law School, Distinguished Professor of Higher Education at Howard University, and Visiting Fellow at the Center for Democratic Institutions), in the November/December 1971 issue of *The Center Magazine*.

4.3 Biracial Education: Two Views

Separate Is Still Unequal
KENNETH B. CLARK

Twenty-five years after the Supreme Court ruled in *Brown v. Board of Education* that "separate educational facilities are inherently unequal," the majority of black students attending colleges in the Southern states are in traditionally black colleges. . . .

Even though the Supreme Court, in a series of decisions before and after *Brown*, made it possible for an increasing number of black students to attend traditionally white state-supported colleges, universities and professional schools, a dual and segregated system of publicly supported higher education is today the dominant and seemingly accepted educational reality in the South. The most visible and dramatic desegregation of traditionally white Southern colleges takes place in varsity sports such as basketball and football. Beyond admitting the potentially outstanding athletes and a small elite minority of black students, the traditionally white colleges remain so; and the colleges attended by the majority of black students remain predominantly, if not exclusively, black.

When one seeks to understand why this uneconomical and educationally unsound dual racial system of state-supported higher educational institutions is not dismantled, one is confronted with a number of justifications for a dual system, justifications that, upon careful analysis, turn out to be rationalizations for maintaining the racial status quo. These rationalizations are inconsistent; they reflect deep fears of change, and a desire to preserve and protect vested interests. Their common denominator is the desire to defy the Constitution of the United States with impunity.*

The most common justification for preserving traditionally black colleges is the claim that they meet "a special educational need" of black college students. The elementary and secondary education most black students receive, the argument runs, does not prepare them to compete with white students in meeting the admissions and academic performance standards demanded by traditionally white colleges. This argument assumes that inferior education of black students persists in the elementary and secondary schools twenty-five years after the *Brown* decision, despite its prime objective of providing equality of educational opportunity for these children. This assumption is, on the whole, correct. But the argument also assumes that black children's educational inferiority is irremediable because they are inherently backward, intellectually or culturally deprived and thus unable to learn, or some other such

Excerpts from two articles in *The Nation* 229: 7–9, July 7, 1979. Used by permission from *The Nation* magazine, copyright © 1979 The Nation Associates, Inc.

Kenneth B. Clark is Professor Emeritus at City College, CUNY, and a member of the New York Board of Regents.

*EDITOR'S NOTE   On this point read Alan David Freeman, "Legitimizing Racial Discrimination Through Antidiscrimination Law: A Critical Review of Supreme Court Doctrine," 62 *Minnesota Law Review* 1048–1120, 1978.

premise. These assumptions are false, but they are self-fulfilling and underlie the perpetuation of separate black and white colleges.

Probably the most difficult and dangerous resistance to the disestablishment of the dual racial system of publicly supported higher education comes from those blacks — particularly blacks now involved in the administration of the black colleges — who plead that segregated colleges should be perpetuated. These black educators present essentially the same arguments for the defiance of the *Brown* decision that white public officials offer, namely that blacks cannot compete in white colleges. They contend further that traditionally black colleges should be perpetuated because they have some special cultural value for black students. They want to isolate black students from premature competition with white students. But in becoming open advocates for the perpetuation of the dual higher education system, they have persuaded many whites that blacks have abandoned the hope of integration. These blacks are encouraged by many reasonable whites and liberal foundations who dangle before them the tantalizing bait of finanical support that will strengthen black colleges and make them "equal" to white colleges.

But invariably the grants to black colleges for such basics as improving the quality of faculty, strengthening and expanding course offerings and generally raising, maintaining and monitoring academic standards are woefully inadequate to meet urgent present needs. . . . If a black college were, in fact, equal or superior to the average white college in a given region of a state, it would quickly become racially integrated. Separate but equal is a contradiction in terms for blacks, as the Court so clearly understood in its *Brown* decision.

There is an understandable vested interest in the maintenance of the racial status quo among blacks now employed in traditionally black colleges. Sometimes this interest is expressed directly and candidly. Many fear that disestablishment of the dual racial system will cause the many black administrators and faculty to lose their jobs and be replaced by less-qualified whites. There is certainly a need to protect the employment rights, status and tenure of those [30,000–40,000] blacks who are qualified by training, experience and ability to compete under a single nonracial standard. And there must be safeguards to prevent whites of mediocre and inferior abilities from displacing blacks. If there is a commitment, this can be done. . . . [Meanwhile, those] who seek to justify the continuation of the dual racial system of education intentionally or inadvertently reinforce the present educational inferiority imposed upon the majority of black students in this country.

There has been no evidence to refute what the Court said in *Brown*: "separate educational facilities are inherently unequal." Whatever might have been the value of black colleges in the seventeenth century and up to World War II, their continuation — particularly state-supported, publicly funded colleges — is a flagrant violation of the letter, the spirit and the goals of the *Brown* decision. It marks a return to *Plessy v. Ferguson*. Black colleges and white colleges are educational anachronisms. Racial considerations intruding upon the educational process contaminate education at the source. Education is the awesome struggle to free the human mind of constrictive parochialisms, superstitions and ignorance.

Integration Can Be Unequal, Too
DERRICK BELL

[It is important to realize that social attitudes change slowly, and that what our Courts declare to be our Nation's ideals and principles are not always realized in fact. In the post-Civil War era, in spite of the clear and unqualified Emancipation Proclamation, Black] survival required self-reliance and great flexibility. A black willing to shoot a Klansman from his horse during a Ku Klux Klan midnight attack on his home, might in town the next noon step off the sidewalk to give way to passing whites. . . .

But it is now 1979. . . . The commitment to the principles of racial equality embodied in the *Brown* decision is not dead . . . [but to achieve genuine equality today requires much flexibility,] risk and sacrifice. This is especially true in urban school districts where the minority population is high, housing segregation is extensive and suburbs offer conveniently available escape routes for middle-class parents when school-desegregation orders take effect. Those who cry that such parents are racist ignore the avoidance by middle-class black parents of involvement in court-ordered desegregation when their means permit. . . .

Today, as during those far more dangerous years after the Hayes-Tilden Compromise of 1877, blacks and those whites who would advance the ideal of racial equality need to eschew rigid slogans and, in the area of education, support policies that are most likely to offer poor black children an effective education. Without it, these children face a future much more bleak for them and ominous for us all than anything envisioned by Chief Justice Earl Warren. In some smaller communities, the best tactic may still be the classical integration remedy: racial balance of pupils and teachers, and busing as needed. But in the cities and suburbs, where rigid adherence to such tactics simply increases the percentage of blacks in the schools, and in some areas threatens the very survival of the school systems, alternative avenues must be explored.

There are now dozens of private and public schools in this country where poverty-level students are learning in trouble-free classrooms, testing at and above national norms, and graduating and going on to college. The educational effectiveness of these schools is not harmed by all-black student enrollments. Indeed, educational programs and materials can be geared to the special learning needs of the students. Educators know that while these schools differ in approach, they share components that seem crucial to their success: strong leadership from the principal, involvement of parents in the educational process and a sense of accountability among teachers. The models these effective black schools present are not easy to duplicate, but they are not impossible either. Certainly they will not engender more resistance than current racial balance remedies, and as some successful magnet schools in black neighborhoods have proved, good schools will attract white students.

Will policies resulting in all-black schools violate the principles of *Brown*? I think not. The landmark 1954 decision voided coerced segregation. Racial balance was a tech-

This response to Kenneth B. Clark also appeared in *The Nation* 229: 9–11, July 7, 1979. Used by permission from *The Nation* magazine, copyright © 1979 The Nation Associates, Inc.

Derrick Bell is a professor of law at Harvard Law School.

nique adopted later to insure that recalcitrant school districts complied with *Brown*. But in most urban districts today, school officials are not entirely responsible for existing racial isolation, and whether or not responsible, there simply are not enough whites to make balance possible. The Supreme Court, moreover, has rejected metropolitan remedies, measures which in any event would likely have sparked a Constitutional amendment against all school desegregation before they succeeded in their educationally questionable goal.

The presence of middle-class whites in a classroom is no guarantee that the money and concern their presence attracts will benefit black students from low-income families. Certainly the presence of white children is no substitute for the involvement in school affairs of black parents, involvement made difficult if their children are assigned to schools far from home.

Not all black parents will agree with my assessment, and thus plans to make black schools educationally effective should permit the voluntary busing of black children to any available mainly white schools. Indeed, some parents may wish to send one child to a black school in the area, and have another bused to a white school across town. The kind of flexibility that makes educational sense within a family is equally worthwhile for the black community. It is, by all odds, the best hope of educating our children until the combination of our demands and the pressure of future events convinces whites that it is time for another major civil rights law.

4.4 Teachers Must Have a Sense of Sacrifice
JESSE JACKSON (and EDWARD B. FISKE)

Most of my notions about education come out of my own experience with the educational process. I came out of a segregated elementary and high school situation in Greenville, S.C. It was a school system where blacks used the books four years after whites had used them. And sometimes for a class of 30 we might have five books, so we would have to read aloud. It was a sheer luxury whenever we were able to take books home from school.

But in that situation there was this love triangle. My mother took me to school, and we met Mrs. Robinson, my first-grade teacher. That Sunday Mrs. Robinson and my mother took me up front to meet the pastor. So there were my parents and my teacher and my church — a love triangle. I was insulated from many of the slings and arrows of hostile segregation.

And I was exposed to some great and dedicated teachers, who have influenced my life tremendously. There was Mrs. Robinson, and secondly, Mrs. Sarah B. Shelton. I went to her class in the sixth grade. The first day in class she put a word on the board

Excerpted from the September issue of *Teacher* Magazine with permission of the publisher. This article is copyrighted. © 1979 by Macmillan Professional Magazines, Inc. All rights reserved.

This article, written by Edward B. Fiske, education writer for the *New York Times*, tells of Fiske's 1979 interview with the Reverend Jesse Jackson. In this interview Fiske put this question to Jackson: "Do the ideas behind 'Push for Excellence' reflect your own experience as a student?" This selection is a summary of Jackson's reply.

larger than any of us understood, and we said, "Uh, you don't understand what grade we're in." (She was a new teacher at the school.) She said, "I know what grade you're in, and I will keep on putting words on there all the year that will chase you to the library, and I'm going to teach you how to use the dictionary." She never talked down to us, and she made great demands and had high expectations.

And the end of that year I looked forward to getting out of her class — to the seventh grade, where I would be a senior and could run the halls and take over. I knew I was going to a teacher who allowed that to happen. One day I came home, and I saw Mrs. Shelton's car in front of our house. I was a bit fearful, but I went in. I ran upstairs and my mother said, "Come on down. Mrs. Shelton wants to talk to you."

"What does she want to talk about?" I asked. "I've already finished her class."

Mrs. Shelton said, "How are things going?"

I said, "Fine, I'm glad I'm through with your class."

Then she said, "I did not feel last year that the class covered adequately what it ought to cover and I think it would be a disservice to allow you children to move up to another grade and play. So I appealed to the principal to move to the seventh grade this year and to take my class with me. Your mother has signed for you to leave the class you were going to go to and come back with me for another year."

"Oh, mother," I said.

And mother said, "Well, that's the class you're going to."

Those were the most pivotal years in my education. I left the sixth and seventh grades ready to go into advanced math, foreign languages and other things because of that teacher.

Then there was my high school coach. He told us that athletics was a developed body and a developed mind. He would run us like wild men on the field, and the next morning he would walk down the hall checking over his list of football players to make certain we were all in our classes.

And in college there was Mrs. Tate. In some ways she was the ultimate teacher because she saw every child as her child. So much so that we ended up rather easily calling her Ma Tate. She taught economics, and she made us write out everything. She gave us extra sentence forms on the writing and spelling of her lectures. It was her way of saying, "You don't have to write enough at our school."

So the impact of dedicated teachers teaching against the odds is part of my personal experience. These teachers taught with conviction. They did not teach in the second and third person. They were teaching in the first person. All great teachers teach in the first person. That's why the attempt to separate ethical values from teaching is virtually impossible.*

---

*EDITOR'S NOTE   The Reverend Jesse Jackson organized, and acts as director of, *Push for Excellence*, Inc., 2525 San Marino St., Los Angeles, CA 90006. The December 1979 *Push for Excellence* "National Support Campaign" brochure contained the following statements.

ON THE MORAL DIMENSION

Moral decadence and ethical collapse are inevitable in a school system that believes it can remain value free and morally neutral. We have seen the result of that philosophy — racial strife and a plague of drugs,

4.5   Voluntary Racial Integration in a Magnet School
JAMES E. ROSENBAUM and STEFAN PRESSER

[With the help of Federal monies, in 1978 at least a dozen cities were planning or initiating] magnet school programs, including Boston, Chicago, Cincinnati, Cleveland, Dayton, Houston, Los Angeles, Mt. Vernon (New York), New York City, Philadelphia, St. Louis, Stamford (Connecticut), and Tacoma (Washington).

Magnet schools are premised on the belief that quality education, not integration, is the real issue and that if they can provide high quality education in an integrated

Excerpts from James E. Rosenbaum (Northwestern University, Evanston, Illinois) and Stefan Presser (Civil Right's Bureau, Attorney General's Office, New York State), "Voluntary Racial Integration in a Magnet School," *School Review* 86: 156–186, February 1979. (Footnotes and bibliographical references are omitted.) By permission.

---

alcohol, teenage pregnancy, venereal disease, and vandalism. We are not going to cure that condition by relying solely on legal and police authority to restore order. Moral authority is required — and that means the restoration of our children's faith and confidence in the trustworthiness of the adults who shape their world.

But there is no way to restore public and student confidence in our schools in the abstract. I often say that a text without a context is a pretext. If we are to restore faith in education it must be seen to contribute purpose and meaning to the lives of those for whom it was intended. We can't restore the confidence of our children if we are only educating them for a jobless existence on welfare. Can we honestly say that education is an upward path, not simply a meaningless respite before the graduate becomes an anonymous digit in rising statistics on black teenage unemployment? . . .

ON FAITH

We must have faith — faith in ourselves, faith in our fellow man, and faith in a power beyond ourselves. If we have faith, the future is ours and cannot be denied or taken from us. If we have faith, disciplined minds and developed characters, there is no limit to what we can accomplish.

ON DEPENDENCY

The national community has become a psychological welfare state, afflicted by a dependency syndrome. Blacks are particularly subject to the syndrome — content to simply *wait* for freedom to come, *wait* for Congress to write new laws, *wait* for the Supreme Court to hand down the right decision, *wait* for the President to take the initiative in expanding the options for the black and the brown and the poor, *wait* for the media to tell our story fairly and fully, *wait* for the business community to give people priority over profits. And when waiting doesn't produce any change we become cynical and pessimistic. We ought to know better. We found out in the days of slavery that freedom was never going to come down from the Big House, and it's not going to come today from the White House, or the Congressional House, or the State House, but from your house and my house.

[Also in 1979, though in a somewhat different context, Jesse Jackson reaffirmed his dedication to self-reliance and to excellence, when he declared: "We're concerned now with the five B's: Blacks, Browns, Busing, Budgets and Buildings." He suggested that it' s time to put the A's where they belong — before the B's—and urged emphasis on "Attendance, Attention, Atmosphere for learning, and Attitudes — all of which lead to Achievement."]

---

setting, then blacks and whites will choose to attend them. [This paper is a report on one of these magnet schools.]. . . .

The opening-day ceremony in the school never mentioned the school's history of racial segregation and the desegregation plan. The only themes that ceremony stressed were how special the school's talent program was and how talented the students were. Nor did the teachers discuss desegregation. . . . It was as if integration was only a side effect of the school's special structure and not the cause of it. In some sense, a myth was being created that told the children and the teachers that this school existed to serve special students who deserved special treatment and not to serve the constitutional principles of integration and equal education.

This emphasis, which the creators of the magnet school expected to defuse the politically difficult issue of integration, did that so well that the goal of integration was almost entirely forgotten. As we shall see, the creation of this myth was to have far-reaching ramifications for the school and its students.

THE TALENTS

If there was one area in which the school had a chance to shine, it was in those classes especially designed for the talents. Each child entered Hess with the understanding that he or she would receive special training in one particular area, designated as a "talent." The school truly offered a rich and varied selection of talent courses: athletics, communication arts, dance, drama, art (both mechanical and fine), music (both vocal and instrumental), math, and science. These classes, which met three hours a week, were particularly well equipped. Furthermore, in these classes all children were proficient, therefore each child could feel that he or she was working in an area of strength. . . .

As the excitement of the first day began to wear off, reality began to intrude on people's perceptions, and an atmosphere of mediocrity began to supplant the initial feelings of specialness. Teachers began to comment that the students, supposed to be so incredibly bright, were not so gifted after all. One teacher reported at great length, with surprise and disappointment, that some students could not spell. . . .

Teachers were obviously becoming frustrated with the wide discrepancies. Some began to say that differential instruction for each student was too difficult and inefficient, and they began dividing the classroom by various means to work with groups rather than individuals. Two of the most prevalent methods used to divide the class were the "work group" and the "work sheet."

In one English class, the teacher handed out composition books to each student, having previously divided the class along program lines. The students in the fast and intensive programs were instructed to read a particular passage silently and then compose their own story as directed by the instructions in the book. Meanwhile, the teacher helped the regular program students to read and discuss a different story. These two groups clearly differed in their racial composition: one of the 15 fast-intensive students was black, while four of the eight regular program students were black. . . .

INEQUALITY, STIGMA, AND THE IRRELEVANCE OF MINORITIES

By the end of the first month of school, one had only to observe a class for a short time to see that the school divisions were being reflected in student behavior. For instance, one math class was working on individual work sheets while the teacher helped a fast-program student. After a few minutes, the teacher called for everyone's attention so that he could help them all with this student's problem by working it out on the board. Having begun to do this, he interrupted his work by saying, "Some of you won't be able to follow this, it's simply beyond you. You can go back to work." This said, almost all black children returned to work. Although no reference had been made to race, the teacher's message seems to have had a clear reference, and the black students had accepted the notion that some work was "simply beyond" them.

Other incidents suggested the same message. In one social studies class, the teacher asked whether anyone had not done the homework. The only Hispanic-looking youth in the room raised his hand and was informed, "Perhaps you weren't meant to be in such a special school. If you aren't going to do your work, I want you to bring your parents to school, and we will have you transferred." Later in the same class period, a white student admitted to not having done the homework, but there was no similar rebuke.

One might discount this and the many other similar incidents as examples of teachers' racial prejudice. But most of these teachers were not prejudiced. Indeed, they tended to be politically liberal and to be quite interested and concerned with helping blacks and Hispanics. Yet they found their liberal inclinations difficult to hold and perhaps inappropriate in this school, which, after all, they conceived to be a school for the talented. As one teacher noted in discussing the grouping in his class, "Look, some of the kids don't even belong in this school; they were only accepted because of color, because the plan stipulated a fixed ratio." The school's myth — that it existed primarily to serve the talented — led to the perception that blacks "don't even belong." . . .

THE INTEGRATION SUCCESSES

There were some encouraging exceptions to the preceding dismal picture. These exceptions are particularly noteworthy, for they not only indicate that magnet schools can accomplish integration, but they also suggest some conditions that may foster it. . . .

We were struck by the fact that the integration successes occurred only for the students in the music, art, and drama talents. The minority students in the academic talents and those in the athletic talents were not integrated into their talent classes nor did they take integrated seating patterns in the lunchroom. In the case of the athletic talents, our observations suggest that the teachers in these talents didn't do much to encourage integration, allowing black and white students to play separate sports. In the case of the academic talents, though, the teachers initially worked quite hard to instruct whole classes or integrated subgroups, and the black and white students initially interacted quite freely. But as time went on, the teachers began to see even the talented black students as less academically talented than the white students, they reported that their efforts at integration were too difficult and weren't working out, and they began to treat blacks and whites differently. The teachers in the academic talents and those in the music, art, and drama talents all began with integrated instruction, but the former all found it unworkable while the latter did not. This suggests that there may be something about the academic talents which militates against integrated instruction or something about the arts that militates for integration.

What this difference might be is a matter about which we can only speculate. It may be that the two sets of talents attract different kinds of teachers or encourage different kinds of instruction. Perhaps music, art, and drama subjects permit more cooperative work than academic subjects, and consequently, they attract the kinds of teachers and encourage the kinds of instruction which foster integrated work groups. Or it may be that blacks and whites in the academic talents are less similar in their level of accomplishment than blacks and whites in music, art, and drama talents are, and this dissimilarity may create greater difficulties for integration in the academic talents.

The difference between the two sets of talent classes is too clear-cut to be merely attributed to chance. . . .

CONCLUSIONS

This magnet school demonstrates that some positive outcomes are possible that were said by critics to be impossible. It also demonstrates that some negative outcomes are possible that advocates had not considered. The following conclusions are offered with this contribution in mind. They are stated in a limited and tentative manner, so that wider generalizability will not be read into them.

1. *A magnet plan, claiming to provide increased resources, special teachers, selective admissions, and a special curriculum to foster talent, can desegregate a formerly black school in a largely black neighborhood, and it can do so without violence.* Regardless of the shortcomings of implementation, this school did enough, or at least was perceived as having done enough, to accomplish its primary goals of attracting whites and to do so without violence. This accomplishment cannot be demeaned. . . .

2. *Although the magnet school was not all that it claimed to be, many of the claims had the effect of becoming self-fulfilling prophesies, and, at least during the crucial first weeks, they transformed ordinary teachers into special teachers and ordinary students into special students.* Although the students were not all special and the teachers were not specifically selected or trained, everyone's high expectations contributed to the success of the school. Admittedly, this could not last for long in the face of a contradicting reality, but, coming as it did during the most important and potentially most tense opening days, the enthusiasm and high expectations may have provided a crucial level of support to the successful and peaceful desegregation of the school.

3. *A talent system can permit integration in music, art, and drama talent classes.* . . .* Interest-

---

*EDITOR'S NOTE   For a specific example of ways in which "art" revitalized interest in school, read Anne Taylor and Rina Swentzel, "Albuquerque Indian School: A Cooperative Renovation Project," *School Arts* 79: 12-16, October 1979; condensed in *Education Digest* 45: 50-53, January 1980.

ingly it is in precisely these subjects that we find the only talent courses with integrated instruction. A drama class of 30 young actors clearly demonstrated that integration can work. The teacher encouraged students to interact with one another, and they readily responded. Particularly impressive was the way students, disregarding race, would help each other in constructing plays and remembering lines. Similar patterns of integrated interaction could be seen in the music and art talent classes. In all of these classes, students helped one another with their work and cooperated on group projects, and no trace of racial groups could be seen.

The teachers of these classes deserve a large amount of credit for these successes. They did not come easily; teachers put a great deal of effort and planning into making them happen. They avoided homogeneous groupings and divided their classes into heterogeneous, integrated work groups. . . .

4. *Given the achievement difference between black and white students formed during the early years of schooling, a magnet school plan based on a talent system may have fundamental drawbacks for accomplishing integration.* . . . Although we could not obtain the achievement scores of the school's applicants, the Coleman report data indicate that the very highest scoring blacks are not even in the top quartile of white scores on standardized achievement tests (for sixth-, ninth-, and twelfth-grade students, see Coleman et al. 1966, pp. 221-45). This suggests that a talent selection policy, recruiting the brightest blacks and the brightest whites, will tend to create a student body with an unusually large gap between black and white achievement in some important academic skills. . . .

The problems posed by desegregation are hard ones. There are no simple answers, and it is unlikely that any form of magnet school offers a completely satisfactory solution. However, magnet schools do present new options to policymakers, and careful analysis is required to determine the advantages and disadvantages of each. Our findings tentatively suggest that a magnet school with different talents may integrate a school but not its classes. Perhaps a school offering a limited range of talents might be more successful at integration, but it might only trade tracking within a school for the tracking of an entire school, posing the risk that the school would limit student composition, breadth of preparation, and students' future opportunities (Rosenbaum 1976). Perhaps a magnet school which offered superior educational resources, but which lacked the distinctions implied by talent programs, might be more promising. Or perhaps an integration effort at younger ages, before the achievement inequalities between whites and blacks become pronounced, is the only way to avoid the difficulties observed here. We do not know the answers to these questions, but we believe that the answers are more likely to come if careful studies are conducted on reform experiments like this one.

4.6 Wingate: Brooklyn's Born-Again High School
DAVID G. SAVAGE

In the early 1970s, George Wingate High School in Brooklyn was chaotic, a "rathole," according to its principal, Robert L. Schain. But that's not what CBS found in 1978.

Instead, Wingate is increasingly referred to as a "model of urban education." The school is neat, the halls are orderly, the lawns are well-kept, and even the bathrooms, once the center of the school's busy drug traffic, are being "used only as bathrooms," says Schain. The order and decorum isn't produced by a cadre of school security officers patrolling the halls. The students simply seem interested in getting an education. . . .

The New York Times, while finding much to criticize about the city's public schools, repeatedly has cited Wingate as an example for other schools to follow.

HOW DID YOU DO IT?

So, what everyone wants to know, Robert Schain, is how did you do it? He shuns any simplistic answers to the questions, but instead prefers to tell how the Wingate program developed.

. . . [When Schain became principal, he] found two things, a school where disruption had won out over education ("I seemed to spend most of my time in suspension hearings") and one where most students could barely read. And the two problems were clearly related. "If you can't read, education has passed you by," Schain observes, "so no wonder they were turned off and disruptive." He began an intensive basic skills mini-school, with his best, young, dedicated teachers working closely with the poorest students. Similarly, the school annually received an influx of French-speaking students from Haiti. For them, Schain established an intensive English program, one of total immersion in the new language, not bilingual education. Both programs paid dividends. The students began to learn, to make progress, and they also realized that the teachers and the school cared about them. Disruption, the symptom of a turned-off school, began to decline.

Then he turned his attention to the rest of Wingate's curriculum. He found it bland, overly traditional, and not really focused on the needs of the students. Schain makes it clear that he doesn't feel it was just the students who hadn't adapted to the school. The teachers hadn't adapted to the students, either. Wingate had a "massive reading problem," but the social studies teachers would say, "I'm not a reading teacher," . . .

So the Wingate staff turned its attention to reading, with the object of integrating reading instruction into all courses. It was everybody's job, not "somebody else's." A by-product of this effort is a handbook, "Developing Reading Skills Through Subject Areas," written, edited, designed, and printed at Wingate. One of the many offshoots of the city's financial crisis has been that schools are shortchanged on funds for

Excerpts from David B. Savage (Associate Editor of *Education U.S.A.,* Washington, D.C.) "Wingate: Brooklyn's Born-Again High School," *Educational Leadership* 36: 541–545, May 1979.

purchasing materials. Schain has partly solved that problem by selling the reading book.[1]

CHALLENGING ALTERNATIVES: LEARNING TO FLY

The Wingate staff also set out to extend the curriculum through alternative courses. The reasons are familiar enough — most high school students get turned off by traditional but unchallenging academic courses. The course offering sheet, once a one-pager, is now four pages long. New courses include psychology in literature, sports literature, Greek mythology, modern dance, photography, advanced algebra, calculus, trigonometry, Carribean-American culture, and anthropology. But Wingate has received the most attention for its "institutes" — specialized programs that are both distinct and integrated into the curriculum.

For example, in a flight training institute taught by an Eastern Airlines pilot, students learn about engines, about aerodynamics, and even learn to fly. A legal institute and an international relations institute feature advanced courses in those areas. The medical science institute features courses in advanced chemistry, microbiology, math, physics, and foreign languages. Students get "hands on" experience working parttime at a nearby hospital, and the students' interest in medicine is incorporated into their entire course of studies. In English, they may read *Arrowsmith*, Sinclair Lewis' novel of a doctor's life.

Most of these programs were developed by the Wingate staff, not by the principal, Schain points out. He has encouraged the staff to come up with new ideas and usually gives them the green light to go ahead. "You've got to involve everyone in the decision-making process, seriously, meaningfully. You've got to get them enthused and thinking about education. That's what leadership is. But we've got creative professionals here. When they're involved, they'll do a good job."

New York City has perhaps the most powerful, best entrenched teacher union in the nation. Schain doesn't minimize that as a problem. "Sure, we've got some teachers who are retired on the job. I've gotten rid of quite a few. In fact, I think I've given out more bad evaluations than any principal in the city. But this, like politics, is the art of the possible. You weed some out. And you encourage and support some, and they become good teachers again."

One of the problems of writing about good school management, or of educational leadership, is that the best ideas, once stated, seem so simple. Sort of the "Elementary, my dear Watson" principle. But the key is not saying it, but doing it, putting the ideas into practice. Like most good schools, the most impressive aspect of Wingate is the attitude of teachers, staff, and students. As an administrator, it is easy to fall into the rut of seeing your job as handling administrative detail, attending meetings, and tackling discipline problems. Education can fall into the cracks. One of Schain's remarkable traits is that he, first and foremost, is still a teacher. He thinks and talks about education, believes he has a "no nonsense approach" to education, but spends

---

[1] Available for $5 a copy from Wingate H.S., 600 Kingston Ave., Brooklyn, N.Y. 11203.

almost no time talking about discipline or administrative trivia. Those are diversions, not the essence of the job. He'll talk at length about "crap courses," how many urban educators, faced with an influx of turned-off minority students, fell back on a "band-aid approach." "They sacrificed content to get the kid's interests. You can't do that. It's like saying I'll teach you to play the piano in 10 easy lessons — there's no such thing. You don't learn to do anything that counts in 10 easy lessons," he says. Instead, he believes good teaching is being able to make learning relevant to the lives of the students. It is this attitude, about the importance of education, even a love of education that Schain passes on to the faculty, staff, and students.*

---

*EDITOR'S NOTE   It is hoped that this article will help to revive confidence and enthusiasm for education. On this point, Ralph W. Tylor wrote (in *Educational Leadership* 36: 163, November 1978):

It's difficult to know all the reasons for the public becoming excited about something, but this has happened several times before. I remember, for example, a national conference on "The Crisis in Education" in 1935. It was called because standards were dropping, discipline was bad, and so on.

What happened this time, I suspect, is that we tried in the 1960s to solve some major problems. We felt there shouldn't be poverty anymore because ours was an affluent society. Our aspirations were heightened by a sense of exhilaration about what could be done. We were committed to reaching everybody, including minority groups. But then we discovered that things don't change that rapidly. So now there is a period of disillusionment, and various social institutions are being blamed.

4.7   Democratic Ideals in a Pluralistic Society
EDITORIAL

Democracy is a form of society whereby men and women may gain confidence in themselves and in their fellow humans, and thus move from force to persuasion, from restriction to liberty, from blind obedience to creative effort. Unlike dictatorial forms of government, democracy has everything to gain and nothing to lose from the intelligence of its citizens. In the words of James Madison:

A popular government without popular information or the means of acquiring it, is but a Prologue to a Farce or a Tragedy, or perhaps both. Knowledge will forever govern ignorance; and a people who mean to be their own Governors must arm themselves with the power which knowledge gives.[1]

In any society progress depends on developed leadership. True leadership must be renewed from the ranks of the unknown, not from the small group of families already famous and powerful. If one class possesses all the wealth and education while the laboring class remains both poor and ignorant, labor will inevitably be servile to capital, and our society will be divided into distinctive, permanent classes. But if education is widely and equally diffused according to ability rather than wealth,

[1] James Madison, Letter to W. T. Barry, Aug. 4, 1822, in *The Complete Madison: His Basic Writings*, edited by Saul K. Padover, (New York: Harper & Row, 1953), p. 337.

children of all classes may attain their maximum potential, and society as a whole will gain from the fuller use of its human resources.

Democracy holds that there is no safe repository of the ultimate powers of society except in the people themselves. If the people make mistakes, the remedy is not to take the power away from them, but to help them in forming their judgment through better education and more open communication. In his First Inaugural Address, Abraham Lincoln expressed democracy's faith in the people as follows:

> Why should there not be a patient confidence in the ultimate justice of the people? Is there any better or equal hope in the world? . . . Truth and justice will surely prevail by the judgment of the great tribunal of the American people.

Democratic education should develop citizens who are "easy to lead, but difficult to drive; easy to govern, but impossible to enslave."[2] It should make them easy to lead by bringing out latent talent and leadership, conceived in cooperative terms. It should make them impossible to enslave — and, we would add, intolerant of enslavement — because their education will have emphasized individual self-reliance, free expression, and unthwarted communication.

The democratic citizen will admit that in specialized areas there are authorities whose technical knowledge may greatly influence decisions concerning public policy. But in a free society the citizen should never relinquish his personal freedom, autonomy, and moral dignity. External guidance may be a means, but self-direction is an end in itself. The mature man wants self-confidence, courage to face all difficulties, and the consciousness of being man in the fullest sense of the word.

> Such a man is possessed by the wish to see the same inner strength develop in others. As he himself abhors alien rule, neither does he wish to rule over others. He is pleased to see life unfolding itself free and strong in his fellow humans. He finds himself happiest in a circle of equals, not surrounded by slaves. In education, his aim is not to exact submissive obedience, but to foster young individuals who in due course will themselves be able to form their own lives with freedom and responsibility.[3]

Such is the democratic ideal which moved our society to broaden suffrage from the wealthy 10 percent or 20 percent to all male adults, to women, and then to all men and women over 18 years old. It is the ideal which inspired our schools in their effort to mold immigrants from various European nationalities throughout the nineteenth and early twentieth centuries. It is the ideal of *liberty, equality,* and *fraternity* which has motivated social progress since 1789.

For the attainment of that ideal, wrote Samuel D. Proctor in 1970,[4] "Education is a corridor through which America's minorities move from rejection, deprivation, and isolation to acceptance, economic efficiency, and inclusion." But this corridor will remain all too narrow so long as the attitude prevails that minority students are social

[2] Lord Henry Peter Broughton, Speech in House of Commons, January 29, 1828.

[3] Alf Ross, *Why Democracy?* (Cambridge, Mass.: Harvard University Press, 1952), p. 104. Compare Harry A. Overstreet, *The Mature Mind,* New York: Norton, 1949.

[4] This quotation by Proctor is from *Black Students in White Schools,* edited by Edgar P. Epps (University of Chicago), (Belmont, CA: Wadsworth, 1972), p. 102.

problems rather than students with problems. Educators can no longer afford to assume that something is wrong with the student as a person, or that something is wrong with his culture. Instead, we must strive to understand and to appreciate the distinctive strengths and weaknesses of each student, and of each culture. And although we tend to think of these problems only in connection with the Native American Indian, the African American, the Chicano, the Puerto Rican, or the South Vietnam Asiatic, we should realize that the largest of all such groups consists of poor, ignored, and lonely whites who are so depressed and harassed that they too need sympathy, understanding, and help.

The poor white today is not "The Man With the Hoe" — the classic poor of the agricultural era. The poor white today is a displaced person, a reject, a person lost in the thickets of a complex technological society, with its mechanized farming, increased automation, and new forms of communications. The poor today are generally the children of small family farmers who could not compete, of farm workers, coal miners, textile workers, and other handicraft occupations that no longer exist.

That our society — and particularly our schools — should strive to equalize the opportunities of children coming from such disadvantaged groups should be axiomatic to anyone in any branch of education. Persons whose language or culture is alien and strange to most Americans obviously suffer the most; but so many diverse groups have been assimilated during the past two centuries that we can surely take hope that further amalgamation and assimilation will occur. In an address before the National Education Association in 1916, John Dewey affirmed the basic meaning of our motto *E Pluribus Unum*:

> No matter how loudly anyone proclaims his Americanism, if he assumes that any one racial strain, any one component culture . . . is to furnish a pattern to which all strains and cultures are to conform, he is a traitor to an American nationalism. . . .
>
> I find that many who talk the loudest about the need of a supreme and unified Americanism of spirit really mean some special code or tradition to which they happen to be attached. They have some pet tradition which they would impose on all.

It is Dewey's concept of an evolving, emerging democracy that teachers should proclaim, both in words and in deeds.

4.8   The Indian Movement: Out of the Wounded Past
VINE DELORIA, JR.

Indians in the last decade would seem to have had more success than the environmen-
talists, the civil rights movement, consumer activists and other citizen constituency
groups. Applying strict standards of judgment to the Indian movement, judging
accomplishments on the basis of fundamental laws controlling Indian life either
passed or blocked — until recently the standard by which many people evaluated
Indian affairs — we can state that Indians in recent years have had fairly good success,
at least until 1974. In the last five years the Taos Pueblo had its Sacred Blue Lake
restored to it. The claims of the Alaska Natives, pending over a century, were finally
resolved. Disputed lands taken by other government agencies in the early part of the
century, such as those at Yakima and Warm Springs, have been returned. The
Menominee tribe, which had been terminated from federal supervision, was restored
to full federal services in 1973.

In the courts Indians have had a number of unexpected successes. The fishing
rights struggle in the Pacific Northwest, which featured seemingly endless litigation
and protest, resulted in a landmark decision in *United States v. Washington* (1973) in which
the treaty fishing rights were upheld. Several very important income and sales tax
cases were won and Indians held their own in the very important field of water rights.
Cases on affirmative action in employing Indians were decided favorably (although
the Bureau of Indian Affairs has been working hard to negate the effect). . . .

[Meanwhile profound] and sometimes heated discussion has been rocking Indian
country concerning the Indian identity. Activist groups seem to maintain a strong
sentiment that a return to traditions is imperative, and raise a broad range of
questions about how Indians can really return to the old ways or stablize Indian
communities by evoking virtues of former days. The most devastating accusation
against anti-Indian Senators and Congressmen has been that they are trying to
extinguish Indian culture, and few people in Congress have ever wished to face this
kind of attack while trying to reorganize the legal status of Indians. The cultural
argument has thus been the most potent counterattack for trying to prevent the
federal government from abandoning or "terminating" the special position of Indians.

Yet it must be apparent to everyone, and particularly to Indians, that times have
indeed changed, and with that change have come irreversible shifts in cultural
outlook. Today we make pottery, carve wood, and carry on many crafts traditions for
the tourist trade. We do not use very many of those products ourselves. We have

Brief excerpts from Vine Deloria, Jr., "The Indian Movement: Out of a Wounded Past," *Ramparts* 13: 28–32,
March 1975. Reprinted by permission of Vine Deloria.

Formerly Executive Director of the National Congress of American Indians, Vine Deloria, Jr., a Standing
Rock Sioux, is author of *Custer Died for Your Sins*, New York: Delacorte, 1969, and *God Is Red*, New York:
Grossett and Dunlap, 1973.

Read also Daniel G. Kelly, Jr., "Indian Title: The Rights of American Indians in Lands They Have
Occupied Since Time Immortal," *Columbia Law Review* 75: 655–686, April 1975; Margaret Szasz, *Education and
the American Indian: the Road to Self-Determination, 1928–1973*, Albuquerque: University of New Mexico Press,
1974; *The American Indian Reader, Book II: Education*, edited by Jeannette Henry, San Francisco: The Indian
Historian Press, 1972; and most of all, Vine Deloria, Jr., *Behind the Trail of Broken Treaties*, New York: Delacorte,
1974.

telephones, go to college, buy cars, and have jobs, and do a great many things that were simply absent in the old culture. In many ways Indians participate in the contemporary technical culture as much as other Americans. But very few Indians have come to realize how drastically this change affects the responsibility of their community as a whole to participate in the formation of a new American identity.

Time and life-styles have changed very rapidly in recent years and the Indian life-style — predominantly rural and perhaps even similar to contemporary folklife-style — is not as exotic as Indians would like to think. While we have been attacking Anglo-Saxon culture as represented by the older generation of white Americans, the immediate past generation of whites has created a new life-style which is quite compatible with many ideas and customs once advocated by Indians alone. Thus as we have worked to sensitize white America, a part of it has made a quantum jump toward our original cultural position. . . .

If Indians are to survive the rapid cultural change that the rest of society is making, the Indian community will simply have to allow some of its members to develop their talents and contacts with the rest of American society. Today there is a feeling of betrayal and jealousy among Indians whenever another Indian attempts to relate to contemporary developments. Individual Indians attempting to succeed at any field unrelated to the general conception of Indian life — be it folk-singing, small business, scholarship, or professional careers — come under tremendous pressure from other Indians and are the object of undeserved ridicule and suspicion. They face accusation of trying to be "better" or "smarter" than other Indians.

The result of this in-group attitude is that an increasing number of younger and educated Indians are becoming discontented at being unable to use their minds and talents in developing their careers as individuals. An unarticulated restlessness exists in Indian country: talented Indians, afraid of social pressure, do not contribute their best efforts toward either the solution of Indian problems or the leading of all Americans to understand the great similarity of Indian dreams and the dreams and goals of other citizens.*

---

*EDITOR'S NOTE: Another Native American Indian, Helen L. Harris, summarizes the contemporary situation as follows:

So long as the nation follows its past pattern of trying to erase Indian consciousness by denying his existence, the Indian will have to exhaust his energies in fighting for identity and survival against some ignorant and some vicious elements of society that take their cue from national policy and feel free to insult, exploit, steal from, and kill Indians.

It is in the schools that children meet the outside world for the first time, and it is here that they are at the mercy of educators and classmates. Educators teach more by "how they teach and how they act," according to Charles E. Silberman, and his findings after three-and-a-half years study reaffirmed this belief. When a child, already shaky in self-confidence, comes to school and learns that his whole background, family, language, and ancestors are treated as something shameful, and his "deficiencies" stressed, his failure is almost certain.

These children require positive direction. Acknowledgment of their people's culture, contributions to the literature, arts, sciences, and philosophy of the country, recognition of their race's outstanding leaders is not too much to ask. Their people have been taught about non-Indian exploits for three hundred years. The schools that Silberman noted as highly successful in maintaining academic achievement as well as a human atmosphere for their Black and Puerto Rican students encouraged the children's pride in their racial and ethnic identity by inviting people of their heritage who were successful in occupations and professions to come and discuss their work and lives, and by teaching their people's achievements.

When will such humane concern be extended to our children, not in a few exceptional schools, but in all schools?

4.9 Bilingual Segregation for Hispanics?
EDITORIAL ESSAY

In recent years, tens of thousands of young teachers, unable to find employment in regular classrooms, have secured teaching positions after taking Special Education courses enabling them to deal with two types of children, the Physically Handicapped and the Mentally Retarded.

Why have they been able to find jobs in these areas? Because Federal Aid supports such programs and because local taxpayers are required to pay only a small portion of the salaries of Special Education teachers.

Recently a third type of Federal Aid has been made available: aid for teaching children who are linguistically handicapped. Such aid is of special importance in southern Florida and in the Southwest, where English-speaking teachers who can also speak Spanish are in great demand.

How did this situation arise? It began shortly after World War II when it became generally recognized that children with English-language deficiencies were not doing well in school and needed special English-language assistance. In 1969, Title VII of the Elementary and Secondary Education Act of 1965 was passed, and it provided federal funds for pilot programs in bilingual education for school districts which wished to apply. This movement came to a head on May 25, 1970, when the Department of Health, Education, and Welfare issued the following clarifying guideline to one of its regulations promultated under Title VI of the 1964 Civil Rights Act:

> Where inability to speak and understand the English language excludes national origin minority group children from effective participation in the educational program offered by a school district, *the district must take affirmative steps to rectify the language deficiency in order to open instructional programs to these students.* (Italics added).

This meant that, in order to secure federal aid for students deficient in their ability to speak or understand English, school districts were now obliged to provide special remedial language assistance to such children.

Ralph Nader has volunteered the present system for educating Indian children as an "ideal prototype" of a blueprint to prevent children from becoming educated. The classroom teachers can [determine] . . . whether American educational attitudes have changed since the seventeenth century or whether it is still following a policy of Indian extermination. . . . Nationwide, the Indian suicide rate is over twice the national average of all other races.

The schools play a major role in children's lives for twelve years; during this time they can accomplish great changes in future national attitudes, both in Indian and non-Indian students. They may not only change the failure and suicide rate of their Indian charges, but they may prevent innumerable children from permanent psychic scars that can be manifested in permanent inferiority feelings or a hatred for the institutions and society that caused them. — Helen L. Harris, "On the Failure of Indian Education." *Clearing House* 48: 242-247, December 1973. By permission of HELDREF Publications.

However there is a growing optimism among contemporary Indians, including Vine Deloria, Jr., who wrote in 1976:

> When that vision [namely, Jefferson's vision that all men are created equal] was renewed and the conflicts between red and white people set aside, America became the greatest demonstration of the vitality of human life that the world has ever seen — a nation of people who truly love others as themselves and who have never shirked their duty to share generously everything they possess. — Vine Deloria, Jr., "Why the U.S. Never Fought the Indians," *Christian Century* 92: 9-12, January 7, 1976.

It should be remembered that these events happened at the very time when the *desegregation of Blacks through Busing* was a major issue in American education. But the Hispanics opposed desegregation through Busing for an obvious reason: If children in need of bilingual education programs were dispersed without consideration of that need, there would not be (in most communities) sufficient numbers of children in any school district or area to justify separate classes for comprehensive bilingual-bicultural instruction.

Thus in the early 1970s arose two contradictory, conflicting movements: One was a movement (designed especially for Blacks) toward *desegregation* through Busing, and sometimes through Magnet Schools. The other was an equally emotion-laden movement (designed especially for Hispanics) toward *segregation*. Faced with such conflicting movements, it was inevitable that the Courts would be called upon to decide what should be done.[1]

In *Lau v. Nichols* [1974] a unanimous Supreme Court agreed with HEW that Title VI required special assistance for students lacking basic English-speaking abilities, as defined by HEW's May 25, 1970, memorandum. And in *Keyes v. School District No. 2* [1974], a Denver school district was ordered to develop a pilot bilingual-bicultural program which was to be implemented in several schools. These two judicial decisions were interpretations of the following HEW regulation:

> Any ability grouping or tracking system employed by the school system to deal with special language skill needs of national origin-minority group children must be designed to meet such language skill needs as soon as possible and must not operate as an educational dead end or permanent track.

The court's mission, of course, is merely to clarify the meaning of laws and regulations set up by the legislative branches of our government. And the court's interpretation was obviously a go-ahead to those who wanted segregated Hispanic schools. But not everyone agreed that this trend was all for the good. Gary Orfield summed up the contemporary situation as follows:

> Noting the low achievement scores of Hispanic children, HEW blamed English-language instruction. English-language tests, and cultural bias in the curriculum. The appropriate remedy was defined as implementation of a bilingual-bicultural school program. Although there appeared to be no evidence that such programs would work and although a large majority of Hispanic children knew sufficient English to function in regular classrooms, HEW halted its investigations into segregated schooling and required school systems to adopt the new educational approach. Scores of districts complied, often relying on federal bilingual program funds to finance the changes. A recent study has found that these bilingual programs are highly segregated and that project directors seldom transfer children back to English-language classrooms after they have mastered the English language. The first national evaluation of federal bilingual programs, published in 1977, found no evidence that the programs improved either academic achievement or attitudes toward school. There was

[1] For a more detailed analysis of this topic, read Peter F. Ross (Director, Education Litigation, Mexican Legal Defense and Educational Fund), "Bilingual Education: The Hispanic Response to Unequal Educational Opportunity," *Law and Contemporary Problems*, 42, 4, Autumn 1978: 111–140. This Autumn 1978 issue is Part II of two complete issues devoted to the topic "School Desegregation: Lessons of the First Twenty-Five Years."
What you are now reading borrows heavily from Ross's article.

even some highly controversial evidence that children enrolled in bilingual programs were less likely to improve their English language skills than children for whom no program was provided. Though the justification for the displacement of desegregation by bilingual remedies was on the basis of educational needs, the movement proceeded without any initial evidence and grew in spite of continued disappointing research results. The advantage of this approach, however, was that it could be implemented with little visibility or controversy since its impact was almost wholly limited to segregated minority communities.[2]

What conclusions may we draw from these two movements, the one, an "affirmative action" movement on the part of Blacks for school desegregation; the other, an "affirmative ethnicity" movement on the part of Hispanics for segregated schools for Spanish-speaking students? One conclusion is an obvious one: America is a large and complex civilization, and we should not expect quick and easy solutions to difficult problems. Problems of racial and linguistic equality, and of cultural unity, have many dimensions, some of which go beyond the realm of government and law. As Samuel Johnson once wrote:

How small, of all that human hearts endure,
That part which laws of kings can cause or cure.

A second conclusion should be of more immediate interest, particularly to young teachers eager to pursue a career in education: In Southern California and in many other areas, there is now a geat need — an excellent job market — for qualified teachers who can read and write Spanish as well as English; or, as critics of the present programs might put it, teachers who can read and write English as well as Spanish. (In Selection 6.6 we return to this topic.)

---

[2] Gary Orfield (Associate Professor of Political Science, University of Illinois), in 42 *Law and Contemporary Problems*, Autumn 1978: 166.

It should be remembered that these issues in American education were occurring at the very same time that Canada was engaged in a life-or-death struggle for national unity and national survival against French-speaking peoples of Quebec who viewed Canada as a nation of two cultures, not one. Quebec is still a part of Canada, and Spanish-speaking Hispanics are still Americans. Even so, there are many who sincerely believe that our national unity is weakened by overemphasis of cultural pluralism. For example:

We once believed that the nation represented values to which immigrants could subscribe — values which transcended ethnic lines. And we believed in the role of the schools in transmitting those values. The advent of bilingual education did not, of course, single-handedly strip us of our faith in an American culture of sufficiently universal appeal to cross ethnic lines. But in promoting the notion that the process of Americanization was helplessly ethnocentric, and in robbing the schools of their traditional integrating function, it has certainly played an important part. — Abigail M. Thernstrom, "E Pluribus Plura — Congress and Bilingual Education," *The Public Interest*, No. 60, September 1980, pp. 3–22.

Read also Tom Bethell, "Why Johnnie Can't Read," *Harper's* 256: 30–33, February 1979.
For more recent developments, read "Education Department Unveils Proposed Rules to Govern Bilingual Education," *Phi Delta Kappan*, 62:150, October 1980.

4.10   The Culturally Undemocratic Character of American Public Education*
ALFREDO CASTAÑEDA

It is possible to identify at least three distinct and major components of educational policy that are designed to implement the socialization function of education. These are (1) language and heritage, (2) cultural values, and (3) teaching styles. In the case of the first component, the goal is to facilitate the development of a healthy self-concept (identity) and one's role in and relationship to society. In the case of the second component, the goal is to facilitate understanding of society's standards of desirability and acceptance as well as the internalization of moral standards, or elements of conscience, which direct behavior along socially appropriate and productive routes. In the case of the third component, the goal is to render teaching styles appropriate to the modes of thinking, remembering, perceiving, and problem-solving desired by society.

If we examine the content of American public education in relation to each of these three components, it becomes eminently clear that what exists in our schools is a picture primarily descriptive of the language, heritage, values, and teaching styles characteristic of Anglo-American middle-class society. It is *monocultural*, or culturally exclusive, in conception, for the content of these three components does not reflect the language, heritage, values, and teaching styles characteristic of other cultural, racial, or social groups. Thus, American public education has failed, in each of these components, to provide the content that would enable minority children to develop healthy self-identities, to minimize cultural or value conflicts, or to learn by means of these preferred modes of cognition and motivation which are the result of their home and community socialization experiences.

Excerpts from "The Educational Needs of Mexican-Americans," in *The Educational Needs of Minority Groups: The Educational Needs of Mexican-Americans, Black Americans and Native American Indians*, by Alfredo Castañeda, Richard L. James, and Webster Robbins, with an introduction by Walter K. Beggs (Lincoln, Nebr.: Professional Educators Publications, 1974), pp. 15–25.) (Footnote references are omitted.) Reprinted by permission.
    Alfredo Castañeda is Professor of Education and Psychology, Stanford University.

*EDITOR'S NOTE   The Hispanics dramatize two streams of thought that are present in nearly all immigrant groups. On the one hand, millions of them come into the United States each year as legal or as illegal immigrants; they see in our industrial society their only hope for a meaningful humane life. On the other hand, in our industry, and especially in our commercial advertising, they note a tendency to love things and to use people, even though they know — as we also know — that we should use things and love people. And so, as a bulwark against such aggressive commercialism, they seek solace in their traditional religion, culture, and language.

In former times, the adage "When in Rome, live like the Romans" was sound advice; until modern times, except for a few soldiers and sailors, nearly everyone spent his or her entire life in an island community. During the Middle Ages the Church helped to establish some reasonably uniform religious standards. But the greatness of America consists in the fact that there are no serious linguistic, religious, economic, or cultural barriers separating the peoples of our fifty states. Insofar as it may be said that we have a common faith, it is this: By using a common language, through dialogue, through free and open discussion, through intermarriages, and by living and working together in a spirit that is both humane and reasonable, we may gradually and continually develop a *new* culture and a *new* civilization appropriate to the world of which all of us are now a part.

Because American public education, operating under the melting-pot theory, has failed to provide culturally democratic educational environments, a new social philosophy must be formulated if the schools are ever to meet the educational needs of children who are products of socialization experiences different from those of the Anglo-American middle class. The basis for this reformulation is implied in the concept of cultural democracy, that is, the right of every American child to remain identified with his own home and community socialization experiences, regardless of whether these experiences are designated ethnic, racial, cultural, or social. This implies that the schools should actively contribute to the positive development and strengthening of these unique home and community socialization experiences *as valuable in their own right.* . . .

[To implement this concept of cultural democracy, the education of Mexican-American students should be built around four clusters of value:] (1) identification with family, community, and ethnic group; (2) personalization of interpersonal relationships; (3) status and role definition in family and community; and (4) Mexican Catholic ideology. . . .

The ability and willingness to speak Spanish is also considered an important criterion of identity with the ethnic group. For this reason, encouraging Spanish fluency in Mexican-American children strengthens their self-concept.

4.11 Ethnicity in a Changing America
THOMAS SOWELL

The rapid and far-reaching changes which swept across the United States in the decades since World War II had especially dramatic impact on racial and ethnic relations. For example, Jews were restricted or excluded from many university faculties before the war, but in the postwar era their representation on such faculties rose far beyond their proportion of the population. Sports which totally excluded black athletes before the war came to be dominated by black athletes after the war; in baseball, for example, there were seven consecutive years in which no white man won the National League's Most Valuable Player award. Anti-Japanese laws, which flourished in California before the war, were resoundingly defeated in a postwar referendum. Attitude surveys showed major reversals of public opinion on race and ethnicity, and rising rates of intermarriage further substantiated these changes. More than 40 percent of all Japanese-American men now marry women who are not Japanese American, and more than half of all Irish-American, German-American, and Polish-American married men are married to women outside their own respective ethnic groups. Ironically, the once popular concept of America as a "melting pot" is

Brief excerpts from "Ethnicity in a Changing America" by Thomas Sowell, Reprinted by permission of the American Academy of Arts and Sciences from *Daedalus* 107: 213–237, Winter, 1978. (Footnote references are omitted.)

Thomas Sowell edited the book *American Ethnic Groups*, New York: Urban Institute, 1978.

now sweepingly dismissed by intellectuals at a time when it is closer to reality than before. . . .

The very concept of ethnic "minorities" is misleading in the United States; and attempts to generalize about minority problems, or to compare one ethnic group to some national average, are still more misleading. Minority is a meaningful designation in countries where there is an ethnic majority, but in the United States the largest specifically identifiable ethnic group — those of British ancestry — constitute only 15 percent of the population, as compared to 13 percent whose ancestry is German, 11 percent Negro, and 8 percent Irish. No small part of the reason why American history has been what it has, is that no one group could achieve overwhelming dominance. Pluralism and toleration were not ideals from which Americans started, but necessities to which they were driven. It was slowest coming in the racial area, where majority-minority lines could be drawn. Nazi racism and its sickening consequences brought racism in general into disrepute in the United States, and set the stage for a series of changes in public opinion and government policy in post-World War II America. The more general and enduring principle of American pluralism was not, however, the result of preachments or "leadership," but of the virtual inescapability of the need to cooperate and the virtual impossibility of achieving the religious, political, or other dominance of any one group — though many tried.

The sheer size of the United States and of American ethnic groups meant that these groups were not mere representatives or appendages of some foreign country or culture. It is a commonplace that there are more people of Italian ancestry in New York than in Rome, more people of Polish ancestry in Detroit than in Cracow, more Jews than in Israel — and so on down the list of American ethnic groups. The distinctive cultures of these ethnic groups are to a large extent creations growing out of their experience on American soil, not mere transplants from other countries. Chow mein, the St. Patrick's Day parade, and the "Afro" hairdo are all American products, some exported back to the homeland from which the groups in question originated. Moreover, the assimilation process has been two-way, with the so-called mainstream American culture incorporating many culinary, vernacular, musical, and other features once specifically and exclusively ethnic. Again, the pluralistic mosaic is more descriptive of American social reality than is a simplistic majority-minority dichotomy. . . .

Despite great qualitative differences in schooling, all the ethnic groups for which data are available show a similar pattern of increasing income with increasing years of schooling, and in all cases a college education means an income above the American national average. Moreover, even before the destruction of various racial barriers in recent decades, black college graduates earned more than the average American, despite many individual stories of blacks with degrees working at menial jobs. . . . More black college students now attend predominantly white schools than attend predominantly black institutions, but again the effects differ among age cohorts or blacks, and it remains true that most black college graduates today are graduates of black colleges.

At the opposite end of the spectrum are the Orientals and the Jews. Orientals not only have quantitatively more education than the national average, they are statistically overrepresented in the more difficult and better-paying areas, such as the natural sciences. In general, Oriental faculty members have the Ph.D more often than either black or white faculty members, and the Orientals' degrees are more often from high-rated departments. Jews are also disproportionately in such demanding fields as law, medicine, and biochemistry, and are educated in the more selective colleges. For Orientals and Jews, statistics on years of schooling understate their real education.

Those ethnic groups attending Catholic colleges and universities are attending institutions which are not included among the top American colleges and universities, either in terms of objective criteria (College Board scores, endowment, library resources. Merit Scholars, faculty publications) or the evaluations of the academic profession. The best of the Catholic institutions rank above the best of the black institutions in these respects, but well below the standards of the Ivy League, of elite colleges such as Amherst and Swarthmore, or of the top state universities. Among those ethnic groups which are predominantly Catholic, only the Irish send half or more of their college students to Catholic institutions, but Italians, Poles, and Germans also send substantial proportions to such Catholic colleges and universities. . . .

What is most clear is that whatever may have determined the past is not inevitably determining the future. There are many objective indications that ethnicity is changing in a changing America. On the whole, and for the present, at least, it is a substantial change for the better.

4.12   Quotations for Further Thought and Discussion

(A)   Full citizenship is incompatible with the dependency of caste. To be a fully respected member of the [free and equal] society, one must be treated as capable of taking responsibility. Conversely, the symbolism of dependency is a primary target of the principle of equal citizenship. . . .

To be a citizen is to be a member of a moral community, to be a responsible person, not a ward of society. . . .

The idea of equal citizenship is not incompatible with all forms of inequality. Indeed, heirarchy itself can be a source of self-respect. In any case, most hierarchies in our society are difficult for the law to reach. Furthermore, the very existence of law necessarily implies inequalities of some kinds, since the enforcement of norms requires a body of enforcers who stand in a relation of dominance over others, at least within the confines of the enforcement system.

— Henry K. Karst, in *Harvard Law Review* 91: 1–68, November 1977.

(B)   Imagine that when New Amsterdam became New York, its inhabitants had stubbornly gone on speaking Dutch. Imagine that in the Pennsylvania Assembly, German had won out over English by a single-vote majority: in Louisiana French had been kept, while Spanish had stayed on in California, Texas, and New Mexico. Imagine that the Indians, instead of dying out, had multiplied under the happy dominion of the White Man and had continued to speak their own languages. Imagine, finally, that American blacks had insisted on keeping their West African tongues. Surely, then, the United States of America — had they united at all — would have become something wholly different from the unilingual America of today. The fact that a single language is spoken from one coast to the other is a unifying trait of the United States, binding the country together despite conflicts between rich and poor, black and white. One glance at neighboring Canada is enough to show the risks of dissolution when two rival languages and cultures battle within a country for preeminence.

— Werner Ross in *Daedalus* 108: 152 f, Spring 1979

(C)   The earliest associations of a child form the basis of his/her cultural heritage. Cultural heritage is the essence of relationship patterns, linguistic and expressive communication, and the fundamental values and attitudes through which each child grows. To ignore or invalidate this living experience for any individual is, in effect, to distort and diminish the possibilities for developing that person's potential. . . .

Cultural pluralism is neither the traditionalist's separatism nor the assimilationist's melting pot. It is a composite that recognizes the uniqueness and value of every culture. Cultural pluralism acknowledges that no group lives in isolation, but that, instead, each group influences and is influenced by others.

In educational terms, the recognition of cultural pluralism has been labeled "multicultural education." The essential goals of multicultural education embrace: (a) recognizing and prizing diversity; (b) developing greater understanding of other cultural patterns; (c) respecting individuals of all cultures; and (d) developing positive and productive interaction among people *and* among experiences of diverse cultural groups.

— from Report of Multicultural Education Commission, reprinted in *Educational Leadership* 54: 288–291, January 1977.

(D)   As societies become more complex in structure and resources, the need of formal or intentional teaching and learning increases. As formal teaching and training grow in extent, there is the danger of creating an undesirable split between the experience gained in more direct associations, and what is required in school. The danger was never greater than at the present time, on account of the rapid growth in the last few centuries of knowledge and technical modes of skills.

— John Dewey, *Democracy and Education* (1916)

(E)   The demand for Afro-American cultural equality is not . . . a threat to public order; instead, it is a threat to the hegemony of the Euro-American intelligentsia in controlling and defining the nature of American life and culture. . . . The Afro-American intelligentsia should support the laws which forbid the exclusion of blacks from public programs, and with equal force they should challenge the laws or customs which compel the inclusion of blacks into a system whose inevitable effect is to shape the opinions and values of their children into the standard Euro-American mold.

— James D. Anderson (University of Illinois), "Black Cultural Equality in American Education" in *Equality and Social Policy*, edited by Walter Feinberg (University of Illinois Press, 1978), pp. 42–65. (Compare this vewpoint with the viewpoints set forth in Selection 4.10.)

(F)   [A free democratic society, in its ideal form, is a method of peaceful change, of nonviolent revolution. To be successful, those who advocate new patterns of thought and behavior must be motivated by a love of truth and of justice which transcends self-interest or the special interests of a particular group. Says Thomas Merton:]

The nonviolent resister is not fighting simply for "his" truth or for "his" pure conscience, or for the right that is in "his side." On the contrary, both his strength and his weakness come from the fact that he is fighting for the *truth*, common to him and to the adversary, *the* right which is objective and universal. He is fighting for *everybody*. . . .

The realism of nonviolence must be made evident by humility and self-restraint which clearly show frankness and open-mindedness and invite the adversary to serious and reasonable discussion. . . . All it seeks is the openness of free exchange in which reason and love have freedom of action. In such a situation the future will take care of itself. . . .

Instead of trying to use the adversary as leverage for one's own effort to realize an ideal, nonviolence seeks only to enter into a dialogue with him in order to attain, together with him, the common good of *man*. . . . In such a confrontation between conflicting parties, on the level of personality, intelligence and freedom, instead of with massive weapons or with trickery and deceit, a fully human solution becomes possible.

— Thomas Merton (Trappist monk). "Blessed are the Meek: The Roots of Nonviolence." *Fellowship* 33: 18–22, May 1967.

(G)   Fondly do we hope — fervently do we pray — that this mighty scourge of [the 1861–65] war may speedily pass away. Yet, if God wills that it continue, until all the wealth piled by the bondman's 250 years of unrequited toil shall be sunk, and every drop of blood drawn with the lash, shall be paid by another drawn with the sword, as was said three thousand years ago, so still it must be said "the judgments of the Lord are true and righteous altogether."

With malice toward none; with charity for all; with firmness in the right, as God gives us to see the right, let us strive on to finish the work we are in; to bind up the nation's wounds; to care for him who shall have borne the battle, and for his widow, and his orphan — to do all which may achieve and cherish a just, and a lasting peace, among ourselves, and with all nations.

— Abraham Lincoln, concluding paragraphs of his Second Inaugural Address. (Read William Lee Miller's analysis of this address in *The Center Magazine* 13: 53–64, July/August 1980.)

(H)   [As we face the future, we should ask three questions concerning pluralism:] Do we want cultures that differ significantly from each other or do we want cultures that differ in name and history only? Do we want schooling that accentuates awareness of cultural differences or do we want schooling that minimizes them? Do we want ethnicity to persist or do we want it to slip away unobtrusively?

— Diana Ravitch, "On the History of Minority Group Education in the United States," *Teachers College Record* 78: 220–227, 1978.

Chapter 5. MEASUREMENT AND EVALUATION

5.1 Introduction: Parable of the Lost Cow
E. F. SCHUMACHER

During the war I was a farm laborer and my task was before breakfast to go to yonder hill and to a field there and count the cattle. I went and I counted the cattle — there were always thirty-two — and then I went back to the bailiff, touched my cap, and said, "Thirty-two, sir," and went and had my breakfast. One day when I arrived at the field an old farmer was standing at the gate, and he said, "Young man, what do you do here every morning?" I said, "Nothing much. I just count the cattle." He shook his head and said, "If you count them every day they won't flourish." I thought, Well, after all, I am a professional statistician, this is only a country yokel, how stupid can he get. One day I went back. I counted and counted again, there were only thirty-one. Well, I didn't want to spend all day there so I went back and reported the thirty-one. The bailiff was very angry. He said, "Have your breakfast and then we'll go up there together." And we went together and we searched the place and indeed, under a bush, was a dead beast. I thought to myself, Why have I been counting them all the time? I haven't prevented this beast's dying. Perhaps that's what the farmer meant. They won't flourish if you don't look and watch the quality of each individual beast. Look him in the eye. Study the sheen on his coat. Then I might have gone back and said, "I don't know how many I saw but one looked mimsey." Then they would have saved the life of this beast.

From E. F. Schumacher, *Good Work*, Harper & Row, 1979. By permission. E. F. Schumacher is best known for his book *Small Is Beautiful*.

5.2 Why Some Children Do Poorly In School
JACOB W. GETZELS

All children acquire their fundamental "codes for future learning" or "learning sets" in the family during the period ascribed to primary socialization. One of the sets is the language code, the other the value code. The language code gives the child the categories for structuring and communicating his experiences. The value code tells him what in his experiences is important. In a sense, language becomes the medium through which the child perceives and expresses experience, and values determine what in his experience he will accept or reject.

Typically, the school requires an achievement ethic, with consequent high valuation on the future, deferred gratification, and symbolic commitment to success. It assumes that every child has had an opportunity to acquire beliefs, that anyone can get to the top if he tries hard enough, and that if he tries he, too, can reach the top. The future, not the present, is what counts; one must use the present to prepare for the future. Time, therefore, is valuable and must not be wasted — "time is money" — and the school assumes that timed tests carry the same urgency for everyone. It is expected that the pupil will be able to defer gratification through symbolic commitment to success; he will study geometry now to become an engineer later. These are the values not only of the school; they are also the values of the families in which many of the children are reared. Such children acquire from their earliest years a value code compatible with the school values, just as they acquire a language code compatible with the school language. There is no reason for them to change, and the school provides no model for change.

In contrast to this, other children have experienced primarily a survival or subsistence ethic, with consequent high valuation on the present rather than the future, on immediate rather than deferred gratification, on concrete rather than symbolic commitment. Where these chldren live, hardly anyone ever gets to the top; often one cannot even move across the street. Time is not important or potentially valuable if there is not going to be anything to do with it anyway. And what does an appeal to symbolic success mean where the only success the child has seen can be measured realistically solely by subsistence and survival? In contrast to the other children, these children face severe discontinuities in values when they come to school — discontinuities which often have a profound effect on their behavior toward school and on the school's behavior toward them.

These children are often accused of failing in school because they are intellectually apathetic and physically aggressive. The issue may be turned around and the question raised whether they may not be intellectually apathetic and physically aggressive

From Jacob W. Getzels, "Schools and Values." Reprinted with permission from the May/June 1976 issue of *The Center Magazine*, a publication of the Robert Maynard Hutchins Center for the Study of Democratic Institutions, Santa Barbara, California.

Jacob W. Getzels is Professor of Education and Behavioral Sciences at the University of Chicago.

In this article Professor Getzels argues that extreme poverty leads to a constant emphasis on survival —on present rather than future values, on immediate rather than deferred gratifications. In contrast, schools emphasize future and deferred values, so that the future, rather than the present, is what counts. This clash of basic values may be the underlying reason why children from poverty-stricken homes frequently do poorly in school.

because they fail. For what can be more tormenting than to be confronted day after day with a situation in which the language and value codes seem different in inexplicable ways from those to which you are accustomed — and more, a situation in which you cannot succeed and from which you are not permitted to escape without threat of severe punishment?

This is a situation in which learning cannot take place, and surely not the learning of new values. The reaction to this type of frustration is hopelessness and rage. In school, the hopelessness is manifested in apathy, intellectual withdrawal from the source of frustration; and the rage is manifested in aggression and in physical attack upon the source of the frustration. The patterns of apathy and aggression maintained over the compulsory school years often become stabilized into deep-seated maladjustment.*

---

*EDITOR'S NOTE   If the parents of disadvantaged children have hope and confidence that, with hard work and effort, their children will be able to enter into the mainstream of American culture, then extra effort may indeed lead to success. Indeed, this has been a major pattern of immigrant children for the past two centuries. In the words of Professor Patricia Albjerg Graham, of Teachers College, Columbia University:

> Despite the disclaimer that the schools are not primarily avenues of social mobility in this country, a recent incident involving the U.S.S.R., a nation that has made a genuine effort to eliminate class distinctions in its society, is illustrative. In 1973 a group of six American professors and one journalist met in the Soviet Union with a counterpart group there to discuss domestic problems of mutual concern. At the opening session each participant — they ranged in age from early 30s to mid 50s — was asked to introduce himself or herself and to say a bit about family background. The Americans, all of whom had been educated at Harvard, Yale, or Columbia, represented a more diverse group in terms of family background than the Soviets. Over half of the Americans were the second generation of their family in this country, and less than half came from families who were professionals. The Soviets, on the other hand, almost unanimously came from families in which the parents had been professionals and had attended college. This was all the more unusual since the proportion of Russians attending college of their parents' generation was very small indeed. Although our educational system clearly has serious limitations as a vehicle for social mobility, it is noteworthy that the most prestigious universities in this country have not limited their enrollments, particularly at the graduate level, to children of the upper middle class. —Patricia Albjerg Graham, "America's Unsystematic Educational System," *American Education* 10: 12–19, July 1974.

In recent decades America's economy has found places for millions of Blacks, Hispanics, Asiatics, and other ethnic minorities — and for women. These changes are not simply movements of lower classes into the middle class; they are also movements of millions of middle-class families into the upper classes:

> The celebration of ethnicity is not so much a recognition of the special contribution of Europeans to America as it is the manufacturing of a new conservatism. Ethnicity gives expression to an organized group of white working-class Americans dedicated to the maintenance of their comparative class positions. As such, ethnicity becomes yet another hurdle for black Americans to jump in order to gain equity in this society. An overt struggle between whites and blacks is intellectually unpalatable; hence ethnicity emerges to defuse racial tension by shifting the struggle to the loftier plane of downtrodden blacks and denigrated ethnics. — Irving Louis Horovitz, (Professor of Sociology and Political Science, Rutgers University), "Race, Class and the New Ethnicity," *Worldview* 18: 46–54, January 1975.

However, the blacks are not the only disadvantaged peoples in America. In 1974 Colin Greer cited these data: "Nationwide, of the 45 million children in the public schools in America,

- More than 9 million children now enrolled in public schools will enter the labor market as functional — for job purposes — illiterates.
- One in four high schoolers drop out before graduation. Estimates vary, but between 25 and 50 percent of those who complete high school are menially employed or unemployed. . . ."

5.3   The Mismatch Between School and Children's Minds
EDITORIAL ESSAY

The late George Conger, for many years professor and head of the University of Minnesota's Department of Philosophy, enjoyed telling of an incident that occurred in the 1930s when Bertrand Russell (1872–1970) was there as a guest speaker. In anticipation of a small and rather selective audience, the lecture was scheduled in a room seating about two hundred students. When Russell had finished his lecture, he asked for questions from the audience. After a considerable lapse of time, one student stood up and asked, "Mr. Russell, what do you think about things in general?" Without a second's hesitation, Russell replied, "In general, I don't think about things in general."

The point of Russell's reply has been well expressed by Albert Camus:

> In psychology as in logic, there are truths but no truth. . . . I realize that if through science I can seize phenomena and enumerate them, I cannot, for all that, apprehend the world.[1]

John Dewey also recognized the empirical, factual, situational basis (and limitation) of thinking. Thinking about thought without reference to *context*, he said, "is in the end but a beating of wings in the void." Dewey insisted that we can understand things and communicate with one another only if there is some temporal or spatial or contextual background for the things about which we think and speak. What Dewey called "selective interest" is generally called "subjective," although E. B. McGilvary preferred the term "perspective." This "subjectivity" is at the core of human individuality or uniqueness; and Dewey viewed individuality as a "mode of selection which determines subject-matter.[1]

What makes the mind so amazing is its ability to move with lightning speed from one context to another. Suppose one overhears two friends, A and B, saying:

A: "Jeet?"
B: "No. Jew?"

---

[1] Quotations from Camus and Dewey in *Tough and Tender Learning*, by David Nyberg (Mayfield Publishing Company, 1971), pp. 55–60. Read also E. B. McGilvary, *Toward a Perspective Realism* (Open Court, 1956).

[But, continues Greer, we do not blame our society or our schools for these failures. We] "blame poor people rather than self-interest, and vested interest, and we use the consequent political stalemates to explain the incapacity of the school to make a positive difference in the lives of those at the bottom of our society. . . . — Colin Greer, *The Great School Legend: A Revisionist Interpretation of American Public Education*, with a foreword by Herbert J. Gans. New York: Basic Books, 1972, Copyright © 1972 by Basic Books, Inc., Publishers.

Unlike Colin Greer and other such critics of the 1970s, we blame neither the "system" of the "schools" nor the "rich" nor anyone else. Instead, we search for constructive programs, for positive steps, and for dedicated parents, teachers, and citizens to work in a variety of ways to improve the situation and to help resolve the difficult problems we face.

We conclude with an observation by Sydney J. Harris (syndicated column, February 12, 1976):

> Utopians of the left make the mistake of assuming that people will act better if you make the 'system' better; while Utopians of the right make the opposite error of assuming that the system will run itself, by some mysterious natural laws, if people don't interfere with it.

If it is known that these two people often eat lunch together, this noonday conversation would immediately be reinterpreted to mean:

A: "Did you eat?"
B: "No. Did you?"

Suppose in a noisy room, one hears a simple statement, which might be any one of the following:

A lot of peas.	Al ought to please.
All out of peas.	Al's auto, please.
All out to please.	Paul's auto, please.

Context will generally enable us to choose the sentence having the "sensible" meaning, even when all that is said is not clearly heard. Considering that each of the above six phrases takes only a second to utter, we may realize how rapidly we interpret and reinterpret what we "hear" by fitting the separate sounds into meaningful patterns.

A person who lacks such mental agility, that is, a person who can see things from only one point of view, is said to have an obsession. The story is told of a high school youth who had such a one-track mind that he was sent to the school psychologist. The psychologist took out a piece of paper, drew a square, and then said to the boy: "When you look at this, what comes to your mind?" "Oh," said the boy, "That is a bed, and on the bed are a man and a woman having sex." The psychologist then drew a circle, and again asked the boy what this made him think of. "That circle," replied the boy, "suggests an Indian wigwam, and inside the wigwam there's an Indian and his squaw having sex." The psychologist drew one more picture, this time, a triangle, and asked the boy once more what came to his mind when he saw that figure. "That triangle," said the boy, "is another wigwam, even though it has a different shape. And inside the wigwam are a man and a woman having. . . ."

"Good God, boy," Don't you ever think of anything but sex?"
"Oh yes, sir," said the boy, "but you keep drawing those suggestive pictures."

Unlike this boy, a normal human mind moves quickly and easily from one context to another. In his *Semantic Account of 570 English Words* (1938), Irving J. Lorge states that these 570 most-used English words average twelve different meanings per word. Of these twelve meanings, let us suppose that six are obsolete and that three are rare. This still leaves three distinct and different meanings for each word. Now suppose we speak a short sentence, four of whose words have three different meanings. This sentence could, in theory, be interpreted in 81 (=3^4) different ways. A little reflection on this point should make us stop and ask: "Why are we sometimes *misunderstood*?" The amazing thing is that we are *ever* able to be *understood*.

Consider this simple example: A horse is "fast" if it is tied to a hitching post. The same horse is "fast" if it breaks loose and gallops away. In the 1920s a woman was "fast" if she smoked cigarettes. The colors on a dress are "fast" if they do not fade. Ascetics "fast" to renounce their bodies. Dieters "fast" in order to keep slender and thus to glorify their bodies.

To conclude this discussion concerning *context*: Unless the viewpoints, or mind sets, of speaker and hearer are quite similar, the same words or phrases may call forth different meanings. "Play" means different things to a musician, an actor, a gambler, or a football player. "Pipe" calls up different ideas to a smoker, a plumber, or an organist. To a card player, "set" suggests an unearned bid; to a poultryman, it calls to mind a hen and eggs; to a logician, it signifies a class of objects or ideas; to a psychologist, it suggests "mind set," a mind's prejudice or outlook.

G. K. Chesterton once declared that the most important thing about a picture is its frame. Educators should adapt Chesterton's statement to read: the most important thing about any student is the mind-set or the background which leads a student to attend to some things and to ignore others.

Basil Bernstein was dealing with this problem when he distinguished between the restricted and the elaborated codes (of thought and language) of children entering school. Stones has summarized Bernstein's views thus:

Bernstein considers the language of the . . . [culturally deprived] family a linguistically *restricted code*. He considers that of the middle class an *elaborated code*. He suggests the main attributes of the restricted code are its syntactical crudity, its repetitiveness, its rigid and limited use of adjectives and adverbs, short, grammatically simple, often unfinished sentences, and above all, much of the meaning is implicit and dependent upon a commonly held system of speech habits.

The elaborated code is a much more flexible instrument. It has an accurate grammar and syntax. It employs a range of subordinate clauses unknown to the restricted code. It makes much more widespread and flexible use of conjunctions, prepositions, adjectives, and adverbs. It is much more discriminating and it has a much greater potentiality of abstraction. . . .

Bernstein illustrates the nature of the restricted code for the learning child. He gives an imaginary example of two conversations on a bus. A mother has a child sitting on her lap.

First conversation: [restricted code]

Mother: Hold on tight.
Child: Why?
Mother: Hold on tight.
Child: Why?
Mother: You'll fall.
Child: Why?
Mother: I told you to hold on tight, didn't I?

Second conversation: [elaborated code]

Mother: Hold on tightly, darling.
Child: Why?
Mother: If you don't you will be thrown forward and you'll fall.
Child: Why?
Mother: Because if the bus suddenly stops you'll jerk forward on to the seat in front.
Child: Why?
Mother: Now darling, hold on tightly and don't make such a fuss.

As can be seen in the restricted code, the symbolic function is slight; the words have little more than signal significance. . . . Later, when he enters school, the language of the [culturally disadvantaged] child acts as a filter to restrict what gets through from the teacher (an elaborated code user) to the elements of the restricted code.

Following from this, Bernstein concludes that the problems facing a. . . . [culturally deprived] child in a school situation aimed at improving his language skills will be very different from that of a middle-class child. The latter has merely to *develop* his linguistic skills, the former has to *change* them. This makes it extremely difficult for the user of a restricted code to schematize the learning he is asked to make, since it is presented in the unfamiliar forms of the elaborated code.[2]

A child's mental and linguistic development may or may not begin, as William James suggested, as a "blooming, buzzing confusion." But we can be quite sure of one thing: Words and meanings are *decoded within specific contexts.* How this happens can be illustrated with an example of adult communication:

Suppose a husband and wife are both familiar with the husband's basement workbench, and that the man's non-mechanically inclined wife says to him, "I put your *thing-a-ma-bob* on the workbench next to your *what-you-may-call-ems.*" With no trouble at all, her husband will intepret this statement to mean "I put your *rat-tail file* on the workbench next to your *pliers.*" If we keep in mind that every word a child learns is a *thing-a-ma-bob* or a *what-you-may-call-em*, we will have a greater sense of wonder and amazement at a child's ability to learn to speak and to communicate.

Even as Wittgenstein said to philosophers, so Margaret Donaldson now says to educators: The mental development of infants and young children begins, not with *words*, but with *situations*, or rather, with *words as part of a total situation.* Children are far more concerned to make sense of what people *do* when they talk and act, than to isolate words and/or to analyze meanings of words. Also, children are generally far more interested in *people* than they are in *words*. Their main endeavor would seem to be this: to discover some structure, and thus to make some sense out of *situations.* Some of these situations include words; others do not. But when words are a part of the total situation, a child's interpretation of these words is strongly influenced by whatever structure the child gives to the total situation which gives that word a specific context:

A child's ability to learn language is indeed something at which we may wonder. But his language-learning skills are not isolated from the rest of his mental growth. There is no reason to suppose that he is born with an "acquisition device" which enables him to structure and make sense of the language he hears while failing to structure and make sense of the other features of his environment. On the contrary it now looks as though he first makes sense of situations (and perhaps especially those involving human intention) and then uses *this* kind of understanding to help him to make sense of what is said to him. . . . [Furthermore, in school:]

A child will have the best chance of starting to consider possibilities of meaning if he is reading a coherent text which contains the right sort of balance between words he already knows well and words he is not sure about, and if, further, the known and familiar parts of the text are so constructed as to guide him towards a manageable set of options when the unknown is encountered. . . .

The process of moving beyond the bounds of human sense is unnatural in the sense that it does not happen spontaneously. The very possibility of this movement is the product of long

[2] E. Stones, *An Introduction to Educational Psychology*, (London: Methuen & Company, Ltd., 1966), pp. 186–187. By permission of Methuen & Company, Ltd., London.

ages of culture; and the possibility is not realized in the life of an individual child unless the resources of the culture are marshalled in a sustained effort directed to that end.[3]

Teachers, like other mature adults, have long since learned to live in a world of disembodied forms of thought — of abstract ideas no longer conjoined with concrete situations. The mismatch between school and children's minds occurs when teachers, overeager for the child to learn, attempt to teach these disembodied abstractions to immature minds — minds still on a level where specific examples and situational thinking persists.

[3] Margaret Donaldson (University of Edinburgh), *Children's Minds* (London and New York: Oxford University Press, 1978), pp. 56, 101, 129.
This book may be said to synthesize, and move beyond the work of Piaget and Chomsky.

5.4 The Hidden IQ
FRANK RIESSMAN

Intelligence tests measure how quickly people can solve relatively unimportant problems, making as few errors as possible, rather than measuring how people grapple with relatively important problems, making as many productive errors as necessary with time no factor.

A few years ago a birthday party for a member of the staff at a well-known psychological clinic played a novel role in the test performance of a Negro child. Prior to the party this boy, whom we shall call James, had been described on the psychological record as "sullen, surly, slow, unresponsive, apathetic, unimaginative, lacking in inner life." This description was based on his behavior in the clinic interviews and on his performance on a number of psychological measures including an intelligence test and a personality test. His was not an unusual record; many culturally deprived children are similarly portrayed.

On the day of the birthday party, James was seated in an adjoining room waiting to go into the clinician's office. It was just after the lunch hour, and James had the first afternoon appointment. The conclusion of the lunch break on this particular day was used by the staff to present a surprise birthday cake to one of the clinicians who happened to be a Negro. The beautifully decorated cake was brought in and handed to the recipient by James' clinician who was white, as were all the other members of the staff. The Negro woman was deeply moved by the cake — and the entire surprise. In a moment of great feeling, she warmly embraced the giver of the cake. James inadvertently perceived all this from his vantage point in the outer office. That afternoon he showed amazing alacrity in taking the tests and responding in the interview. He was no longer sullen and dull. On the contrary, he seemed alive, enthusiastic, and he answered questions readily. His psychologist was astonished at the change and in the

Excerpts from *The New Assault on Equality: I.Q. and Social Stratification* (pp. 206-216), edited by Alan Gartner, Colin Greer, and Frank Riessman of *Social Policy* magazine. Copyright © 1974 by Social Policy Corporation. (Footnote references are omitted.) Reprinted by permission of Harper & Row, Publishers, Inc.
Frank Riessman is at Queens College, New York City.

course of the next few weeks retested James on the tests on which he had done so poorly. He now showed marked improvement, and she quickly revised not only the test appraisal of him on the clinical record card, but her general personality description of him as well.

The high point of their new, positive relationship came some months later when he confided to her that she had gotten off on the wrong foot with him on the first day in the first three minutes of contact. She was taken aback and said, "What do you mean? I was very friendly, I told you my name and asked you yours." He responded, "Yeh, and I said James Watson and right away you called me Jimmy and you bin callin' me Jimmy every since. My name is James, 'cept to my very good friends maybe. Even my mother calls me James." Then he went on to tell her how he had changed his opinion of her on the day of the birthday party because of the close relationship he had seen widened between her and the Negro psychologist.

This little story illustrates a number of things. First, it shows that *the test is a social situation.* The testing situation, whether it be a psychological test or any other kind of test, for that matter, reflects a relationship between people, a relationship that is often remarkably subtle. And when anything hampers this relationship, the result is likely to show in the test score itself. This can occur on an individual test as well as a group test, an IQ test as well as a personality test, a subject matter examination as well as a psychological measure. . . . It also shows [that children] from different cultural backgrounds respond very differently to clinical situations and to the idea of being tested or evaluated.

The anecdote also points up the fact that a well-meaning, clinically trained, unprejudiced psychologist can have poor rapport with a deprived child, not because of deficient psychological technique, but because of limited knowledge about certain cultural attitudes. In this case, the attitude in question is the feeling held by many Negro people that the informality intended by shortened nicknames signifies a lack of respect when it takes place across cultural lines. This does not suggest that the child himself was aware of this reasoning, but that, rather, he was simply reflecting his parents' wish that he be called by his full name.

The importance of having Negro psychologists on the staff of a clinic is shown in a pertinent way by the anecdote. The Negro child need not himself have a Negro clinician, but her presence in the clinic was indirectly influential.

Finally, the story neatly illustrates the fact that scores on tests are not fixed and can be reversed dramatically when the relationship to the tester is improved. There is apparently a hidden IQ and a hidden personality that is often not revealed by the test and the clinical interview. In our story, James's IQ score rose considerably in the retesting and his personality began to appear in a totally new light.*

---

*EDITOR'S NOTE Compare the following statement by David Harman, of Center for Studies in Development, Harvard University:

[Japan], Israel, and England, among other countries, have become disenchanted with standardized testing in general, and [they] have recently abolished national standardized examinations that served as indicators of potential and, hence, education beyond the primary school years. Research in all three countries has indicated the importance of parental involvement in the teaching of reading. Great importance is attached to the role of parents as reading motivators, stimulators, and, in many cases, instructors. Parents also play an important role in identifying reading difficulties and,

5.5 The Case for I.Q. Tests
ARTHUR R. JENSEN

[Many] arguments against I.Q. tests ignore a large number of scientifically established facts. Below I have listed some of these that seem most germane; except the first, all items are amply substantiated by research published in the scientific journals. . . .

1. The level of technology needed to maintain the standard of living enjoyed in North America and Europe, given their present populations, demands that a substantial proportion (say, 15 percent) of the population possess a high level of the kind of mental ability measured by intelligence tests. We could get along without this kind and amount of intelligence in the population only if we drastically reduced population size and returned to a simple agrarian way of life or became hunters and gatherers of food, as in primitive societies. The present population could not be sustained without the technology (food production, transportation, health services, sanitation, and so on) and the kinds of brains needed to maintain it. Thus, to denigrate intelligence is to abandon civilization as we know it.

2. Intelligence tests do, in fact, predict socially and occupationally significant criteria. I.Q. is in a sense a measure of a person's ability to compete successfully in the world of work in all known civilized societies. When the "man in the street" is asked to rank various occupations in order of their "prestige," "desirability," and so on, it turns out that the rank order of the average I.Q. of persons in those occupations closely corresponds to the rank order of their desirability. For example, most of the practical business executives to whom McClelland refers have an average I.Q. that places them above approximately 96 percent of the rest of the population.

3. Persons would still differ in intelligence even if there were no intelligence tests. Any merit system based on performance reveals these differences. I.Q. tests reveal

Excerpts from "The Case for I.Q. Tests: Reply to [David C.] McClelland," by Arthur R. Jensen, *The Humanist* 32: 14. Reprinted with permission from *The Humanist*, January/February 1972.

Arthur R. Jensen is Professor of Educational Psychology and Research Psychology in the Institute of Human Learning, University of California, Berkeley. His article "How Much Can We Boast I.Q. and Scholastic Achievement?" (*Harvard Educational Review* 39: 1-123, 1969) created such a stir that in June 1969 *HER* published a special issue, *Environment, Heredity and Intelligence*, with numerous writers presenting pros and cons on the Heredity-Environment issue.

The present excerpt passes over the genetics dispute, and deals only with I.Q. in the narrower, less theoretical sense.

through working in tandem with schools, they serve significant roles in alleviating them. Also of importance in all three countries is the attempt to determine areas of interest to school children so that reading material might be suitably planned and published.

These observations are not intended to imply that reading difficulties and failure do not occur in Japan, Israel, and England. They do, however, show the emphasis in areas such as parental involvement, student motivation and interests, and individualized — rather than standardized — approaches to student reading development might be more profitable avenues to the attainment of reading and comprehension abilities. The less frequent use of standardized exams in these countries has certainly not hindered instruction or caused greater general reading failure. — David Harman, "Reading Tests," *National Elementary Principal* 54: 81–87, July/August 1975.

A number of studies by Christopher Jencks and other indicate that scholastic aptitude may be relatively unimportant in business, industry, agriculture, and many other occupations, particularly nonprofessional ones.

the same differences to the extent that the performance involves mental capabilities. They are not intended to predict performance based on physical capacities or on special talents such as artistic and musical ability. Bright persons and dull persons were recognized long before intelligence tests came into existence, and there has always been a marked relationship between mental characteristics and occupational attainments. Throwing out intelligence tests will not improve a person's intelligence or reduce differences between persons, just as throwing away the thermometer will not cure a patient's fever.

4. The use of intelligence tests in the armed forces shows that they are highly correlated with the kinds and levels of skills for which men can be trained and the time they need to achieve certain levels of skill. Reversing the assignments of recruits in mental Categories I and IV would guarantee the greatest snafu in military history.

5. Intelligence tests do not reflect only the accidents of cultural and social privilege; they get at some quite basic biological capacity underlying the ability to reason, to organize and utilize one's knowledge, and so on. Hereditary or genetic factors account for more of the I.Q. differences among persons than do cultural and environmental factors. In the white European and North American populations, where this has been studied most extensively, it has been found that genetic factors are about twice as important as environment as a cause of individual differences in I.Q.

6. Intelligence is positively related to other nonintellectual traits of personality and character that are also involved in competing successfully for what most persons in our society — rich or poor, black or white — regard as the "good things in life."

7. Various intelligence tests differ in their degree of "culture loading." Contrary to popular belief, blacks perform *better* on the *more* culture-loaded than on the more culture-free tests. (The opposite is true for other minorities.) Blacks also do better on verbal than on nonverbal tests. Thus, on some nonverbal I.Q. tests, about 85 percent of American blacks score below the average for whites, while the culturally very different Arctic Eskimos score on a par with white norms. This shows that the higher scores on these tests do not depend upon having experienced a white, middle-class American background.

8. Just as no one has been able to make up a test of mental ability that favors younger children (say, 10-year-olds) over older children (say, 12-year-olds), so no one has been able to make up a test that favors persons of low socioeconomic status over persons of middle- and upper-class status. If the reasons for social-class intelligence differences were due to status-biased content, it should be possible to make tests that reverse the differences. Yet, despite many attempts, no one has succeeded in devising such tests.

9. Language and dialect do not have the importance in intelligence tests attributed to them by popular belief, especially where nonverbal I.Q. tests are used. Urban black children tested on the Stanford-Binet I.Q. Test by a black tester using ghetto dialect do not score appreciably higher than when the test is administered in standard English. Children who are born deaf, though scoring poorly on verbal tests because of their severe language deprivation, score no differently from children with normal hearing on the nonverbal tests.

10. College aptitude tests, such as the S.A.T., predict college grades for blacks as well as for whites, for rich as well as for poor. The tests are colorblind. Black

individuals and white individuals, rich or poor, with the same I.Q. can be expected to perform equally well in school or on the job — insofar as the job depends upon intellectual ability. In predicting a person's scholastic performance, knowledge of his race or social class adds little or nothing to what is predicted by his I.Q.*

---

*EDITOR'S NOTE   For some more recent pros and cons on this topic, read "Trouble over Testing," *Educational Leadership* 37: 639-653, May 1980.

5.6   National Achievement Profiles in Ten Learning Areas
J. STANLEY AHMANN

On the basis of what you know about our educational enterprise today and the students it serves, do you believe that most of the nine-year-olds 1) understand fractions, 2) know what an atom is, 3) can determine the main idea in a reading passage, and 4) are able to read musical notation? Also, would you guess that most of the thirteen-year-olds 1) understand the structure and function of the legislative branch of the government, 2) can express feelings in writing, 3) understand the transfer of energy, and 4) are able to show perspective by drawing objects larger and smaller to show distance? Finally, do you believe that most seventeen-year-olds 1) understand simple probability or statistics, 2) know basic geographic relationships, 3) can sing from printed music with acceptable rhythm and pitch, and 4) are able to evaluate poetry and prose with care?

The answer to each of the foregoing questions is "no." Less than one-third of the nine-year-olds, thirteen-year-olds, and seventeen-year-olds respectively can perform the tasks listed. These are but a few of the findings of the National Assessment of Educational Progress (NAEP) which is assessing the levels of achievement of young Americans on a national basis in ten learning areas during the 1970s. NAEP is an information gathering project which annually surveys the educational attainments of four age groups, namely, the three mentioned plus young adults (ages twenty-six —thirty-five). The primary purpose of the assessments is to describe the trends in educational achievement in America today. Specifically, the assessment tries to discover what young Americans know and what they can do. In other words, it is not designed to sort or rank individuals as is the case of norm-referenced testing, but to describe the kinds and levels of achievement which exist, thereby giving us a detailed survey of the behavior changes which young Americans are experiencing.

NATIONAL ASSESSMENT METHODS

The achievements of the four age groups are assessed in ten learning areas which can be conveniently classified into three categories. The first category, the basic skill area,

Excerpts from J. Stanley Ahmann (Iowa State University), "National Achievement Profiles in Ten Learning Areas," *Educational Studies* 9: 351-364, Winter 1979. (Footnote and bibliographical references are omitted.) Reprinted by permission of the American Educational Studies Association.

includes reading, writing, and mathematics. The second, the general subject-matter areas, is composed of four learning areas, namely, social studies, citizenship, science, and career and occupational development. Finally, three learning areas are included in humanities and the fine arts, that is, literature, art, and music.

The number of learning areas assessed each year varies from one to three, and typically is two. The assessment schedule is shown in Table 1.

Each assessment is a product of many years of work by a large number of educators, specialists, and concerned laymen from all over the country. . . . All areas are periodically reassessed in order to measure any changes in levels of educational achievement which might exist. . . . The second and third assessments reveal changes in levels of achievement, thereby providing significant information with regard to achievement trends which may exist. . . . The study of wrong answers offers insights into the origin of faulty learning and hints as to possible remedial actions. . . .

TABLE 1   Schedule for Assessing All Learning Areas

Learning Areas	Assessments		
	First	*Second*	*Third*
Basic Skill Areas			
Reading	1970-71	1974-75	1979-80
Writing	1969-70	1973-74	1978-79
Mathematics	1972-73	1977-78	
General Subject-Matter Areas			
Social Studies	1971-72	1975-76*	1980-81
Citizenship	1969-70	1975-76*	1980-81
Science	1969-70	1972-73	1976-77
Career and Occupational Development	1973-74		
Humanities and Fine Arts Areas			
Literature	1970-71	1979-80	
Art	1974-75	1978-79	
Music	1971-72	1978-79	

*Citizenship and Social Studies were combined after the first assessment.

ACHIEVING EDUCATIONAL OBJECTIVES ON A NATIONAL BASIS

As interesting as it is to identify the relative position of various subgroups of students and to measure the sizes of the differences which exist, in many ways these data do not represent the central thrust of the National Assessment of Educational Progress. Instead, the National Assessment seeks to *describe* the actual achievements of young Americans and thereby permit inferences to be drawn as to the degree to which important educational objectives are being achieved. Ideally such an inference can be based on the data from each exercise in each assessment.

The highlights of what nine-year-olds, thirteen-year-olds, and seventeen-year-olds in the nation know and can do in the ten learning areas included in the assessment have been identified. . . .

[Table 2 is omitted as not applicable to this condensation.]

Needless to say the lists are long. The illustrations of these are the samples of mathematics achievement shown in Tables 3, 4, and 5.

TABLE 3   Selected Findings in Mathematics for Nine-Year-Olds

Many (more than 67%)
1. Can add two-digit numbers.
2. Know the properties of zero.
3. Can tell time.

Some (approximately 33% to 67%)
1. Can subtract two-digit numbers.
2. Can add a series of three- and four-digit numbers.
3. Can solve single-digit multiplication word problems.

Few (less than 33%)
1. Can multiply and divide.
2. Understand fractions.
3. Can subtract three- and four-digit numbers.

TABLE 4   Selected Findings in Mathematics for Thirteen-Year-Olds

Many (more than 67%)
1. Can add, subtract, multiply, and divide whole numbers.
2. Can make comparisons using common units of measurement.
3. Can make change.

Some (approximately 33% to 67%)
1. Understand and can compute with fractions.
2. Can solve story or word problems.
3. Can manipulate algebraic expressions.

Few (less than 33%)
1. Understand probability or statistics.
2. Can choose the most economical purchase at a supermarket.

TABLE 5   Selected Findings in Mathematics for Seventeen-Year-Olds

Many (more than 67%)
1. Can multiply fractions and reduce them to lowest terms.
2. Can add, subtract, multiply, and divide decimals.
3. Can evaluate simple algebraic expressions and solve first-degree equations and inequalities.

Some (approximately 33% to 67%
1. Can convert decimals to common fractions.
2. Can add fractions.
3. Can recognize the graph for $y = x$.

Few (less than 33%
1. Can calculate the area of a square given its perimeter.
2. Can simplify algebraic expressions.
3. Understand probability or statistics.

In general, the reviewers feel that there is reason to be cautiously optimistic about the well being of the elementary school mathematics program. However, for the elementary and secondary school programs a number of questions have been raised which should receive additional attention. For instance, there needs to be a greater emphasis on percents, better coverage of consumer mathematics, and better student performance with fractions. How can these be accomplished? One possibility mentioned is new alternative curriculum in the seventh- through ninth-grades which would lead to a better feel for mathematics and quantitative thinking. Such a change would be a massive one and require considerable discussion and preparation. . . .

Surveys such as NAEP are not designed to investigate causal relationships directly. Instead, they serve as a means for generating hypotheses with respect to possible causes of achievement patterns, which can then be studied more intensively by designing appropriate experiments or conducting thorough case studies. In a very real way large-scale assessment programs are beginning points, not end points, in our search for answers with regard to the improvement of student achievement in our schools.

5.7 Down with Remediation
MIRIAM T. CHAPLIN

Remediation, when applied to education, is an unfortunate word. It implies that there is a malfunction that needs to be corrected, and that students with this disorder must receive special treatment. Who is a remedial learner is decided on the basis of standards arbitrarily set for all students. Those who attain these standards are average or above; those who do not are cases for remediation. Thus, the connotation of remediation is negative.

Once labeled, few learners are ever cured and are, therefore, damned in their school years to a life of suffering from a metaphoric malady. It is for this reason that remediation can be detrimental, for when the realities of growth and development are perceived in terms of those who do and those who don't, a problem is created that is difficult to solve. It is wise to look closely at some of the pitfalls of remedial education so they can be avoided.

First, *remedial education can be in direct opposition to developmental education.* Each child is different and progresses at his own rate of speed. The task of educators should be to [help each student move forward at his or her own proper pace,* and thus to] . . . engage in a process of development. Movement is the primary consideration involved in development, and education must enhance movement in every child. The inherent

Excerpts from Miriam T. Chaplin (Rutgers University), "Down with Remedieation", *Kappa Delta Pi Record* 15: 81-83, 91, February 1979; and condensed in *Education Digest* 44: 11-15, May 1979. By permission of Kappa Delta Pi Record.

Read also George R. Knight, "Reschooling Society," *Phi Delta Kappan* 60: 289-291, December 1978.

*EDITOR'S NOTE   Selection 5.8 tells of some new methods by which to measure and to speed up a student's pace.

danger in setting limits or minimum standards is the possibility that movement may be inhibited or, in some cases, eliminated.

Remedial education always comes after children have been allowed to fail. The alternative to remediation is to prevent failure in the first place. There are steps that can be taken to do this.

First is to engage in programs of mass professional inservice education for teachers and administrators in an attempt to create a fertile climate for student growth. These programs must include an emphasis on human growth and development with particular emphasis on individual learning styles. . . .

Teachers must be part of the planning process as active participants.

Also, instruction must be truly individualized through an eclectic approach which allows the instructional method to be geared to the learning style of the child to be taught. All methods are good for someone in class, but one method is not good for everyone.

Teachers will ask how this is possible, and this points to a dichotomy. Presently, there is a surplus of teachers; at the same time, too many students are graduated without basic skills necessary to lead productive lives. With schools in this predicament, do we need fewer teachers or more? Why not use decreased population to reduce class size to a level which makes individualization possible? Or why not have more than one teacher in a classroom so students can have the benefits of an education that comes as a result of shared expertise and responsibility? Why not use experienced Master Teachers as resources for regular classroom teachers?

Needy students are not the primary factors in a learning situation. Emphasis should be directed toward all students and their potential for full development, in an attempt to prevent the need for remediation. . . .

NEED TO APPLY SKILLS

Second, *remediation, as presently conceived, refers to an isolation of skill deficits and instruction aimed at eliminating those deficits.* While this may lead to acquisition of isolated skills, it may not lead to application of skills in real situations. The reason it is so difficult to bring students up to an acceptable level in remediation is that students cannot comprehend the isolated skills as meaningful to their academic or personal lives.

Students must practice the skills of reading, writing, and mathematics in experiences in which they are involved — not in isolation from their lives. Learning is the vocation of students in their school years. If we fail to teach application of skills to life situations in the early grades, it is not fair to expect that students will make these applications in a graduation requirement test. Isolated skill instruction does not provide an opportunity for students to use what they learn to make sense of their lives. . . .

This underscores the need for more professionals in the classroom so that there can be human interaction is an interdisciplinary approach to learning. A history teacher and a reading teacher in the same classroom can make students aware that disciplines and the skills for acquiring knowledge in these disciplines are independent. Skills can, thus, be applied when and where they are needed. If, at the same time, the progress expectations of students are varied enough to accommodate individual learning styles, there will be no need for a separation and isolation for remedial instruction.

TEACHING FOR THE TEST?

Finally, *remediation may lead to teaching for the test rather than for growth.* . . . [for] basic skills cannot always be measured by a paper-and-pencil test. But these skills can be taught, and, if policy-making bodies identify these broad-based performances instead of narrowly isolated skills as those which are necessary for student success and follow through in their conviction by upgrading the skills of teachers in service (supplying the professional personnel and financial resources necessary), then there will be no need for vast remedial programs.

Then educators can stop trying to find out what is wrong with students through testing and will begin to capitalize on what's right with them. The attention will be placed on providing an educational environment in which intellectual growth occurs as naturally as physical growth. The efforts toward remediation can subside and be replaced by techniques which help children to develop strong, healthy, and inquisitive minds.

5.8 New Directions in Educational Research
BENJAMIN S. BLOOM

A major revolution has taken place during the past decade in educational research and our understanding of some of the factors that directly influence learning in or out of the schools. As a result, student learning can now be improved greatly, and it is possible to describe the favorable learning conditions that can enable virtually all students to learn to a high standard. Researchers who were at one time concerned about providing equality of educational opportunity for students now speak of the learning conditions that can bring about equality of educational outcomes for students. And such educational outcomes are at very high levels of attainment. . . .

At least four methodological features account for the striking qualities of these new research developments. The simplest of these is the movement from a study of the characteristics of teachers and students to direct observation of learning taking place in the interactions between teachers and students in the classroom. Perhaps, to put it in the most direct terms, it is a movement from the study of the actors (teachers and students) to the study of teaching and learning as they take place under specific environmental conditions.

Increasingly, educational researchers are performing experimental studies under classroom conditions in which selected variables are studied in terms of the processes involved as well as the changes they produce in both teachers and learners. Central to these studies is the concern about the causal links between the process variables and the qualitative and quantitative changes in the learning of students.

From Benjamin S. Bloom (University of Chicago), "The New Direction in Educational Research: Alterable Variables," *Phi Delta Kappan* 61: 382-385, February 1980. This article is adapted from the introduction of Bloom's book *All Our Children Learning*. (Footnote references are omitted.) (New York: McGraw-Hill, 1980. Copyright © 1980 by Benjamin S. Bloom.) By permission.

But perhaps the most important methodological change is the movement from what I have termed stable or static variables to variables that are alterable either before the teaching and learning processes or as a part of these processes. I consider this shift in the variables used as central to the new view of education. This shift enables researchers to move from an emphasis on prediction and classification to a concern for causality and the relations between means and ends in teaching and learning. This new concern has resulted in new ways of understanding, explaining, and altering human learning. The search for alterable variables, and the causal processes by which they can be altered, is a relatively recent step in educational research. I am confident it will be central in educational research of the next decade. . . .

AVAILABLE TIME VERSUS TIME-ON-TASK

We have always recognized time as a central factor in all learning. Schools have allocated a certain number of years for different subjects such as reading, literature, arithmetic, science, or social studies. In addition, the schools determine the number of school days in each school year and the number of hours per day or week that will be assigned to each part of the curriculum. Time in the sense of years, days, and hours available for school learning becomes a relatively fixed or stable variable. To make significant alterations in these time allocations requires major legal, economic, and other policy changes at the state or local level. Only rarely can a group of teachers or local school administrators make drastic changes in these time allocations. And, since these time allocations are much the same for most students, they account for only small differences in the learning of individual students within a classroom or school.

Quite in contrast to the concept of time *available* for learning is the variable of *time-on-task* (i.e., active learning time, time that students are engaged in learning). If two students are in the same classroom and one is actively engaged in learning for 90% of the classroom hour while the other is actively engaged for only 30% of that hour, there will be quantitative as well as qualitative differences in their learning during that hour.

One method of appraising time-on-task is to determine at various intervals whether or not a particular student is *overtly* engaged in the learning — paying attention, doing work assigned, or in some way responding in a relevant way to the instruction and the instructional material. A second method is to determine the extent to which the student is *covertly* engaged in the learning. This is done by various methods (stimulated recall, interviews, or questionnaires) of determining whether the student is *thinking* in relevant ways about what is going on in the classroom or whether his thoughts are unrelated to the classroom teaching/learning processes. Most studies report an index of time-on-task as the proportion of the classroom hour the individual student was on task — overtly, covertly, or an average of the two.

Studies of this variable show that the percentage of engaged time (for individual students or groups of students) is highly related to subsequent measures of achievement and to subsequent indices of interests or attitudes toward the learning. In turn, time-on-task is largely determined by the quality of instruction and the extent to which the students have the cognitive prerequisites for each new learning task. To put it another way, students cannot actively engage in learning if the instruction is poor and/or they are unable to comprehend what is being taught and what they are to do.

For the purposes of this article, what is most important is the strong evidence that the amount of active engaged time in the classroom can be altered during a sequence of learning tasks. Consider two groups of students who are comparable in aptitude or previous achievement at the beginning of a new course. One group learns the subject under conventional conditions while the second learns under a very high quality of instruction (mastery learning or some other procedure that maximizes learning). During the first learning task both groups are likely to be very similar in percentage of time-on-task. On the second learning task, the percentage of time-on-task will tend to be greater for the group with high-quality instruction and lower for the group with poorer instruction. If both groups are followed over a series of learning tasks, the high-quality instruction group will be found to increase greatly in percentage of time-on-task while the low-quality instruction group decreases greatly in percentage of time-on-task. On the final learning task the two groups (who were very similar on the first learning task) will be very different. These differences will be reflected in achievement differentials, motivation for further learning of the subject, and self-confidence in learning ability.

Time-on-task is then one of the variables that account for learning differences between students, between classes, and even between nations. Time-on-task can be altered positively (or negatively) by the instructional process, and this has direct consequences for the learning that will take place.

INTELLIGENCE VERSUS COGNITIVE ENTRY

During much of this century educators have used intelligence and aptitude tests to predict school achievement. In general, the correlations between these tests and later achievement have been found to be about +.50 to +.70. Most researchers and educators have interpreted these relations as indications that intelligence and aptitude *determine* the individual's potential for learning. Many educators use these test scores as a basis for making long-term decisions about selection, grouping, and even about the types of school programs to which individual students are assigned. All too frequently, intelligence and aptitude scores determine opportunities for further education, student support and encouragement, and even the types of interaction between teachers and students.

There is some evidence that intelligence test scores are alterable in the early years (ages 3–7), but there is little evidence of significant alteration in levels of intelligence as a result of school experiences in the later years. Less is known about the alterability of performance on specific aptitude tests. On the basis of present evidence, we may regard both intelligence and aptitude as highly stable characteristics.

Quite in contrast to intelligence and aptitude indices are *cognitive entry characteristics*. These are the specific knowledge, abilities, or skills that are the essential prerequisites for the learning of a particular school subject or a particular learning task. Such prerequisites typically correlate +.70 or higher with measures of achievement in a subject. Furthermore, when they are identified and measured, they *replace* intelligence and aptitude tests in the prediction of later achievement. That is, intelligence or aptitude tests add little or nothing to cognitive entry measures for the prediction of school learning. All of this is to say that cognitive entry characteristics have a high relation to achievement, and they have an obvious causal effect on later achievement. This is especially true when sequential learning tasks are involved, where it may be impossible to learn task B without prior adequate learning of task A.

Cognitive entry characteristics are highly alterable, because they represent particular content and skills that may be learned if they are absent, reviewed if they have been forgotten, and learned to a criterion level if they have been learned to a lesser level. In the next section of this article I shall refer to feedback-corrective procedures as one major method for insuring that cognitive entry characteristics are developed adequately for almost all students. Much of mastery learning research in the schools demonstrates that the large gains in final achievement for mastery versus control groups are attributable to the fact that the mastery students were brought to high levels of achievement on the *prerequisites* for each new learning task. This was not done for the control students.

Much of the variation in school learning is directly determined by the variation in students' cognitive entry characteristics. When means are found for insuring that students reach adequate levels of competence on the essential cognitive entry behaviors, most students can be assured of high levels of school learning with very little variation in their achievement. The alterability of cognitive entry characteristics has the most profound implications for instruction, curriculum, and our views about the learning potential of almost all students in the schools.

SUMMATIVE VERSUS FORMATIVE TESTING

In most classrooms achievement tests are used for summative purposes. The summative test evidence is primarily used to classify or judge the student on the extent to which he has learned the content and objectives set for the course. The students' scores on each test are converted into school marks or other indices that compare each student with norms or standards set by the teacher or the test makers. Typically, once a student has taken a test, he is marked and rarely is given an opportunity for correcting his errors or being retested. The basic notion is that the students have had equal opportunity to learn the subject over a defined period of time and are then to be judged on what they have learned. This is repeated again and again during the school year.

Test results and school marks are frequently assumed to be the primary motivators for learning in the school. Marks based on tests are also assumed to be sound estimates of the *quality of learning* as well as a proper index of the *quality of the learners*. Such marks are eventually the basis for many decisions about learners, including school programs and further opportunities for education.

The use of summative testing/grading procedures results in highly predictable measures of school achievement. Typically, correlations between achievement tests in the same subject at two points in time are above +.70 (depending upon the reliability of the separate tests). If carefully made standardized tests are used over a number of subjects, the correlations over a five-year period or longer tend to be +.80 or higher. That is, the ranks of the students in a school remain very constant over many years of schooling. Many researchers and educators infer from this that differentials in achievement are nonalterable and that they are fixed by intelligence, heredity, home influences, or other conditions outside the school. It is assumed that the student and his background explain this remarkable stability of achievement and that the causes or remedies are not to be found within the schools. It is the student who has failed (or succeeded), and the teacher, the instruction, the curriculum, or the school is not to be held responsible.

In contrast to tests used for grading and judging is the use of tests and other evidence as an integral part of the formation of the learning. Formative tests are used primarily as feedback, to inform the student about what he has learned well and what he still needs to learn. When feedback is provided in relation to corrective procedures to help the student correct the learning, then with additional time and help most students do reach the standard of achievement set by the teacher. Typically, teachers use a parallel formative test to determine when the student has completed the corrective process to the set standard. Various studies have found that if 20% of a group of students reach the mastery standard on a formative test given at the end of a particular learning task, then with an hour or two of corrective effort most of the students reach the same mastery standard, when they are retested on a parallel formative test.

When formative tests and corrective procedures are used in this way over a series of learning tasks, the proportion of students reaching the mastery standard (before correctives) increases on each subsequent task until as high as 80% or 90% of the students are able to reach the mastery standard on the final learning tasks in the series. The amount of corrective help needed becomes smaller on successive learning tasks, until only a few students need such corrective procedures. The students appear to be "learning to learn."

This use of formative tests insures that most of the students have the necessary cognitive prerequisites for each new learning task, that students have increased interest in the learning and greater confidence in their own ability to learn, and that · they use more of the classroom time to engage actively in the learning process.

Formative tests are also useful in helping the teacher determine which aspects of the learning task were learned well by the majority of the students and which were learned poorly by most of the students. This gives the teacher feedback in order to determine which ideas and skills need to be reviewed or retaught in a different way if the majority of students are to learn them to a high standard. The major change is that teachers do less in the way of judging and grading students on what they had learned by a particular date and they do more to see to it that each student learns what he or she needs as preparation for the next learning task(s). . . .

Periodic formative testing and corrective procedures can be effective as one way of insuring that excellent learning takes place. However, in the long run, the basic problem of group learning is to find ways of providing feedback-corrective processes as an integral part of the classroom teaching/learning interactions.

TEACHERS VERSUS TEACHING

Over the past four decades there has been a great deal of research on teacher characteristics and their relations with student learning. This research has been concerned with such variables as the age of the teachers, their training, teaching experience, membership in teacher organizations, personality and attitudes, and even performance on achievement tests related to their field of teaching. In general, the relationship between teacher characteristics and student learning has typically been represented by correlations of less than +.20. Researchers in the past may not have selected the right teacher characteristics for study. However, based on the research done to date, we may conclude that the characteristics of teachers have little to do with the learning of their students. And, even if they did show higher relations, most of the characteristics of teachers studied so far are static variables not directly alterable by in-service or other teacher training programs.

Different from these many studies of teacher characteristics is the more recent research on the qualities of teaching that have a direct causal relation with student learning in the classroom. This research on the qualities of *teaching* (rather than on qualities of the *teachers*) consists largely of observational and experimental studies of teachers interacting with their students. Although there are many ways of doing this research, the theoretical approach of John Dollard and Neal Miller has been found very useful. Dollard and Miller have emphasized three major characteristics of all teaching: *cues, reinforcement*, and *participation. Cues* include instruction as to what is to be learned as well as directions as to what the learner is to do in the learning process. Much of the research relates student learning to the clarity, variety, meaningfulness, and strength of the explanations and directions provided by the teacher and/or the instructional material. *Reinforcement* includes the extent to which the student is rewarded or reinforced in his learning. Much of the research relates student learning to the variety of reinforcements provided, the frequency with which reinforcement is used, and the amount and kind of reinforcement given to different students in the class. *Participation* includes the extent to which the student actively participates or engages in the learning. The research relates student learning to the extent to which he actively participates in using the cues, makes appropriate responses, and practices the responses until they have become a part of his repertoire. The research also includes the extent to which the instructor and/or the instructional method engages the different students in the class in overt as well as covert participation and response to the learning.

Observations of teacher interaction with students in the classroom reveal that teachers frequently direct their teaching and explanations to some students and ignore others. They give much positive reinforcement and encouragement to some students but not to others, and they encourage active participation in the classroom interaction from some students and discourage it from others. The studies find that typically the students in the top third of the class are given the greatest attention by teachers, while the students in the bottom third receive the least attention and support. These differences in the interaction between teachers and students provide some students with much greater opportunity and encouragement for learning than is provided other students in the same classroom.

These qualities of teaching are alterable as a result of in-service education that provides teachers with feedback on what they are doing (or not doing) and what they can do to alter the situation. Studies have found that when these interactions of teachers with their students are altered, there are significant improvements in student learning. . . .

SUMMARY

If we are convinced that little or nothing can be done to improve the learning of individual students, then our major effort must be invested in predicting school achievement and classifying children at an early age. Stable variables are ideal for this purpose. Such efforts result in a school system that is quite effective for a small proportion of the students while at the same time it dooms most students to a deep sense of inadequacy and a dislike for school and school learning. Such a school system must invest much in the way of human and material resources with very small returns to the society or to the majority of its students.

If we are convinced that a good education is necessary for all who live in modern society, then we must search for the alterable variables that can make a difference in the learning of children and adults in or out of the school. Such alterable variables will do much to explain the learning process, and they will do even more to directly improve the teaching and learning processes in the schools. Our basic research task is to further understand how such alterable variables can be altered and their consequent effect on students, teachers, and learning.

The small number of alterable variables I have discussed here are only a few of the variables that have already been studied by researchers and used by teachers. These have already made a great difference in our understanding of school learning. But, also, they have brought about major changes in our views of learners and their amazing potential for learning. I hope that this small list will be rapidly expanded in the next decade and that they will become equally central for teachers, parents, and researchers. When they are thoroughly understood and well used, they will bring about the most profound changes in the schools and in the society.*

---

*EDITOR'S NOTE   Lauren B. Resnick (University of Pittsburgh) comments on Mastery Learning as follows:

. . . While Bloom may be overly enthusiastic [about Mastery Learning], the evidence does support his first claim that mastery learning procedures can make it possible for most students to learn what is in the curriculum. But with his second claim, that variability in learning rates can and should reach negligible levels under mastery instruction, I disagree. Mastery learning strategies shift school organizations from allowing equal amounts of time for all students for any particular topic to allowing as much time as each individual needs to master that topic. Unless variability in time actually does reduce to zero, the very possibilities of mastery learning raise important questions for educational goals and priorities which must be considered. The students who learn fastest have a cumulating amount of "extra" time as the

5.9   Multiple-Choice Tests: The American Way
THOMAS C. WHEELER

Until the 1950's, students wrote essays in schools because they were expected to write essays on college entrance exams. But the university abandoned the essay requirement by adopting, a generation ago, the entirely objective test for admission, the Scholastic Aptitude Test (S.A.T.).

Before World War II, the objective S.A.T had been a supplement to written achievement tests in various subjects. But when the S.A.T. became dominant, the achievement tests became objective, too, and also optional. When the university dropped the essay requirement, it failed to recognize the power of the system it launched. Once the college entrance exams were objective, secondary schools asked for less writing. Urged on by test manufacturers, high schools began to use objective tests both to prepare their students and for their own examinations. The university, by sanctioning the objective system, bears a terrible responsibility for the decline of writing in the United States. . . .

[Today, most] Americans are probably tested more than they are taught. Compositions, essay questions, term papers — vigorous thinking — all have yielded to one

From Thomas C. Wheeler, "The American Way of Testing," *New York Times Magazine* September 2, 1979, p. 40–42.

Reprinted by permission of Viking Penguin Inc. from *The Great American Writing Block* by Thomas C. Wheeler. Copyright © 1979 by Thomas C. Wheeler.

Thomas C. Wheeler teaches writing and literature at York College, the City University of New York.

---

course proceeds. Educators must consider what these faster learners will do with the time not needed for mastering the prescribed curriculum.

To clarify this question we need only consider another tradition of instruction that is also in accord with the basic assumptions underlying mastery learning. The individualized instruction tradition, which relies heavily on self-instruction, has developed instructional programs that are designed both to assure mastery of prerequisites for successive units of instruction and to allow individual students to proceed at their own "optimal" rates. Both computer-assisted instruction programs and workbook-based programs, such as Individually Prescribed Instruction, qualify as mastery programs. The course is divided into learning units; students are tested and provided with all instruction necessary to reach mastery on each unit; through appropriate sequencing of the units, mastery of prerequisites for successive units is largely assured. The use of self-instructional procedures in these programs makes it possible to allow students to proceed onward through the sequence as soon as they demonstrate mastery of a particular unit.

As a result, students spread out through the curriculum increasingly over time, with faster students moving further and further ahead as the slower ones carefully master the earlier units. If students are allowed to proceed onward in the curriculum rather than waiting for slower classmates to catch up, variability increases instead of decreases. . . .

If a "waiting to catch up" strategy is used, variability will be reduced, but so will the topmost levels of achievement. In that case equality of learning outcome could be achieved only at the expense of high-level achievement for the most able. Unless future studies demonstrate that variability in time needed to learn can indeed be reduced to zero, this will remain a dilemma from which mastery learning offers no escape. It is an issue we can no more afford to ignore than we can afford to continue ignoring the possibility, highlighted by Bloom's book, that all students can learn the basic skills if the schools will only organize themselves seriously for the task of teaching — Lauren B. Resnick, "Assuming That Everyone Can Learn Everything, Will Some Learn Less?" *School Review* 85: 445–451, May 1977. Read also Daniel J. Mueller (Indiana University), "Mastery Learning: Partly Boon, Partly Boondoggle," *Teachers College Record* 78: 49f, September 1976.

It should be noted that these criticisms deal with the likely applications — and missapplications — of Mastery Learning in classes of 20 to 40 students. These criticisms were not directed to Bloom's new methods of research.

---

right answer out of four, to boxes to be checked, blanks to be filled. Objective tests not only carry the prestige of being scientifically accurate — when they aren't — but also provide an easy way of handling the masses by machine. The results might have been predictable to an educational system that valued education. The national S.A.T. verbal-aptitude scores have shown a steady decline over a 14-year period. If the scores show anything, they show how poor teacher objective tests are. The American language — supple, imaginative and alive — has lost ground to the pretense of measurement. "Nobody ever cared about my writing" is a refrain I, as a teacher, have heard in several accents. After two decades of objective education, the "educationally disadvantaged" are not merely the poor and minority groups, but the supposedly well-educated and the well-to-do.

Many colleges now profess doubts about S.A.T. scores and say that in admissions considerations high-school grades and teacher recommendations are more important. One distinguished liberal-arts college, Bowdoin College in Maine, found there was no correlation between high test scores and college performance. Finding the "predictive value of standardized tests" questionable and test scores misleading, it has abandoned the test requirement for admission. . . .

To give the devil his due, it must be said that the S.A.T. asks for an ability to make fine distinctions, as in this analogy:

Impregnable: Aggression =
(A) imperfect: revision
(B) invincible: defense
(C) inequitable: criticism
(D) indivisible: separation
(E) immutable: preservation

Thirty percent of the near-median scorers chose the right answer, D. Just as something is *impregnable* against *aggression*, so is something *indivisible* if *separation* is tried.

S.A.T. sentences, with their blanks filled in correctly, read well enough in this one released test; even the reading passages do not assault the ear of the sensitive reader. But even though verbal sections of the S.A.T. are well enough written, the test is still obnoxious. Its verbal part, like other objective tests in language, does not ask for writing; and because it doesn't, the act of writing has withered in our schools. . . .

Vainly, E.T.S.[1] tries to measure writing ability objectively in a 30-minute part of the S.A.T. called the Test of Standard Written English (T.S.W.E.). The test asks the student to spot the grammatical errors in underlined sections of sentences; it also asks him to choose from among five possibilities the best way to phrase an underlined part. A student who can spot an error in an underlined section may still commit the same error in the frenzy of unaccustomed composition. Even if a student has a sure knowledge of grammar as shown on an objective test, the test still won't determine whether he can write an essay. For writing requires not only grammar but ideas and the ability to organize material. These abilities show up only in actual writing. The test is in many ways an exercise in futility. The student's score is not counted in the S.A.T. but sent to the college, supposedly to determine what level of freshman English the student should take. Good colleges will not use the score for placement purposes, as

[1] Education Testing Service.

E.T.S. recommends. Most colleges administer their own written essay exams to determine what level of composition course a student needs.

E.T.S. does ask for a 250-word essay in one of the five annual offerings of the optional Achievement Tests in English Composition. But of the 1.4 million students who took the S.A.T. in 1977-78, only 85,000 students [6%] wrote the essay. In the multiple-choice English Achievement Test, the student marks errors in "diction," "usage," "idiom," "wordiness," "sentence structure" and "metaphor" without ever demonstrating that he can avoid making such errors in his own writing. Many good writers, students or not, may be unsure of academic terminology but write well out of their sense of language. That kind of talent would do poorly on the test.

The test encourages schools to teach primarily by terminology, since the final test asks for it. For example, the student must choose from several possibilities the right rephrasing of a sentence if a subordinate clause is changed to a participle, or if one sentence is changed to a clause. He is told, in effect, that writing is a juggling act, without purpose.

The testing services that dominate our educational system may be able to justify tests in mathematics, but they shouldn't be allowed to sap the strength from our language with objective tests in writing. If we are given another generation of tests, writing will become a rare art. The responsibility for salvaging writing falls to the American university, which instituted the objective tests for college admission 25 years ago and sanctioned their use throughout the school system.

The antidote is to restore writing requirements on college entrance exams. But the task is formidable: E.T.S. has a vested interest in protecting its contracts; it is marshaling every "social science" argument it can in defense of existing tests and challenging the "scoring reliability" of essay tests. Justifying the multiple-choice approach, E.T.S. declares that "students who recognize the problems in the writing of others are likely not to have those problems in their essays, an assumption confirmed by careful research." English teachers know this is often not the case. The real problem seems to be money. E.T.S. throws up its hands at the cost of grading written exams, but surely a way exists to pay readers to read written essays.

No critic has defined the shortcomings of the S.A.T. better than Ralph Nader. "E.T.S. has us all locked into a test that doesn't look for creativity, stamina, motivation or ethics — which are the four qualities on which man's greatest achievements are based." Our mania for measurement, our naïve assumption that we will discover a true meritocracy through objective standards, contradicts the original American idea. When Jefferson wrote of a "natural aristocracy" emerging from an elementary and then a "higher degree" of education in preparation for the university, he thought that "worth and genius would thus have been sought from every condition of life." "Virtue and talent" were to be relentlessly encouraged and sought in schools at all levels. What worth, what talent, what virtue, does objective testing measure? Rather than rewarding visible intellectual work done in the classroom, the tests reward a cleverness that even the clever can doubt. . . .

Though E.T.S. announces that the S.A.T. is not designed to judge the "worth" of anyone, the tests set implicit standards of worth by becoming a passport to education, income and social status. An S.A.T. score — the score on a single test — can set the direction of a lifetime. . . . To "learn" to take the test, students spend valuable hours in cram schools and crash courses — and even attend summer school. Though the coaching sessions can be helpful, they also teach an appropriate cynicism toward "the system." Substantial education — the history of man or nation — is set aside in order to beat the test. The test is "the system," to be overcome by studying vocabulary lists, by taking practice tests, by learning the technique of test taking. Resentment and cynicism are two lessons taught by the American way of testing.

5.10   Why Johnny Can Read
ROSINA SPITZER

It seemed unbelievable to listen to five- and six-year-old British boys and girls read so fluently and write so easily, as I observed them on a recent visit to England. And even more incredible as I looked around was the absence of textbooks, ability grouping, reading circles, pre and post tests, and report cards or grades! What a striking contrast to the average American school!

What techniques were the British using with such success? The American parent is bombarded with the importance of reading scores. The American student is subjected to formal standardized tests to get the "magic number" that will rate him into supposedly accurate reading levels. The American student, regardless of our devious ways, always knows if he is in the low, average or high reading group. Many text books are prescribed for the child to read, along with answering specific questions at the end of each story, along with daily use of workbooks and lesson sheets which are, in essence, more testing.

In England I looked for workbooks and dittoes and found none! I looked for phonic books and drills and found none! I looked for five- and six-year-olds copying dictation taken by their teacher, but instead found them perfectly capable of writing down their own thoughts. I couldn't find children in reading groups because there was no ability grouping.

I noted how curious, eager and interested the boys and girls were and how delighted they seemed to be in school. I set about to find the key to such success in reading in an atmosphere I found so free and relaxed.

Each child was treated as a unique individual, in spite of the fact that I saw as many as 38 youngsters with one teacher. What was the structure of this? Many teachers in America say it is impossible to individualize instruction, as their classes of 28 to 35 are too large. I observed that each child was involved and busy and the teacher went around and helped each child individually. How, precisely, was she able to do this?

The key to this ease of learning and teaching, as I saw it, was, first of all, the attitude of the teacher. She was not an autocratic authority at a desk, but moved easily among

From Rosina Spitzer, "Why Johnny Can Read," *The Clearing House* 51: 234-239, January 1978. By permission.

Rosina Spitzer is currently associated with the Montebello Intermediate School as a project director for Educationally Disadvantaged Youth. She has taught grades 1-8 and is an instructor for the University of California, Los Angeles and Pepperdine on "Learning Centers."

the children, helping, guiding, listening and discovering their particular interests. The children were allowed to learn to read "naturally" through their own background, experiences and interests. Instead of texts or formal reading material, they had their own blank composition books where they recorded daily their own thoughts and activities. A "speller" was another little blank book in which words were entered by the teacher, peers, or themselves as they needed them for their own writing. No one sat in straight rows, nor were they ability grouped, nor were they necessarily working at the same task. There was no need for the "right" answer because their reading emanated from their own understandings. I counted the words in six-year-old Sharon's "speller" and found 350.

The methods and procedures of the British are obviously child-centered. British teachers have the backing of their headmasters (principals) to use their judgments in assessing a child's progress. They are not subjected to the American pressures of reading scores, standardized tests, or other outside factors. British teachers are held in high regard in their society and are not the scapegoats of the ills of society. They also believe direct contact with the parents is the best way to report progress, as grades do not explain what the child is doing. . . .

[It was] at Ravenscote Middle School in Frimley, Surrey, where I met Arthur Razzell, headmaster of 700 pupils ages 8 to 12 and a staff of 28 teachers. Arthur Razzell opened this school in 1972 with the determination to make Ravenscote a pleasant place in which teachers and children learn with a sense of joy, pleasure and excitement and inspiration in their work. Razzell stated the primary aims (no long lists of objectives) of his school as follows:

- to have good relations with parents
- to cultivate excellence
- to create joy in learning

No specific curriculum is written down. For instance, in social studies there are broad aims, such as:

- to study something nearby (students and teacher decide)
- to study something far away by vicarious sources (writing to people, seeing films, etc.)
- to draw from both resources and compare

Razzell's school is organized with "year group leaders" who are floating teachers working with teachers in the classroom from one to four days a week, sometimes planning together, teaching together, or taking over the class so the teacher has planning time. All teacher talents are shared. Meetings of the staff are held regularly, away from school in a social atmosphere, to discuss:

- individual children
- purpose of teaching a particular subject so as to keep in sharp-focus direction
- priorities

Also staff meetings regularly consider:

- what they want the children to come to know (body of knowledge)
- what they want the children to come to know how to do (skills and abilities)
- what they hope the child might become (interests, attitudes, concepts, values, judgments)

Instead of having set objectives, studies evolve from the needs and interests of the students. In the field of math, the first broad aim at this school is to ensure that children find it to be an enjoyable study. Razzell says, "The blunt facts are that unless children find some joy or satisfaction in the work, they are hardly likely to put their full energies into a greater understanding of it. For many thousands of children, math failure begins by unimaginative teaching, and the distaste grows." Instead of thinking in terms of "what ought to be covered," Ravenscote staff feel their "high flyers" (gifted children) should be able to fly as high as the teachers' capacity to lead them. The child becomes an active agent of his own learning. They feel children can make little progress by a series of drills. "They can do no more than bark at numbers," states Razzell. "Drills are a facility based on the ability to remember the rules, not on a complete understanding of what happens."

The teachers feel there is no sense in having a team situation if children are going to be following a prescribed course of instruction from text books or work cards. If teachers are given a basic chunk of assignments, the danger is that their talents will not be used. They do not see how one can individualize using small booths or carrells, as they have heard about in some American schools. Teachers here use their keen perception and judgment on what is happening daily in the classroom by being closely involved, moving around the room and encouraging children to progress.

Again, I saw the children using their composition books for reading and math, with much writing going on daily, no ability grouping, no phonics books or texts. Ravenscote does have one reporting form a year, but along with it goes a letter informing parents that it "shows no more than the way in which your child's teacher and group leader feel the wind has been blowing this year. Children who are good at math at our level are not necessarily the mathematicians of the future. More important are the attitudes and the levels of interest shown." The letter goes on to include these extracts from "Lessons from Childhood" (by Illingworth & Illingworth, E. S. Livingstone, Ltd., 1966):

> Beethoven's tutor wrote, "Beethoven has never learnt anything and never will learn anything. As a composer he is hopeless." Frederick Delius "spent all his time reading tales of the Wild West and crime thrillers." Sir Isaac Newton was "inattentive and a bad scholar." James Watt was "dull and inept." Charles Darwin was considered at school to be "rather below the common standard in intellect." Edison was always at the bottom of his class, and his father thought he was stupid. Albert Einstein at the age of nine had in his school report, "He is mentally slow, unsociable and adrift for ever in his foolish dreams." William Smellie, the famous obstetrician was "very idle and dull at school." Sir John Hunter's teachers described him as "an idle, surly, dullard, irredeemable by punishment or reward." Louis Pasteur was conscientious and worked hard but proved only a mediocre pupil. Oliver Goldsmith was described as a "stupid heavy blockhead, little better than a fool." Sir Walter Scott was "well below average." George Borrow was "slow of comprehension and almost dull witted." Winston Churchill's entrance examination paper to Harrow contained nothing but a figure I in brackets, two smudges and a blot. He was bottom of the lowest form and never moved out of Lower School for the whole five years he was there. Baden-Powell was pretty heavily slated — "Mathematics — has to all intents given up; Science — not paid the slightest attention; French — could do well but has become very lazy" — and so on.

Peter Redwood, headmaster of St. Paul's Church School, graciously greeted the

"American," as I was the first American visitor in ten years to his lovely country-side school in Dorking. There were 360 children, ages 5 to 12, and 15 teachers in this combined "first" and "middle" school. The curriculum was broad, definite aims showing purpose and direction without lists of specifics. Again, I saw great flexibility in allowing the teachers to meet the interests of their class in all subjects. All reporting to parents was done in conversations with parents. . . .

Since I expressed much interest in children who found it difficult to read, Mr. Redwood graciously offered to drive me to a nearby remedial school where students received special help. I was totally surprised at the striking difference with American remedial classes. Again, I saw no workbooks, dittoes, phonics books, basal texts. Instead, I found children cooking, playing games, role playing, and acting. As I talked with Mrs. Tindle, the Director, she said the first priority in her school was to restore the self-confidence of the child, and the second priority was to give children many opportunities to talk with their peers and adults. On checking students' backgrounds, she felt all had psychological or emotional problems resulting from home conditions.

Her first request for this school was equipment for cooking, as "language is related to mothering, and cooking is an activity where language can flow naturally." As we were conversing, students came over from time to time to offer us something they had just made.

Another priority at this school is having children spend about one hour a day here and during their first half-hour they are free to choose what they want to do in this rich environment. Mrs. Tindle took me over to a closed door and we heard two girls chatting away. She told me these girls never spoke in class and elatedly said they were planning a play. She knocked, then went in and asked if we could see their play in a little while. They smiled and said, "Yes." When we returned, we brought an audience of two staff members and two children and all gave their undivided attention to the two girls pretending they were mommies, using dress-up clothes, dolls and a doll carriage. One would never suspect they were non-talkers.

The second half-hour for students is devoted to one-to-one tutoring by the teacher using whatever approach is good for that child, with no set programs prescribed for all. The child at this school was not viewed as having a 'reading problem,' but rather looked upon as a whole child that needed attention as a whole person.

My experience in English schools gave me deep insight into why children as young as five and six are reading and writing. These points were very apparent:

- In the English schools I visited, the teacher is aware of the whole child and regards reading as a natural function.
- Reading is allowed to happen naturally, drawing upon a child's personal language and beginning with a child's own background and experiences.
- Children listen, read, write, talk every single day, getting continual practice in the total reading process.
- Teachers provide a natural, relaxed meaningful environment in which children are free from pressure of ability grouping, labelling and grades.
- Teachers are keenly aware of every child's needs and interests and view each child as a unique human being.
- Teachers are happy, relaxed and confident.

- The headmaster's major goal for schooling is that each child will enjoy learning for a lifetime.
- Children do not have to conform to one way of doing their tasks and have choices in deciding when and how they will do them.

In concluding, I think it appropriate to share a quote from an English school:

We have them in school for quite a short time. How can we ensure that what we have to offer them counts in their thinking the rest of their lives?

5.11   Integrity in the Teaching of Writing
JAMES MOFFETT

It is impossible to understand the teaching of writing in America if one does not realize that, in one form or another, from first grade through graduate school, it serves mostly to test reading. In elementary school the main form of writing is the book report, which becomes dignified in high school and college as the "research paper" or "critical paper," then deified in graduate school as the "survey of the literature" in the doctoral dissertation. The real goal of writing instruction in the U.S. is to prepare for term papers and essay questions (though secondary and college teachers increasingly fall back today on multiple-choice "objective" tests, partly because "the kids can't write"). We have always been far more interested in reading than in writing, so much so that writing in schools has hardly existed except as a means to demonstrate either reading comprehension or the comprehensiveness of one's reading. Because writing produces an external result, it is a natural testing instrument if one wishes to regard it so, whereas the receptive activity of reading leaves no traces outside. Using writing to test reading, then, seems the perfect solution to an institution so bedeviled by managing and monitoring problems that it resists student productivity tooth and nail and regards testing as the solution to everything. Writing about reading quite effectively kills two birds with one stone. . . .

[The following definitions of the ambiguous term "writing" are scaled upward toward true authoring. Authentic writing must embrace *all* these activities.]

- Revising inner speech — starts with inchoate thought.
- Crafting conventional or given subject matter — starts with topics and language forms.
- Paraphrasing, summarizing, plagiarizing — starts with other writers' material and ideas.
- Transcribing and copying — starts verbatim with others' speech and texts. . . .

[The teaching of writing should make certain that the highest definition should not only be included with the others but should govern the others, as is not the case with conventional composition instruction in the United States.]

The processes of writing cannot be realistically perceived and taught so long as we

Brief excerpts from James Moffett (author and consultant in education, now living at Mariposa, Calif.), "Integrity in the Teaching of Writing," *Phi Delta Kappan* 61: 276–279, October 1979. (Footnote references are omitted.) By permission. © 1979, Phi Delta Kappa, Inc.
Read also Ronald Berman, *The Literacy of Ideas*, New York: New American Library, 1980.

try to work from the outside in. The most fundamental and effective way to improve compositional "decisions" about word choice, phrasing, sentence structure, and over-all organization is to clarify, enrich, and harmonize the thinking that predetermines the student's initial choices of these. We must never forget, no matter how much a technocratic mentality and an uncontrolled educational-industrial complex bully us the other way, that the heart of writing beats deep within a subjective inner life that, while neither audible nor visible at the time the most important action is occurring, governs all of those choices that a composition course tries belatedly to straighten out. . . .

If we concentrate our forces on fostering the highest development of inner speech, we shall automatically not only teach excellence in writing but lift other subjects along with it into a new learning integration, for the quality and qualities of inner speech determine and are determined by all mental activities.*

---

*EDITOR'S NOTE   In an article "Why Johnnie Can't Think" (*Change* magazine, Vol. 9, No. 9, 1977) Daniel Shanahan explains the relationship between writing and thinking:

> Writing is an unsettling and disconcerting task for most people. It forces them to think — something they have little confidence about doing — and this makes them self-conscious. . . . When we write we have no eye contact, no body language, no sound, nothing. Faced with silence, the expectant paper, and our own thoughts, we are suddenly forced to listen to ourselves and to be good critical judges of what we say. In other words, writing is thought speech, and since most of us feel at some level that our faculties of thought — let alone our writing skills — are not what they should be, we become self-conscious when we pick up a pen and must listen to ourselves think.

5.12   Some Principles of Self-Education
MAURICE GIBBONS AND OTHERS

[After careful study of the lives of over 450 famous self-educated people in all walks of life, we come to the following principles of self-education:]

1. In self-education the locus of control is in the self-educator whereas in formal education the locus of control is in institutions, their representatives, or their prescriptions. *Teaching for self-education involves helping students to internalize control over their own learning.* . . .

. . . .

6. Self-educators tend to settle on the particular field in which their interests, talents, past experiences, and opportunities are combined. *Teaching for self-education involves patterns of exploration which enable students to try out a wide range of fields of activity.* . . .

. . . .

Excerpts from "Toward a Theory of Self-Directed Learning: A Study of Experts Without Formal Training," by Maurice Gibbons and others (Simon Frazer University, Burnaby, British Columbia, Canada), *Journal of Humanistic Psychology* 20: 41-56, Spring 1980. (Bibliography is omitted.) By permission.

We place this brief excerpt (which will be included in a forthcoming book on *Self-Education*) in Chapter 5 because its conclusions are *not* based on statistical correlations or on quantitative measurements of any kind, but are based on biographies. For brevity's sake, we include only five of the original fourteen principles.

8. Self-education involves the development of attributes traditionally associated with people of character: integrity, self-discipline, perseverance, industriousness, altruism, sensitivity to others, and strong guiding principles. *Teaching for self-education should promote, model, and reward the development of personal integrity rather than the opportunistic pursuit of offered rewards, of self-discipline rather than obedience, of inner drive rather than the avoidance of punishment or the pursuit of artificial rewards, of caring rather than sustained competition and of strong internalized principles rather than externally imposed rules. . . .*

. . . .

12. Self-education is best cultivated in a warm, supportive, coherent environment in which people generally are active and there is a close relationship with at least one other person. *Teaching for self-education involves creating an active environment in which a student's self-directed activities are warmly supported and there are many opportunities to form close working relationships. . . .*

. . . .

14. . . . . *Teaching for self-education involves helping each student to become an expert, a participant, and a person.*

5.13 Two Ways to Cultivate Great Minds
GILBERT HIGHET

We can never tell how great minds arise, and it is very hard to tell how to detect and encourage them when they do appear. But we do know two methods of feeding them as they grow.

One is to give them constant challenge and stimulus. Put problems before them. Make things difficult for them. They need to think. Produce things for them to think about and question their thinking at every stage. They are inventive and original. Propose experiments for them. Tell them to discover what is hidden.

The second method is to bring them into contact with other eminent minds. It is not enough, not nearly enough, for a clever boy or girl to meet his fellows and his teachers and his parents. He or she must meet men and women of real and undeniable distinction. [They must be privileged to] . . . meet the immortals. . . .

The life of every teacher is partly dedicated to discovering and encouraging those few powerful minds who will influence our future, and the secret of education is never to forget the possibility of greatness.

Brief excerpts from Gilbert Highet, *Man's Unconquerable Mind* (New York: Columbia University Press, 1960), pp. 40-45, 75-76.

Groucho Marx said he once resigned from a club immediately after being elected to membership. Why? Because, he reasoned, any club which would accept *him* as a member was a club that wasn't worth joining.

Many children feel the same way about the clubs we call schools. For children realize that they are immature, and they "join the club" (that is, willingly go to school) only if they are fully aware that its primary goal is, not merely to accept them as they *are*, but to discipline and cultivate their *potential* thought and behavior.

Gilbert Highet's remarks are concerned with this problem.

5.14   Quotations for Further Thought and Discussion

(A)   The term *disadvantaged youth* has been a disaster . . . because it has permitted school systems to stereotype students who are suffering from multiple and varied learning problems and treat them as if their problems were homogeneous. You cannot seriously hope to achieve success when you group together students who have low verbal intelligence, students who speak English as a second language, students who suffer from malnutrition, and students who have not learned to read well; label them as if their problems were one and the same; and give them identical educational treatment. . . .

These students don't need labels; they need teaching. They need a teacher with enough knowledge and skill to diagnose their learning problems and help them overcome those problems.

We don't need any more special programs for disadvantaged youth. We need programs to help bilingual students develop greater skill in standard English. We need programs to help those with specific reading problems, and we need programs to help those with specific arithmetic problems. It is time to stop labeling students and start teaching them.
— Robert A. Schultheis, "Time to Stop Labeling and Start Teaching," *American Vocational Journal* 50: 53–57, October 1975; condensed in *Education Digest,* January 1976. Read also "Handicapped — According to Whom?" by Rachel M. Lauer, *The Humanist* 41: 16–17, November/December 1980.

(B)   Open education . . . is not a place where anything goes. Rules are established and the teacher must uphold them and see that each student is able to move, explore, and choose freely. Although the teacher has final responsibility for making decisions and handling discipline, the atmosphere of mutual trust leads to an individual and group responsibility. The teacher has to plan a variety of programs, sometimes one for each student, and then be flexible enough to change plans on the spot with a changing situation. The teacher will give information when it is needed to an individual student, a small group of students, or the total class. The teacher is basically a stimulator, guide, and evaluator. . . .

Evaluation is a major area of concern for proponents of open education. Most feel that objective achievement measures are inappropriate and many have a negative effect on learning. Evaluation should be in terms of each student's progress. Observation of the student's interaction with materials and people and what he produces should be the basis for the evaluation and it should cover a long range of time. It is subjective in nature.
— James W. Bell, "Open Education: Are High Schools Buying It?" *Clearing House* 48: 332–338, February 1974.

(C)   The Principles Outstanding Principals Stand For:

1. The unshakable belief that every child can learn. The school must be held responsible if the youngster has not acquired the basic skills or gone beyond the three R's. In educator Allan Glatthorn's words, learning is "a journey, not a destination," which requires "questioning the answers" as well as "answering the questions."
2. The belief that teachers and principals must be life-long learners. If the faculty is not learning, it is the principal who must do a better job of teaching his teachers, and constantly learning himself.
3. The belief that people must always come before paper work. A distressed student, a troubled teacher, an anxious parent should take priority in the life of a principal.
4. The conviction that school must be an encouraging, supportive place, where people feel free to take risks, knowing that they won't be ridiculed if they are wrong and that they will

be respected for trying. Without this kind of atmosphere, all else fails. With it, everything is possible.

> — From *Ladies Home Journal*, October 1974, and from the *NASSP Bulletin* 59: 45, March 1975.

(D)   [In 1948 Clyde Kuckhokn and Henry Murray affirmed what has since become an axiom among anthropologists:] "Everyone is in certain respects (a) like all other men, (b) like some other men, and (c) like no other man." These observations can be used as a point of departure from which to show how early prodigious achievement is (a) like all other developmental phenomena, (b) like some other developmental phenomena, and (c) like no other developmental phenomenon. . . . We must face the fact that perhaps as many as a fifth of our nation's children are bored and frustrated in classrooms where their gifts, talents and needs are ignored. The child from the educationally and/or economically deprived background may be the most overlooked. If children can be viewed as our nation's greatest natural resource, we should not ask if we can afford special programs for the gifted student, but rather if we can afford not to provide them. . . .

During the past two decades much attention has been given to handicapped children, but almost none to the gifted or the talented. Of the five states which had programs for the gifted, relative expenditures in 1970 were as follows: The excess cost, over and above the normal cost of schooling, ranged from $92 per child for the intellectually gifted to $1,729 per child for the physically and multiply handicapped. Of all exceptional children, the programs for the gifted cost the least, but these costs are often enough above the average to be significant in hindering the development of special programs.

> — From *The Gifted and the Talented: Their Education and Development: The Seventy-Eighth Yearbook of the National Society for the Study of Education*, Part I, edited by A. Harry Passow (University of Chicago Press, 1979), pp. 42, 126, 344. Read also Dorothy Sisk and Ken Bilerly, "Every Child in a Gifted Program," *Instructor* 88: 84-92, April 1979.

(E)   We must face up to the idea that the intellectual human resources of any nation are finite; that not more than a third of the individuals in any age group can be educated for intellectual work; that from this segment of the population come nearly all of our scientists, scholars, lawyers, teachers, writers, inventors, artists, musicians, etc.; that individuals from the top third contribute to civilization out of all proportion to their number; that manpower shortages have developed in almost every professional and technical field; and that these shortages are a real danger to our way of life. Our great concern for the proper education of high-ability youth stems from the critical need for conserving human talent and resources.

> — Robert G. Andree and Morris Meister, "What Are Some Promising Programs for Gifted Students?" *National Association of Secondary School Principals Bulletin*, April 1954, p. 314.

(F)   [The heritage of mankind is tremendously large and complex, and it can hardly be overemphasized how much there is for each oncoming generation to learn. Yet by himself alone, no individual would be able to acquire such knowledge, or to become even reasonably aware of his own rightful heritage.]

Without the guiding patterns of human culture, man's intellectual life would be but the buzzing, blooming confusion that William James called it; cognition in man depends upon the existence of objective, external symbolic models of reality in a way no ape's does. Emotionally, the case is the same. Without the guidance of the public images of sentiment found in ritual, myth, and art we would, quite literally, not know how to feel. Like the expanded forebrain itself, ideas and emotions are cultural artifacts in man.

What this heralds, I think, is a fundamental revision in the theory of culture itself. We are going, in the next few decades, to look at culture patterns less and less in terms of the way in which they constrain human nature, and more and more in the way in which, for better or for worse, they actualize it; less and less as an accumulation of ingenious devices to extend preexisting innate capacities, and more and more as part and parcel of those capacities themselves; less and less as a superorganic cake of custom, and more and more as, in a vivid phrase of the late Clyde Kluckhohn's, designs for living. Man is the only living animal who needs such designs for he is the only living animal whose evolutionary history has been such that his physical being has been significantly shaped by their existence and is, therefore, irrevocably predicated upon them. As the full import of this fact becomes recognized, the tension between the view of man as but a talented animal and the view of him as an unaccountably unique one should evaporate, along with the theoretical misconceptions which gave rise to it.

— Clifford Geertz, "The Transition to Humanity," in *Horizons of Anthropology,* edited by Sol Tax (Chicago: Aldine, 1960, 1973), p. 47.

Chapter 6. EDUCATION FOR WORK AND FOR LEISURE

6.1 Introduction: Three Stages in the Reduction of Educational Inequality
HAROLD R. BOWEN

Historical changes in educational attainment may be viewed in three stages. The first was typified by the American frontier where differences in education were small because almost no one had much. The range, with few exceptions, was from illiteracy to fourth grade. There were differences, of course, in other aspects of socioeconomic background and in what was learned through experience. But differences in formal education on the whole were quite small.

The second stage, through which we are now passing, has been a period in which differences in educational level have become very great. The adult population now ranges from illiterates and recent immigrants with limited educational backgrounds to persons with PhDs, and there are many people at every intermediate level. During this second stage the whole population has not been advancing together in educational level, one grade at a time. While the educational level of young people has been increasing rapidly, that of older people has not changed much, and the educational progress of some groups of young people has been much more rapid than that of others, the difference being largely related to differences in socioeconomic background. The result is a very unequal distribution of educational attainment.

In the third stage, which we are now slowly approaching, virtually the entire population will have completed several years of high school; one half to two thirds will have attended college; and perhaps 10 percent will have obtained some postbaccalaureate study. At this third stage, the differences in educational level can be expected to diminish because nearly everyone will have achieved considerable education.

These changes in the distribution of educational attainment may be illustrated in the following table showing estimated percentages of the adult population by education levels at various historic stages:

	Grade School: 0 to 8th grade	High School: 9th to 12th grade	College: 13th grade or above	Total
Stage I, 1825 (hypothetical)	95%	4%	1%	100%
Stage II, 1975 (actual)	23%	53%	24%	100%
Stage III, 2025 (projected)	3%	37%	60%	100%

Concluding portion of an article by Harold R. Bowen (Claremont University, California), "Higher Education and Human Equality," in *The Third Century: 26 Prominent Americans Speculate on the Educational Future* (New Rochelle, N.Y.: Change Magazine Press, 1977), pp. 90–97. Reprinted with permission from Change Magazine Press. Copyrighted by the Council on Learning (Change Magazine Press).

As shown in the table, educational attainment was distributed quite equally at Stage I in that most of the population had very little of it. It will again be distributed quite equally at Stage III when virtually all the population will have a great deal of it. But at present, in transitional Stage II, differences in educational level are very great (perhaps just past the maximum). The process of moving large numbers from lower levels of education to higher levels of education can only be accomplished over several generations. One of the costs of going through Stage II is a widening of educational differences and a concomitant widening of differences in social position. Little wonder that inequality is today a major social issue.

It may be imagined that the transitional process will go on indefinitely as more people seek advanced education. But this trend is limited by the fact that formal education, like other kinds of resource use, is subject to diminishing returns. As one's educational level rises, the incremental gains in desirable abilities and traits diminish. This is reflected in the fact that additions to income, power, privilege, and status diminish as education is lengthened. Studies of the economic return on education uniformly show that the return is greatest at the elementary level, next at the secondary level, next at the college level, and least at the higher levels. The reason for this is that people can scarcely function in an industrial society without the elementary rudiments of literacy and "numeracy." But at each subsequent stage of education the economic returns fall because cost rises, and the incremental benefits decline.

Diminishing returns also occur as a result of the extension of higher education to more people. As more people receive college education, the supply of persons available for the preferred positions in our society increases and the salaries and prestige from these positions tend to fall; correspondingly, the number of less-educated persons available for the less-desirable positions declines and their wages rise. For example, the earnings of coal miners and truck drivers may exceed those of teachers and junior bank officers. As a result, the relative economic gain from college diminishes. There is considerable evidence that the relative returns on investments in higher education have been declining in recent years.

As differences in educational levels within the population become narrower, the role of higher education as a credentialing and screening device for job placement will become less important. For example, if almost everyone were a high school graduate, and large numbers had college degrees, then these particular credentials would lose much of their significance for screening and specific qualifications related less closely to formal education would become more important. Also, if higher education were widened and deepened, it would yield less not only in income but also in power, privilege, and status.

The conclusion is that if higher education were extended to more people, inequality would be lessened. On the other hand, if the spread of higher education were to cease, as is often advocated on grounds that there are not enough jobs of the kind traditionally reserved for the college educated, then present differences in educational level and the present degree of inequality would be maintained, and the American dream of equality through education would have been effectively frustrated. To maintain the higher educational system at Stage II would simply perpetuate present inequality.

A common criticism of mass higher education is that only part of the population is qualified for higher learning. This, of course, is true. However, differences in scholastic aptitude are probably due in considerable part to socioeconomic background, which could be changed over time. Indeed, the percentage of the population with scholastic aptitude up to college standards has grown steadily throughout the twentieth century. I have heard informed guesses that if further progress could be made in improving the socioeconomic background of disadvantaged persons, perhaps 75 percent or more of the population would be qualified to do college work at reasonable standards.

The percentage of the population that may be considered educable at the college level will also depend on our conception of higher learning. That conception has been steadily broadening as we have moved from a classical education characteristic of the nineteenth century to an education that encompasses natural sciences, social studies, many interdisciplinary fields, and many professional and vocational areas. The conception has been broadening also as methods of instruction have been diversified to include various forms of independent study, self-paced learning, internships, experiential learning, and mechanized instruction, and as higher education has become increasingly available to older adults and to part-time students of all ages. There are possibilities of broadening the conception even further.

As I have pointed out, however, the present system of higher education is at transitional Stage II. One of its main tasks is to introduce millions of persons of widely varying backgrounds and cultural levels into higher education. As Stage III is approached, and, the general educational level of the population becomes higher and more equal, then the student population will again be more homogeneous, and the goals and standards of higher education can be less varied.

At the same time, the degree to which human equality can be approached will be determined in part by the range and variety of interests that are considered in measuring or judging differences among individuals. For example, if differences are measured in terms of a single criterion, such as income, differences will be very pronounced. But if other interests, such as scholarly learning, moral virtue, religious commitment, sociability, artistic talent, skill in handicrafts, a green thumb, civic participation, athletic ability, mechanical skill, and adventurous spirit, were all valued qualities in addition to income, then overall inequality would be greatly lessened. The greater the number of dimensions along which excellence is measured, the less the inequality.

If education were viewed as a way of serving people of widely different traits and abilities, of helping them to discover their talents and interests and values, and of helping them develop themselves along lines compatible with their varied interests, then education could be an instrument for widening the range of human expression and reducing inequality among persons. A pluralistic culture cannot encompass every interest and every temperament; society would simply lose its coherence and integrity. But the range of permitted interests need not be so narrow as to condemn large numbers of its people to the role of incompetents or second-class citizens or deviants. Higher education could be an instrument for broadening our notion of valued interests and thus of reducing the sense of social inequality. . . .

[If this third stage should come to pass, America would indeed become the learning society, the achieving society; and it would have brought to completion the historic aims of our schools, namely, to serve as portals] through which children of all classes would find equal opportunity [in their struggle for security, for self fulfillment, and for social position].

6.2   The Career Education Debate: Where the Differences Lie
STEPHEN P. HEYNEMAN

A basic tenet of Career Education is that every pupil should leave formal schooling with a skill that is salable.

To accomplish this is not easy, and the efficacy of Career Education is particularly suspect when salable skills are taken to include those provided through vocational education. According to Foster, adults rarely locate employment by the vocational skills they received in school. In fact, 50 percent of all Americans receive their first jobs through personal contacts. This leads Berg to conclude that there can be no such thing as a school-to-work "network," affected by the school.

Other critics say that the most practical skills are those that make the recipient adaptable to the widest variety of employment possibilities and to technical changes in occupations over time; and that this adaptability cannot be learned through metal shop, or plumbing, but through more exposure to language, mathematics, and science.

According to Barth, predicting the salability of vocational skills is less than 50 percent accurate. The costs of teachers, equipment, laboratories, about 40 percent more than mathematics or language, are so high that vocational investments, either for the individual or the society, are frequently negative. Bobrow says that this is particularly true because only a small fraction of jobs open to high school graduates require skills that cannot be learned in about three or four weeks. Moreover, knowing how to type, cut hair, keypunch, or weld a pipe does not create a demand for those skills. When protagonists meet, the debates proceed as follows:

Pro	Con
1. Unemployment occurs because of a mismatch of skill supply and demand.	Unemployment does not occur because of a mismatch of skill, but because of insufficient demand.
2. If only we had better information we could advise (plan) accurately.	We have been saying this for fifty years; countries that spend much more than we do on information do not advise accurately at all.
3. Other countries do much more than we do in the area of manpower prediction and planning.	Yes, and look at the trouble they have gotten themselves into because of it.

Excerpts from Stephen P. Heyneman (The World Bank, Washington, D.C.), "The Career Education Debate: Where the Differences Lie," *Teachers College Record* 80: 659–686, May 1979. (Footnote references are omitted.) By permission.

Pro	*Con*
4. Children of the poor, children in rural areas, and children of less-educated parents all need special help in deciding career options.	Children and parents show remarkable awareness of their own interests and the market factors affecting them; it is efforts to influence them that, in retrospect, appear naive.
5. Bringing schools closer to the work place and sponsoring cooperation between employers and school officials can iron out the difficulties in where to train and in what skills to supply.	Employers will not agree to pay for training not specific to their firm, for that would amount to self-taxation. Having schools teach highly specialized skills lays more burden on the taxpayer than the taxpayer receives in benefits.

[All parties agree that students learn best when the subjects they study are not only interesting in themselves, but are also recognized as relevant to real life. But then the question arises:] Must the school now find a clear connection between science, history, languages, math, and work in order to justify their place in a student's program? . . .

Career Educators argue that they are not motivated because their courses are not relevant to work; detractors argue that students are not motivated because of a lack of definitive priorities in what is required of them to learn. Sides divide as follows:

Pro	*Con*
1. Forcing children into school for longer amounts of time breeds resentments and boredom.	If children are resentful and bored it does not mean that too much is being asked of them; it means that not enough is being asked of them.
2. The traditional "bookish" way of teaching is not sufficient incentive for a classroom.	That there is something which every child should know is not to say that children should be taught in a way devoid of curiosity and self-motivation.
3. Students need to see the application of what is learned; then they will become excited and desire to learn more.	Correct. But to assume that "application" means "career" is incorrect.
4. Experiencing the world of work first-hand will assist minorities and other disadvantaged categories of children to define their goals carefully and realistically; it will help them to avoid occupational drift, and it will help them to achieve more. Thus, Career Education is *not* a tracking mechanism; in fact it works in the interest of minority children.	Not only are programs like Career Education not the solution, they are the cause of the problem. They dupe the less motivated into believing that all occupations and skills can be equally valuable. They approach youth from a position of career *neutrality* and occupational agnosticism. Consequently, Career Education does not provide an avenue in which the young are challenged to do what they do want to do.

If one agrees with the Career Educators, then making subjects career relevant is the answer to student boredom. If one takes the opposite view, then time spent on developing "career" awareness, "decision-making," or "exploration" is time spent away from endeavors with higher priority. In fact some might go so far as to suggest that a minimum level of achievement be maintained if a student wishes to engage in Career Education activities, just as participation in high school sports requires a B average. They believe that efforts spent on basic skills should be top priority; and Career Educators argue that Career Education is a part of learning basic skills. . . .

[For example, long before the advent of Career Education, English teachers were using] bulletin boards showing today's youth meeting today's problems through some aspect of English: What English department does not have current magazines, newspapers, films, film strips and AV equipment as signs of that real world? Which ones do not have course descriptions of the practical: Consumer English, Business English, Happenings in Language, Vocabulary Power, How to Win an Argument, Basic Composition, Vocational and Technical Writing? . . .

Teachers are particularly resentful of reform movements that do not recognize current efforts. This is particularly true in the case of Career Education. The differences between them:

Pro	*Con*
1. Career Education will make history and English meaningful.	There is nothing in Career Education that a good English teacher does not already do, in addition to other laudable techniques for making the subject meaningful.
2. No subject should be taught if the teacher cannot explain why it is important for a student to know.	True. And this always has been true. But there are many reasons to know history. "Career" is one reason, and perhaps a very small one.
3. Career Education will improve teaching because it will provide a rationale for re-training teachers.	There have always been schemes for re-training teachers; some have been helpful, others not. Improving the quality of teaching is not the monopoly of Career Education.
4. Career Education will expose teachers to the meaning of work.	Teachers know full well what work is and find it insulting to have anyone suggest otherwise.
5. Career Education will inform all teachers about employment requirements in their local community.	Physics teachers need not know any more about employment opportunities than should employers about how to do well in physics class.
6. Career Education will bring the world of the classroom closer to the world of reality.	The classroom is a real world. It involves work; it is relevant; it is useful. It needs no further justification to make it meaningful, nor does it need representatives of work outside of school to produce good teaching. . . .

SUMMARY

Rarely has support for an educational movement been universal, and it would be naive to expect Career Education to generate universal support. The question is whether the misgivings of its detractors carry sufficient weight to prevent future investment, and so prevent a waste of resources.

6.3   Where Vocationalists Go Wrong
JAMES O'TOOLE

[It] is easy to demonstrate that work affects education, and education affects work. And that is enough for America's educators. They have used this particle of truth as a springboard to take a prodigious leap of logic: Ergo, they conclude, we must *improve* the fit between education and work. This goal is pursued in many and various ways, including career education in the elementary schools, vocational education in the high schools, professional education in undergraduate colleges, and dozens of "nontraditional" efforts to import work-place concerns into classrooms at all levels. Since none of these activities have worked terribly well, educators far and near are now intensifying their efforts. "We *will* make education relevant for work," educators are saying with Germanic resolve.

But how? Vocationalism has a long and unglorious history of failure. And the reasons for these well-documented failures are hardly addressed by increasing the commitment to do more of the same. After decades of trying, it still seems nearly impossible to train young people appropriately in schools and colleges for specific jobs because:

1. It is impossible to forecast labor-market demand more than a few months into the future. Thus, by the time schools can gear up to train anvil salesmen, all the available jobs in this field will be filled before the first A.A.'s in Anvils have their degrees.
2. There are tens of thousands of different types of jobs, and it is unclear which skills are needed to do most of these jobs successfully. Consequently, it is also unclear how schools should go about training people for most jobs. What, for example, is the proper academic curriculum for one who aspires to repair roofs?
3. Most skills needed in lower-level jobs are taught to workers on the job in a matter of a couple of weeks. Hence, students who will be looking for such jobs upon graduation do not require specific skills training in educational institutions. For such semiskilled jobs as roof repairing, a year's fully-paid apprenticeship will leave one an expert on every house cover from tiles to tar paper, while even eighteen years of unpaid formal education will leave one still falling off the roof. And most upper-level jobs that undeniably require specific skills training are at the graduate level where professional schools are already fully geared to the world of work.
4. Although there is a small, residual category of technical, nonprofessional jobs that *might* require some formal classroom training, this training is provided by proprietary schools. But, in fact, almost none of these licensed, nonprofessional jobs actually *require* any specific

Excerpts from a lecture by James O'Toole (University of Southern California), "Education is Education, and Work is Work — Shall Ever the Twain Meet?" delivered at Teachers College as part of the Spring 1979 series: "Education Tomorrow: Changes, Challenges and Conflicts," reprinted in *Teachers College Record* 81: 5–21, Fall 1979; and in *Education Tomorrow: Changes, Challenges and Conflicts*, edited by Frederick R. Brodzinski, New York: Columbia University Press, 1980. Used by permission.

training. For example, anybody with a decent high school education can learn almost all he needs to know about selling real estate by reading a single, short book. Phony educational qualifications for selling real estate are erected in some states solely as self-serving barriers to entry, not for the altruistic reason of "protecting consumers by insuring highly trained real estate agents." As far as I can tell, the only real value of real estate schools is as compensatory education for those who did not learn how to read well enough in high school or college to get through the how-to manual on the occupation. . . .

What must be recognized is that there has never been a problem of "fitting education to the world of work" during periods of labor shortages. During World War II, for example, minorities, youth, and women went productively to work on the nation's assembly lines *without* the benefit of vocational training. Clearly, then, the problems young people have had getting entry-level jobs during the last fifteen years have not been the result of lack of skills training in the schools. . . .

Somehow, amidst all the brouhaha about work relevance, the message has not gotten through to educators that the problems most people face at work are complex, interdependent, and above all have to do with working with people cooperatively and ethically. Most of the really tough problems that people encounter at work are not technical — the computer can be made to solve those. Indeed, the tough questions are not problems at all, if a problem is defined as having a single solution. For there are no solutions to the tough policy and organizational problems of work — there is only a spectrum of alternative responses, some more appropriate than others, but none that are simply either right or wrong. Significantly, it is problems of this nature that have deep precedents in the history of social affairs. It is such problems that a broadly educated, truly encultured worker is best equipped to handle. (For example, Mortimer Adler constantly amazes business leaders in his Aspen Executive Programs by demonstrating the "relevance" of Greek philosophy to their business problems. Adler, of course, would never use the word "relevance.")

If what I am claiming is right, it is a special shame that trans-disciplinary education is the revolution that never occurred in academia. A major reason why this once-heralded change never came about is that professors would themselves have to be broadly educated to teach such a curriculum. And most American educators have not been so prepared for over a quarter of a century.*

---

*EDITOR'S NOTE   Compare:

    The great majority of all jobs can be learned through practice by almost any literate person. The number of esoteric specialties "requiring" unusually extensive training or skill is relatively small. . . .

    It has been by the use of educational credentials that the lucrative professions have closed their ranks and upgraded their salaries; and it has been by imitation of their methods that other occupations have "professionalized." — Randall Collins, *The Credential Society: An Historical Sociology of Education and Stratification*, New York: Academic Press, 1979.

6.4   Careers, Competencies, and Liberal Education
H. BRADLEY SAGEN

If liberal arts programs accept, as one aim, the preparation of students for entry level positions appropriate to their level of educational attainment, such programs must also accept the fact that appropriate positions increasingly will demand at least moderate amounts of specialized knowledge and skills.

Finally, the current liberal arts transcript in most fields provides too little evidence of what the student can do that is of much interest to an employer. Liberal arts education must devise more effective ways for students to demonstrate and credential their competence in ways that potential employers will accept as valid predictors of effectiveness on the job.

SOME INITIAL PROPOSITIONS

Based upon an analysis of the current and projected labor market for college graduates and an examination of the adequacy of a liberal arts degree as preparation for that market, seven basic propositions appear to represent the conditions necessary for maintaining the liberal arts as a viable route to employment for large numbers of students.

The first proposition represents a fundamental guiding assumption: that liberal arts education will continue to constitute the most effective career preparation for significant numbers of students and that career preparation can be carried out without violating the traditional aims of the liberal arts. . . .

A second proposition is that career preparation must play a more significant role in liberal education. Career-oriented courses will occupy a greater portion of the typical student's program and choices among liberal arts majors and courses will be made with career preparation as one goal in mind. The difficult task will be to maintain the traditional aims so that future employment does not dominate the student's planning or the curriculum itself. . . .

Third, liberal arts education must become more competency oriented, although not necessarily more competency based as that term is now used. Development of generalized competencies should characterize both the general education and the academic major components of the curriculum. These competencies should include a wider array of cognitive skills than the skills currently emphasized in academic scholarship. More of the broad problem solving, decision making, and other intervention techniques of the several professions can and should be introduced in the liberal arts curriculum. Examples of such techniques include legal reasoning, operations research, engineering design, and assessment of human and group behavior.

Fourth, more emphasis must be placed upon the acquisition of the moderate amounts of specialized knowledge and expertise required to obtain an entry-level position appropriate to a baccalaureate degree. Students must gain some knowledge

From "Trends for the 80s." (Footnote references are omitted.) Excerpted from *Liberal Education*, Vol. 65, No. 2 (pp. 150–166). © 1979 Association of American Colleges. By permission.
  H. B. Sagen is Professor of Higher Education at the University of Iowa, and editor of *Liberal Education*.

of the economic system and of the nature of business and other organizations as well as competence in specialized functions such as marketing or finance. They must also acquire specialized tools such as accounting and technical writing skills which permit general abilities to be applied to specific occupational tasks. For this reason, professional knowledge and skills should be introduced in greater amounts into traditional liberal arts programs, and relationships between liberal arts and professional programs strengthened.

Fifth, competence, to be credible, must eventually be credentialed in work-related settings. The recommended emphasis upon competence is unlikely to have significant effect unless the generalized competencies promoted through the liberal arts can be validated in a range of occupational tasks. Internships will probably remain the most widely used method of demonstrating competence in work settings, but alternative methods of assessment should be developed.

The sixth proposition is perhaps the most complex and the most difficult to achieve. The proposition is that career-related competencies and specialized knowledge must be developed and credentialed at relatively high levels of intellectual functioning if students are to compete successfully for jobs appropriate to a baccalaureate degree. If the liberal arts experience is to continue as the dominant element in the curriculum, it follows that career preparation and the liberal arts must be integrated to a considerable degree and that the career elements must draw heavily upon the competencies developed in the liberal arts. . . .

A final basic proposition for successful career preparation is that effective programs require careful though not rigid career guidance and planning for the individual student. As the student progresses through the liberal arts degree, he or she should be aware of the career implications of each educational decision. Opportunities for career exploration through field experience and discussion should be offered early in the program and career advising must be linked with academic advising. Liberal arts programs should retain a high degree of flexibility to avoid locking the student into premature career choices. . . .

How effectively liberal arts institutions respond to the challenge of career preparation will determine in large measure the future of liberal learning. Capitulation to narrow specialization will deprive both the individual student and society of the humanizing influence of the liberal arts. Rejecting career preparation as a major goal, however, will result in desertion of the liberal arts by our most promising students who are striving to fulfill their potential as human beings through productive and meaningful careers. The challenge to educational leadership is to unite the liberal and the practical in a more effective pursuit of each as a worthy aim of human achievement.

6.5 Lifelong Learning
A. J. CROWLEY

[Lifelong learners may be described as:]

1. Highly skilled at locating information.
2. Highly effective in applying knowledge they already possess in a variety of situations.
3. Accustomed to setting their own objectives.
4. Efficient in evaluating their own learning.
5. More highly motivated to continue learning than is usually the case.
6. Possessing self concepts favourable to continual learning. . . .

Implications of lifelong education for teaching and learning methods and materials:

Organizational Aspect of Curriculum	Action Guidelines for Curriculum	Examples of Practices	Objectives
Vertical Integration	1. Future knowledge is presented as the outcome of present learning	Schoolwork includes study of post-school learning facilities	Pupils acquire self-image as continuing learners
	2. Knowledge is presented as subject to change	Organization of curriculum permits rapid and easy modification	Change produces positive motivation for further learning
Horizontal Integration	1. Learning is presented as a useful device for dealing with real life	Teaching aids, examples, etc., are taken from real life	Pupils are motivated to apply school learning to real life
	2. The non-school world is presented as a source of important learning	Some learning relevant to school occurs in out-of-school settings such as zoos, libraries, museums	Pupils regard learning in life as relevant to school

Brief excerpts from A. J. Crowley (University of Regina, Saskatchewan, Canada), "Some Guidelines for the Reform of School Curricula in the Perspective of Lifelong Learning," *International Review of Education* 24: 21–33, 1978. By permission.

Compare:

Richard Boles of career education fame has recently published a book about the three boxes of life. Almost all human activity falls within the categories of preparation or education, work, and play. These three constitute what we are about as human beings. Instead of blending and intermingling these activities we tend to segregate and sequentialize them. First, we go to school for twelve—sixteen—twenty years, then we work, and finally, we retire to the eternal playground, the nonending vacation, and wait to die.

Lifelong learning is the recognition that life is not a boxed affair. It means that education is regarded as an integral part of the texture of living and thus, like living, extends from birth to death. It is an affirmation that people learn at various times, in different places, at diverse paces. The role of the school or formal education institution remains significant but there is a new awareness of the educational roles of media, industry, on-the-job training, community agencies, libraries, and so forth. — Sister Ruth Dowd (Director, School of New Resources, New Rochelle, N.Y.), "The Challenge of Lifelong Learning, *Liberal Education* 65: 135–140, Summer 1979.

6.6   Language as a Vocational Subject
SYLVIA PORTER, S. FREDERICK STARR, AND OTHERS

It Will Pay You to Know a Second Language
SYLVIA PORTER

With a language skill added to your other skills, you might double your chances of getting the job you want. There are openings for an auto mechanic who also speaks Arabic; and electronic radio expert who knows Japanese, a chef (even woman chef) who understands French. It even could be [that] a foreign language would be more useful to you during the next ten years than a college diploma. . . . You should weigh the judgment of one executive: "A person who speaks two languages is worth two people." Language is, in fact, your hidden job insurance.

English Dethroned
S. FREDERICK STARR

The rise of English is one of the most striking developments of the modern world. In Shakespeare's day it was a minor tongue spoken only in the British Isles by fewer than six million people — scarcely a fraction of the numbers speaking French, German, Spanish, or Italian, not to mention numerous non-European languages. Today, the total stands at approximately 350 million throughout the world. Only Chinese surpasses English in the number of native speakers, but Chinese is far less standardized, its speakers far more concentrated geographically.

The expansion of English has been a remarkably recent phenomenon. As late as 1800 the number of English speakers still lagged behind the number who spoke most of the principal European and Asian languages. Since then, however, the growth has been astonishingly rapid; while the number of native speakers of Spanish has doubled, German trebled, and Russian multiplied by five, English has expanded by a factor of ten. Sociolinguists cite three factors to account for this. First, the British Empire carried the language to numerous shores where it had not previously been spoken. Second, the North American and Australian frontiers attracted millions of non-English speakers, who were quickly assimilated; and third, the early rise of medicine in the English-speaking world prolonged life expectancies for several generations without a corresponding diminution in the birth rates.

Whatever its causes, the expansion of English has changed the world. Not only are first-language speakers of English the second most numerous language group on

This selection is taken from three sources. The opening paragraph by Sylvia Porter, "Foreign Language Is Job Insurance for Future" is from her Field Newspapers Syndicated column, 1978, and is cited in the Seventy-Ninth Yearbook of the National Society for the Study of Education (NSSE) *Learning a Second Language*, (Chicago: University of Chicago Press, 1980), pp. 31–32.

The second portion is from S. Frederick Starr (Secretary of the Kennan Institute for Advanced Russian Studies in the Woodrow Wilson Center at Washington, D.C.), "English Dethroned." Reprinted with permission from *Change* Magazine; Vol. 10, No. 5 (May 1978). Copyright by the Council of Learning, 271 North Avenue, New Rochelle, New York 10801.

The third excerpt "The 'Scandal' in Language Training in the United States" is from the November 19, 1979 *U.S. News & World Report*, 87: 99, November 19, 1979. By permission.

earth, but the societies they have created far outrank those of other language groups with respect to practically any measure of wealth or modernization.

Beyond its numerical strength as a native language, in a large number of countries where English is not the mother tongue for the majority of the population it has been designated the official language or otherwise accorded a privileged position in public affairs. The inhabitants in nations where it has official status number over 700 million, approximately a third of the world's population. Granted that 550 million of these are in India, the countries where English is either an official or semiofficial language include such emerging powers as Nigeria, Pakistan, and the Philippines.

For the most part, of course, the strength of English as an official language is a direct legacy of the British Empire. . . . Of some 93 million secondary school students in the non-English-speaking world, excluding China, 71 million — 76 percent — are studying English. Now that English has supplanted Russian as the most studied foreign language in China, the gross figures must be revised substantially upward. English has also replaced Dutch in Indonesia, Spanish in the Philippines, and both German and French in the USSR.

A recent survey found that one out of four articles produced by French scientists is now written in English. . . .

This trend is directly reflected in publishing activity around the world. By 1967 one out of three books published in Asia and Africa appeared in English. A generation ago Russians denounced this phenomenon as a sinister plot by the Anglo-Saxon world. Today the USSR surpasses all other non-English-speaking countries except India in the number of English language titles it publishes. . . .

[However, communication is a two-way affair, and] it is hard to escape the conclusion that in coming years Americans will have far greater need to know foreign languages. Industry recognizes that this is so, even if educators do not. In 1974 *Business International* reported that 80 percent of the firms sending personnel abroad were providing opportunities for foreign language training. . . . [For when he is unable to speak his potential customer's language, however] cordial the conversation, to some extent the American will be an outsider to the other's world. . . .

More and more, Americans will find themselves in contact with persons who speak English as a second language, if at all. More and more, Americans will be seeking in such meetings to persuade the other party, or gain his consent to proposals advanced by the American side. As second-language speakers of English, most of these people will do their thinking in another language, maintain their closest fellowship and deepest allegiances through another language, and conduct their private lives in another language. . . .

Faced with changes in their competitive position and the rise of linguistic nationalism in many quarters, American businessmen are finding it useful to use local languages, even when their official counterparts have a nominal command of school English. English is, after all, principally a white-collar language outside of the English-speaking world. American interests abroad, whether economic, political, or cultural, are increasingly affected by developments originating beyond the white-collar elites. Corporate leaders with international contacts are coming to appreciate the implications of this situation, and educators would do well to follow suit.

We will not know precisely how greatly English will slip, and in what specific areas, until it actually happens. But we can scarcely afford to gamble on the outcome. Those Americans who very likely will function in a world of linguistic egalitarianism are already in school today. They should not be handicapped by a continuing neglect of their needs.

The "Scandal" in Language Training in the United States
U.S. NEWS & WORLD REPORT

America's status as a world leader is in jeopardy because so few of its citizens can speak a foreign language.

That conclusion was reported November 7 by the President's Commission on Foreign Language and International Studies, which spent a year assessing the nation's language skills.

"Americans' incompetence in foreign languages is nothing short of scandalous, and it is becoming worse," the commission said. Among its findings —

• Only 15 percent of students in public high schools in the U.S. study a foreign language, compared with 24 percent in 1965. Only 1 student in 20 takes French, German or Russian beyond the second year.

• Fewer than 900 U.S. business people working in Japan speak Japanese, while nearly 10,000 Japanese assigned to the U.S. are proficient in English.

• It is getting harder and harder to recruit foreign-service personnel with foreign-language skills.

At issue "Security." Incompetence in foreign languages, the commission found, has helped create a "dangerously inadequate understanding of world affairs" and has damaged U.S. economic and diplomatic influence. Asserted the experts: "Nothing less is at issue than the nation's security."

The commission, headed by former Cornell University President James A. Perkins, noted that educators have cut back foreign-language programs in recent years. The teaching of foreign tongues has "virtually disappeared" in elementary schools, the panel reported, and only 8 percent of U.S. colleges and universities now require a foreign language for admission, compared with 34 percent in 1966.

[The commission concluded its report by making several specific recommendations, namely, that more foreign language courses be available to students from kindergarten through twelfth grade; that larger cities build "international studies high schools" comparable to the special schools for music, art, and vocational subjects; and that special grants be allowed to college students who pursue a foreign language. The commission stated that the $200 to $300 million needed to implement the recommended programs would be a small price to pay for helping students "cope with the changing world."]*

---

*EDITOR'S NOTE   Language is only one of many types of *new* well-paying positions available to persons who are *well prepared.*

6.7   Economic Justice in an Era of Technological Change
EDITORIAL

Any social system may be viewed as an assemblage of statuses and roles. A *status* is a position in a social system. Each position (place, occupation) is associated with one or more roles. A *role* is a cluster of group obligations or functions which a member of the social group is expected to fulfill. For example, in the nursery rhyme

Rich man, poor man, beggar man, thief,
Doctor, lawyer, merchant, chief

the first line refers to four social roles based on wealth; and the second line refers to roles based on vocations. The same individual may have several roles: a doctor may be a surgeon, an executive of a hospital, a member of the school board, and a husband and father — or a wife and mother — in a family.

In all societies, careers are very important in establishing social status. "The Man With the Hoe" has less status than a workman driving a powerful tractor. A welder working 500 feet in the air to help build a skyscraper has more status than an unskilled laborer working on the ground below. Changes in economics (for example, producing cloth by looms instead of spinning wheels) result in changes in occupations, in family and community relationships, in politics, and even in language and religion. Such changes mean that traditional ideals of social justice and of human excellence must be restudied, reinterpreted, and reformulated in order to apply to our fast-changing world.

Justice demands fair treatment for all members of society — and, in the emerging world community, for all peoples of the world. But the attainment of justice is extremely difficult and complex because new and improved technologies put people out of work, thus depriving them of any useful role and of any social status. In the late 1920s, for example, when the "talkies" replaced silent movies, over 2,000,000 theater musicians lost their jobs; and many of them remained unemployed and became maladjusted for the rest of their lives. This is not an unusual event. Within less than a hundred years, prefabricated clothing, prepackaged foods, automatic washers and dryers, and 101 other timesaving and laborsaving devices have made it possible for tens of millions of women to join the labor force. Indeed, in 1980 more than 51 percent of the United States labor force consisted of women. These women do not merely wish to earn money; they also desire to find more meaningful roles for themselves in the community, and to help gain greater social status for their families.

As a result of many new inventions — and (let us be fair!) as a result of capitalistic investment — within less than a century the average work week has been reduced from over 70 hours to less than 40. Whether it be the man with the hoe replaced with a farmer using a horse-drawn plow, or a one-furrow plow being replaced by a seven-furrow tractor; whether it be hotel doormen replaced by electronic door-openers, or . . . — the list could go on and on — efficiency is the word for success. And we should not discredit it. Surely, it represents progress. Surely it is a positive gain.

But progress has its negative side. What are we to do for the millions who, being out of work — and even having no hope for finding meaningful work — become alienated outcasts? This problem is especially acute for blacks and native American Indians.

Thus, during the decade from 1965 to 1975 the average unemployment rate for whites was 7 percent, whereas that for blacks was over 15 percent. Over 40 percent of black teenagers between the ages of 16 and 19 years were unemployed in 1976, as compared to 18 percent for white teenagers. It is in this unemployed group that arrests for criminal offenses are greatest. Further, the probability of a black American being arrested for crime is more than three times greater than that of a white — and that of a native American Indian is almost ten times greater.

Nonacceptance often results in disillusionment, fear, hate, and crime. Far from being a land of hope and opportunity, where the downtrodden are able to rise "from rags to riches" and "from the log cabin to the White House," the nation seems to be merely the scene of ruthless competition, of a brutal power struggle between individuals and groups vying for wealth, power, and prestige — with no holds barred. For the alienated and the downtrodden, living in a society where power and wealth seem to be the be-all and end-all of life, it becomes difficult to distinguish between robbers and robber barons, between underground and Mafia organizations, and business and labor leaders who "pull strings", or even cripple the entire economy, in order to gain advantages for their own vested groups. Once a person can see no real difference between business profiteering and bureaucratic empire building on the one hand, and piracy, kidnapping, robbery, and hijacking on the other, "success at any price" becomes his slogan too — and crime becomes his only "solution."

Such societal problems are reflected in our schools in many ways, for example, in the alienated youth and the problems of school discipline discussed in Chapter 2. They are also reflected in the varied efforts of educators to make schooling more meaningful and relevant, to show the relation (if any!) of memorized book learning to the ever-changing occupations of modern industry. The need for such readjustments and adaptations is so great and so imminent that it is often called a crisis. But every crisis is also an opportunity. In this case it is an opportunity to remove the cleavages between labor and leisure, work and play, and the long "unproductive" waiting period of adolescence from the active productive life of adulthood.

Whereas selections 6.1-6.6 are mainly concerned with career education, selections 6.7-6.11 deal with the larger problems of unemployment, of democratic equality, and of social justice.

6.8 The Despair of Unemployment
SHARON FERGUSON

I want to ask my own question and then answer it. "What is it like to be unemployed?"

My brother is unemployed. He's 21 years old. He tries day in and day out to find a job. Every morning, he dresses up, shaves, and takes off. He goes anywhere and everywhere.

Excerpt from a letter from a reader of *Solidarity* (a publication of United Auto Workers). Reprinted from *UAW Solidarity*, November 11, 1977; also reprinted in *Moving On: Monthly Magazine of the New American*, September 1978, p. 4.

Sharon Ferguson's father is a UAW member at Pontiac Motors in Pontiac, Michigan.

When he gets home, he's either excited or depressed. It just depends on how many promises of employment he gets. Some days he comes home and cries like a baby. Or he'll crawl into a shell, not talking or eating. He'll just lay staring at the ceiling. Once in awhile he gets so short-tempered that he will yell at the boys or hit them. One day we found him in my parents' room, with a gun to his head. It was even loaded.

He was hired for full-time work, but when the emergency was over, they fired him. He enjoys machinery. There is a local sawmill here that's had four owners in five years. Everytime he goes up to find work, they'll hire him for a day or two; then, boom, he's fired. He'll come home angry and take it out on everyone else.

He makes all of us climb the walls with his moods. Everytime he's out of work, he's moody — and it changes from being in a shell to crying to being angry. But when he's working, he's always smiling or excited. He comes home and he has to tell us about his day.

Others who have a job sometimes forget the unemployed. And the bosses aren't willing to train people. My parents and I know how it is with my brother. We try to be patient with him. But how long does our government think we can hold up? He's an ogre when he's unemployed.

Every day we hear the same thing, "If you were a woman or black, you could have the job." Or "you're not trained." Or "there are plenty of jobs; you've just got to look." I believe the people who say these things are blind, deaf, or dumb.

I'm a 20-year old woman and I haven't a job. The one thing they ask is "Are you a libber?" No, I'd prefer to wait for a job until my brother has one first. I'm not in as bad a need as he is. Besides, I have parents. I keep telling my brother that some day his ship will come in and he'll have a job. He'll say, "It sunk, so shut up."

America is supposed to be the best and richest country. Then how come there's supposed to be jobs and there aren't? We don't even know what money is in our family. So you can add my brother and me to your unemployed list.

Thank you for your time. I didn't get into the unemployment scene as well as I wanted to in this letter, I failed to put in that children whose parents are selling everything to survive are afraid of being sold. Or that unemployed parents often take out anger on innocent children. Or that the unemployed often get depressed and commit suicide.*

---

*EDITOR'S NOTE Compare:
The drowning man in the river
answered the man on the bridge:
"I don't want to die,
    I'll lose my job in the molding room of
    the Malleable Iron and Castings Works."
And the living man on the bridge
hotfooted to the molding room foreman
of the Malleable Iron and Castings Works
and got a short answer:
"You're ten minutes late. The man who
    pushed that fellow off the bridge
    is already on the job."
— Carl Sandburg, *The People, Yes* (New York: Harcourt Brace Jovanovich, 1936, 1965), p. 74. Reprinted by permission.

6.9   Two Caustic Catechisms
AUGUST STRINDBERG AND FREDERICK DOUGLASS

A Catechism for Workers
AUGUST STRINDBERG

. . . *What is history?*
The story of the past, presented in a light favorable to the interests of the upper classes.

Suppose the light is unfavorable?
That is scandalous.

What is a scandal?
Anything offending the upper classes.

What is esthetics?
The art of praising or belittling works of art.

What works of art must be praised?
Those that glorify the upper classes.
Therefore Raphael and Michelangelo are the most famous artists, for they glorified the religious falsehoods of the upper classes. Shakespeare magnified kings, and Goethe magnified himself, the writer for the upper classes.

But how about other works of art?
There must not be others.

A Slave Catechism
FREDERICK DOUGLASS

Q: Who keeps the snakes and all bad things from hurting you?
A: God does.
Q: Who gave you a master and a mistress?
A: God gave them to me.
Q: Who says that you must obey them?
A: God says that I must.
Q: What book tells you these things?
A: The Bible.
Q: How does God do all his work?
A: He always does it right.
Q: Does God love to work?
A: Yes, God is always at work.
Q: Do the angels work?
A: Yes, they do what God tells them.
Q: Do they love to work?
A: Yes, they love to please God.
Q: What does God say about your work?
A: He that will not work shall not eat.
Q: Did Adam and Eve have to work?
A: Yes, they had to keep the garden.
Q: Was it hard to keep that garden?
A: No, it was very easy.
Q: What makes the crops so hard to grow now?
A: Sin makes it.

The Strindberg "catechism" was taken from *A Cry for Justice: An Anthology of the Literature of Social Protest*, edited by Upton Sinclair (1873–1968). New York: Lyle Stuart, rev. ed. 1963. August Strindberg, (1849–1913), was a Swedish dramatist — here protesting against the enslavement of workers.
"A Slave Catechism" by Frederick Douglass is from *From Freedom to Freedom: African Roots in American Soil* (Selected Readings based on Alex Haley's *Roots*), New York: Bantam Books, 1977.
These two "catechisms" should remind us how recently not only negro slaves but white workers as well have gained "emancipation." And the gains already made should encourage hope that further gains may be made in the future.

Q: What makes you lazy?
A: My wicked heart.
Q: How do you know your heart is wicked?
A: I feel it every day.

Q: Who teaches you so many wicked things?
A: The Devil.
Q: Must you let the Devil teach you?
A: No, I must not.

6.10   A Theory of Liberal Education
ELIZABETH STEINER

Thesis: Educology of the Oppressor: Education as a Means of Social Stratification

Every act of conquest implies a conqueror and someone or something which is conquered. The conqueror imposes his objectives on the vanquished, and makes of them his possession. He imposes his own contours on the vanquished . . . [and] reduces men to the status of things. . . . [To achieve this end,] the oppressors develop a series of methods precluding any presentation of the world as a problem and showing it rather as a fixed entity, as something given — something to which men, as mere spectators, must adapt.

It is necessary for the oppressors to approach the people in order, via subjugation, to keep them passive. This approximation, however, does not involve *being with* the people, or require true communication. It is accomplished by the oppressors' depositing myths indispensable to the preservation of the status quo: for example, the myth that the oppressive order is a "free society"; the myth that all men are free to work where they wish, that if they don't like their boss they can leave him and look for another job; the myth that this order respects human rights and is therefore worthy of esteem; the myth that anyone who is industrious can become an entrepreneur — worse yet, the myth that the street vendor is as much an entrepreneur as the owner of a large factory; . . . the myth of the heroism of the oppressor classes as defenders of "Western Christian civilization" against "materialist barbarism;" . . . the myth that the dominant elites, "recognizing their duties," promote the advancement of the people, so that the people, in a gesture of gratitude, should accept the words of the elites and be conformed to them; the myth that rebellion is a sin against God; the myth of private property as fundamental to personal human development (so long as oppressors are the only true human beings); the myth of the industriousness of the oppressors and the laziness and dishonesty of the oppressed, as well as the myth of the natural inferiority of the latter and the superiority of the former. . . .

[The *methods* of teaching, as well as the *content* of education, reflect the conqueror's

Adapted and greatly shortened from Elizabeth Steiner (Indiana University), "Educology of the Free: A Theory of Liberal Education," presented at the Philosophy of Education Society, San Francisco, April 1, 1980, and reprinted in the Philosophy of Education *Proceedings*, College of Education, University of Illinois, 1981. (Footnote references are omitted.) By permission.

This paper is structured around the Thesis-Antithesis-Synthesis dialectic of Hegel and Marx. The thesis is educology (that is, a theory of education) of the oppressor; the antithesis is educology of the oppressed; the synthesis is educology of the free. The net result is a theory of liberal education.

The Thesis and Antithesis are, in the main, summaries of *Pedagogy of the Oppressed* by the Brazilian educator Paulo Freire, pp. 58–75, 134–136; revised edition, 1972, pp. 27–68. Copyright © 1970 by the author. Used by permission of The Continuum Publishing Corporation.

mentality.] Narration (with the teacher as narrator) leads the students to memorize mechanically the narrated content. Worse yet, it turns them into "containers," into "receptacles" to be "filled" by the teacher. The more completely he fills the receptacles, the better a teacher he is. The more meekly the receptacles permit themselves to be filled, the better students they are.

Education thus becomes an act of depositing, in which the students are the depositories and the teacher is the depositor. Instead of communicating the teacher issues communiqués and makes deposits which the students patiently receive, memorize, and repeat. This is the "banking" concept of education, in which the scope of action allowed to the students extends only as far as receiving, filing, and storing the deposits. . . . ["Banking education" manifests] the following attitudes and practices, which mirror oppressive society as a whole:

   (a) the teacher teaches and the students are taught;
   (b) the teacher knows everything and the students know nothing;
   (c) the teacher thinks and the students are thought about;
   (d) the teacher talks and the students listen — meekly;
   (e) the teacher disciplines and the students are disciplined;
   (f) the teacher chooses and enforces his choice, and the students comply.

Antithesis: Educology of the Oppressed: Education as a Means Whereby the Oppressed May Gain Control of Society

Education of the oppressor — the thesis, above — attempts to control thinking and action, leads men to adjust to the world, inhibits their creative powers, and (by alienating men from their own decision-making) changes men from persons into things or objects.

In contrast, education of the oppressed (the antithesis) maintains that genuine education consists in acts of cognition, not transferrals of information. . . . Through dialogue, the teacher-of-the-students and the students-of-the-teacher cease to exist and a new term emerges: teacher-student with students-teachers. The teacher is no longer merely the-one-who-teaches, but one who is himself taught in dialogue with the students, who in turn while being taught also teach. They become jointly responsible for a process in which all grow.

In such education, the teacher-student and the students-teachers reflect simultaneously on themselves and the world without dichotomizing this reflection from action, and thus establish an authentic form of thought and action. For the essence of a dialogue consists in words, and to speak a true word is to transform the world: Through critical awareness, transformation of the world can occur.

Transformation is revolutionary too. The interests of the oppressors cannot be served, and so revolution is required. Indeed, the pedagogy of the oppressed is a task for radicals.

Synthesis: Freedom through Liberal Education

Friere's pedagory of the oppressor and of the oppressed recognizes only two viewpoints, those of the oppressor (sectarianism) and those of the oppressed (radicalization). The conservative is Freire's rightist sectarian who attempts to domesticate the present so that (he hopes) the future will reproduce this domesticated present. The radical, on the other hand, enters into reality to transform it and so fights at the side of the oppressed.

A synthesis between educology of the oppressor and educology of the oppressed requires recognition of yet a third category — a category we shall call "liberalism" or "liberal education" — a category which contains three elements of permanent value: liberty, individuality and intelligence.

Intelligence or rationality can be explicated by stating that subjective choosing ought to be objective. Kant set forth this principle as follows:

"Act only on the maxim whereby thou canst at the same time will that it should become a universal law." The method of intelligence requires that the beliefs we hold should be held for good reasons, i.e., reasons that would be compelling to other rational beings. Only on this basis can our reasons be recognized as fair and objective, rather than as partisan and subjective.

But freedom of choice involves not merely the intellect, but also the will: Only subjective choosing which is objective is also a will conditioning itself so as to be a good will. Kant's expression of this principle is known as the principle of autonomy: "So act that the will could at the same time regard itself as giving in its maxims universal laws."

Unless the will is conjoined with the intellect in the search for principles of behavior that apply equally to all men and women, the will cannot be said to be truly free. Rather it is a slave to inclination and to prejudice. Kant reemphasized this point in his third rule, which he called the principle of humanity: "So act as to treat humanity, whether in thine own person or that of any other, in every case as end withal, never as a means only."

This third principle establishes personhood as inviolability. It is this third principle which makes genuine dialogue — and genuine education — possible. Since a decision-maker is a subject (an end) and not an object (merely a means), and since objectivity implies other selves, individuality must be honored and a community of selves acknowledged.

But for the above three principles of liberalism to be viable, they must be given an interpretation that makes them relevant to our time. Consider *laissez faire* liberalism. Under this kind of liberalism, liberty was interpreted as free economic activity of individuals leading through competition to effective production of the socially needed commodities and services. But, as Dewey noted,

> . . . in identifying the extension of liberty in all its modes with extension of their particular brand of economic liberty, they completely failed to anticipate the bearing of private control of the means of production and distribution upon the effective liberty of the masses in industry as well as in cultural goods. An era of power possessed by the few took the place of the era of liberty for all envisaged by the liberals of the early nineteenth century.

No wonder that *laissez faire* liberalism is today's conservatism. For, under this kind of liberalism, the individual standpoint not the social is emphasized. For example, intelligence is seen, in Dewey's words, as ". . . an individualistic possession, at best enlarged by public discussion." To counter such an individualistic interpretation of liberalism, John Rawls has reformulated Kant's principles of justice into the following three summary statements:

General Conception: All social primary goods — liberty and opportunity, income and wealth, and the bases of self-respect — are to be distributed equally unless an unequal distribution of any or all of these goods is to the advantage of the least favored.

First Principle: Each person is to have an equal right to the most extensive total system of equal basic liberties compatible with a similar system of liberty for all.

Second Principle: Social and economic inequalities are to be arranged so that they are both: (a) to the greatest benefit of the least advantaged. . . . and (b) attached to offices and positions open to all under conditions of fair equality and opportunity.[1]

The above "Synthesis" by Kant, by Dewey, and by Rawls of principles of justice are in close accord with those expressed by Aristotle in Book I of his *Nicomachean Ethics*. For, like Aristotle, they recognize that happiness comes as a result of learning; hence, that liberal education signifies the guidance of one's rational development. John Cardinal Newman defined liberal education in Aristotelian terms when he wrote:

. . . Liberal Education, viewed in itself, is simply the cultivation of the intellect, as such, and its object is nothing more or less than intellectual excellence.

Such a notion of liberal education does not separate thought from action, as Freire believed — and as Marx implied in his famous statement that philosophers have hitherto tried to *understand* the world, whereas he seeks to *change* it. For, as Newman noted, a truly liberal education is also a useful one:

I say that a [liberally] cultivated intellect, because it is a good in itself, brings with it a power and a grace to every work and occupation which it undertakes, and enables us to be more useful, and to a greater number.

This view of liberal education was reaffirmed by Whitehead in a discussion of "wisdom":

. . . wisdom is the way knowledge is held. It concerns the handling of knowledge, its selection for the determination of relevant issues, its employment to add value to our immediate experience. This mastery of knowledge, which is wisdom, is the most intimate freedom available.

If we make knowledge subordinate to wisdom, then we may conclude as follows: The concept of liberal education evolves from

[*Thesis:*] cultivation of the intellects of Free Men for their enjoyment (educology of the oppressor)
    and
[*Antithesis:*] cultivation of the words of Slaves for their transformation of the world through revolution (educology of the oppressed)
    to

---

[1] John Rawls, *A Theory of Justice*, Cambridge, Mass.: Harvard University Press, 1971; excerpts from pages 60–62, 83 and 95, as formulated by R. Freeman Butts in "The Search for Purpose in American Education," *Today's Education* 65: 76–85, March-April 1976.

Compare: "A sense of justice is grounded in the mental operation by which a person puts himself in someone else's shoes." — Herbert Spiegelberg (Washington University, St. Louis) in *Mid-Twentieth Century American Philosophy*, Peter A. Bertossi, editor, New York: Humanities Press, 1974, p. 193.

For two excellent contrasts of Rawls' theory with two other theories of justice, read Ronald M. Dworkin (interviewed by B. Magee), "Three Concepts of Liberalism," *New Republic* 180: 41–49, April 1979. Read also Robert L. Heilbroner, review of *Schooling in Capitalist America* (1976) by Samuel Bowles and Herbert Gintis, *New York Review of Books* 23: 13–14, April 15, 1976.

[*Synthesis:*] cultivation of the social intelligence of human beings for their freedom (educology of the free).*

---

*EDITOR'S NOTE   Professor Steiner's thesis — or rather, her synthesis — is quite similar to one also affirmed by Jean Francois Revel:

> The optimum conditions for the realization of revolution are those in which the forces of change exist in an atmosphere of constitutional benevolence that allows them to make enormous progress without the necessity of provoking an actual civil war. In other words, the more that change is possible through legal means, the better the chances of [peaceful, and therefore lasting] revolution. — Jean Francois Revel, *Without Marx or Jesus* (New York: Doubleday, 1971), p. 185 (Translated from the French)

We agree with Albert Einstein in emphasizing the creative individual as the source of human progress:

> The real source of all technical progress is divine inquisitiveness and the instinct for play of the constructing and pondering researcher, and no less the constructive imagination of the technical inventor.
> They [technicians] not only ease the daily work of humans, but also make available the works of the finest thinkers and artists to the general public, whose enjoyment only a short time ago was a privilege of the great, and thus awaken the peoples from a sleepy stupor.

Even in a free society, care must be taken lest the clumsiness of bureaucracy overshadows the creativity of individuals. On this point Robert Coles has written:

> People such as myself who want government intervention in certain areas of life need to come to grips with the dangers of bureaucracy: Its impersonal manipulation of lives; its coldness, arrogance and insensitivity. I've seen poor families I've worked with who have been treated as rudely and inconsiderately and manipulatively by those who were supposed to be helping them as by those who were oppressing them. . . . Liberals and progressives have not given enough thought to the haunting dilemma that some of the programs and agencies they embrace to implement justice create new forms of injustice and callousness. — Robert Coles (Harvard University), in *U.S. News & World Report*, February 25, 1980.

6.11   QUOTATIONS FOR FURTHER THOUGHT AND DISCUSSION

(A)   That work shall be with man as long as man is mortal is a view we may well accept. That it follows from this that life should be organized into a Work Society is another matter. . . . "The benefits of leisure are ultimately the benefits of cultivating the free mind: creativeness, truth and freedom. They are benefits of which our nation and our civilization stand in constant and pressing need; nor are we conspicuous for their cultivation.
  — Sebastian de Grazia (1963)

(B)   Democracy has many meanings, but if it has a moral meaning, it is found in resolving that the supreme test of all political institutions *and* industrial arrangements shall be the contribution they make to the all-around growth of every member of society. . . .
  It is impossible for a highly industrialized society to attain a widespread excellence of mind when multitudes are excluded from occasion for the use of thought and emotion in their daily occupations. . . . We must wrest our general culture from an industrialized civilization; and this fact signifies that industry itself must become a primary educative and cultural force for those engaged in it.
  — Arthur G. Wirth, "Issues Affecting Education and Work in the Eighties: Industrial Democracy, A Historical Perspective," *Teachers College Record* 79: 55-63, September 1977.

(C)   The prison *cell* and the commercial *sell* explain much of the current *Hell* in our society.
  — Michael G. Cooke, in *Yale Review* 67: 166, Winter 1968. (Slightly adapted)

(D)   [The distinction between *intrinsic* and *extrinsic* educational values may be understood by considering] . . . two questions: What is good chemistry or history or literary criticism? What is good chemistry, history or literary criticism *good for?*

> — Harry S. Broudy, "The Brightest and the Best," *Phi Delta Kappan* 60: 640-644, May 1979.

(E)   A university is a center of independent thought. Since it is a center of independent thought, it is also a center of criticism. The freedom of the modern university in a democratic society is based not on the remnants of a medieval tradition but on the proposition that societies require centers of independent thought and criticism if they are to progress or even to survive.

> — Robert M. Hutchins, "The American Way of Life," *School and Society* 70: 130, 1949.

(F)   In England, there are "livery companies" still in existence that bear the names — but not the functions — of old occupations that were chartered and guilded by the king. How many of these occupations can a modern person even recognize or identify today?

Bowyers, Broderers, Cordwainers, Curriers, Farriers, Fletchers, Horners, Loriners, Mercers, Paviers, Poulters, Salters, Turners, Tylers, and Upholders, among others.

I can pick out no more than a half-dozen of the more obvious — but what did Horners do, or Paviers, or Broderers? What did Turners turn, and what did Upholders uphold? Hardly anyone knows any more. And so, soon, with the linotypist — not to mention the genially indispensable servant for a century — the Pullman car porter. . . .

Now, riding the crest of the automation and cybernetic revolution, we may expect many more ancient skills to become obsolescent, and people as young as their 40s to find that their occupations have been pulled out from under their feet. The early Luddites broke the new weaving-machines they felt would do them out of jobs, but nothing has been able to stop the steady march of technology.

> — Sydney J. Harris (1979).

(G)   In 1970, only 0.7 percent of women had salaries of $15,000 or over; with comparable salaries of $25,000 in 1978, only 0.8 percent were women.

Even if there are more women in visible positions, they have not necessarily got there at the expense of men. This can be seen particularly in the professions. Between 1970 and 1978, the number of women lawyers trebled, from 13,078 to 45,026, rising from 4.8 percent to 9.4 percent of that profession. Progress, of a sort. But in this period while 31,948 new women became lawyers, so did 174,592 new men. The same held in banking and financial management, where 119,702 new women joined the field, and so did 143,698 new men. Between 1970 and 1977 the women's proportion more than doubled among persons receiving medical degrees. However total medical enrollments also rose, adding 5,147 new places, of which 36 percent went to women and 64 percent to men.

In some fields women made net gains. In graduate studies as a whole, new entries by women (380,000) have not been matched by equal numbers of new men (160,000). The same happened with certain occupations, such as real estate and personnel relations. With women's admissions increasing at medical and business schools, and with total enrollments holding steady, the time will certainly arrive when women will start taking at least some men's places in the higher income levels. (Complaints have already been heard that employers are more likely to use white women for their affirmative action quotas than black men.)

> — from Andrew Hacker, review of several population studies, including *Employment and Earnings*, Vol. 26, No. 1 (U.S. Government Printing Office, 1979) (Table 23), *Digest of Education Statistics* (U.S. Government Printing Office, 1979), (Table 110) in *The New York Review* 27: 20-27, March 20, 1980.

(H)   Three themes have dominated the history of group child care and early childhood education in the United States: (1) child care as welfare, (2) early childhood education as socialized play, and (3) integration into the public schools as a necessary prerequisite for universalization. . . .

The welfare basis of child-care services has been pervasive. . . . [A major] issue, we believe, is whether the public is willing to subsidize child care at a level similar to its subsidization of public education without permitting the monolithic conditions that presently exist in public schooling, allowing instead for diverse delivery systems, a large range of choices, and sufficient information upon which to make choices.

— W. Norton Grubb and Marvin Lazerson, "Child Care, Government Financing, and the Public Schools," *School Reveiw* 86: 5-31, November 1977.

(I)   Although contemporary adaptations of basic values as they relate to children and family may not always coincide with traditional notions, people do seem to be reaffirming the existence of two perennial family-building truths: they do want children, and they do value them.

Parental love seems to be strong and is likely to remain an enduring trait in the American character. The survival of some kind of familiar community in the United States seems assured, despite statistics that are apparently antagonistic or detrimental to such community.

— Eulah C. Lauchs, in *The Center Magazine* 27: 20-27, March 20, 1980.

(J)   Marriage is a community consisting of a master, a mistress, and two slaves — making in all two.

— Ambrose Bierce

(K)   Modernity has produced a world of affluence and comfort unparalleled in human history; yet the very material abundance mankind has struggled for since the beginning of history seems to create new problems. Modernity has liberated human beings from the narrow confines of family, tribe, and tradition and this very liberation has brought with it new forms of loneliness and despair. Modernity has opened up a hitherto unimagined range of options, yet their very number has resulted in more confusion than happiness.

Nowhere is this more apparent than in the lives of some American women today, who seem to grow angrier and angrier the closer their demands for total liberation come to be fulfilled. The first step to liberation of any kind of women is indeed the modification of cultural barriers and social constraints. But once "liberated," women (and men) begin to discover something very unexpected — that meaning is not necessarily to be found out there in the public world. Rather, it may more likely be found in a private sphere that is somewhat protected from the turbulence of modern society. . . .

Unless and until the Women's Liberation movement in this country has grasped this fundamental fact, its advocates will continue to impose an empty rhetoric on a reality they fail to understand.

— Brigitte Berger (Professor of Sociology, Long Island University), "What Women Want," *Commentary* 69: 62-66, March 1979.

(L)   We in the United States have developed a pattern in which these two central human activities (work and child-bearing) are placed in conflict with each other.

— Urie Bronfenbrenner, in *Character* 2: 1-7, December 1980.

PART THREE

FRATERNITY

Laws are made that the stronger might not in all things have their way.
— Latin

If each sweeps before his own door, the whole street is clean.

Let each reform himself and not his neighbor.

Opinion in good men is but knowledge in the making. — John Milton

The love of liberty is the love of others; the love of power is the love of ourselves. — William Hazlett

President Lincoln defined democracy to be "government of the people, by the people, for the people." This is a sufficiently compact statement of it as a political arrangement. Theodore Parker said that "Democracy meant not 'I'm as good as you are,' but 'you're as good as I am.' " And this is the ethical conception of it, necessary as a complement to the other. — James Russell Lowell, Essay on "Democracy."

The mass media, with their cult of celebrity and their attempt to surround it with glamour and excitement, have made Americans a nation of fans, moviegoers. The media give substance to and thus intensify narcissistic dreams of fame and glory, encourage the common man to identify himself with the stars and to hate the 'herd,' and make it more and more difficult for him to accept the banality of everyday existence. . . .

To live for the moment is the prevailing passion — to live for yourself, not for your predecessors or posterity. We are fast losing the sense of historical continuity, the sense of belonging to a succession of generations originating in the past and stretching into the future. — from *The Culture of Narcissum* by Christopher Lasch, New York: Norton, 1979

EDITOR'S NOTE   *Reminder:* Chapter 3 may be conjoined with Chapters 7, 8, and 9.

Chapter 7.   SOME NONACADEMIC ASPECTS OF EDUCATION

7.1   Introduction: Two Cultures: The Instrumental and the Expressive
ROBERT STROM

I wish to propose a way for more teenagers to achieve identity, an alternative by which favorable self impression can be sustained during adult life even if one's employment is boring and routine. Let's begin by reminding ourselves that the school has two cultures — one expressive and the other instrumental.

The instrumental culture is made up of those activities that lead to the skills, knowledge, and values that are stated as goals of schooling. A student participates in the instrumental culture for the sake of obtaining or achieving something outside of and beyond the process of study and learning — to be promoted, to be praised by the family, to get a diploma, to become a doctor or an engineer. The school consists in part of a set of instrumental procedures that produce an individual who is a reader, mathematician, or master of a foreign language. On the other hand, the expressive culture at school includes those activities that students take part in for the sake of the activity itself rather than for some purpose beyond the activity. Intramural athletics, art, music and so on are all part of the expressive culture.

Although the expressive culture sometimes involves the learning of knowledge and skills, these outcomes are generally not as important as they are in the instrumental culture. Youngsters can enjoy singing in the chorus, working with clay, or playing volleyball without acquiring much knowledge or skill. The criterion of success is not so much how well they can do as it is how much they enjoy doing it. To be sure, the instrumental culture sometimes has expressive impact — for instance, when a student learns to enjoy reading or performing science experiments or doing algebra and will do these things for their own sake. Conversely, there is an instrumental undertone to most expressive activities. But students usually distinguish the expressive from the instrumental culture. Since most students can succeed in the expressive

Robert Strom (Arizona State University), "Work, Leisure and Identity," From THE HIGH SCHOOL JOURNAL, Volume 61, (393-401), May 1978. Copyright 1978 by the University of North Carolina Press. Reprinted by permission of the publisher. Compare Selection 4.5.
    This selection might have been placed in Part 2 on Equality, because it expands on a statement by Harold R. Bowen (see Selection 6.1): "The greater the number of dimensions along which excellence is measured [or judged], the less the inequality." But we place it here because, almost by definition, "the expressive" involves communication, and thus encourages Fraternity.

culture, where there is not such rigorous and explicit competition, it follows that this realm is especially good for teaching values. In this context some youngsters can learn to appreciate school, to become committed to learning, to value successful participation in the expressive as well as in the instrumental culture. Then, too, even the parents with little formal education can take part in the expressive aspects of school without embarrassment.

There are various combinations of success and failure in the expressive and instrumental cultures of the school. The social and intellectual development of a student depend on his or her particular combination of successes. A high level of success in both cultures is characteristic of the good student who also finds satisfaction as a social leader. A high instrumental/low expressive combination describes the bookworm who is socially invisible but does well at scholarly pursuits. A low instrumental/high expressive combination defines the mediocre student who still is able to obtain satisfaction at school because of participation in extracurricular activities. There are young people whose interest in athletics or band is the only incentive for staying in school. It is foolish to tell such persons that unless they maintain a "B" average on the instrumental side they can no longer take part in the expressive realm. Finally, a low instrumental/low expressive combination represents the students who can find no satisfaction or reward in the school. Often these youngsters decide to quit formal education as early as legally possible.

Through a creative use of the expressive culture, the school can become a place of satisfaction for more children, and it can teach certain values more effectively as well as improve performance within the instrumental culture. A dramatic illustration of these possiblities was recorded a few years ago in New York City. The setting was Junior High School 43, located in a slum section of Harlem. About 50% of the student body were Black, and nearly 40% were Puerto Rican. The most successful half from the entire school population of 1400 were selected to participate in the Higher Horizons project. These students had a median IQ of 95 and were, on the average, a year and a half below grade level in reading and mathematics. Instead of increasing the amount of time these students spent on math or reading by eliminating the so-called "frill" areas of education, an opposite approach was taken. That is, a number of motivating influences from the expressive culture were introduced to increase satisfaction with school and desire for learning. The boys and girls were brought to sporting events, concerts and movies. They went to parks and museums and on sightseeing trips.

Follow-up studies showed that the project members who entered senior high school graduated in substantially greater numbers than had those from the same junior high school in pre-project years. Furthermore, 168 of the graduates went on to an institution of higher education, compared with 47 from the three classes preceding the experiment. It seems that the expressive activities gave rise to some important value changes in the experimental group that in turn led to improved performance in the instrumental culture. Findings like these ought to cause more of us to take the extracurricular, the nonacademic, the expressive aspects of schooling far more seriously than we do. . . .

[In contemporary America work is often supposed to be the only avenue to self-identity and self-esteem. As a result, parents] who are anxious about the occupational futures of sons or daughters may not recognize the need for a balance of academic and expressive activities. Consequently, they often urge the school to reduce or give up expressive offerings. In turn, when teachers are held accountable for scholastic attainment only, other important aspects of a student's personal development are neglected. By encouraging all students to participate in the expressive culture for fun, we can help them develop self-esteem and avoid boredom.*

7.2   Bertrand Russell's Four Aims For Education
JOE PARK

The four universal characteristics which jointly constitute Russell's aim for education are vitality, courage, sensitiveness and intelligence.

VITALITY

"Vitality is rather a physiological than a mental characteristic; it is presumably always present where there is perfect health, but it tends to ebb with advancing years. . . . Where it exists, there is pleasure in feeling alive, quite apart from any specific pleasant circumstance. It heightens pleasures and diminishes pains. It makes it easy to take an interest in whatever occurs, and thus promotes objectivity, which is an essential of sanity. Human beings are prone to become absorbed in themselves, unable to be interested in what they see and hear or in anything outside their own skins. . . . Vitality promotes interest in the outside world; it also promotes the power of hard work." (E) "Consistent purpose (embodied mainly in work) is an indispensable condition of a happy life. . . . A too-powerful ego is a prison from which a man must escape if he is to enjoy the world to the full." (CH)

COURAGE

Russell has made courage his second aim of education and has defined it as the absence of irrational fear. He is convinced that all men and women can be so educated as to enable them to live without irrational fear. "What is wanted is a combination of

Adapted from Joe Park, *Bertrand Russell on Education*, Studies in Educational Theory of the John Dewey Society, No. 1. (Columbus: Ohio State University Press, 1963), pp. 97–121. Sentences in quote are from Russell's *On Education* (E) and *The Conquest of Happiness* (CH) (1930). By permission of the publisher.

Read also *Bertrand Russell, A. S. Neill, Homer Lane, W. H. Kilpatrick: Four Progressive Educators*, London and New York: Macmillan-Collier, 1967.

This selection briefly summarizes the four major purposes of education as understood by one of the great analytical minds of all times. Observe that only one of Bertrand Russell's four aims of education is amenable to I.Q. tests. Like many other selections in this anthology, especially in Chapters 7, 8 and 9, selection 7.2 deals only peripherally, if at all, with "what to do" problems. But "what's it all about" selections are also important, because they deal with the intellectual and cultural backgrounds of parents and of students which are often the cause of more specific problems.

self-respect with an impersonal outlook on life. To begin with self-respect: Some men live from within while others are mere mirrors of what is felt and said by their neighbors. The latter can never have true courage: They must have admiration, and are haunted by the fear of losing it . . . The highest courage [requires] . . . an impersonal outlook on life. There are certain things in human nature which take us beyond the Self without effort. The commonest of these is love. . . . Another is knowledge. . . . The perfection of courage is found in the man of many interests, who *feels* his ego to be but a small part of the world, not through despising himself, but through valuing much that is not himself. . . . " (E)

SENSITIVENESS

[Sensitiveness, the third of Russell's four universal characteristics,] is the corrective or counterbalance to mere courage. "An expansive and generous attitude towards other people, including all their natural qualities or traits, not only gives happiness to others, but is an immense source of happiness to its possessor. But such an attitude is scarcely possible to a man haunted by a sense of sin. . . . [because] Conscious self-denial is often a form of egoism, leaving a man self-absorbed and vividly aware of what he has sacrificed. To escape from the smallness of yourself, you must develop *genuine* interests — not merely simulated, or pretended interests, adopted merely as a medicine. . . . Whoever wishes to increase human happiness must wish to increase admiration and to diminish envy." (CH)

What he wished his teachers to have, and what he wanted them to develop in their students, was "reverence," which he defined as the feeling that there exists "in all that lives, but especially in human beings, and most of all in children, something sacred, indefinable, unlimited, something individual and strangely precious, the growing principle of life, an embodied fragment of the dumb striving world." (E)

"One of the great drawbacks to self-centered passions is that they afford so little variety to life. The man who loves only himself cannot, it is true, be accused of promiscuity in his affections, but he is bound in the end to suffer intolerable boredom from the invariable sameness of the object of his devotion. . . . The happy man is the man who lives objectively, who has free affections and wide interests, who secures his happiness through these interests and affections and through the fact that they, in turn, make him an object of interest and affection to many others. (CH)

"Such a man feels himself a citizen of the universe, enjoying freely the spectacle that it offers and the joys that it affords, untroubled by the thought of death because he feels himself not really separate from those who will come after him. It is in such profound instinctive union with the stream of life that the greatest joy is to be found." (CH)

INTELLIGENCE

[Intelligence is the last of Russell's four aims of education]. The instinctive foundation of the intellectual life is curiosity. . . . If curiosity is to be fruitful, there must be habits of observation, belief in the possibility of knowledge, patience, . . . industry and open-mindedness. . . .

"Nothing is more fatiguing nor, in the long run, more exasperating than the daily effort to believe things which daily become more incredible. To be done with such efforts is an indispensable condition of lasting happiness." (CH)

Russell opposes the control of education by the church on the grounds that the church tends to undermine and underestimate the intellectual virtues of toleration and impartiality, and so contributes liberally to prejudice, religious bigotry and bias. . . . [However] Russell does not think that science has dealt a death blow to beliefs in God and immortality, for they are such pleasant beliefs that people will wish to continue them. Also, he admits that he does not pretend to be able to prove that there is no God.

[As a supreme moral maxim, Russell proposed the following]: "Act so as to produce harmonious rather than discordant desires." [e.g., The desires of any one individual should, if possible, harmonize with desires of other individuals. The truths of science should harmonize with the teachings of ethics and religion.] Russell has concluded that the good life is one inspired by love and guided by knowledge. . . . Although both love and knowledge are necessary, in a sense love is more necessary and fundamental, since it is love that leads intelligent people to seek knowledge in order to discover how they may better help those whom they love. If people do not have knowledge, however, they may be content to believe what they have been told and may as a consequence do harm, in spite of a genuine spirit of love." (CH)*

---

*EDITOR'S NOTE   Russell lived to be 98 years old. His last major work was *The Autobiography of Bertrand Russell* (London: George Allen & Unwin, 1967–1971; Boston: Little, Brown, 1968, two volumes). The *Preface* to this work contains a summary of Russell's most mature views, and might be titled "What I have lived for."

Three passions, simple but overwhelmingly strong, have governed my life: the longing for love, the search for knowledge, and unbearable pity for the suffering of mankind. These passions, like great winds, have blown me hither and thither, in a wayward course, over a deep ocean of anguish, reaching to the very verge of despair.

I have sought love, first, because it brings ecstasy — ecstasy so great that I would often have sacrificed all the rest of life for a few hours of this joy. I have sought it, next, because it relieves loneliness — that terrible loneliness in which one shivering consciousness looks over the rim of the world into the cold unfathomable lifeless abyss. I have sought it, finally, because in the union of love I have seen, in a mystic miniature, the prefiguring vision of the heaven that saints and poets have imagined. This is what I sought, and though it might seem too good for human life, this is what — at last — I have found.

With equal passion I have sought knowledge. I have wished to understand the hearts of men. I have wished to know why the stars shine. And I have tried to apprehend the Pythagorean power by which number holds sway above the flux. A little of this, but not much, I have achieved.

Love and knowledge, so far as they were possible, led upward toward the heavens. But always pity brought me back to earth. Echoes of cries of pain reverberate in my heart. Children in famine, victims tortured by oppressors, helpless old people a hated burden to their sons, and the whole world of loneliness, poverty, and pain make a mockery of what human life should be. I long to alleviate the evil, but I cannot, and I too suffer.

This has been my life. I have found it worth living, and would gladly live it again if the chance were offered me.

7.3   Individualism, Collectivism, and Radical Educational Reform
ELIZABETH CAGAN

Suggesting the American notions of individualism may be at the heart of the failure of radical school reform, Elizabeth Cagan argues that educators must actively foster in children a collectivist character —one based on altruism, cooperation, and concern for the welfare of others. In support of this, she reviews a diverse body of literature ranging from observations of education in socialist nations to experimental research on cooperative behavior among children. Concluding that a moral commitment to collectivist ideals is the essence of radical reform, she offers a series of educational activities and methods designed both to reflect and to promote such ideals.

In the past decade we have witnessed the emergence of an impressive array of ideas and activities related to educational reform. Much of this is an outgrowth of the social criticism and activism of the 1960s and reflects a radical orientation at least in style and sympathy, if not more explicitly in ideology. Those who mobilized against an unresponsive and inequitable social system found schools a logical target, since education was so clearly a vehicle for the perpetuation of the very social institutions and relationships which were under criticism. Alternative schools sprang up, traditional pedagogical practices were challenged, and numerous programs for reschooling and deschooling society were offered.

Although the actual pedagogy in alternative schools has borrowed more from the writings of A. S. Neill and John Dewey than from those of Che Guevara, it was the latter whose pictures hung on the walls of many free-school classrooms. The Cuban and Chinese revolutions rekindled an interest in socialism as a viable alternative to corporate capitalism, particularly among those who rejected the Soviet model of a better society. However, the actual practice of education in China, Cuba, and other socialist nations has had a suprisingly limited impact on radical education in the United States. This is apparent in the strikingly different conceptions of character development held by radical reformers and by socialist educators. Schools in socialist societies place great emphasis on the development of collectivist values and behavior, whereas radical education reform has largely retained the individualism of American culture. . . .

Although the term "character development" is unfashionable, especially in the rhetoric of radical school reform, a radical pedagogy nevertheless implies that a particular kind of person is desirable — an individual who is nonauthoritarian, independent, and self-directed. How educators are to create such an individual is problematic since radicals have been reluctant to develop a pedagogy which deliberately shapes values and consciousness. The notion that adults have the right and responsibility to direct the moral or character development of young children is inimical to many radicals, who see this merely as the substitution of a different set of illegitimate adult constraints. A. S. Neill, for one, was quite adamant on this point: "I hold that moulding of the young mind is criminal, whether the moulding is moral or religious or political. Free education must allow a free mind."

Neill's sentiments are apparently rather widely shared among American radical

Brief excerpts from Elizabeth Cagan (Cleveland State University)" Individualism, Collectivism, and Radical Educational Reform," *Harvard Educational Review*: 48, 227-267, May 1978, (extract). (Footnote references are omitted.)

educators. Graubard comments, "Reacting against authoritarianism . . . some new-schools people took their affirmation of freedom to imply never interfering with children, never asserting values and priorities with the knowledge that one was quite possibly influencing the young people. . . . " The new liberated individual, then, is to be created simply by abandoning the old structures and constraints. The role of the educator is at times reduced to the simplistic formula of "rejecting the bad things, like *knowledge, authority,* and *structure* and accepting the good things, like *freedom, sharing* and *creativity."*

This extreme stance in favor of freedom and against authority has appealed to those who are thoroughly antagonistic toward existing social institutions and the authority relationships they rest upon. But it too often precludes any meaningful consideration of the kinds of values, consciousness, and behaviors which are necessary to create a new society. By sentimentalizing the concept of the natural development of the child, radical educational theory assumes that a new consciousness would develop with relatively little struggle or deliberate intervention. Ironically, activists and educators who would never accept a laissez-faire approach toward economic or social organization have embraced that concept for education. . . .

[There are exceptions to this. In *School in Capitalist America* (1976) Bowles and Gintis note the] dialectical relationship between the individual and community at the heart of Marxist theory. . . .

> Human development is not the simple "unfolding of innate humanity." Human potential is realized only through the confrontation of genetic constitution and social experience. Dogma consists precisely in suppressing one pole of a contradiction. The dogma of repressive education is the dogma of necessity which denies freedom. But we must avoid the alternative dogma of freedom which denies necessity. Indeed freedom and individuality arise only through a confrontation with necessity, and personal powers develop only when pitted against a recalcitrant reality. . . . Independence, creativity, individuality and physical prowess are, in this sense, developed in institutionalized settings, as are docility, subservience, conformity, and weakness. Differences must lie not in the presence or absence of authority, but in the type of authority relations governing activity.

Furthermore, an educational program that has as its goal humanistic interaction cannot ignore the relationship between schools and society. . . .

Radical school reformers must define their work as part of a larger political movement that seeks to change society as well as the schools. Pedagogical practices must derive from these long-range goals as well as from the desire to offer children the experience of freedom. . . .

[However, most radical educational reformers of the 1960s and 1970s seemed to believe that "the free and happy student," left to himself, would "naturally" develop into a cooperative, social, and morally responsible adult. At the same time, many of these same radicals paid homage to the educational systems of communist societies like Cuba or China. But they did not actually examine what was actually being done in those schools. Let us try to learn the truth about education in socialist and communist societies.]

My own research suggests, in fact, that [social, cooperative] behavior does not arise spontaneously, even in nurturant group settings, but rather must be deliberately

cultivated. Furthermore, to do so requires structures and adult interventions different from those that appear to enhance personal freedom. The focus on liberating
children from adult control that characterizes radical pedagogy may actually be
antithetical to preparing children for a more collective orientation. The goals of
freedom and personal liberation on the one hand, and social responsibility and
collective participation on the other, may appear contradictory, at least in the short
run.

We must consider, however, that true freedom and individuality are not necessarily
ensured or defined by the absence of constraints and controls. It is in the nature of
being human that we can grow and develop only in a social context, only by participating in a human community. This necessarily means the imposition of certain restric-
tions and demands on the individual by the community. However, such participation
also provides the preconditions necessary for self-actualization. . . . [For example:]

The absence of aggressiveness and restlessness in Chinese schools, which has
impressed American observers because it is in such contrast to the "normal" behavior
of young children in this country, appears related to this high degree of adult control
and direction. As a team of American child-development specialists visiting Chinese
schools suggests:

> The low incidence of anti-social behavior may be ascribable in part to the highly structured
> environment in which the children lived. More important, however, it seemed to us that the
> teachers were unusually alert and involved, and did not leave the children on their own for
> any length of time or with any great frequency. . . .

Sidel describes how Chinese nursery-school techers carefully encourage young
children to help each other:

> We were told repeatedly that if a child falls down, other children are taught to help him up.
> The teacher does not run to him but encourages the other children to go to him and help him.
> At the moment the child falls, the teacher says to the other children, "We have to help each
> other," and encourages them to do so right then. . . . In the winter the children wear jackets
> with buttons up the back; since they cannot reach their own buttons, they button each
> other's up; again they are encouraged to help each other.

Common to many of the moral lessons in socialist pedagogies is the idea that bad
conduct can be rectified. Children might display selfishness or meanness, but they can
be persuaded — not through punishment, bur rather by a combination of gentle
guidance, group pressure, and self-criticism — to mend their ways. Expectations for
children are very high, but forgiveness is always possible and rewards are forthcoming as long as the lesson is learned. In this description of a Vietnamese children's book,
we can note how these themes are conveyed:

> A nursery school child has been hitting other children. When "Uncle Ho" visits the school
> in the story and offers the children candy, the misbehaving child refuses. He has been
> naughty, he says, and does not deserve a reward. Ho Chi Minh commends him for his
> self-criticism, pats the child gently on the shoulder, and gives him his candy.

The use of "Uncle Ho" in this story illustrates the way in which socialist societies
encourage identification with exemplary figures. These typically are people who have
become popular cultural heroes and who serve as models of desirable conduct for
children and adults. . . .

Adults can have a significant impact on the development of moral autonomy and commitment in children, but they can do this only in an atmosphere of mutual respect and equality. If morality and social consciousness are treated as a set of catechisms to be recited and taken on faith, it is clear that children will not learn to use their critical faculties and that their moral sentiments will be shallow and easily manipulated. Adults have a responsibility for providing experiences that will encourage moral reasoning as well as moral concern, but this can be done only with an understanding of what is effective and why it is necessary. The basis for collectivist education is that we can use both the structure and the content of the educational experience to move children to an appreciation of the human bonds of sympathy and caring, and that we can build a vision of a society in which these bonds can be realized. . . .

[Our conclusion is that adults generally, and teachers especially, should organize] children into cooperative group activities, provide specific moral instruction, present themselves as models of humanistic interaction, encourage moral reasoning and committment and, more generally, establish a climate in which values of social responsiblity, caring, and respect are highlighted.

7.4 Plain Talk about Art in Basic Education
ROBERT J. SAUNDERS

Because art teachers — however unwittingly — often do ignore the intellectual activity of children, it is important that they do more than choose among the approaches to art lessons (*concepts, media, techniques, projects*). They must make provision in their lessons for what art-educator Viktor Lowenfeld and psychologist J. P. Guilford call criteria for creativity. These comprehend *sensitivity to problems, fluency, flexibility, originality, ability to redefine and rearrange, analysis, synthesis,* and *coherence of organization.* These talents or qualities have application to virtually all learning, of course, and call for explanation here.

Sensitivity to problems is the ability to recognize a problem before it becomes obvious or something dangerous happens, to forecast or prophesy, to empathize with feelings outside oneself. . . . When Johnny paints a starving child in a mural on world hunger, and Janie paints slaves working, they may begin to have empathy with starving and oppressed people.

Fluency is the ability to think of many solutions to a problem, many uses for a particular material or thing, and to provide alternative solutions in a short period of time. A teacher who asks students to make ten thumb-nail sketches for a design is saying "Solve this problem ten ways." And when a student makes cut-paper designs and moves shapes around for different arrangements before choosing the best one,

From Robert J. Saunders (Art Consultant, Connecticut State Department of Education), "Plain Talk about Art in Basic Education," in *Art in Basic Education: Two Papers,* by Jacques Barzun and Robert J. Saunders, Washington, D.C., Council for Basic Education, 1979.

Permission granted by Robert J. Saunders and the Council for Basic Education.

In the opening paragraph, the reference to Viktor Lowenfeld and J. P. Guilford may be found in *A Source Book for Creative Thinking,* edited by Sidney P. Parnes and Harold G. Harding, New York: Scribner's, 1962.

he is using the ability to try different ideas and delay decision. To be able to change directions in midstream is to be *flexible* — to use a mistake as the basis of a new idea, for example, or to change a plan that clearly is leading nowhere. Janie learns to be flexible when paint drops from her brush on a landscape painting and she turns the drops into flowers rather than destroy the picture. . . .

A student who can think of solutions and ideas not suggested by the teacher or copied from others has the talent called *originality*. Originality is often difficult to recognize because we never really know what students see or experience outside the classroom. The last idea of ten may be a student's most original simply because he had to think hardest to come up with the tenth. Like imagination, originality cannot come from nothing, but grows from many experiences. A teacher can encourage originality by not letting chilrden copy the pictures of others, but by expecting them to draw on resources within themselves. To *redefine and rearrange* is to find other meanings or solutions by rearranging various parts of a whole, or various factors and elements. When boys and girls rearrange wire or clay to change an elephant into a giraffe, or cut pictures from magazines to create a face montage, they are redefining those objects. In surrealistic art, where objects take on symbolic meanings, or when a student makes a sculpture or a print from found objects, he is learning to redefine and rearrange.

Analysis is a matter of noticing details, separating parts from the whole, identifying evidence inside contour outlines, extracting meaning from symbols in contrast to merely identifying objects and details. Johnny is analyzing a work of art when he looks for examples of the principles and elements of design. When tracing movement, finding repetitions and contrast of colors, textures, or shapes in a painting, he separates abstract concepts from the subject matter. Following a line of complex movement in a painting is not unlike following the route of a highway on a road map. Johnny uses analysis when he carves away in sculpting, or models in clay by forming the arms and legs from the whole. If the teacher asks him to draw something from memory, he activates his visual memory, an analytical process. On the other hand to put divergent parts together again, often with a new meaning, is to make a *synthesis*. Janie synthesizes when she works jig-saw puzzles (which also require visual analysis), makes a collage, mosaic, or montage. . . .

Coherence of organization has to do with giving order, unity, design and overall meaning to a statement, product or concept. The principles of design, such as balance, movement, emphasis, subordination, contrast, and repetition, are parts of coherence in a visual work of art. When students make designs using such factors, or analyze paintings according to such principles to determine its quality, they are finding a new sense of order.

In whatever art activity Johnny and Janie take part, they use one or more of these creative mental processes. . . .

Such programs are not, in my opinion, based on inflated notions about art; rather, they treat art as a basic learning process requiring hard work, discipline, and demonstrated achievement. In today's society, we can ask for nothing less. No person is truly educated unless he is also educated in art.

7.5   In Praise of Cognitive Emotions
ISRAEL SCHEFFLER

Rational Passions. The life of reason is one in which cognitive processes are organized in accord with controlling rational ideals and norms. Such organization involves characteristic patterns of thought, action, and evaluation comprising what may be called rational character. It also thus requires suitable emotional dispositions. It demands, for example, a love of truth and a contempt of lying, a concern for accuracy in observation and inference, and a corresponding repugnance of error in logic or fact. It demands revulsion at distortion, disgust at evasion, admiration of theoretical achievement, respect for the considered arguments of others. Failing such demands, we incur rational shame; fulfilling them makes for rational self-respect.

Like moral character, rational character requires that the right acts and judgments be habitual; it also requires that the right emotions be attached to the right acts and judgments. . . . [Indeed, we do not consider a person as morally or intellectually mature if he does not have feelings of guilt or uneasiness after doing a "bad" act, or if he does not have feelings of joy and inner satisfaction after performing a "good" deed.] The wonder is not that *rational* character is thus related to the emotions but that anyone should ever have supposed it to be an exception to the general rule. . . .

Perceptive Feelings . . . are also intimately tied to our vision of the external world. Indeed they help to construct that vision and to define the critical features of that world. . . . [For example, we may] describe a certain situation as *terrifying*, ascribing to it, *independently of our own state*, the capacity to arouse fear. Thus employing the emotions as parameters, we gain enormous new powers of fundamental description, while abstracting from actual conditions of feeling. . . .

Theoretical Imagination . . . [We come now] to the third role of emotions in the service of cognition, that of stimulus to the scientific imagination. This role is virtually annihilated by the stereotyped emotion-cognition dichotomy. For this dichotomy assigns all feeling and flair, all fantasy and fun, to the arts and humanities, conceiving the sciences as grim and humorless grind. The method of science is miserly caution — to gather the facts and guard the hoard. Imagination is a seductive distraction — a hindrance to serious scientific business.

This doctrine is, in fact, the death of theory. Theory is not reducible to mere fact-gathering, and theoretical creation is beyond the reach of any mechanical routine. Science controls theory by credibility, logic, and simplicity; it does not provide rules for the creation of theoretical ideas. Scientific objectivity demands allegiance to fair controls over theory, but fair controls cannot substitute for ideas. "All our thinking," said Albert Einstein, "is of this nature of a free play with concepts; the justification for this play lying in the measure of survey over the experience of the senses which we are able to achieve with its aid."

The ideal theorist, loyal to the demands of rational character and the institutions of

Brief excerpts from Israel Scheffler (Harvard University), "In Praise of Cognitive Emotions," *Teachers College Record* 79: 171-186, December 1977. (Footnote references are omitted.)

By permission of the author and *Teachers College Record.*

Even as Selection 7.4 shows the analytical, cognitive requirements of artistic creation, so Scheffler's article shows the emotional dimensions of scientific and intellectual achievement.

scientific objectivity, is not therefore passionless and prim. Theoretical inventiveness requires not caution but boldness, verve, speculative daring. Imagination is no hindrance but the very life of theory, without which there *is* no science.

Now the emotions relate to imaginative theorizing in a variety of ways. The emotional life, to begin with, is a rich source of substantive ideas. Drawing from the obscure wellsprings of this life, the mind's free play casts up novel patterns and images, exotic figures and analogies that, in an investigative context, may serve to place old facts in a new light. The dream of the nineteenth-century chemist F. A. Kekulé will provide a striking illustration. He had been trying for a long time to find a structural formula for the benzene molecule. Dozing in front of his fireplace one evening in 1865, he seemed, as he looked into the flames, "to see atoms dancing in snakelike arrays. Suddenly, one of the snakes formed a ring by seizing hold of its own tail and then whirled mockingly before him. Kekulé awoke in a flash: he had hit upon the now famous and familiar idea of representing the molecular structure of benzene by a hexagonal ring. He spent the rest of the night working out the consequences of this hypothesis."

The emotions serve not merely as a *source* of imaginative patterns; they fulfill also a *selective* function, facilitating choice among these patterns, defining their salient features, focusing attention accordingly. The patterns develop in imagination, that is, carry their own emotive values; these values guide selection and emphasis. They help imagined patterns to structure the phenomena, highlighting factual features of interest to further inquiry. "Passions," as Michael Polanyi has said, "charge objects with emotions, making them repulsive or attractive: . . . only a tiny fraction of all knowable facts are of interest to scientists, and scientific passion serves . . . as a guide in the assessment of what is of higher and what of lesser interest.

Finally, the emotions play a directive role in the process of *applying* the fruits of imagination to the solution of problems. The course of problem-solving, as has already been intimated, is continually monitored by the theorist's cues of feeling, his sense of excitement or anticipation, his elation or suspicion or gloom. Moreover, imagined objects encountered in thought by the problem-solver affect his deliberation emotively, as real objects do, and influence his decisions in analogous ways. "In thought as well as in overt action," says Dewey, "the objects experienced in following out a course of action attract, repel, satisfy, annoy, promote and retard. Thus deliberation proceeds." There is, no doubt, much yet to be learned about the interaction of emotions and imagination in all the ways I have sketched, and in others as well. It should, however, even now, be evident that creation is fed by the emotional life in the sphere of science no less than in the spheres of poetry and the arts.

COGNITIVE EMOTIONS

. . . . I want now to deal with two emotions that are, in a sense to be explained, *specifically cognitive* in their bearing — the *joy of verification* and the *feeling of surprise*. . . .

The Joy of Verification. In his well-known paper of 1934 on "The Foundation of Knowledge," Moritz Schlick . . . [gave great emphasis] to the joy that accompanies the fulfillment of an expectation . . . "With the confirmation of prediction the scientific goal is achieved: the joy in cognition is the joy of verification, the triumphant feeling of having guessed correctly." . . .

This joyful feeling [which we here call a] cognitive emotion . . . [results from the fact] that what has happened is what had, in fact, been predicted. . . . [And, of course, there are feelings of disappointment when we are mistaken — when the things we expect to occur do not occur.]

It is undeniable that our beliefs greatly influence our perceptions, but neither psychology nor philosphy offers any proof of a preestablished harmony between what we believe and what we see. Expectations have the function of orienting us selectively toward the future, but this function does not require that they blind us to the unforeseen. Indeed, the presumption of mismatch between experience and expectation underlies another cognitive emotion: *surprise*. The existence of this emotion testifies that we are not, in principle, beyond acknowledging the predictive failures of our own theories, that we are not debarred by nature from capitalizing upon such failures in order to learn from experience. The genius of science is, in fact, to institutionalize such learning by wedding the free theoretical imagination to the rigorous probing for predictive failures.

The Significance of Surprise. Suprise is a cognitive emotion, resting on the (epistemologically relevant) supposition that what has happened conflicts with prior expectation. Without such presumption, surprise cannot be supposed to occur, although the truth of the presumption may, of course, be questioned in particular cases. . . .

How we cope with surprise, once it is acknowledged, is of critical importance. Surpise may be dissipated and evaporate into lethargy. It may culminate in confusion or panic. It may be swiftly overcome by a redoubled dogmatism. Or it may be transformed into wonder or curiosity, and so become an educative occasion. Curiosity replaces the impact of surprise with the demand for explanation; it turns confusion into question. To answer the question is to reconstruct initial beliefs so that they may consistently incorporate what had earlier been unassimilable. It is to provide an improved framework of premises by which the surprising event might have been anticipated and for which parallel events will no longer surprise.

Critical inquiry in pursuit of explanation is a constructive outcome of surprise, transforming initial disorientation into motivated search. There is, as we have seen, no mechanical routine that guarantees success in the search for explanatory theory. Yet, an emotional value of each search is to offer mature consolation for the stress of surprise and the renunciation of inadequate beliefs. . . . Cognition is thus two-sided and has its own rhythm; it stabilizes and coordinates; it also unsettles and divides. It is responsible for shaping our patterned orientations to the future, but it must also be responsive to the insistent need to learn from the future. Establishing habits, it must stand ready to break them. Unlearning old ways of thought, it must also power the quest for new, and greater, expectations. These stringent demands upon our cognitive processes also constitute stringent demands upon our emotional capacities. The growth of cognition is thus, in fact, inseparable from the education of the emotions.

7.6 The Union of Cognitive and Noncognitive Learning (illustrated in some Jewish Fables, Parables, Legends, and Traditions)

(A)   Why Only One Adam? (Adapted from the Agada in the Talmud.)

Why did God create only one Adam and not many at a time?

He did this to demonstrate that one man in himself is an entire universe. Also He wished to teach mankind that he who kills one human being is as guilty as if he had destroyed the entire world. Similarly, he who saves the life of one single human being is as worthy as if he had saved all of humanity.

God created only one man so that people should not try to feel superior to one another and boast of their lineage in this wise: "I am descended from a more distinguished Adam than you."

He also did this so that the heathen should not be able to say that, since many men had been created at the same time, it was conclusive proof that there was more than one God.

Lastly, He did this in order to establish His own power and glory. When a maker of coins does his work he uses only one mould and all the coins emerge alike. But the King of Kings, blessed be His name, has created all mankind in the mould of Adam, and even so no man is identical to another. For this reason each person must respect himself and say with dignity:

"God created the world on my account. Therefore let me not lose eternal life because of some vain passion!"

(B)   Equal Justice

Rabbi Wolf of Zbaraz had a stern sense of justice. Far and wide he was famed as an incorruptible judge. One day, his own wife raised an outcry that her maid had stolen an object of great value. The servant, an orphan, tearfully denied the accusation.

"We will let the Rabbinical Court settle this!" said her mistress angrily.

When Rabbi Wolf saw his wife preparing to go to the Court he forthwith began putting on his Sabbath robe.

"Why do you do that?" she asked in surprise. "You know it is undignified for a man of your position to come to Court with me. I can very well plead my own case."

"I'm sure you can," answered the rabbi. "But who will plead the case of your maid, the poor orphan? I must see that full justice be done to her."

There are hundreds of excellent collections of folklore. We chose this one because we believe that folklore, legends, and long-standing traditions, no less than the Bible itself, have helped to unite the Jewish people, even though they live in all parts of the world. The first story "Why Only One Adam," illustrates the manner in which, over hundreds of years, a variety of meanings can be read into a story. Whether that story is fact or fiction, history or myth is of little consequence when compared to the *meanings* that are read into it.

Except for this first example, we leave it to the reader to decide what meaning or meanings the story contains. We wish to point out, however, that we should be able to derive inspiring meanings from the third story, "The Foresighted Father" without condoning the fact that, in ancient times, slavery was almost universally accepted as "moral."

(C)   The Foresighted Father (from the Midrash*)*

It chanced that a wealthy merchant, accompanied by his steward, a slave, left the Holy Land on a long ocean journey. Being a widower he left behind him only a son, who was pious and a student of Holy Lore.

On the way the merchant fell sick. At the point of death he made a will, leaving all his possessions to his steward. To his son he wrote that he could choose one thing only among all his possessions.

After the merchant's death the steward-slave took all his money and the will and returned to the land of Israel. He told his master's son, "Your father is dead. He has left a will bequeathing his entire fortune to me. He allows you, however, to choose any one thing from all his possessions."

When he heard the words of his father's slave the orphaned son was sorely troubled. He went to the rabbi and told him all that had happened. The rabbi then said to him, "Your father was a sage and had great foresight. I believe he must have thought to himself: 'If I leave my fortune to my son, my slave, as the steward, will pilfer it. Far better that I make the slave my heir. In that case he will guard it as the apple of his eye. Therefore, it will be enough for my son if he chooses but one of my possessions.'

"My advice to you," concluded the rabbi, "is that when you go to the judges and the slave shows them the will, you must say to them, 'My father has stipulated that I can choose only one thing from his possessions. I therefore choose this slave.'

"Rest certain," continued the rabbi, "that if your slave belongs to you, all the wealth he has inherited from your father is also yours."

The orphan son did as the rabbi told him. Consequently, he came into all of his father's possessions, for the law is that whatever a slave owns belongs to his master.

(D)   The Poor Are Willing

The rabbi had prayed long and fervently.

"And what have you prayed for today?" asked his wife.

"My prayer is that the rich should give bigger alms to the poor," answered the rabbi.

"Do you think God has heard your prayer?" his wife asked.

"I'm sure He has heard at least half of it," replied the rabbi. "The poor have agreed to accept."

(E)   Where Is Paradise?

A rabbi fell asleep and dreamt that he had entered Paradise. There, to his surprise, he found the sages discussing a knotty problem in the Talmud.

"Is this the reward of Paradise?" cried the rabbi. "Why, they did the very same thing on earth!"

At this he heard a voice chiding him, "You foolish man! You think the sages are in Paradise. It's just the opposite! Paradise is in the sages."

(F)   The Virtue of the Commonplace

A rabbi once had a dispute with a Jew-baiting theologian. Said the latter, "You Jews brag about your world-mission and are proud of the fact that you are God's Chosen

People — yet everybody tramples you underfoot! Aren't you deceiving yourselves?"

The rabbi replied, "When our Father Jacob fled before the wrath of Esau, God appeared to him in a dream and said: 'And thy seed shall be as the dust of the earth.' What, may I ask, brings greater use to man than the earth? Just the same — men trample it underfoot. . . ."

(G)   The Blemish on the Diamond

A king once owned a great diamond of the purest water. He was very proud of it for it had no peer in the world. But one day an accident happened and the diamond became deeply scratched. The king then consulted with several diamond cutters, artists in their line. They told him that even if they were to polish the stone they would never be able to remove the imperfection.

Some time later, at the king's command, the greatest lapidary in the country arrived in the capital and undertook to make the diamond look even more beautiful than it was before the accident.

With the greatest art he engraved a delicate rosebud around the imperfection, and out of the deep scratch he cut a stem. When the king and the diamond cutters saw what he had wrought with so much ingenuity they were filled with admiration.

(H)   It Could Always Be Worse

The poor Jew had come to the end of his rope. So he went to his rabbi for advice.

"Holy Rabbi!" he cried. "Things are in a bad way with me, and are getting worse all the time! We are poor, so poor, that my wife, my six children, my in-laws and I have to live in a one-room hut. We get in each other's way all the time. Our nerves are frayed and, because we have plenty of troubles, we quarrel. Believe me — my home is a hell and I'd sooner die than continue living this way?"

The rabbi pondered the matter gravely. "My son," he said, "promise to do as I tell you and your condition will improve."

"I promise, Rabbi," answered the troubled man. "I'll do anything you say."

"Tell me — what animals do you own?"

"I have a cow, a goat and some chickens."

"Very well! Go home now and take all these animals into your house to live with you."

The poor man was dumbfounded, but since he had promised the rabbi, he went home and brought all the animals into his house.

The following day the poor man returned to the rabbi and cried, "Rabbi, what misfortune have you brought upon me! I did as you told me and brought the animals into the house. And now what have I got? Things are worse than ever? My life is a perfect hell — the house is turned into a barn! Save me, Rabbi — help me!"

"My son," replied the rabbi serenely, "go home and take the chickens out of your house. God will help you!"

So the poor man went home and took the chickens out of his house. But it was not long before he again came running to the rabbi.

"Holy Rabbi!" he wailed. "Help me, save me! The goat is smashing everything in the house — she's turning my life into a nightmare."

"Go home," said the rabbi gently, "and take the goat out of the house. God will help you!"

The poor man returned to his house and removed the goat. But it wasn't long before he again came running to the rabbi, lamenting loudly, "What a misfortune you've brought upon my head, Rabbi! The cow has turned my house into a stable! How can you expect a human being to live side by side with an animal?"

"You're right — a hundred times right!" agreed the rabbi. "Go straight home and take the cow out of the house?"

And the poor unfortunate hastened home and took the cow out of his house.

Not a day had passed before he came running again to the rabbi. "Rabbi!" cried the poor man, his face beaming. "You've made life sweet again for me. With all the animals out, the house is so quiet, so roomy, and so clean! What a pleasure!"

(J)   A Clever Jewish Tailor*

In a small town where racial and religious feelings ran high, a Jewish tailor had the temerity to open his little shop on the main street. To drive him out of town, some of the leading citizens set a gang of little ragmuffins to annoy him. Day after day they stood at the entrance of his shop. "Jew! Jew!" they hooted at him. The situation looked serious for the tailor. He took the matter so much to heart that he began to brood and spent sleepless nights over it. Finally out of desperation he evolved a plan.

The following day, when the little hoodlums came to jeer at him, he came to the door and said to them, "From today on any boy who calls me 'Jew' will get a dime from me." Then he put his hand in his pocket and gave each boy a dime.

Delighted with their booty, the boys came back the following day and began to shrill, "Jew! Jew!" The tailor came out smiling. He put his hand in his pocket and gave each of the boys a nickel, saying, "A dime is too much — I can only afford a nickel today." The boys went away satisfied because, after all, a nickel was money, too.

However, when they returned the next day to hoot at him, the tailor gave them only a penny each.

"Why do we only get a penny today?" they yelled.

"That's all I can afford."

"But two days ago you gave us a dime, and yesterday we got a nickel. It's not fair, mister."

"Take it or leave it. That's all you're going to get!"

"Do you think we're going to call you 'Jew' for one lousy penny?"

"So don't!"

And they didn't.*

---

*EDITOR'S NOTE   This story about the Jewish tailor is used by Edward Deci in his book *Intrinsic Motivation* (New York: Plenum Press, 1975), pp. 157-158, to illustrate the power of intrinsic, as opposed to extrinsic, motivation. In *Children's Minds* [New York: Norton, 1978, pp. 124-125 (See Selection 5.3.)] Margaret Donaldson also uses the story, and introduces it with these comments:

> . . . we enjoy best and engage most readily in activities which *we experience as freely chosen.* We do not like being controlled, we like controlling ourselves. Insofar as reward is seen as a means of controlling our behavior, it tends to diminish our interest and our pleasure. Of course we may work hard to get the reward at the time and for so long as we expect more reward to be forthcoming, but we will be less likely to go on with the activity when the reward is withdrawn.

7.7 Some Practical Advice for Teachers
RUTH TSCHUDIN

What's an A+ teacher? Is it possible to distinguish between great and merely adequate teachers? [Ruth Tschudin] thinks she can.

[Tschudin] identified 311 "A+" teachers using three criteria: 73% were nominees or winners of the Teacher of the Year program; 16% were recommended by administrators or fellow teachers; and 11% were chosen because of media coverage of their activities. A control group of 109 teachers was chosen by asking entire school faculties to participate. *Instructor* magazine published the results.

After data from the 420 completed questionnaires were tabulated, 17 statistically significant differences between A+ teachers and ordinary teachers emerged. They were:

- A+ teachers set goals that develop student confidence.
- They gather ideas from a wide variety of sources.
- They create better plans and are more willing to deviate from them.
- They are better classroom designers.
- They use common materials in uncommon ways.
- They discipline students with less punishment.
- They work harder at individualizing instruction.
- They use a wider variety of teaching activities.
- They provide an appealing array of activities.
- They get students actively involved.
- They use all the help they can get.
- They assign less homework.
- They use teacher-made tests sparingly.
- They use checklists, student folders, and a variety of alternatives to the "little red gradebook."
- They are more involved in activities outside the classroom.
- They are more humorous and more enthusiastic.*
- They succeed through hard work.

This condensed summary of a lengthy survey is taken from the *Phi Delta Kappan* 60: 267, December 1978. By permission.

A much longer and more detailed summary of Ruth Tschudin's survey of the traits that characterize "A+ teachers" may be found in the *Instructor* 88: 65-74, September 1978.

We place this selection in Chapter 7 to call attention to the fact that it is possible to be a very effective teacher without having elaborate theoretical constructs of paradigms.

---

*EDITOR'S NOTE: We consider a sense of humor of great importance, not only to help teachers maintain poise and avoid anxiety, but also to help reduce monotony and to decrease tension in students. As you read the examples of humor found in the following pages, ask yourself if they do not help to restore a sense of joy and relaxation. Most important, keep in mind that if you and your students are full of zeal and enthusiasm, with a sense of power and control over circumstances, hard work neither bores, brutalizes, nor alienates.

7.8 Humor: A Way of Building Class Morale
EDITORIAL

The essence of wit or humor is to begin with something rather commonplace and to imaginatively reconstruct it so it becomes absurd or ridiculous. Such imaginative reconstruction requires intelligence, and except in early infancy, joy and laughter from wit and humor characterize self-development both in children and in adults. Here are a few examples from America's rich heritage of humor.

Early to bed and early to rise makes a man — not watch TV.

Early to bed and early to rise —
Until you can afford to do otherwise.

Don't wait for your ship to come in. Row out and get it.

If you give some people a free beer, they would want an egg in it.

That animal ought to have its tail cut off right behind its ears.

The quickest way to do many things is to do one thing at a time.

In times like these, it helps to recall that there have always been times like these.

There are two sides to every argument, until you take one.

Education can broaden a narrow mind, but there is no cure for a big head.[1]

Bore: A person who talks when you want him to listen.

Education: That which discloses to the wise and disguises from the foolish their lack of understanding.

Egoist: A person of low taste, more interested in himself than in me.

Incompatibility: In matrimony a similarity of tastes, particularly the taste for domination.

Saint: A dead sinner revised and edited.

Wit: The salt with which the American humorist spoils his intellectual cookery by leaving it out.[2]

Humor requires an ability to recognize why some ideas are coherent and harmonious with one another, and why other ideas are incoherent or contradictory. Very early in life, a child acquires schema (that is, patterns of thought); and an infant finds joy in matching a stimulus to a schema, for example, in recognizing — re-*cognizing* — its mother. Some degree of mismatch between events and schema is inevitable — a moderate amount of mismatch provides the pleasure of surprise; and an extreme amount of mismatch gives rise to humor and causes laughter.

It is sometimes said that children lack a sense of humor. Insofar as this is true, it is not so much because young children are unable to recognize incompatible ideas or situations. It is rather because they do not have clear and distinct ideas about the subject matter of the joke.

To evoke laughter, what is said must be neither too easy nor too difficult. If too easy, a joke is repetitious or commonplace. If too difficult, it involves concepts which

[1]From R. A. Bodkin ed., *Folklore on the American Land* (Boston: Little, Brown, 1972), pp. 61-68.
[2]From *The Devil's Dictionary*, by Ambrose Bierce (1842-1914?):

the hearer does not comprehend. Here are three examples of Chinese humor. Observe that (a) requires some knowledge of etiquette, (b) requires distinguishing between dreams and reality, and (c) requires appreciation of the role of Taoist priests in warding off evil spirits.

(a) A Foolish Bird

A guest at a dinner sat tight and showed no signs of leaving. At length the host called his visitor's attention to a bird on a tree and said, "As our last course has been served, wait till I cut down the tree, catch the bird, have it cooked, and tell the butler to bring up some wine. What do you say to that?"

"Well," replied the guest, "I expect that by the time the tree is down, the bird will have flown."

"No, no," said the host, "that is a foolish bird, and doesn't know when to go."

(b) Cold Wine

A man who loved to drink found a jug of cold wine in his dream. He was about to warm it up and drink it when all of a sudden he awoke.

"I should have had it cold!" he said with profound regret.

(c) Evil Spirits

A Taoist priest, who was walking through the burial ground of a prince's palace, was bewitched by a host of evil spirits. He obtained the help of a passer-by, who saw him safely home. Said the priest to his rescuer:

"I am deeply indebted to you for rescuing me, but I have no means of rewarding you. Here is an amulet which will keep off evil spirits. I beg you to accept it with my best thanks."[3]

We laugh for many reasons: sometimes in sympathy, sometimes in scorn, sometimes as a relief to anger or frustration. To be able to laugh at our own follies is a mark of maturity; and to be able to laugh only at the expense of others signifies immaturity. We must realize that laughter can be a very cruel weapon, causing injury if it undeservedly strikes a defenseless human being. As Sidney Smith once noted, "There are few who would not rather be hated than laughed at."

Furthermore, it is altogether different to laugh *at* than to laugh *with* someone. When we laugh *with* someone, as Thomas Carlyle once wrote, "Humor is not contempt, its essence is love. . . . It is a sort of inverse sublimity, exalting, as it were, into our affection what is below. . . . [or sublimely drawing] down into our affection what is above us."

Humor is a wonderful outlet for the downtrodden and the oppressed, because it serves to inhibit outright aggressiveness in favor of fun and fancy. If by fantasy or by clever word play the humorist is able to surmount imaginatively his social disadvantages, humor helps the downtrodden group or the alienated individual to regain confidence and self-esteem, even if only momentarily and imaginatively. In this sense, humor is far more than a manifestation of cleverness and wit. Used judiciously in a

[3]From *Chinese Wit and Humor*, edited by George Kao (New York: Coward-McCann & Geoghegan, 1946), pp. 229-268.

classroom, it is an expression of a sincere desire to make students feel at ease and to recover from whatever frustrations or difficulties that may have weakened their desire to learn.

7.9   A Laugh That Meant Freedom

There were some slaves who had a reputation for keeping out of work because of their wit and humor. These slaves kept their masters laughing most of the time, and were able, if not to keep from working altogether, at least to draw the lighter tasks.

Nehemiah was a clever slave, and no master who had owned him had ever been able to keep him at work, or succeeded in getting him to do heavy work. He would always have some funny story to tell or some humorous remark to make in response to the master's question or scolding. Because of this faculty for avoiding work, Nehemiah was constantly being transferred from one master to another. As soon as an owner found out that Nehemiah was outwitting him, he sold Nehemiah to some other slaveholder. One day David Wharton, known as the most cruel slave master in Southwest Texas, heard about him.

"I bet I can make that rascal work," said David Wharton, and he went to Nehemiah's master and bargained to buy him.

The morning of the first day after his purchase, David Wharton walked over to where Nehemiah was standing and said, "Now you are going to work, you understand. You are going to pick four hundred pounds of cotton today."

"Wal, Massa, dat's aw right," answered Nehemiah, "but ef Ah meks you laff, won' yuh lemme off fo' terday?"

"Well," said David Wharton, who had never been known to laugh, "if you make me laugh, I won't only let you off for today, but I'll give you your freedom."

"Ah decla', Boss," said Nehemiah, "yuh sho' is uh goodlookin' man."

"I am sorry I can't say the same thing about you," retorted David Wharton.

"Oh, yes, Boss, yuh could," Nehemiah laughed out, "yuh could, if yuh tole ez big uh lie ez Ah did."

David Wharton could not help laughing at this; he laughed before he thought. Nehemiah got his freedom.

From *The Book of Negro Folklore*, edited by Langston Hughes and Arna Bontemps (New York: Dodd, Mead, 1958), pp. 67-68.
    This book contains many examples of black humor in the United States.

7.10 Swapping Dreams

Master Jim Turner, an unusually good-natured master, had a fondness for telling long stories woven out of what he claimed to be his dreams, and especially did he like to "swap" dreams with Ike, a witty slave who was a house servant. Every morning he would set Ike to telling about what he had dreamed the night before. It always seemed, however, that the master could tell the best dream tale, and Ike had to admit that he was beaten most of the time.

One morning, when Ike entered the master's room to clean it, he found the master just preparing to get out of bed. "Ike," he said, "I certainly did have a strange dream last night."

"Sez yuh did, Massa, sez yuh did?" answered Ike. "Lemme hyeah it."

"All right," replied the master. "It was like this: I dreamed I went to Nigger Heaven last night, and saw there a lot of garbage, some old torn-down houses, a few old broken-down, rotten fences, the muddiest, sloppiest streets I ever saw, and a big bunch of ragged, dirty Negroes walking around."

"Umph, umph, Massa," said Ike, "yuh sho' musta et de same t'ing Ah did las' night, 'case Ah dreamed Ah went up ter de white man's paradise, an' de streets wuz all ob gol' an' silvah, and dey wuz lots o' milk and' honey dere, an' putty pearly gates, but dey wuzn't uh soul in de whole place."*

From *The Book of Negro Folklore*, edited by Langston Hughes and Arna Bontemps, New York: Dodd, Mead, 1958), p. 71.

Some contemporary readers may object to the inclusion of stories which refer to blacks as "niggers." But we should realize that such salutations were but one of many ways in which sixteenth-, seventeenth-, eighteenth-, and nineteenth-century slaves were "kept in their proper place." Realization of this fact should make all the more evident the courage implicit in this story.

---

*EDITOR'S NOTE   At this point, the reader may wish that this anthology had included more stories with a humorous flavor and fewer essays. But we merely call attention to the fact that humor is a remarkably effective device for keeping people calm and cool, and thus for securing needed social changes (or personal wants) in a peaceful way. The reason for humor's effectiveness was clearly stated by Sigmund Freud:

In every epoch of history those who have had something to say but could not say it without peril have eagerly assumed the fool's cap. The audience to whom their forbidden speech was aimed tolerated it more easily if they could at the same time laugh and flatter themselves with the reflection that the unwelcome words were clearly nonsensical.

7.11   Story of a Good Brahmin
VOLTAIRE

On my travels I met an old Brahmin, a very wise man, of marked intellect and great learning. Furthermore, he was rich and, consequently, all the wiser, because, lacking nothing, he needed to deceive nobody. His household was very well managed by three handsome women who set themselves out to please him. When he was not amusing himself with his women, he passed the time in philosophizing. Near his house, which was beautifully decorated and had charming gardens attached, there lived a narrow-minded old Indian woman: she was a simpleton, and rather poor.

Said the Brahmin to me one day: "I wish I had never been born!" On my asking why, he answered: "I have been studying forty years, and that is forty years wasted. I teach others and myself am ignorant of everything. Such a state of affairs fills my soul with so much humiliation and disgust that my life is intolerable. I was born in Time, I live in Time, and yet I do not know what Time is. I am at a point between two eternities, as our wise men say, and I have no conception of eternity. I am composed of matter: I think, but I have never been able to learn what produces my thought. I do not know whether or no my understanding is a simple faculty inside me, such as those of walking and digesting, and whether or no I think with my head as I grip with my hands. Not only is the cause of my thought unknown to me; the cause of my actions is equally a mystery. I do not know why I exist, and yet every day people ask me questions on all these points. I have to reply, and as I have nothing really worth saying, I talk a great deal; and am ashamed of myself afterward for having talked.

"It is worse still when I am asked if Brahma was born of Vishnu or if they are both eternal. God is my witness that I have not the remotest idea, and my ignorance shows itself in my replies. 'Ah, Holy One,' people say to me, 'tell us why evil pervades the earth.' I am in as great a difficulty as those who ask me this question. Sometimes I tell them that everything is as well as can be, but those who have been ruined and broken in the wars do not believe a word of it — and no more do I. I retire to my home stricken at my own curiosity and ignorance. I read our ancient books, and they double my darkness. I talk to my companions: some answer me that we must enjoy life and make game of mankind; others think they know a lot and lose themselves in a maze of wild ideas. Everything increases my anguish. I am ready sometimes to despair when I think that after all my seeking I do not know whence I came, whither I go, what I am nor what I shall become."

The good man's condition really worried me. Nobody was more rational or more sincere than he. I perceived that his unhappiness increased in proportion as his understanding developed and his insight grew.

The same day I saw the old woman who lived near him. I asked her if she had ever been troubled by the thought that she was ignorant of the nature of her soul. She did not even understand my question. Never in all her life had she reflected for one single moment on one single point of all those which tormented the Brahmin. She believed with all her heart in the metamorphoses of Vishnu and, provided she could obtain a little Ganges water wherewith to wash herself, thought herself the happiest of women.

Struck with this mean creature's happiness, I returned to my wretched philosopher. "Are you not ashamed," said I, "to be unhappy when at your very door there lives an old automaton who thinks about nothing, and yet lives contentedly?"

"You are right," he replied. "I have told myself a hundred times that I should be happy if I were as brainless as my neighbor, and yet I do not desire such happiness."

My Brahmin's answer impressed me more than all the rest. I set to examining myself, and I saw that in truth I would not care to be happy at the price of being a simpleton.

I put the matter before some philosophers, and they were of my opinion. "Nevertheless," said I, "there is a tremendous contradiction in this mode of thought, for, after all, the problem is — how to be happy. What does it matter whether one has brains or not? Further, those who are contented with their lot are certain of their contentment, whereas those who reason are not certain that they reason correctly. It is quite clear, therefore," I continued, "that we must choose not to have common sense, however little common sense may contribute to our discomfort." Everyone agreed with me, but I found nobody, notwithstanding, who was willing to accept the bargain of becoming a simpleton in order to become contented. From which I conclude that if we consider the question of happiness we must consider still more the question of reason.

But on reflection it seems that to prefer reason to felicity is to be very senseless. How can this contradiction be explained? Like all the other contradictions. It is matter for much talk.*

---

*EDITOR'S NOTE   The story's contradictions, and its humor, are a consequence of dealing with knowledge and ignorance as if they were black and white. But the resulting contradictions compel us to think, as we probably would not otherwise do, about the relative merits of knowledge and ignorance.

7.12   Objective Truth Is Not Confined to Things That are Quantifiable and Measurable
W. T. STACE

There is no difference in objectivity between the botanical statement that fertilizers tend to produce healthy plants and the psychological statement that malice and hate tend to produce unhappy human beings, love and affection happy ones. Nor is there in principle any difference as regards empirical verifiability. Both the results produced by fertilizers and the results produced by malice or love are known in the same way — by observing the facts. And just as when an agriculturist says, "Fertilize your plants," his advice has a solid foundation in known facts about plants, so when the moralist says "Love your neighbor," his advice has a solid foundation in known facts about human beings.

Miss Ruth Benedict in her book — *Patterns of Culture* — tells us that the Dobu Islanders disagree with this advice of Jesus Christ about loving your neighbor. They found their culture on treachery and ill-will. They act as if they supposed that treachery and ill-will are likely to produce the sort of society in which they will be most happy. Miss Benedict seems to conclude that treachery and ill-will *are*, for the Dobu Islanders, good. My own conclusion is that the Dobu Islanders are simply mistaken. They would find, if they could be induced to try, that good faith and good-will would produce in their society a much happier state of affairs for them than exists at present. People are often mistaken about what is good for the health of their bodies. That is why we have doctors. And people are just as likely to be mistaken about what will be good for the happiness of their souls. That is why we have moralists. The Dobu Islanders need someone to correct their moral or sociological mistakes.

I have compared moral laws to scientific principles. In respect of objectivity they are entirely comparable, but in respect of precision of course they are not. Love and hate are vague concepts and they can never be reduced to mathematical equations. But love and hate are just as real and objective as oxygen and hydrogen; and they just as truly produce effects in the world. And to know these effects is just as much knowledge although it may never be capable of the precision of mathematics and physics.

Also we know much less about the laws of personality than we do about the laws of physics. This means that our moral knowledge is very elementary. But this is no

Brief excerpt from W. T. Stace (Princeton University), "Science and Faith," reprinted from *Mid-Century: The Social Implications of Scientific Progress*, edited by J. E. Burchard, by permission of the MIT Press, Cambridge, Massachusetts, 1950. Copyright 1950 by the Massachusetts Institute of Technology.

Perhaps this selection belongs in Chapter 5, because it deals with the limitations of measurement. It may also be viewed as a response to the widely held view that "anything which exists exists in some measurable degree" or that "everything that exists can be measured." These statements have exactly the same meaning as "anything which cannot be measured does not exist."

We place W. T. Stace's statement here as an adjunct to this chapter's *Quotations for Further Thought and Discussion*, and as a prelude to Chapters 8 and 9. It deals briefly with the problem of moral relativism, already briefly discussed in Selections 4.10 and 4.12, and to be discussed again in Selection 9.6. For two other interesting discussions of moral relativism, read "Normative Absolutism vs. Sociological Relativism: An Investigation of Two World Views," by Frank R. Westie and Richard Hummel, *Educational Studies* 2: 25–36, Spring, 1980; and articles by Robert Hogan, David Schroeder, and others in the August and September 1980 issues of *Character*, the magazine cited in Selection 2.3

reason for declaring that what knowledge we have is baseless. What we have to do is to advance in this knowledge.*

---

*EDITOR'S NOTE   In connection with Stace's affirmation that moral truths, no less than truths of the mathematical and physical sciences, are *objective*, consider the following:

> The great ethical force of science has proved to be the dissemination of the idea that truth is a thing which will in some way help us all. In this, we don't have to claim that truth is good, or beautiful, or absolute. We simply recognize that men have found that it is easier to run a society made up of independent individuals if they all acknowledge what is true. . . . We have now learned to acknowledge that to be truthful makes it easier for man to be both solitarily creative and socially sustained than any alternative behavior. I regard this as a major step that science has made in producing an ethic. — Jacob Bronowski, *Man and His Future*, (Boston: Little Brown, 1963), pp. 370-371.

> The fallacy of cultural bias is that of improperly using the standards of one culture to judge a very different culture. The fallacy of cultural relativism is that all standards of a cultural sort are relative, and, therefore, there are no standards for judging any culture. These two fallacies are two sides of the same coin. A pseudo-version of the fallacy of cultural bias exalts the status quo of any given society and confuses mores (customs) with morals. What is the case in a society is taken as right and just. It would prohibit judging slavery to be wrong in slaved-based societies. The fallacy of cultural relativism does virtually the same thing by making the absolutist claim that all values are relative. Where all values are relative, then the value of slavery is relative to time, place and circumstance. The pseudo-fallacy of cultural bias says in effect: "judge me by no standards except my customs" and that of cultural realtivism says "judge me by no standards at all." One supports bias and propaganda, with special pleading for immunity from criticism, and the other supports license and irresponsibility. — George Newsom (University of Georgia, Athens), "Bias, Censorship, and Freedom in the Academic Press," *Educational Theory* 29: 229-236, Summer 1979.

> It is the *reasoned* judgment of the majority that obligates our compliance with its decisions, not the *will* of the majority as such. To the extent, therefore, that the rule of the majority becomes more an expression of will and less an expression of reasoned judgment, to that degree it becomes less democratic and more tyrannical. — John H. Hallowell, "The Meaning of Majority Rule," *Commonweal* 56: 167-169, May 25, 1962.

7.13   Quotations for Further Thought and Discussion

(A)   We used to think that our civilization should be guarded, and even that at times it should advance, so that our soldiers were heroes, but now we think of our generals only as stupid and knavish and war-hungry. We used to believe that our civilization should act with great authority in the world, so that we found heroes among our politicians to speak for it, but now we regard our politicians only as petty and self-serving. We once believed that our writers and artists should speak of and to the common values of our civilization and be bearers of it, so that we found heroes among them even down to the 1930s, but now we think that our writers and artists should stay on the margins and entertain us. . . .

Great peoples who in the past have done great deeds have had great heroes whom they honored. Just as Alexander and the Hellenistic world had the *Iliad*, so did the Norsemen have their sagas, and the Jews made a scripture of the deeds of their heroes. Can we imagine Rome without the *pietas* with which it celebrated its founders? To think of France without Joan is hardly to think of France at all. England without Alfred! Scotland without the Bruce! Italy without Garibaldi! Holland without William the Silent! Sweden without Charles XII! America without Lincoln! Spain without . . . Don Quixote! (Before you say that Quixote did not live, you had better ask a Spaniard.) Such countries stripped of their heroes cease to be historical countries. We have to deserve our history, otherwise it becomes a mere shadow; if we ourselves are unheroic, we will be cut off from our heroic pasts. So we become smaller than life. . . .

— Henry Fairlie, "Too Rich for Heroes," *Harper's* 257: 33-44. Copyright © 1978 by Harper's Magazine. All rights reserved. Reprinted from the November 1978 issue by special permission.

(B)   There are two basic myths about modernity, and both derive in part at least from Rousseau. I call them the myth of the Long Revolution and the myth of Lost Community — using the word myth to indicate that these are ideological, as well as analytic, concepts, organizing belief and action, as well as thought. The myth of the Long Revolution portrays modern Western history as a steady advance in the values of autonomy, equality, and rationality. This is the modernizing myth that has generally prevailed in America's booster past, a parable of progress. The myth of Lost Community, on the other hand, takes the form of a critique of the consequences of this very progress. Its central value is community, and it tells the story of the West since the Middle Ages (usually) as a tale on growing alienation, disenchantment, and anomie, a vast uprooting amounting to a human catastrophe. The Long Revolution applauds the sundering of old unities; the Lost Community perspective sees the splintered, broken modern world as a disaster, and the division of labor as the great source of mystification and alienation.

Proponents of the Long Revolution speak of gains in the standard of living, the development of science, the slow extension of the revolutionary ideals of liberty, equality, and fraternity into the realms of child-rearing and the family, and in recent years the evidence (in the advanced Western countries) of higher standards of child care, health, social services. Those who mourn the Lost Community point to alienation, disenchantment, the collapse of authority, bureaucratization, and anomie — all the costs of progress. . . .

— Joseph Featherstone (Harvard University), "Rousseau and Modernity," *Daedalus* 117: 167-193, Summer 1978. Reprinted by permission of the American Academy of Arts and Sciences, Summer 1978.

(C)   Democracy has many meanings, but if it has a moral meaning, it is found in resolving that the supreme test of all political institutions and industrial arrangements shall be the contribution they make to the all-around growth of every member of society. . . .

If we do not go on and go far in the positive direction of providing a body of subject matter much richer, more varied and flexible, and also in truth more definite . . . than traditional education supplied, we shall tend to leave an educational vacuum in which anything can happen.

— John Dewey, cited in *Value Development . . . As the Aim of Education*, edited by Norman A. Sprinthall and Ralph L. Mosher, (Schenectady, New York: Character Research Press, 1978), pp. 21, 82

(D)   [All over the world, men, women and children are] seeking a fuller and richer human life, a greater fulfillment of their humanity . . . [They] want the freedom to create new things, new socieites, new cultures and new purposes. In fact if we look at the last three to four hundred years of modern history, men have revolted against religions primarily because in the name of a fixed divinely ordained order they prevented men's creativity in science, arts, and morality. In fact, many doctrines of the creator-God have been so defined as to give no room for the creativity of men, so that men had to revolt against God himself to affirm human creativity. In a sense, the process of secularization in the modern world and a good deal even of militant secularism have been primarily an affirmation of man's humanity as essentially creative.

[Throughout the world today] there is the search for freedom as the awareness of a responsible selfhood. Self-determination, self-development and self-identity are phrases charged with great meaning in the life of individuals as well as groups in the modern world. Men and women ask for their fundamental rights of responsibility as human persons. Nations and races and cultures are in the struggle for their self-identity and for the power and responsibility to exercise their selfhood.

[There is also] among all people the search for a love which is different from paternalism. Paternalism is a form of love, no doubt. But today, it appears to men and women in all situations to be lacking in true reverence for the dignity of the person. Young people revolt against paternalism in the family; and there is revolt against paternalism of caste, class and race. In fact we shall misinterpret even the struggle of the poorer classes, races and nations against poverty, if it is seen only as a search for bread to satisfy hunger. Of course it is that, but it is the search for bread as the expression of justice to man's manhood.

[Finally,] men everywhere have become conscious of a sense of history. On the one hand, there is the awareness of a universal history of mankind, and, on the other, every nation, race and group is becoming conscious of its own historical mission and vocation in the world, and is struggling to define it.

In this seeking for creativity, selfhood, love and historical mission, men are driven in the deepest levels of their spirit by the vision of new dimensions of human existence; and this new humanism is the spiritual ferment within the cultural revolutions of our contemporary world.

> — M. M. Thomas, "Ecumenism and the Cultural Revolution," *Religious Education* 42: 93-97, March-April 1967. Used by permission of the publisher, the Religious Education Association, New York, N.Y.
> M. M. Thomas is Director, Christian Institute for the Study of Religion and Society, Bangelore, India. In 1966-1967 he was Henry W. Luce Visiting Professor of World Christianity at Union Theological Seminary, New York, N.Y.

(E)   Science is founded on uncertainty. Each time we learn something new and surprising, the astonishment comes with the realization that we were wrong before. The body of science is not, as it is sometimes thought, a huge coherent mass of facts, neatly arranged in sequence, each one attached to the next by a logical string. In truth, whenever we discover a new fact it involves the elimination of old ones. We are always, as it turns out, fundamentally in error.

I cannot think of a single field in biology or medicine in which we can claim genuine understanding, and it seems to me the more we learn about living creatures, especially ourselves, the stranger life becomes. . . . The world is not a simple place, and we are not simple instruments.

> — Lewis Thomas (M.D., Chancellor of the Memorial Sloan-Kettering Cancer Center in Manhattan), "On Science and Uncertainty," *Discover: A Newsmagazine of Science*, Vol. 1, No. 1, October 1980, pp. 58-59.

(F)   The assumption that anything is knowable with completeness and certainty arrests inquiry and closes the channels that lead on to deeper and wider insight. . . .

The teacher who is spiritually aware does not seek to protect himself from the insecurity of uncertainty, perplexity, and irremediable ignorance. He does not try to hide behind a screen of academic presumption and professional expertise, embellished with mystifying jargon. Nor does he confuse the role of teacher with that of authoritative oracle. He does not expect or encourage his students supinely to accept his beliefs or directions. On the other hand, he shares with conviction and enthusiasm the light that he believes he possesses, and encourages his students to do the same, resolutely resisting in himself and in his students the paralysis and sense of futility associated with skepticism and indifference.

> — Philip H. Phenix (Teachers College, Columbia University), "Transcendence and the Curriculum," *Teachers College Record* 73: 271-283, December 1971.

(G)   In sciences in which men come to agreement, when a theory has been broached it is considered to be on probation until . . . agreement is reached. After it is reached, the question of certainty becomes an idle one, because there is no one left who doubts it. We individually cannot reasonably hope to attain the ultimate philosophy which we pursue; we can only seek it, therefore, for the *community* of philosphers [i.e., the community of all people dedicated to the pursuit of truth]. . . .

So the social principle is rooted intrinsically in logic. . . . For he who recognizes the necessity of complete self-identification of one's interests with those of the community, and its potential existence in man, even if he has it not himself, will perceive that only the inferences of that man who has it are logical, and so views his own inferences as being valid only so far as they would be accepted by that man. But so far as he has this belief, he becomes identified with that man. And that ideal perfection of knowledge by which we have seen that reality is constituted must thus belong to a community in which this identification is complete.

> — Charles Sanders Peirce, cited in a discussion of "The Great Community" by Max H. Fisch, editor, *Classic American Philosphers*, (Appleton-Century-Crofts, 1951), pp. 36–39 — an outstanding reference.

(H)   Modern educational technologies, if conjoined with lower student/teacher ratios, should make it possible for us to do the kinds of things that classroom teachers have previously seldom been able to do: to discover the special interests and abilities and needs of each student, and then to satisfy these needs and stimulate these abilities by providing for each student a tailor-made series of programs from a central computer terminal having tens of thousands of such programs for each grade level. All of this must be matched, of course, by the teachers' personal concern and loving care for each individual student.

> — the Editor (a paraphrase of statements by William E. Gardner, Dean, College of Education, University of Minnesota, Minneapolis.)

Chapter 8. ADAPTING TRADITIONAL VALUES TO MODERN EDUCATION

8.1 The American Tradition of Separation of Church and State

INTRODUCTION

Any attempt to understand the American tradition of church and state should keep in mind the fact that secularization has its historical roots in the Bible itself. By denuding the cosmos of its divinity and placing God totally beyond its confines, the biblical tradition prepared the way for the process we now call secularization. It was during the Colonial period of American history that Renaissance, Reformation, and Enlightenment thinkers, both in Europe and in America, repudiated magic and superstition as means toward moral integrity or toward religious salvation. They insisted that a viable religion must now abandon the pretentions covered up by Pomp and Ceremony, or — to use Dostoevski's phrase, by "miracle, mystery and authority." No longer are service and sacrifice to be viewed as something to be endured until better times come in Heaven; they are to be viewed now as duties which responsible citizens embrace in order that better times may come on Earth. In religion no less than in politics, each of us is a human being and remains one, both when we embrace (or reject) some religious tradition and when we become responsible citizens of a political community.

Although shared by most of the Founding Fathers in 1789, such notions were quite unorthodox. For they implied that the basis of law, order, and morality is no longer to be justified by an appeal to Heaven; it is to be justified by an appeal to reason.

In contrasting the American constitutional system with earlier systems of government, Edmund Cahn writes that the American system represents a change:

	As to Objective	As to Content	As to Sanction
From:	perpetuity	immutability	appeal to heaven
To:	efficacy	adaptation	appeal to the courts[1]

---

[1] Edmund Cahn, *Confronting Injustice* (Boston: Little, Brown, 1962), p. 68. See also pp. 168–175, 216 f.

230

In a study of the American tradition of church and state, it is well to remember that 1789 is a halfway mark between 1607 and 1976. In the colonial period of American history, values — called moral and spiritual values — were almost universally equated with religious belief. But by the time our nation was founded there had been a movement from Religious Establishment to Multiple Establishment to Disestablishment.[2]

The reason why disestablishment was chosen in preference to other alternatives has been well stated by Zechariah Chaffee, Jr.:

> We have made our choice and chosen the dream of Roger Williams. It was not a choice between a good dream and a bad dream but between a good dream which on the whole works and a good dream which occasionally turned into a nightmare of the . . . hanging of Mary Dyer on Boston Common. Sometimes nostalgia for what we have given up creeps over us. Men sometimes lament, for instance, that our public schools are godless. Suppose we admit frankly that this is a loss to the public schools, that one very important part of our nature has to be wholly neglected in the place where we receive much of the shaping of our characters and minds. It is a price to pay, but we must look at all which we have bought thereby. We cannot reject a portion of the bargain and insist on keeping the rest. If the noble ideal of the Puritan had persisted, there would be no godless schools in Massachusetts and there would be nobody in her churches except Congregationalists. Through the choice which all of the United States has made, it becomes possible for men of many different faiths to live and work together for many noble ends without allowing their divisions in spiritual matters to become, as in the old days, unbridgeable chasms running through every aspect of human lives.[3]

Or, as Justice Robert H. Jackson put it, the purpose of the First Amendment was

> . . . not only to keep the states' hands out of religion, but to keep religion's hands off the state, and, above all, to keep bitter religious controversy out of public life by denying to every denomination any advantage from getting control of public policy or the public purse. . . .
>
> This policy of our Federal Constitution has never been wholly pleasing to most religious groups. They all are quick to invoke its protections; they all are irked when they feel its restraints. . . .
>
> But we cannot have it both ways. Religious teaching cannot be a private affair when the state seeks to impose regulations which infringe on it indirectly, and a public affair when it comes to taxing citizens of one faith to aid another, or those of no faith to aid all. If these principles seem harsh in prohibiting aid to Catholic education, it must not be forgotten that it is the same Constitution that alone assures Catholics the right to maintain these schools at all when predominant local sentiment would forbid them. *Pierce v. Society of Sisters*, 268 U.S. 510. Nor should I think that those who have done so well without this aid would want to see this separation between Church and State broken down. If the state may aid these religious schools, it may therefore regulate them.[4]

The public school, well named "the common school," reflected the changes in the

---

[2] For an excellent summary of these three movements in colonial America, read R. Freeman Butts and Lawrence A. Cremin, *A History of Education in American Culture* (New York: Holt, Rinehart and Winston, 1953), pp. 98–99, 152, 153.

[3] Zechariah Chaffee, Jr., *The Blessings of Liberty*, pp. 255–256. Copyright © 1956 by Zechariah Chaffee, Jr. Reprinted by permission of J. B. Lippincott Co.

[4] *Everson v. Board of Education*, 330 U.S. 1 (1946). This is part of a dissenting opinion in a 5–4 decision which gave constitutional sanction for the public transportation of children to parochial schools.

direction of religious tolerance, and helped bring about the broadening base of citizenship in our country from Puritan to Protestant, to Christian, to Christian and Jew, to adherents of all religions, and, finally, to all men. The United States Supreme Court, and the several state courts, also reflected the changing attitudes of the American people. In 1844, Mr. Justice Story, for a unanimous Court, could assume that this is "a Christian country" and refer to "Judaism, or Deism, or any other form of infidelity." *Vidal v. Girard's Ex'rs.*, 43 U.S. (2 How.) 127, 198 (1844). A century later the Court declared only that "we are a religious people," *Zorach v. Clauson*, 343 U.S. 306, 313 (1952), and just a few years ago it unanimously struck down a requirement "of belief in the existence of God," *Torcaso v. Watkins*, 367 U.S. 488, 495 (1961), as a condition to eligibility for public office. . . . More and more, the law has come to respect the human spirit and the dignity and worth of man.[5]

THE MEANING OF RELIGIOUS PLURALISM

When we say that the United States is a pluralistic society, we mean that it contains a variety of societies, organizations and religious sects, some of whose beliefs are hostile to those of other groups. To maintain law and order in such a society, the Courts have consistently interpreted the United States Constitution to mean that the state must refrain from intervention into the religious beliefs of its citizens. The only exceptions are cases in which religious beliefs upset the peace and order of society. Thus in *Davis v. Beason*, 133 U.S. 333 (1890), the Court classified bigamy and polygamy as crimes, not as religious rights. In *Zucht v. King*, 260 U.S. 174 (1922), the Court declared that school officials have a constitutional right and responsibility to require vaccination as a means of protecting public health.

However, the Court has consistently refused to act as an arbiter as to whether a religious belief is true or false. In *Watson v. Jones*, 13 Wallace, 679 (1872), which dealt with a dispute between two Louisville Presbyterian church factions, the Court held that the freedom and independence of churches would be in grave danger if *the Court* undertook to define religious heresy or orthodoxy or to decide which of two factions was the "true faith." A somewhat similar opinion is found in *Kedroff v. Saint Nicholas Cathedral*, 344 U.S. 94 (1952). Again, although laws against the fraudulent use of the mail are constitutional, the Court in *United States v. Ballard*, 322 U.S. 78 (1944), ruled that secular authorities may not use such laws to determine the truth of religious claims and beliefs — in this case, the "I am" movement; for, no matter how "prepos-

---

[5] These and other cases are from a lengthy article on religious freedom by Arner Brodie and Harold P. Southerland, 1966 *Wisconsin Law Review*, pp. 214–330.

In *Torcaso v. Watkins*, 367 U.S. 499 (1961), the U.S. Supreme Court held that a state could not make declaration of belief in God a condition for appointment as a notary public. Such a condition on any public benefit would put state power "on the side of one particular sort of believers. . . . " This is a forbidden establishment, since . . . neither a State nor the Federal Government can constitutionally force a person "to profess a belief or disbelief in any religion." Neither can constitutionally pose laws nor impose requirements which aid all religions as against non-believers, and neither can aid those religions based on a belief in the existence of God as against those religions founded on different beliefs. (Among religions in this country which do not teach what would generally be considered a belief in the existence of God are Buddhism, Taoism, Ethical Culture, Secular Humanism.).

terous" or "incredible" these claims may be, religious beliefs are not subject to findings of "truth" by fact-finding bodies.

Wherever possible, the Court has sought to accommodate secular laws to religious traditions. In *McGowan v. Maryland* and three other similar cases, 366 U.S. 420 (1961), the Court upheld the constitutionality of "Sunday Closing Laws" on the grounds that such laws were "preeminently secular" and could thus be upheld as general welfare regulations. "To say that the States cannot prescribe Sunday as a day of rest for these purposes [that is, as a day of relaxation for all citizens] solely because centuries ago such laws had their genesis in religion would give a constitutional interpretation of hostility to the public welfare rather than one of mere separation of church and state."

The separation of church and state with respect to education has given rise to a long succession of court rulings, including such issues as public funds for busing, school lunches, and public health services for parochial school students (*Everson*, 1946), released time for religious studies [*McCullom* (1948) and *Zorach* (1951)], official public school prayers (*Engel*, 1962), Bible reading (*Schempp*, 1963), the provision of secular textbooks to parochial schools (*Allen*, 1968), exemption of church properties from taxation (*Walz*, 1970), public monies to parochial schools for science buildings, counselors, and other "secular educational services" [*DiAnso, Lemon, Tilton* (1971), *Brusca* (1972), *Norwood* (1973) and *Meek* (1975)]. In these and other such rulings, the basic principles were these: that there should be strict political noninvolvement in religion, and that there should be no trace of ecclesiastical interference by political authorities. In a concurring opinion in *Schempp* (1968), Justice Brennan noted that the types of involvement the drafters of the Constitution meant to avoid were those which (a) serve essentially religious activities of religious institutions, (b) employ the organs of government for religious purposes, or (c) use religious means where secular means would suffice. We must remember, too, that the state allows generous tax exemptions for contributions to nonprofit charitable organizations and that most of such tax exemptions are allowed to religious organizations.

It should be obvious that the American tradition of separation of church and state is based on ethical values. In the words of Ivan Shapiro:

> Strict separation is a proper and meaningful belief only if it is founded on an overarching ethical view of the relationship between a government and its citizens. . . . If one is not free to examine, select, and reexamine one's deepest values, one is not a free person and has therefore lost a portion of one's humanity. If government insists upon directing belief or lending its weight to private groups desirous of inculcating religious beliefs, then such actions are destructive of individual freedom. In a related context, Abraham Lincoln declared that "As I would not be a slave, so I would not be a master. This expresses my idea of democracy — whatever differs from this, to the extent of the difference, is not democracy." If we would preserve our own right to believe what we will and to support only such beliefs as we wish, we have no right to offer less to the next person. The ad hoc stands taken on church/state questions by various groups, to the extent that they are not wholly consistent with this concept of individual freedom, can be destructive of freedom and are ethically unacceptable.[6]

[6] Ivan Shapiro (President of the New York Society for Ethical Culture), "The Ethical Case for Separation of Church and State," *The Humanist* 35: 33, November/December 1975. Reprinted by permission. For longer treatments of this topic, read Leo Pfeffer, *God, Caesar and the Constitution*, Boston: Beacon Press, 1975; Frank J. Sorauf, *The Wall of Separation: The Constitutional Politics of Church and State*, Princeton, N.J.: Princeton University Press, 1976; and Thayer S. Warshaw, *Religion, Education, and the Supreme Court*. Nashville, Tenn.: Abingdon, 1979.

To conclude: Many of the traditions inherited from a Mediterranean civilization are not applicable to our multivalued nation, and are probably not applicable to any world civilization of the foreseeable future. At the same time, however, the extreme individualism of the past two centuries seems to be equally unsuited to contemporary needs. So we conclude these remarks with a theme which John Dewey expressed in the concluding paragraph of *A Common Faith* (1934):

> The things in civilization we most prize are not of ourselves. The exist by grace of the doings and sufferings of the continuous human community in which we are a link. Ours is the responsibility of conserving, transmitting, rectifying and expanding the heritage of values we have received that those who come after us may receive it more solid and secure, more widely accessible and more generously shared than we have received it.

8.2   The Supreme Court's Efforts To Define Religion
HARVARD LAW REVIEW

[The American tradition of separation of church and state began with Roger Williams, continued with Jefferson and Madison, and has been adapted as our nation assimilated a wider and wider variety of immigrant groups. By the time of *Everson v. Board of Education* (1947), the Court had come to recognize] two fundamental principles: voluntarism (that belief should be free, not coerced) and separatism (that neither government nor religion should involve itself in the work of the other). . . .

The establishment clause combines the principles of voluntarism and separatism. Three goals predominate: (1) protecting religious freedom of choice, (2) avoiding the political strife that might result if religion and politics were intertwined, and (3) insuring the integrity of both church and state by immunizing each from contamination by the other. . . .

[Until] fairly recently the predominant judicial image of religion stressed traditional elements like theologies, sacraments, and, above all, worship of a deity. In 1890, the Supreme Court in *Davis v. Beason* stated: "[T]he term 'religion' has reference to one's views of his relations to his Creator, and to the obligations they impose of reverence for his being and character, and of obedience to his will." As late as 1931, Chief Justice Hughes concluded that "[t]he essence of religion is belief in a relation to God involving duties superior to those arising from any human relation." State courts have generally echoed this interpretation.

Beginning in the 1940's, however, this traditional understanding was increasingly challenged. A signal departure came in *United States v. Kauten* [1943]. Interpreting the conscientious objector exemption of the Selective Service Act of 1940. Judge Augustus Hand ventured this definition:

Brief excerpts from "Notes: Toward a Constitutional Definition of Religion," 91 *Harvard Law Review* 1056–1089 (1978). (Footnote references are omitted.) By permission.

To avoid duplicating materials covered in the preceding selection, the period from 1789 to 1940 is dealt with very briefly. The emphasis of these excepts is on the period from about 1940 to 1978.

Religious belief arises from a sense of the inadequacy of reason as a means of relating the individual to his fellow-men and to his universe. . . . It is a belief finding expression in a conscience which categorically requires the believer to disregard elementary self-interest and to accept martyrdom in preference to transgressing its tenets. . . .

. . . [Conscientious objection] may justly be regarded as a response of the individual to an inward mentor, call it conscience or God, that is for many persons at the present time the equivalent of what has always been thought a religious impulse.

The *Kauten* interpretation represents a dramatic shift in emphasis. Whereas *Davis* saw religion as relating man to God. *Kauten* examined the relationship of man to the broad universe and to other men. Where most other courts had considered the external attributes of a denomination — its dogma, doctrines, and creeds — the Second Circuit focused on the psychological function of the belief in the life of the individual.

The Second Circuit's new conception was not accepted immediately. Interpreting the same statute, the Ninth Circuit in *Berman v. United States* [1946] reiterated the traditional definition of religion. The court declared that "religious training and belief" is something apart from conscience or "high moralistic philosophy." Gradually, however, the expansive approach began to gain ground. The *Kauten* language was quoted with approval in Justice Frankfurter's dissent in *West Virginia State Board of Education v. Barnette* [1943]. Justice Jackson, writing the opinion of the Court in the same case, signaled the Court's reluctance to impose orthodoxy of thought: "If there is any fixed star in our constitutional constellation, it is that no official, high or petty, can prescribe what shall be orthodox in politics, nationalism, religion, or other matters of opinion or force citizens to confess by word or act their faith therein." The year after this declaration, Justice Douglas wrote for the majority in *United States v. Ballard* [1944] that freedom of religion

embraces the right to maintain theories of life and of death and of the hereafter which are rank heresy to followers of the orthodox faiths. . . . Men may believe what they cannot prove. They may not be put to the proof of their religious doctrines or beliefs. Religious experiences which are as real as life to some may be incomprehensible to others. Yet the fact that they may be beyond the ken of mortals does not mean that they can be made suspect before the law.

Ballard makes clear that the classification of a belief as religion does not depend upon the tenets of its creed. . . .

[Again, in *Torcaso v. Watson* (1961),] a unanimous Court struck down a provision of the Maryland Constitution which had been used to deny a Secular Humanist appointment as a notary public because he refused to declare belief in God. The Court reasoned that, under the establishment clause, government cannot force a person to profess either belief or disbelief in any religion, aid all religions against nonreligions, or aid theistic religions against nontheistic faiths. The Court thus gave wide reach to the term "religion." Among the beliefs the Court explicitly identified as religious were Buddhism, Taoism, Ethical Culture, and Secular Humanism.

The Court shortly made it clear that *Torcaso* was not an eccentric ruling. *United States v. Seeger* [1965] and *Welsh v. United States* [1970] were the occasions for the most detailed consideration of the definition of religion yet given by the Supreme Court.

In *Seeger* [1976], the Court resolved a conflict between circuits regarding the interpretation of section 6(j) of the Universal Military Training and Service Act of 1948. Construing the statute's requirement of belief "in a relation to a Supreme Being." the court characterized the question as

> whether a given belief that is sincere and meaningful occupies a place in the life of its possessor parallel to that filled by the orthodox belief in God of one who clearly qualifies for the exemption. Where such beliefs have parallel positions in the lives of their respective holders we cannot say that one is "in a relation to a Supreme Being" and the other is not.

Although the *Seeger* Court couched the issue narrowly as one of statutory construction, its holding appears to have been constitutionally required. Certainly the Court violently strained the plain meaning of words and disregarded the evident intention of Congress to exclude nontheists from exemption. The Court presumably found such a distortion necessary because a literal construction, discriminating between theists and followers of other traditions, would have, as Justice Douglas noted in his concurrence, rendered the provision constitutionally vulnerable. . . .

In *Welsh*, which also construed section 6(j), the Court extended *Seeger*. First, by holding that purely ethical and moral considerations were religious, it further blurred the distinction between religion and morality, at least when the conviction with which the latter is entertained approximates the intensity usually associated with more conventional religious belief. Second, it held that a sincere petitioner might be denied the exemption only if his system of beliefs does "not rest at all upon moral, ethical, or religious principle but instead rests *solely* upon considerations of policy, pragmatism, or expediency." *Seeger* had denied exemption to those whose views were "essentially" nonreligious, suggesting that a petitioner could have been denied an exemption even though his views had a substantial moral-religious component if the secular component were more substantial. *Welsh* foreclosed this interpretation.

THE COURT'S DEFINITION AND CONTEMPORARY RELIGIOUS EXPERIENCE

Arguably, there are as many definitions of religion as there are students of religion. Nonetheless, the Court simply cannot avoid the problem of definition. *Torcaso* [1965], *Seeger*, and *Welsh* [1970] suggest a willingness, in contexts raising free exercise questions, to adopt an expansive definition of religion. That willingness comports both with the free exercise clause's concern for inviolability of conscience and with the diversity of contemporary religious experience. . . .

[For example, Paul Tillich and other twentieth century existentialists, have defined "religion" as "ultimate concern," recognizing] that the concern must be of an unconditional, absolute, or unqualified character. The meaning of the term "ultimate" is to be found in a particular human's experience rather than in some objective reality. . . .

[Another contemporary controversy deals with the "death of God." There were several advocates of this view in the 1960s. Thus Thomas Altizer (1966) sees the hallmark of Christianity as its assertion that the sacred is reached only through the profane. For Altizer, the death of God is an actual event, not to be confused with an eclipse of God or a withdrawal of God from history. The theology of Altizer differs from the views of other "death of God" theologians in important details, of course; but it shares with them a major precept — that the concept of a God, a concept long presumed to be the irreducible core of the Christian religion, is not only unnecessary but also undesirable for the true Christian.

While the "death of God" theologians concerned themselves with the place of God in religion, another equally notable group of Christian theologians debated the role of the church in the modern world. A popular spokesman for this group, Harvey Cox, heralds the "epoch of the secular city." His secularization theology "bypasses and undercuts religion and goes on to other things. It has relativized religious world views and thus rendered them innocuous." Cox locates the essence of Christianity in "just those forms which many religious people consider evil or occasions for evil, that most of the rest consider to be at least morally indifferent." He argues that the starting point for any theology of the church today must be a theology of social change. . . .

[Although the number of adherents to such views may be small, the Court cannot ignore them, because] notable thinkers, unquestionably within the Christian tradition, are espousing them as *their* Christian religion. . . .

THE "NEW RELIGIONS"

The essence of American religion is its diversity and radical pluralism. In 1960 there existed "more than 400 more or less definitely organized bodies . . . [not including] the multitude of store-front churches, local sects, cults, and unclassifiable quasi-religious associations which operate ephemerally but often vigorously in the American scene." Moreover, the "spiritual explosion" of the 1960's and 1970's has generated untold additional diversification.

The "religions of the perimeter," it has been argued, stand for creative religion in the hands of the people and represent the truest expression of religious life. Since many of these religions do not speak in the familiar terms of classical traditions, cannot be tested by logic, and doubtless appear deviant to some, it is extraordinarily important that they be approached generously and without religious chauvinism. In each of the instances that follow, the only claim is that the beliefs involved are religious to *some*; there are certainly individuals for whom they do not rise to the level of ultimate concern.

The Court has recognized humanism as religious. One study goes further and asserts a religious dimension (for some) in the Human Potential Movement, a movement claiming more than six million adherents who seek to transcend the oppressiveness of culture by transforming themselves as individuals. Believers see human potential as including greater insight, body awareness and communication with others.

Witchcraft is often put forth as the world's oldest living religion, and one commentator puts the number of witches practicing in groups at close to 5,000. The practice of witchcraft takes many forms, ranging from what might be called simple nature worship, to the use of plant-based hallucinatory ointments (such as hebain, mandrake, and atropine) to create a trance state, or to the similar use of LSD in "Acid Satanism."

Of course, witchcraft does not stand alone in claiming religious use of LSD or drugs. At least three psychedelic churches have been founded around the use of LSD. While the probabilities may be that an individual using LSD or drugs is not doing so for religious reasons, it has been forcefully argued that, once again, *for some* the choice is made for reasons of ultimate concern.

Even political and social beliefs may be religious. Tillich suggests: "If a national group makes the life and growth of the nation its ultimate concern . . . [e]verything is centered in the only god, the nation. . . ." This point has been variously made about "civil religion in America," Communism, Marxism, Nazism, Italian Facism, and Japanese militarism.

Against a background of such heterogeneity, it becomes increasingly difficult to disregard the claim of a group that it is a "new religion." Clearly, a test of religiosity grounded in the phenomenological approach of Tillich is compatible with that background. And, equally clearly, there is the danger that content-based tests will arbitrarily excise what may be significant segments of contemporary religious experience. . . .

THE APPROPRIATENESS OF A FUNCTIONAL DEFINITION. . . .

To remain true to the free exercise clause . . . a definition must proceed at a level of inquiry that does not discriminate among creeds on the basis of content, that does not circumscribe the very choices which the Constitution renders inviolate. What those choices are — and thus the meaning of religion for free exercise purposes — can therefore be limited only by a broader inquiry which looks at the role played by a system of belief in an individual's life and which seeks to identify those functions worthy of preferred status in the constitutional scheme. This is precisely the kind of inquiry at the root of the ultimate concern test espoused by Tillich and relied upon by the Court in *Seeger* and *Welsh*.*

This approach is appropriate for at least four reasons. First, as noted above, it does not violate the idea of free exercise itself because it focuses on functional rather than content-oriented criteria. Second, it is not hopelessly open ended; on the contrary, it rejects any belief which for the individual is subordinate or capable of compromise. Third, while parochial to the extent that any definition formulated on the basis of human experience must be, the ultimate concern approach does as much as possible to avoid the dangers of religious chauvinism. Fourth, and most importantly, this test is peculiarly appropriate to the preferred status given to religious freedom by the first amendment. Indeed, what concerns could be more deserving of preferred status than those deemed by the individual to be ultimate? . . .

Since many untraditional concerns could be viewed as religious under an expansive definition, it might be feared that the required exceptions and accommodations will imperil the effective implementation of government programs. Combining the im-

---

*EDITOR'S NOTE   Read also *The Sociology of Religion*, by Harold Fallding, New York: McGraw-Hill, 1974.

pact of *Sherbert* with that of *Seeger*, one observer remarked: "[W]hen this forbearance toward religious objection is combined with the new permissiveness in defining religion . . . [d]issidents of all kinds — nudists, LSD users, racists, utopians, and groups as yet unimagined — can be expected to present claims for religious freedom." Further, it is contended that if individuals could receive exemption from particular statutes merely by joining a particular cult, they would be given a right of private nullification of the law.

These fears are overdrawn. Under *Sherbert* [1963] exemption from observance of the law is not automatic. The accommodation concept entails an assessment of the magnitude of the state interest in denying the exemption. The mere fact that an individual's religious practices would be inconvenienced is unlikely to prove sufficient should claims for exceptions or accommodations truly threaten the viability of a valid scheme of regulation. . . .

Possibility of Fraudulent Claims

The more common objection to an expansive definition is that including "fringe" beliefs will encourage fraudulent claims for exemptions or privileges. If insincere assertions became frequent, and if no satisfactory means could be found to recognize them, the courts would be confronted with the hard choice between, on the one hand, granting all claims (and perhaps producing so many exemptions that government programs would be emasculated) and, on the other hand, denying all free exercise claims (and thus rejecting many that are sincerely religious). . . .

One deterrent to the unscrupulous is the fact that pressing a false claim could lead to legal liability. An individual will find it difficult to prevail on a claim of ultimate concern without taking the stand, and false testimony could expose him to prosecution for perjury. Clearly such prosecutions would be appropriate only in unusual and blatant cases lest perjury become a technique for religious persecution. But the mere possibility of prosecution might deter some false claims.

Further, the courts are not completely powerless to resist false claims. Insincerity may sometimes be discovered through examination of extrinsic evidence, including patterns of inconsistent actions of statements. . . .

To further discourage insincerity, free exercise claims might, in appropriate cases, be allowed only if the petitioner agrees in the imposition of some alternative duty or burden. This is done in selective service statutes. Analogously, in *Sherbert*, it might have been reasonable to condition receipt of unemployment compensation on Sherbert's willingness to do volunteer work or perform some other service useful to the state on non-Sabbath days during the week. The use of alternative burdens would promote three desirable ends: it would discourage insincere claims, minimize the cost of the state of engaging in accommodation, and accord roughly equivalent treatment to exempted and unexempted persons. . . .

8.3 Can Transcendental Meditation Be Taught in Public Schools? No!

Transcendental Meditation (TM) is an effective relaxation teaching that involves "thinking" a special sound, or "mantra". . . [to] achieve a deep state of wakeful rest . . . [so that] both TM and its underlying theory, the Science of Creative Intelligence (SCI), have . . . achieved a remarkable degree of popularity. . . .

[However, school TM programs have] drawn severe criticism from those who have labeled TM religious on the basis of its resemblance to various Hindu practices. . . .

[In *Malnak v. Mahesh* the U.S. Supreme] Court likened TM preja to a form of prayer and SCI's concept of Creative Intelligence to the traditional [Western] concepts of God. Since it apparently was not disputed that the public schools were promoting SCI/TM, these analogies compelled the conclusion that teaching SCI/TM in the public schools was an establishment of religion [forbidden by the First Amendment]. . . .

The possibility of preferential treatment is diminished if SCI is taught in a comparative religion or philosophy course. In this situation, the high school administrator may easily maintain that the school's curriculum, as a whole, is neutral among religions. Moreover, as several Supreme Court Justices have indicated, religion is a subject worthy of objective study. . . .

[For example, in a concurring opinion in *McCollum v. Board of Education* {333 U.S. 203 (1948)} Justice Robert H. Jackson observed:]

> The fact is that, for good or ill, nearly everything in our culture worth transmitting, everything which gives meaning to life, is saturated with religious influences derived from paganism, Judaism, Christianity — both Catholic and Protestant — and other faiths accepted by a large part of the world's peoples. One can hardly respect a system of education that would leave the student wholly ignorant of the currents of religious thought that move the world for a part in which he is being prepared.

It is not clear that even the existence of a legitimate secular purpose will save a program involving a religious practice in the public schools. In *School District v. Schempp* [344 U.S. 203 (1963)], for instance, the state attempted to justify its Bible reading program as an effort to promote various secular civic virtues . . . but the Court, in effect, dismissed the contention [when it said:]

> [Even if the program's] purpose is not strictly religious, it is sought to be accomplished through readings . . . from the Bible. Surely the Bible as an instrument of religion cannot be gainsaid, and the state's recognition of the pervading religious character of the ceremony is evident from the rule's specific permission of the alternative use of the Catholic Douay version . . . [and] the . . . amendment permitting nonattendance [for nonbelievers] . . . None of these factors is consistent with the contention that the Bible is here used either as an instrument for nonreligious moral inspiration or as a reference for the teaching of secular subjects.

Brief excerpts from "Notes: Transcendental Meditation and the Meaning of Religion Under the Establishment Clause," 62 *Minnesota Law Review* 887–949, June 1978, especially pp. 887, 889, 940, 941, 956. By permission.

Although the article refers to numerous court decisions, the chief one is *Malnak v. Mahesh* 440 F. Supp. 1284 at 1315–1325 (1977, 1978)

[In the *Schempp* case, then,] the Court simply did not believe that the state's purpose was secular, [and in the *Malnak* decision of 1977 and 1978 the Court judged that]

> . . . a course of instruction in TM, which is as much "an instrument of" SCI as Bible reading is an instrument of the Christian religion, violates the establishment clause as interpreted in *Schempp.*

It was apparently not the use of the Bible per se, but the failure of school authorities to present the Bible in a secular context, that was fatal to the school Bible reading in *School District v. Schempp*:

> It certainly may be said that the Bible is worthy of study for its literary and historic qualities. Nothing we have said here indicates that such study of the Bible or of religion, when presented objectively as part of a secular program of education, may not be effected consistently with the First Amendment. But the exercises here do not fall into these categories. They are religious exercises. [343 U.S. at 225 (1963)].*

---

*EDITOR'S NOTE   In the *Lemon* and *Tilton* cases of 1971 and in the *Meek v. Pettinger* case of 1975, the Supreme Court also clearly enunciated the three criteria which were to be employed in the determination of the constitutionality under the establishment clause of public aid to church schools: (1) The statute must have a secular legislative purpose; (2) the principal or primary effect of the statute must be one that neither advances nor inhibits religion; (3) the statute must not foster an excessive government entanglement with religion. If any of the three criteria is not complied with, the legislation is unconstitutional as a law respecting the establishment of religion.

8.4   The Nation's Second School System
NEIL A. McCLUSKEY

Until very recent years, parochial school attendance . . . was required by church law. . . . Historically . . . the bishops and clergy were at the forefront in the creation of the parochial schools and subsequently in their operation and staffing. There was little alternative and large precedent for this dominance. Even had there been ample funds to pay the salaries commanded by lay teachers, modest though they were, the tradition of clerical and religious involvement in education was as old as the monastic schools of the early Middle Ages. Thus for many years the parochial schools were staffed almost exclusively by nonsalaried teaching orders of religious men and women.

During the past two decades, however, the lay teacher has come more and more to replace the religious or clerical teacher, a move that started after World War II when the great expansion of parochial schools took place. It was heightened subsequently by the sharp decline in the numbers of men and women entering the religious state.

Excerpts from Neil A. McCluskey, S. J., "The Nation's Second School System," *American Education* 10: 16–19, December 1974.

Dr. McCluskey is Dean of Teacher Education, Herbert H. Lehman College, City University of New York.

The net result was that the percentage of lay teachers in the Nation's Catholic schools rose from ten percent in 1950 to 26 percent by 1960 and to more than 50 percent by 1970, the further result being a huge increase in the cost of Catholic education.

The scarcity of religious teachers (and its impact on costs) is the chief reason regularly advanced by Catholic school superintendents for closing a school or curtailing classes, but changing viewpoints would appear to be involved also. Large numbers of Catholics today, for example, seem to have decided that Catholic youngsters who attend public school will not for that reason turn out to be something less than good Catholics.

The consequence of such factors as these has been a steady decline in Catholic school enrollments. . . . Within a decade the fall-off has come to 35 percent, more than one-third. . . .

But what lies ahead? Research has become an important new ingredient in Catholic planning for the future. Sparked by a Carnegie-Notre Dame national study completed in 1966, some 57 dioceses and dozens of religious teaching orders have undertaken in-depth examinations of their own educational situations. Out of these various research enterprises have come several important findings that begin to sketch out the future of the Catholic schools. Four would appear to be of pivotal significance:

1. The schools which have withstood the winnowing process of the past ten years have generally been the schools that had on their own account initiated needed reforms. They have larger and better qualified staffs. Their teacher-pupil ratio has achieved or is approaching the accepted professional optimum — on the elementary level in Catholic schools today the ratio is one to 28; on the secondary level, one to 19. These advances plus new instructional methods and imaginative reorganization suggest the pattern by which the parochial schools can attract the necessary measure of local community support.

2. The contemporary Catholic school has largely shed its narrow confessional image as it has moved more and more into the mainstream of American education. There is new emphasis on civic concern, especially in taking responsibility for the schooling of minority-group children, including a heavy proportion of youngsters from non-Catholic families.

3. Increasing numbers of Catholic leaders are taking the position that there are other ways of discharging pastoral responsibility outside the parochial school setting. . . .

4. Not only has the lay teacher gained equal footing in the staffing of the schools but lay people are rapidly becoming full partners in policy-making. The fastest growing movement in Catholic education is the development of parish and diocesan school boards. As a side effect, the increasingly lay image of the Catholic school may greatly broaden its appeal for whatever constitutionally valid forms of public assistance may be forthcoming in the years ahead.

Such findings and the continuing research behind them inspire in many observers the conviction that although Catholic schools may not again enroll the numbers of the students of former years, they will continue to be an important element in American education.*

---

*EDITOR'S NOTE   In discussing "American Catholic Education Science Vatican II" (an article written especially for the fourth edition of *Crucial Issues in Education*, 1969, pp. 136-145), John W. Donohue, S.J. (Fordham University) observes that

> as Catholic colleges become academically more sophisticated they also become more secularized, just as Protestant colleges did some generations ago. . . . Since they are schools, they are fully committed to secular values and share all the specifically educational problems of American higher education. In addition, they encounter special issues of their own, which may be summed up in three questions asked with varying degrees of seriousness. Is there a definable sense in which an institution can be truly Catholic and truly a university? If so, what precisely makes such a university *Catholic*? Even if it is possible to have a Catholic university, is it desirable? Might not Catholics simply conduct good secular institutions that are no more Catholic than Harvard is Congregational?
>
> Questions of this sort are posed more insistently after the Second Vatican Council. . . . [from which there seem to emerge] four nuclear ideas that are already shaping Catholic school theory and practice. These are the themes of (1) the endorsement of the process of secularization; (2) the importance of the role and responsibility of the laity both in the Church and in the whole of human society; (3) freedom as the root of personal worth and dignity; and (4) community as a focal value flowing from the human family's oneness and common destiny — demanding expression in friendship and cooperation across all lines and at all levels, including not least the international.

To more fully appreciate the meaning of such post-Vatican II statements, consider the 1948 Catholic position as it appeared in Rome in the Jesuit fortnightly *La Civiltà Cattolica*:

> The Roman Catholic Church, convinced, through its divine prerogatives, of being the only true church, must demand the right to freedom for herself alone, because such a right can only be possessed by truth, never by error. As to other religions, the church will certainly never draw the sword, but she will require that by legitimate means they shall not be allowed to propagate false doctrine. Consequently, in a state where the majority of the people are Catholic, the church will require that legal existence be denied to error, and that if religious minorities actually exist, they shall have only a *de facto* existence without opportunity to spread their beliefs. If, however, actual circumstances . . . make the complete application of this principle impossible, then the church will require for herself all possible concessions. . . .
>
> In some countries, Catholics will be obliged to ask full religious freedom for all, resigned at being forced to cohabitate where they alone should rightfully be allowed to live. But in doing this the Church does not renounce her thesis . . . but merely adapts herself. . . . Hence arises the great scandal among Protestants. . . . We ask Protestants to understand that the Catholic church would betray her trust if she were to proclaim . . . that error can have the same rights as truth. . . . The church cannot blush for her own want of tolerance, as she asserts it in principle and applies it in practice.
> — La Civiltà *Cattolica*, quoted in *Time* 51: 70, June 28, 1948.

Such intolerance of Catholic toward Protestant, and of Protestant toward Catholic, still survives in Northern Ireland in the year 1977. But such intolerance — and such inhumanity — are as nothing compared to the treatment of the American Indian by the Catholic Hernando Cortez in Mexico or by the Protestant Andrew Jackson in the United States. If the Christian religion is an integral element of Western Civilization, then a revision of Christian theology is a most urgent need. For an excellent discussion of this problem, read René Dubos, *The God Within*, New York: Scribners, 1972.

Compare also the following statement from Ralph Barton Perry's book *Characteristically American* (New York: Knopf, 1949):

> The history of Catholicism . . . [in] the United States reveals two broad trends: a trend coinciding broadly with contemporary political, social, and economic progress; and a trend toward a more rigid and highly centralized ecclesiastical authority. And whenever these two trends have come into conflict, it is the second which appears to have prevailed in Rome, while it is the first which has prevailed in America.

8.5 Evolution Versus Creation in the Public Schools
RICHARD H. UTT

Evolution, like its opposite philosophy, creationism, is unprovable, and lies outside the realm of science. Ultimately both theories are explanations of origins heavily influenced by one's personal faith and world view. Neither is more or less scientific than the other, in that neither can be observed or tested today. It is surprising how often leading defenders of evolutionism, when it comes to the ultimate explanations, use words like "faith," "mystery," and even "magic." If either theory is used in the teaching of science, certainly the other should have equal time. To refuse discussion of alternative views of origins is to display, not devotion to science, but dogmatism.

WHAT ABOUT THE FIRST AMENDMENT?

If creationism is to be presented as an alternate theory of origins, does this not breach the wall of church and state?

Decidedly not! — not if it is taught as *scientific* creationism, in a nonreligious way. How is this done?

Mr. Louis Goodgame, an experienced teacher in the Crescent City, California, public schools, has been teaching creationism as an alternate theory to evolutionism for a number of years — with widespread community approval. How does he do it

From Richard H. Utt (Wrightville, California), "Evolution versus Creation in the Public Schools," *Liberty* (Seventh Day Adventist Church Magazine), January/February 1980, pp. 13–15. (Bibliographical footnotes are omitted.) Reprinted with permission from *Liberty*.

Martin E. Marty (*Saturday Review* 7: 37–38, May 1980) notes why this issue is important: It is because in the year 1980 there are many uprooted moderns who " . . . seek authority, discipline, a kind of earnest religious experience." Marty observes how, using TV for entertainment, conversion, healing, positive thinking, and political signal calling, such fundamentalists as the Reverend Jerry Falwall and Pat Robertson are now taking in more money than the Republican and Democratic parties combined.

In an article "More Than Segregated Academies: The Growing Protestant Fundamentalist Schools" (*Phi Delta Kappan* 61: 391–393, February 1980), Virginia Davis Nordin and William Lloyd Turner (both at the University of Wisconsin, Madison) remind us that Fundamentalist Protestantism:

> . . . is a sober and devout belief that their religious faith should and does pervade every aspect of their lives, their churches and [their] Academies]. . . . [Fundamentalists] perceive a basic philosophical difference between themselves and the leaders of public education. Like the seventeenth-century Puritans, they believe in the "innate depravity of man." Because they believe that the corrupt nature of humanity can be changed only through a supernatural infusion of Divine grace, religious "conversion" becomes the basis of all education. Furthermore, since human nature is utterly depraved, children require strict supervision and authoritarian guidance if they are not to be overcome by Satan and the evil within their own nature.

> Fundamentalists see public education, by contrast, as proceeding on John Dewey's conviction that human nature is basically good, that students will naturally seek the highest and best if left to themselves, and that the adversary is therefore not Satan or an evil nature but poverty, ignorance, and prejudice. Fundamentalists try to approach the educational task from a different philosophical perspective, using different methodology and pursing different goals.

> Because they perceive that the Protestant ethic has disappeared from public education philosophy, fundamentalists have voiced an increasing nostalgia and a desire to return to the practices of former days. One hears frequent references to the "old-time religion," "old-fashioned" virtues, and the "faith of our fathers." This has produced schools that attempt to recreate the environment of past generations.

Thomas Torrance, Professor of Christian Dogmatics at the University of Edinburgh, holds that the conflict between evolutionary theory and the recent Creationist movement " . . . is a conflict between bad science and bad theology." (*Zygon Newsletter*, Summer 1980.) Perhaps so. But many do not understand this. And for them, and for educators who must deal with them, programs such as the one described here may help us to move from insulation to dialogue and from ignorance to understanding.

legally? The same way, he says, as the place of God and Christian faith in American history is discussed without apology and without sectarianism. The Declaration of Independence, for example, appeals to the "Laws of Nature and of Nature's God." The document's signers closed the Declaration by committing themselves to the "Protection of divine Providence."

The Liberty Bell in Philadelphia is inscribed with a Bible verse: "Proclaim liberty throughout all the land unto all the inhabitants thereof."

The speeches of Abraham Lincoln, including the Gettysburg Address, abound in references to God, and the Second Inaugural quotes liberally from the Bible, King James Version. Thanksgiving and Christmas, rich in religious meaning, are observed in various ways in the schools.

In other words, it is not only possible but desirable to present the important part the religious faith of our founding fathers played in our history. Of course, this must be done without sectarianism or proselytism, without turning public school classes into some kind of evangelistic meeting or Sunday school class.

In exactly the same way, the concept of a great Creator and Designer — the same divine Providence invoked in the Declaration of Independence, the same Creator who endowed human beings with "certain unalienable Rights" — is one prominent explanation of the origin of the world and life upon it. This alternate theory can be discussed without calling for any commitment to the doctrines or rituals of Catholics, Baptists, Jews, Moslems, Unitarians, or Madalyn O'Hair. The data from geology, biology, genetics, paleontology, and other branches of science are discussed in relation to the two models — creation and evolution — and each student can decide for himself which model he accepts as more true and persuasive.

WILL THE PUBLIC ACCEPT IT?

Does the public wish both the theory of evolution and that of creation taught in the tax-supported schools? Yes, according to several limited polls. A 1973 survey of 1,500 people in Crescent City, California, showed that 89 percent believed that creation should be taught; 79 percent favored teaching both theories; and 10 percent wanted only creation.

A random telephone survey of 526 people in five Midwestern states yielded the following results: Both creation and evolution should be taught, 68 percent; creation only, 15 percent; evolution only, 6 percent; no opinion, 11 percent.

WILL THE COURTS PERMIT IT?

There is evidence that the courts would favor neutrality and fairness in the presentation of theories of origins in the public schools. Supreme Court concurrences have stated:

> We agree of course that the State may not establish a 'religion of secularism' in the sense of affirmatively opposing or showing hostility to religion, thus 'preferring those who believe in no religion over those who believe.'

The fullest realization of true religious liberty requires that government neither engage in nor compel religious practices, that it effect no favoritism among sects or between religion and nonreligion, and that it work deterrence of no religious belief. . . .

It is said, and I agree, that the attitude of the State toward religion must be one of neutrality. But untutored devotion to the concept of neutrality can lead to invocation or approval of results which partake not simply of that noninterference and noninvolvement with the religious which the Constitution commands, but of a brooding and pervasive devotion to the secular and a passive, or even active, hostility to the religious. Such results are not only not compelled by the Constitution, but, it seems to me, are prohibited by it.*

WATCH OUT FOR SEMANTICS

The old vocabulary in the evolution-creation controversy needs to be discarded and a new one adopted. Defenders of "evolution only" in the schools represent the issue as one of science versus religion, which it is not. They overuse the pejorative term *fundamentalist* because they know that to most people the word evokes images of Bible-thumping bigots. They resurrect the specter of the Scopes "Monkey Trial" of 1925, with John Scopes and Clarence Darrow as heroes on one side and William Jennings Bryan and a backdrop of hillbilly preachers as villains on the other.

Whatever may be said for the stereotypes, this is 1980, not 1925. The scenario is now vastly changed. Now there are hundreds of scientists with doctorates from Harvard, Berkeley, and most points between who are firmly on the creationist side. Nowadays attempt to bring fairness into the teaching of origins in public school science classes will have the support of a significant number of trained scientists. These men and women are familiar with the scientific method and can intelligently discuss the strengths and weaknesses of both creation and evolution as hypotheses of origins.

WHAT DIFFERENCE DOES IT MAKE?

Whether or not we have stopped to think about it, one's understanding of evolution and creation affects, directly or indirectly, every area of human thought and conduct. Joseph LeConte, in his *Evolution, Its Nature, Its Evidences, and Its Relation to Religious Thought*, wrote,

---

*EDITOR'S NOTE   These quotations are from the *Schempp* and *Murray* cases, U.S. 807-944, (1963). It should be noted that the majority opinion was written by Justice Tom C. Clark, a Presbyterian active in the affairs of his church. Concurring opinions included those by Justice Arthur J. Goldberg, the Court's only Jew, and by Justice William J. Brennan, the Court's only Roman Catholic. These Supreme Court rulings affirmed that *compulsory* recitation of the Lord's Prayer, or even *compulsory* reading of some particular translation of the Bible, is unconstitutional.

Serious students should read the entire series of opinions defending *both* freedom *from* and freedom *for* religion.

The process of evolution pervades the whole universe, and the doctrine concerns alike every department of science — yea, every department of human thought. It is literally one half of all science. Therefore, its truth or falseness, its acceptance or rejection, is not a trifling matter, affecting only one small corner of the thought realm. On the contrary, it affects profoundly the foundations of philosophy, and therefore the whole domain of thought. It determines the whole attitude of the mind toward nature and God.

The evolution-creation issue looms ever larger in American education. Parents have a right to be concerned about the world view their children receive at school. Taxpayers have a right to protest when their tax dollars are used for lopsided indoctrination of a philosophy they themselves reject.

In the next few years the controversy will undoubtedly involve many levels of government, the courts, the public schools, and every teacher, parent, and student in the land. Is it not time for every citizen to become well informed on the issue — *both* sides of it?*

---

*EDITOR'S NOTE   For further discussion of "secular humanism" and the "creation versus evolution" controversy, read articles by J. Charles Park, Richard H. Stewart, Connaught Marshner, Gerald Skoog, Wendell R. Bird, and William B. Mayer in *Educational Leadership*, 38: 146–159, November 1980 (bibliography).

8.6   Teaching About Religion — With No Indoctrination
MARGHERITE LAPOTA

The "taboo" against the study of religion in American public education has been imposed largely by educators themselves. This fact has grown out of confusion about what is legal and what is not . . . *Abington v. Schempp* (1963) [did rule out from use in public schools both compulsory Bible reading and compulsory school prayers. At the same time, the majority opinion written by Justice Tom C. Clark] specifically pointed out in the decision the following often-quoted guidelines:

> It might well be said that one's education is not complete without a study of comparative religion or the history of religion and its relation to the advancement of civilization. It certainly may be said that the Bible is worthy of study for its literary and historic qualities. Nothing we have said here indicates that such study of the Bible or of religion, *when presented objectively as part of a secular program of education, may not be affected consistently with the First Amendment.* (Italics added.)

Concurring statements were made by Justices William J. Brennan and Arthur J. Goldberg. Those by Brennan follow:

Excerpts from Margherite LaPota, "(The 'Taboo' Can Be Lifted): Religion: Not 'Teaching' but 'Teaching About,' " *Education Leadership* 31: 30–33, October 1973. (Slightly adapted.) Reprinted with permission of the Association for Supervision and Curriculum Development and Margherite LaPota. Copyright © 1973 by the Association for Supervision and Curriculum Development.
Margherite LaPota is Supervisor of Language Arts and English, K–12, Tulsa (Oklahoma) Public Schools.

The holding of the Court today plainly does not foreclose teaching about Holy Scriptures or the differences between religious sects in classes of literature or history. . . . *To what extent, and at what points in the curriculum, religious materials should be cited are matters which the courts ought to entrust very largely to the experienced officials who superintend our Nation's public schools. They are the experts in such matters, and we are not.* (Italics added.)

These opinions were tested in 1970 when the Supreme Court upheld (by refusing to rehear) the state supreme court ruling that the University of Washington did not violate the First Amendment in offering and teaching an elective course, "English 309: The Bible as Literature" (*Calvary Bible Presbyterian Church v. Board of Regents of the University of Washington*).

Since the Abington-Schempp decision cleared away legal doubts about the objective use of the Bible and religion as academic study, many school boards, administrators, and teachers around the nation have become active in implementing such study in their schools. They have acted upon their belief that a truly complete and effective education must include the study of religion. . . .

The educator who wishes to initiate courses about religion in his school must be concerned about the *how*, *who*, and *what*. The *how* was mandated by Justice Clark when he stipulated that (a) *objectivity* is the only acceptable approach to teaching about religion in public schools, and that (b) such study must be a *part* of a secular program of education. It is essential not only that *objectivity* be clearly defined by the administrators and the course instructor(s), but also that input be encouraged from the community. . . .

[As for the *who*, the teacher must] be comitted to objectivity in the classroom, and be knowledgeable in the history of religions and their sacred writings. Many classroom teachers do not qualify and some do not even want to qualify. For those who want to qualify but who lack sufficient scholarship, special in-service training could be offered locally; or, better still, more summer institutes at universities and colleges (such as the one offered at Indiana University and directed by James Ackerman and Thayer Warshaw) could be made available to teachers. . . .

[As for the *what*, materials are in plentiful supply, for example, from the University of Nebraska Press, 901 N. 17th St., Lincoln, NB 68508; Augsburg Publishing House, 426 S. 5th St., Minneapolis, MN 55415; Allyn and Bacon, Inc., Rockleigh, N.J. 07648; Addison-Wesley Publishing Co., Reading, MA 01867; Indiana University Press, Bloomington, IN 47401; Harcourt Brace Jovanovich, Inc., 757 Third Ave., New York, N.Y. 10017.*

---

*EDITOR'S NOTE   In societies where there is a union of church and state, "values" and "religious values" are often used almost synonymously. But such is not the case in the United States, where there is separation of church and state. Selections 8.1-8.6 have presented some of the problems and limitations faced by public schools when approaching the teaching of values by way of religion. Selections 8.7-8.15 are also concerned with the teaching of values, but approach the problem from a neutral or secular (but not from an "antireligious") point of view.

8.7   Toward a Clarification of Our Values
MILTON ROKEACH

. . . From a values clarification perspective, the school is seen to have value-clarifying functions but not value-transmitting and value-implementing functions. In fact, the latter functions are more or less explicitly denied, because the only social instructions that are recognized to have such functions are the family and organized religion:

> In our society, families and organized religions will not allow the school to usurp their role and teach a particular set of values. Therefore, modern values education as it has evolved in the school has, for the most part, emphasized the teaching of a *process* of valuing, rather than any one value or value system.
>
> Values clarification, stemming from the pioneer work of Louis Raths, is one approach to teaching a process of valuing — in schools, in homes, or in any setting where *values* issues may be present. (Simon and Kirschenbaum, 1973, p. 2)

Not all educators would, however, agree that the family and religion are the main or sole transmitters of values. Wagschal, for instance, writes that ". . . a society transfers values to its members through its political, social, and educational structures . . ." (Wagschal, 1975). But for those educators who do accept this view, and for those who agree that the school ought not attempt to usurp the family's and church's traditional functions, it is perhaps inevitable that they would adopt a doctrine of value neutrality, and a concomitant opposition to moralizing, value inculcation, and value modification. About all that would be thus left is to focus on the "process of valuing" and on the teaching of "value process skills."

Value clarification's insistence about value neutrality notwithstanding, an examination of its basic tenets suggests that it nonetheless has certain value commitments that remain silent, and that it moreover attempts through the back door to inculcate students with these values. The seven "valuing process" skills that it attempts to teach: (1) seeking alternatives when faced with a choice, (2) looking ahead to probable consequences before choosing, (3) making choices on one's own, without depending on others, (4) being aware of one's own preferences and valuations, (5) being willing to affirm one's choices and preferences publicly, (6) acting in ways that are consistent with choices and preferences, and (7) acting in these ways repeatedly, can readily be translated as attempts to inculcate students with the following value preferences: (1) broadmindedness or openmindedness rather than narrowmindedness or closed mindedness, (2) a future rather than past or present time perspective, (3) independence and freedom rather than dependence or obedience, (4) self-awareness rather than self-deception, (5) a courageous standing up for one's beliefs rather than cowardice, (6) logical consistency rather than an indifference to logical consistency, and (7) reliability and dependability rather than unreliability and undependability. All these refer to values that are not all that different from those that I have empirically identified as educational values. But a question remains: Is it not value-obfuscating rather than value-clarifying to teach such values through the back door, and at the same time give the impression of value neutrality through the front door?

From Milton Rokeach, "Toward a Philosophy of Value Clarification," in J. R. Meyer (ed.), *Values Education: Theory/Practice/Problems/Prospects*, © 1975 by Wilfred Laurier University Press, Waterloo, Ontario, pp. 117–26. Used by permission.

Closely related to value clarification's position on value neutrality is its position on value change: The purpose of value clarification is to clarify but not to change values. Such a view is, I believe, an untenable one. How would one proceed to demonstrate the effectiveness of a classroom procedure that seeks to clarify but not to change values? If it is demonstrated to not affect values, can it be claimed to be effective? If it does have effects, it must surely affect values to one extent or another, in which case, can it be claimed to be value-free? . . .

All such reservations about values clarification notwithstanding, I believe that the values clarification movement has made an extremely important contribution to modern education. It has succeeded in getting across the proposition that beyond making students aware of facts and concepts it is also important to make them aware of their own values. Such a broadening of educational objectives now has a universal face validity, largely because of the pioneering work of proponents of values clarification.*

---

*EDITOR'S NOTE   Subjects not usually associated with morality and ethics may often be made more interesting if the pros and cons of related disputed topics are studied. When this is done, it is important that teachers avoid using such discussions merely to air their own prejudices, but treat each topic as objectively as possible. Here are a few examples, taken from an article "Social Issues Serve as Unifying Theme in a Biology Course," by Melba James, Edward Schmidt, and Thomas Conley in *The American Biology Teacher* 36: 347, September 1974:

Biologic Content	Social Issue
1. Flow of matter and energy	1. Should solid refuse be disposed of in landfills?
2. Relation of organisms to each other and their environment	2. Should we continue the use of pesticides to control agricultural pests?
3. Population growth and regulation	3. Should the human race be considered too populous?
4. Succession	4. Should humans continue the use of strip mining?
. . . .	. . . .
10. Mendelian laws	10. Should geneticists be allowed to alter the genes of humans?
. . . .	. . . .
14. Plants: classification and structure	14. Should we allow technologic progress to continue the destruction of natural plant life?
. . . .	. . . .

8.8   Kohlberg's Theories of Moral Development
EDITORIAL SUMMARY

Lawrence Kohlberg's theories represent the culmination of several earlier movements. First of all were the ethical theories of Dewey and Tufts, which postulated three levels of moral development:

This brief sketch is condensed from varied sources, especially from Lawrence Kohlberg, "Moral Education for a Society in Moral Transition." *Educational Leadership* 33: 46–52, October 1975; and from *Moral Development and Behavior*, edited by Thomas Lickona, (New York: Holt, Rinehart and Winston, 1976), pp. 5, 10, 71, 161.

1. a premoral or preconventional level of "behavior motivated by biological and social impulses with results for morals,"
2. the conventional level of behavior "in which the individual accepts with little critical reflection the standards of his group," and
3. the autonomous level of behavior in which "conduct is guided by the individual thinking and judging for himself whether a purpose is good, and does not accept the standard of his group without reflection."

The French psychologist Jean Piaget was another major influence. Piaget claimed:

1. There is an invariant order of stages of human growth and development.
2. These stages form a hierarchy, in which each higher stage integrates and includes those which precede it.
3. There is a progression, so that each new level signifies a higher level.

Piaget's third point may be viewed as an answer to moral relativism, for it affirms that some stages or levels of intellectual and moral development are both higher and superior to others.

It is also a response to the "Is — Ought" dichotomy which, for nearly a century, had excluded anything having to do with "ought" from the realm of scientific inquiry. Kohlberg spelled out, with greater clarity and precision than Piaget, the fact that "Is" psychology is restricted to the here and now, to stimulus-response behavior, and neglects the future-oriented — the "ought" motivated — levels which are built around rational principles and moral ideals. The editor would like to believe that Kohlberg's theories spell out in detail some of the notions set forth in "Human Freedom and the Sense of Duty" (Selection 3.15).

Here in capsule form are Kohlberg's levels and stages of moral development:

LEVELS AND STAGES	BEHAVIORAL MOTIVATION
I. Preconventional Level	
Stage 1. Seek pleasure. Avoid pain.	1. Self-gratification; egocentrism.
Stage 2. More prudent and more socially oriented self-gratification. Some awareness of fairness and reciprocity.	2. It pays to consider the desires of others as well as of oneself. "You scratch my back, and I'll scratch yours."
II. Conventional Level	
Stage 3. Good behavior is that which is approved by others; bad behavior is that which is not approved.	3. Behave so as to avoid social disapproval. Even as stage 1 would avoid pain, so stage 3 would avoid social disapproval or condemnation.
Stage 4. The "law and order" orientation: Conformity to authority.	4. Follow social rules and help to maintain them. You cannot make exceptions, because everyone else would start making them too.
III. Post-Conventional, Autonomous, Moral Principle Level	
Stage 5. The social contract, legalistic orientation. Right actions are defined in terms of general individual rights and standards which have been examined and agreed upon by society.	5. The overall aim is equality and opportunity under civil law. Right actions should be derived by mutual agreement, as they are under our American constitutional system.

Stage 6. The universal-ethical-principle orientation. In stage 6 moral principles are judged according to their comprehensiveness, universality and consistency. Examples: The Ten Commandments, the Golden Rule, Kant's categorical imperative.

6. Emphasis is placed on the sacredness of life; on compassion for fellow humans, including all races, creeds, nations and cultures; and on the rationality of moral principles.

Kohlberg's sixth stage is morality based on the principle of justice, namely, to treat every man's claim impartially regardless of the man. For Kohlberg, a moral principle is not only a rule of action but a reason for action. As a reason for action, justice (stage 6) means respect for persons.

It may be instructive to compare Kohlberg's six stages with Urie Bronfenbrenner's *Five Types of Moral Judgment and Behavior*, namely: (1) Self-oriented, (2) Authority-oriented, (3) Peer-oriented, (4) Collective-oriented, and (5) Objectively oriented. In Bronfenbrenner's fifth type, the individual responds to situations on the basis of principles rather than on the basis of orientations to self-interests, to group loyalties or toward social agents.

Elizabeth Leonie Simpson also calls our attention to the following:

Parallels between Motivational Aspects of Kohlberg's and Maslow's Theories:

Kohlberg's *Stages of Motives for Moral Action*
1. Fear of punishment by another
2. Desire to manipulate goods and obtain rewards from another
3. Anticipation of approval or disapproval by others
4. Anticipation of censure by legitimate authorities, followed by guilt feelings
5. Concern about respect of equals and of community
6. Concern about self-condemnation

Maslow *Hierarchy of Needs* [see Selection 3.3]
1. Physiological needs
2. Security needs

3. Belongingness or affiliation needs

4. Need for esteem from others

5. Need for self-esteem from sense of competence
6. Need for self-actualization

Maslow emphasizes an important point: It is only when the more elementary or basic needs (namely, *survival, security, belongingness* or *affiliation,* and *esteem*) can be taken for granted that a person is freed to utilize his abilities to the fullest, that is, to actualize his potential as a human being. The needs which then motivate him are growth producing rather than deficiency compensating.

In conclusion, in his attempt to find something universal in moral development, Kohlberg makes a distinction between *structure,* held to be universal and to follow laws of development, and *content,* held to vary with specific patterns of experience and to follow the laws of learning. Content tells us *what* a person believes, which is obviously dependent upon cultural variable experiences, whereas structure tells how a person *thinks about* the content of his beliefs, which reasoning, according to Kohlberg's theory, is universal.

The weakness of Kohlberg's theory arises from the fact that, although he may have avoided ethical relativism with respect to the *psychology* or *structure* of moral development, his methods have little or nothing to say with respect to *content.* This criticism is elaborated in the following selection.

8.9 Providing Content to Moral Education
CORNELL M. HAMM

The venerable tradition of inculcating into our children specific moral virtues has received a fresh challenge in recent years from Lawrence Kohlberg. In his emphasis on the development of a rational form of universal morality by means of providing children with "cognitive stimulation" to help them progress through invariant necessary stages of moral development, Kohlberg has discarded as fruitless and irrelevant the practice of teaching and enforcing specific rules of behavior. He has demeaningly labeled the contents of morality as nothing but a "bag of virtues." The imagery itself suggests artificiality, superficiality, and arbitrariness. This is as misleading as it is unfortunate; for failure to inculcate moral virtue is morally debilitating and socially hazardous. In what follows I shall argue that . . . the bag of virtues approach to moral education is not only compatible with, but necessary to, his theory of stimulating moral development through cognitive stimulation. Thereafter, I specify some content which could legitimately comprise part of the bag of virtues. . . .

A moral virtue, as I shall use the term and as is reflected in ordinary usage, is the disposition to behave in a morally desirable manner. While there might be some point in taking Kohlberg seriously when he says, "I have no idea what virtue really is" (Kohlberg 1970, p. 57), it is nevertheless evident that he himself has a fair grasp of what virtue consists. He cites honesty, fair play, loyalty, courage, and many others as examples.

The legitimate point I think he wants to make is that not all people who display these qualities of character are necessarily in the full sense of the term morally "educated." To have internalized certain morally acceptable rules and to behave according to them as a matter of habit is not yet necessarily to have grasped the principle which constitutes the reason for those rules. In this sense there is certainly something morally amiss; and moral education is to that extent incomplete. . . .

[What] makes a quality a virtue is not how one views a rule but how morally acceptable a certain practice is (based on whether or not it is an instance of a moral principle) and how thoroughly a rule enjoining that practice has become internalized as a feature of one's character. Thus it is appropriate to talk of virtue at every level of Kohlberg's developmental stages. A person may be said to have the virtue honesty if he has learnt to be honest; and whether he views honesty as a practice required by his peers or one required by a fundamental moral principle does not detract from his having the virtue. What matters is that honesty be morally justifiable and that it has become dispositional. . . . I would like it clearly understood that I share Kohlberg's ideal of the autonomous moral agent whose action flows from self-adopted universal moral principles, such as justice and respect for persons. What I argue is that the teaching of content, and all that this implies for moral virtues, is both compatible with Kohlberg's stage theory of moral development and required by it. . . .

Excerpts from Cornel M. Hamm (Simon Fraser University, Vancouver, B. C.), "The Content of Moral Education, or the 'Bag of Virtues,' " pp. 37–46 in A. C. Kazepides (ed.), *The Teaching of Values in Canadian Education*, Second Yearbook of the Canadian Society for the Study of Education, Edmonton, Alberta: The Society, 1975. (Reprinted in *School Review* 85: 218–228, February 1977.) (Footnote references are omitted. Also omitted are some specific suggestions by Professor Hamm for the teaching of moral content.) By permission of The Society, the University of Chicago Press, and Cornell M. Hamm.

Empirical evidence supports prima facie evidence that children learn situation-specific rules of behavior before they grasp the principles which cover a wide range of cases. They learn to walk before they run, so to speak, even in matters of morals. . . .

[It is] absurd to suggest that generalizations can be made without particulars. To have understood a principle means to have understood that instances (at least more than one) have common characteristics which make them fall within the same class. Principles of morality could not operate without concrete content. Peters puts it nicely when he says, "by calling something like respect for persons a 'principle' we mean that it embodies a consideration to which appeal is made when criticizing, justifying, or explaining some determinate content of behaviour or belief" (1973, pp. 60-61). From a logical standpoint, content, then, must be learnt prior to, or at least simultaneously with, principles. . . .

[That] content is important should be obvious from the fact that children must act long before they are able to make complete sense of rules and before they understand the validity of rules. And this must also be true of those adults who never reach stages beyond rule conformity. There are then social reasons why moral rule and moral habit must bridge the gap. Before children reach the age of reason, rules must be set down for them for purposes of their own safety and security, and to protect them and others from their misconduct. The same applies to adults whose development is arrested at the rule conformity level. Ideally, of course, one would hope that most people could reach the autonomous stage where they would do the morally right thing for the morally right reason. That is, indeed, how one might define the morally educated person. Failing that, it is still better, for socially desirable reasons, that people do the right thing for the wrong reason rather than the wrong thing for the wrong reason. (I take it that doing the wrong thing for the right reason is an impossibility.) There is point, then, to the teaching of rules. But the point is not merely to have memorized the rules, but to have internalized them and to have become habituated in them. If it is the case, as is commonly held, that bad habit militates against good habit, then we have a very good reason to instill reasonable habits in children in their heteronomous stage so that they can cash in or capitalize on their training when they reach the autonomous stage of morality and come to realize that the habits they have are indeed reasonable. They will then, as Plato suggests, "greet (reason) as a friend" (*Republic* 402a). Or one could sum it up in Peter's (1974, p. 274) terms as entering the palace of reason through the courtyard of habit.

THE CONTENTS OF THE BAG OF VIRTUES

Disagreement about the contents of moral education is not nearly as widespread as sometimes supposed. Such disagreement as there is usually occurs with respect to very specific and local rules at a fairly distant remove from more basic rules and principles. Such rules as *don't swear, don't drink, don't smoke, don't pollute the environment, don't engage in extra- or premarital sexual activity, don't take drugs, obey your parents and others in authority* are controversial because their justifiability depends on differing situations and on relevant information which is often unavailable. Here one must be cautious. There is, however, no need to focus on these controversial rules at the initial stages of teaching for virtue any more than there is need to start a child's science education by introducing him to the difficulties of the particle and wave theories of light.

In any case, if, as I have argued, it is impossible to proceed with moral education without content, then we as educators and parents shall simply have to work out a common body of rules which are generally acceptable on moral grounds. It should never be said of us that we failed to rear our children properly because we failed to do our homework, or lacked nerve, or couldn't risk making errors. We shall simply have to select the best rules we can think of. What more can be asked of us? If we make mistakes, so be it. That is part of the human condition.*

It is in the spirit of seeking such agreement that I venture to submit for consideration a body of content for which I believe there is ample moral justification.

---

*EDITOR'S NOTE   Hamm's criticisms of Kohlberg apply also to Raths, Simon, and other exponents of "value clarification." If a student should ask a "value clarification" teacher how he might best study values, the dialogue would be like that of the mother and daughter in the old song:

Mother, dear, may I go swimming? Oh, yes, my darling daughter:
Just hang your clothes on a hickory limb — but don't go near the water!

For another fine article dealing with this problem, read Israela Ettenberg Aron (Albert Einstein College of Medicine), "Moral Philosophy and Moral Education: The Formalist Tradition and the Deweyan Alternative," *School Review* 85: 513-524, April 1977.

Peter Scharf, a follower of Lawrence Kohlberg, notes the following difficulty in applying Kohlberg's "six-stages-of-moral-development" approach to teaching:

The theory suggests that only a teacher at the Stage 5 level of moral judgment is capable of formulating genuinely developmental educational objectives. At the same time, however, the theory encourages democratic dialogue and full participation in the formulating of educational goals. While the conflict between stage theory and democracy probably is potentially resolvable, it does generate some tension in the minds of many teachers. The teacher is asked to act as a moral philosopher, viewing classroom conflict from a lofty level of abstraction (and knowing that the student does not understand the reasoning involved), while at the same time encouraging full democratic participation of the students. This can lead to several problematic outcomes. The teacher may become an elitist, dismissing even the reasonable claims of students as "lower stage." On the other hand, the teacher may succumb to the immediate will of the group. — Peter Scharf, *Moral Education*, Davis, CA: Responsible Action Press, 1978. Pages 168-221 of this book include the above paragraph, and also other good and bad features of Kohlberg's approach.

Similarly, Eric Beversluis notes the contradiction involved in asserting that children (1) should be free to *choose* their own values, but (2) are not free to *act* on them. — Eric H. Beversluis (Capitol University), "The Dilemma of Value Clarification," *Philosophy of Education Yearbook 1978*, Philosophy of Education Society, University of Illinois, Champaign, Illinois, 1979, pp. 417-427.

A bolder approach is that of M. Donald Thomas and Rafael Lewy who cut the Gordian knot and insist that a teaching of the American way of life is the best way to make moral conduct pervade the school curriculum. Their curriculum at Salt Lake City affirms that

. . . on the whole, the establishment and development of the United States has been beneficial to Americans in particular, and mankind in general. This is not to say that the image of our present and past should be presented as flawless. However, the presumption of virtue for the traditional American ideals is justified because (a) it represents the beliefs of the overwhelming proportion of Americans, (b) it is ridiculous to rear children as adversaries to the culture of their homeland, where most of them will spend their adult lives, and (c) it reflects the belief of the persons administering the school district, who are charged with bringing their best judgment to bear on the policies governing our schools. —M. Donald Thomas and Rafael Lewy (both at Salt Lake City, Utah), "Education and Moral Conduct: Re-Discovering America," *Character* 1, 3: 2-7, January 1980. By permission.

At the most general level there can be little doubt about these basic principles: *be just, fair, and impartial; consider other people's interests; do not without warrant interfere with another's freedom; respect your fellow man.* Surely anyone even vaguely interested in morality would find these acceptable, for these constitutive rules are moral almost by definition. Nor do I think there would be any hesitation to accept such basic rules as: *don't kill or disable others; do not injure or wantonly cause pain; be honest; keep promises and abide by contracts; don't cheat; don't lie; don't steal; do not discriminate against others on the basis of irrelevant differences such as color, sex, or ethnic origin.*

It seems entirely legitimate to include also such virtues as: courage, politeness, punctuality, kindness, perseverance, integrity, loyalty, thoughtfulness, lawfulness, toleration, respecting others' privacy, self-respect. Even at the more mundane and childish level there is little fault to be found with such rules as: *take turns* (at the swing, at bats, etc.): *don't jump the queue; don't needlessly make a mess; don't talk out of turn; don't damage property; don't be selfish; don't deceive; don't be lazy; obey school and family rules.*

It is not a serious criticism to suggest that these rules have exceptions. Possibly all moral rules do, as Kurt Baier (1965, p. 97) has noted. To have learnt a rule is also to have learnt the exceptions. Children can and do easily learn the legitimate exceptions.

It will be noted that this list is neither complete nor organized according to types and classes of virtues. What I have attempted to show is merely that with a little thought one can come up with quite a substantial body of rules which are generally acceptable on moral grounds. Moral education need not flounder for lack of agreed-upon virtues. I do not, of course, expect all thoughtful and reasonable people to agree on this content. But I do think the onus is on those who disagree to give good cause for objecting. Simply to call these "old-fashioned middle-class virtues" will not do.

8.10   The Role of Applied Ethics in Learning
DANIEL CALLAHAN AND SISSELA BOK

[Attempts to teach ethics in today's schools should embody] five basic goals:

1. [Encourage] students to understand that there is, as Kurt Baier states, a "moral point of view," that human beings live in a web of moral relationships, that a consequence of moral positions and rules can be actual suffering or happiness, and that moral conflicts are frequently inevitable and difficult. . . . [also that] sensitivity to other humans, empathy, and feelings are critical to the moral life.

2. [Recognize] ethical issues. [Become aware] that many technical, social, psychological, or political problems raise fundamental questions of right and wrong. . . .

3. [Strive to] understand the difference between cogent and slipshod arguments and the kinds of justification required for moral assertions.

4. [Endeavor to develop] a sense of moral obligation and personal responsibility. "Why ought I to be moral?" is a fundamental and complex question in ethics . . . Any

Brief excerpts from Daniel Callahan and Sissela Bok: "The Role of Applied Ethics in Learning." Reprinted with permission from *Change* magazine, Vol. 11, No. 6 (September, 1979). Copyrighted by the Council of Learning, 271 North Avenue, New Rochelle, New York 10801.

course in applied ethics must explore the role, in practice, of freedom and personal responsibility. . . .

5. [Learn to tolerate — and to resist —] disagreement and ambiguity . . . [Strive] to find civil and rational ways of handling moral disagreements. . . .

One goal frequently proposed for courses in ethics is missing from our list: that of changing student behavior. . . . [Admitting that it is the ultimate goal, we do not consider it to be] an appropriate explicit goal [for a school course] in ethics.*

---

*EDITOR'S NOTE   We fully agree that "changing student behavior" should not constitute the *subject matter of a course in ethics*. It is enough that such a course attempt to understand the goals of life as enunciated by some of the world's great moralists. Moreover, from a more personal point of view, students should come to understand that moral behavior is the most essential ingredient in their search for happiness and for self-fulfillment.

But it does not seem altogether out of line for students to learn how some people, whose greatness is universally recognized, developed their own moral character. For this reason, we include as our next selection, a brief summary of Benjamin Franklin's plan for self-improvement.

8.11   Benjamin Franklin's Self-Development Through Habit Formation

In his early youth, Benjamin Franklin hit upon an important truth. He found that bad habits often take precedence over good intentions, and that the temptations or inclinations of the moment often caused him to abandon his own ideals of good behavior. Franklin combined this fact with another truth: Even as the skills of an artisan are not purely inborn but are developed by practice, so it must be with the development of moral character.

But what is moral character? A person's character, Franklin discovered, was nothing more than a bundle of specific habits. So Franklin listed thirteen specific traits of character that he would try to build into his own character. Here they are, each one briefly defined:

1. *Temperance.* Eat not to dullness; drink not to elevation.
2. *Silence.* Speak not but what may benefit others or yourself.
3. *Order.* Let all your things have their places; each activity its time.
4. *Resolution.* Resolve to perform what you ought. Perform what you resolve.
5. *Frugality.* Make no expense but to do good to others or yourself.
6. *Industry.* Lose no time; be always employed in something useful.
7. *Sincerity.* Think and speak justly.
8. *Justice.* Wrong none by doing injuries, or omitting benefits that are your duty.
9. *Moderation.* Avoid extremes.
10. *Cleanliness.* Tolerate no uncleanliness in body, clothes, or habitation.
11. *Tranquility.* Be not disturbed at trifles, or at unavoidable accidents.
12. *Chastity.* Clean thoughts and wholesome activities lead to clean living.
13. *Humility.* Imitate Jesus and Socrates.

Realizing that he could not concentrate on all thirteen virtues at the same time he decided to concentrate on one each week; May 1-7, Temperance; May 8-14, Silence; May 15-21, Order; May 22-28, Resolution; and so on for thirteen weeks, four times each year.

To carry out this *Resolution*, Franklin graded himself each night, using a chart something like this:

	S M T W T F S	S M T W T F S	S M T W T F S
Temperance			
Silence			
Order			
Resolution			
Frugality			
Industry			
Sincerity			
Justice			
Moderation			
Cleanliness			
Tranquility			
Chasity			
Humility			

Question: What was the outcome? *Answer*: Benjamin Franklin!

8.12   Morality in Art and Literature
JOHN GARDNER

It was said in the old days that every year Thor made a circle around Middle-earth, beating back the enemies of order. Thor got older every year, and the circle occupied by gods and men grew smaller. The wisdom god, Woden, went out to the king of the trolls, got him in an armlock, and demanded to know of him how order might triumph over chaos.

> "Give me your left eye," said the king of the trolls, "and I'll tell you."
> Without hesitation, Woden gave up his left eye. "Now tell me."
> The troll said, "The secret is, *Watch with both eyes!*"

Woden's left eye was the last sure hope of gods and men in their kingdom of light surrounded on all sides by darkness. All we have left is Thor's hammer, which represents not brute force but art, or, counting both hammerheads, art and criticism. Thor is no help. Like other gods, he has withdrawn from our immediate view. We have only his weapon, abandoned beside a fencepost in high weeds, if we can figure out how to use it. . . .

In a world where nearly everything that passes for art is tinny and commercial and often, in addition, hollow and academic, I argue — by reason and by banging the table — for an old-fashioned view of what art is and does and what the fundamental business of critics ought therefore to be. . . .

The traditional view is that true art is moral: it seeks to improve life, not debase it. It seeks to hold off, at least for a while, the twilight of the gods and us. I do not deny that art, like criticism, may legitimately celebrate the trifling. It may joke, or mock, or while away the time. But trivial art has no meaning or value except in the shadow of more serious art, the kind of art that beats back the monsters and, if you will, makes the world safe for triviality. That art which tends toward destruction, the art of nihilists, cynics, and merdistes, is not properly art at all. Art is essentially serious and beneficial, a game played against chaos and death, against entropy. . . .

I do not mean that what the world needs is didactic art. Didacticism and true art are immiscible; and in any case, nothing guarantees that didacticism will be moral. Think of *Mein Kampf.* True art is *by its nature* moral. We recognize true art by its careful, thoroughly honest search for and analysis of values. It is not didactic because, instead of teaching by authority and force, it explores, open-mindedly, to learn what it should teach. It clarifies, like an experiment in a chemistry lab, and confirms. As a chemist's experiment tests the laws of nature and dramatically reveals the truth or falsity of scientific hypotheses, moral art tests values and rouses trustworthy feelings about the better and the worse in human action. . . .

One man's understanding is as good as another's not because each is equally valid but because right understanding does not submit to any proof. If Mr. Smith empathizes well with strangers and Mr. Perkins is convinced that everyone is out to steal

Excerpts from John Gardner, *On Moral Fiction* (New York: Basic Books, 1977), pp. 3–4, 5–6, 19, 41–42, 101, 135, 204–205. Used by permission of Basic Books, Inc., Publishers.
Gardner's essay explains how art and literature embody moral values without being either pedantic or didactic.

his shoes, Mr. Smith's understanding is more correct than Mr. Perkins', but it gives Mr. Perkins no good reason to stop glancing at his feet. Thus healthy society is pluralistic, allowing every man his opinion as long as the opinion does not infringe on the rights of others . . .

Unlike the fascist in uniform, the artist never forces anyone to anything. He merely makes his case, the strongest case possible. He lights up the darkness with a lightning flash, protects his friends the gods — that is, values — and all humanity without exception, and then moves on. . . .

True art's divine madness is shot through with love: love of the good, a love proved not by some airy and abstract high-mindedness but by active celebration of whatever good or trace of good can be found by a quick and compassionate eye in this always corrupt and corruptible but god-freighted world. To return one last time to the image of Thor's hammer with which I launched all this, it strikes outward at the trolls, or inward when the trolls have made incursions, not blindly in all directions. It smashes to construct.*

---

*EDITOR'S NOTE   The psychologist Bruno Bettelheim explains the morality of children's literature in quite similar terms:

> [A child learns] the advantages of moral behavior, not through abstract ethical concepts but through that which seems tangibly right and therefore meaningful to him. . . .
> The figures and events of fairy tales. . . . [are] presented in a simple homely way; no demands are made on the listener. This prevents even the smallest child from feeling compelled to act in specific ways, and he is never made to feel inferior. Far from making demands, the fairy tale reassures, gives hope for the future, and holds out the promise of a happy ending. . . .
> The question for the child is not "Do I want to be good?" but "Who do I want to be like?" The child decides this on the basis of projecting himself wholeheartedly into one character. If this fairy tale figure is a very good person, then the child decides that he wants to be good, too. . . . Morality is not the issue in these tales, but rather, assurance that one can succeed. — Bruno Bettelheim, *The Uses of Enchantment: The Meaning and Importance of Fairy Tales*, (New York: Knopf, 1975), pp. 5, 10, 26, 117.

That Bettelheim's analysis may apply to adults as well as to children is suggested in *The Myth of God Incarnate*, edited by John Hick (Philadelphia: Westminster Press, 1977), p. 34.

8.13   The Place of the Humanities as Aids to Moral Growth and Self-Knowledge
JOHN S. MORRIS

[This article examines] the consequences of the sixties' denial of the traditional view of the university as keeper of the culture, the subsequent demand for practicality in curriculum and evaluation, and the problems this has raised for the humanistic disciplines.

[In his 1970 book] *The Cultural Contradictions of Capitalism* . . . Daniel Bell has argued that we are living in the shadow of the "sensibility" of the sixties . . . [and that]

Excerpts from an article by this title by John S. Morris (Provost, Colgate University) in *Liberal Education* 64: 44–54, March 1978. (Footnote references are omitted.) By permission.

although the sensibility of the sixties appeared in the guise of an attack upon the "technocratic society," it was really an attack upon reason itself. Bell says:

> In a place of reason we were told to give ourselves over to one form or other of pre-rational spontaneity — whether under the heading of Charles Reich's Consciousness III, the Shamanistic Vision of Theodore Roszak, or the like. Nothing less is required, said Mr. Roszak, one of the movement's most articulate spokesmen, than the subversion of the scientific world view with its entrenched commitment to an egocentric and cerebral mode of consciousness. In its place, there must be a new culture in which the non-intellective capacities of personality —those capacities that take fire from visionary splendor and the experience of human communion — become the arbiter of the true, the good, and the beautiful.

With the denial of reason came a retreat from the world; for the denial of the intellect was a *denial* of the world as an objective order. This was a fascinating side to the revolt. It was not only the order of society that was rejected, but the ordered nature of an objective world. With the form of the world taken away, one was able to live within oneself without the onerous weight of structure that intellect and our culture bring. All that was left, however, was a distorted self. In Bell's words: "All that there was, was the pathetic celebration of the self — the self that had been emptied of content and which masqueraded as being vital through the play acting of revolution."

To live within this kind of world was to live within an order that was not ordered, which had no past and which could not entertain the future. The apocalyptic visions of this time were in reality a rejection of the future. The alarming futuristic pictures made the present uncontrollable and made us unable to handle a present in which the past was irrelevant. The sixties were characterized by an anti-intellectualism and an overriding emotionalism, and in the consequent disorder there was a denial of the roots of social order and the culture which gives shape and structure to life. . . .

An interesting feature of the last decade was the claim that anything American was in some way evil; and the rebellion rejected every element of our cultural style. This was accompanied by a rejection of the past, the well-spring of the culture, which, if taken seriously, can only result in nihilism. All the norms of common behavior are lost, the moral glue goes out of our lives, and when you also refuse to look into the past, into the sources of our culture, there is nowhere else to go. It is no wonder that the chief sufferer of this nihilism was the university. For the university has, for good or ill, been thought of as the modern keeper of the culture in our secular society. This was once the function of religion, but more and more the scientific temper of our times has brought us to an awareness of the breadth as well as the depth of our cultural heritage which is rooted in the movements of intellectual thought. How could one countenance this holy of holies, then, if it was the fount of all evil, and if one had to reject all that it contained? One could only destroy the past and turn to the evanescence of the moment, the moment of experience. But experience is not itself meaningful, nor does it harbor meaning, however much one strives to find it there. Experience is set within the matrix of culture which gives experience a system of language to make it a meaningful whole. . . .

Tradition provides the context within which we understand the relevance and importance of the values by which we judge our decisions. Only insofar as we discern this context within the literature, the philosophy, the theologies of the past can we understand ourselves. Our students must know how to formulate these relevant questions so they can find themselves. For, only through our discovery of our human past in all its many facets, in the awareness of the roots of our philosphy, of our theology, of our history, and of our art, can we find ourselves. And it is only through this discovery that we can help ourselves find out humanity. . . . As A. W. Levi says:

> The Humanities cannot be dismissed. Far from being outmoded, they are eternally relevant precisely because they are the arts of communication, the arts of continuity, and the arts of criticism. Language remains the indispensable medium within which we move and breathe. History provides that group memory which makes the communal bond possible. Philosophic criticism is the only activity through which man's self-reflection modifies the condition of his existence. The cup of the humanities, therefore, must be the vessel from which we drink our life.

Unless we drink of that vessel, we can never fully appreciate our present, and in these complicated times, the need to understand our present predicament grows more urgent every day.*

---

*EDITOR'S NOTE   Compare:

> The moral and religious roots of our civilization should receive no less attention in our education than the study of galaxies, genetics, or constitutions. The sad fact is that study of those roots is often neglected entirely. . . . We have so exaggerated what is true, namely, that values cannot be "taught" after the fashion of mathematics or chemistry, that we fail even to teach students *about* the values that have in fact sustained our civilization. Through the teaching of history, philosophy, and religious studies, each new generation needs to be made aware of both our debt to and the contemporary importance of the moral and religious sources upon which our lives have depended — the norms of justice, mercy, righteousness, and love derived from the Judeo-Christian tradition; the ideals of truth and of virtue bequeathed by the Graeco-Roman traditions; the convictions of the Enlightenment concerning inalienable rights, human equality, and the need for representative forms of government; the experience of democracy and free institutions. Even more important, we have failed, largely because of a fear of bias and partisanship in a pluralistic society, to focus on the reality of the moral situations that constantly confront us so that the ethical dimension is obscured and moral sensitivity erodes — John E. Smith, in *Teachers College Record* 80: 556–563, February 1979. Read also *The Humanities and Humanistic Education* by James L. Jarrett, Reading, MA.: Addison-Wesley, 1973.

8.14   Quotations for Further Thought and Discussion

(A)   We are incredibly heedless in the formation of our beliefs, but find ourselves filled with an illicit passion for them when anyone proposes to rob us of their companionship. It is obviously not the ideas themselves that are dear to us, but our self-esteem, which is threatened. We are by nature stubbornly pledged to defend our own from attack, whether it be our person, our family, our property, or our opinion.

— James Harvey Robinson

(B)   Whenever two people meet there are really six people present. There is each man as he sees himself, each man as the other person sees him, and each man as he really is.

— William James

(C)   Our judges are not monks or scientists, but participants in the living stream of our national life, steering the law between the dangers of rigidity on the one hand and of formlessness on the other. Our system faces no theoretical dilemma but the single continuous problem: how to apply to ever-changing conditions the never-changing principles of freedom.

— Earl Warren (1955)

(D)   Self-restraint and tolerance are not to be identified with bewilderment or spinelessness. Yet for some contemporaries lack of commitment is sported as the hallmark of philosophical depth and, adopting that modish idiom in which *bad* and *good* become *sick* and *healthy* . . . even the notorious underground "families" are to be appreciated as "patterns of culture."

— Edward G. Rozycki (1979)

(E)   The voice of intelligence is soft and weak, said Freud. It is drowned out by the roar of fear. It is ignored by the voice of desire. It is contradicted by the voice of shame. It is hissed away by hate, and extinguished by anger. Most of all, it is silenced by ignorance. Nevertheless, we believe as Freud did, that it is man's best hope for rising to a higher level of existence.

— Karl Menninger

(F)   The traditional American emphasis on individualism and self-determination entails a weakening of institutional forms of restraint with the consequence of a relatively high statistical incidence of aberrant behavior. . . . Freedom from external restraint means that the individual must internalize the values of the culture, and restrain himself. He must be, as we say, self-governing; he must repress his antisocial impulses in order to remain free.

A society such as ours, which increasingly rejects the sanctions of tradition, the family, the church, and the power of the state, necessarily must create the kind of personality who is self-governing, self-restraining, self-repressive. The founding fathers, following the Roman model, defined the essential quality as virtue; Emerson called it character; the Protestant evangelical tradition named it benevolence. The tradition is a long one, and we may respond warmly to some of its phrases, but we should not in our self-congratulation ignore the enormous psychic burden such an ideal places upon the individual. Until we reach the millennium of American democratic hopes, we must accept the probable instability of our society, especially when it denies the opportunity and self-respect which its ideology constantly celebrates.

— John William Ward, "The Problem of Violence and American Ideals," in *Up the Mainstream*, edited by Herbert G. Reid (New York: David McKay, 1974), p. 259.

(G)   In an important sense this world of ours is a new world, in which the unity of knowledge, the nature of human communities, the order of society, the order of ideas, the very notions of society and culture have changed and will not return to what they have been in the past. What is new is new not because it has never been there before, but because it has changed in quality. One thing that is new is the prevalence of newness, the changing scale and scope of change itself, so that the world alters as we walk in it, so that the years of man's life measure not some small growth or rearrangement or moderation of what he learned in childhood, but a great upheaval. . . . To assail the changes that have unmoored us from the past is futile, and in a deep sense, I think, it is wicked. We need to recognize the change and learn what resources we have.

— Robert Oppenheimer, "Prospects in the Arts and Sciences," *Perspectives* USA: 11, Spring 1955, pp. 5–14 at 10–11.

(H)   [As for the unity of science, and of culture, there is more than] one way of bringing a wider unity to our time: That unity, I think, can be based only on a rather different kind of structure than the one that most of us have in mind when we talk of the unity of culture. I think that it cannot be an architectonic unity, in which there is a central chamber into which all else leads, the central chamber which is the repository of the common knowledge of the world. . . .

I think that the unity we can seek lies really in two things. One is that the knowledge which comes to us at such a terrifyingly, inhumanly rapid rate, has some order in it. We are allowed to forget a great deal, as well as to learn. This order is never adequate. The mass of un-understood things, which cannot be summarized, or wholly ordered, always grows greater; but a great deal does get understood.

The second is simply this: we can have each other to dinner. We ourselves, and with each other by our converse, can create not an architecture of global scope, but an immense, intricate network of intimacy, illumination, and understanding.

— Robert Oppenheimer, quoted by Gerald Holton in *Daedalus*, 106: vi, Fall 1977.

(I)   You should have education enough so that you won't have to look up to people, and then more education so that you will be wise enough not to look down on people.

— M. L. Boron

(J)   Conscience is the pulse of reason.

— Coleridge

A man's conscience and his judgment are the same thing, and as the judgment, so also the conscience, may be erroneous.

— Thomas Hobbes

A sense of duty is useful in work, but offensive in personal relations.

— Bertrand Russell

[We speak of "the Puritan conscience" with good reason.] Puritanism was the cutting edge which hewed liberty, democracy, humanitarianism and universal education out of the black forest of feudal Europe and the American wilderness. . . . Puritanism, therefore, is an American heritage to be grateful for.

— Samuel Eliot Morison

(K)   It was the best of times, it was the worst of times; it was the age of wisdom, it was the age of foolishness; it was the epoch of belief, it was the epoch of incredulity; it was the season of light, it was the season of darkness; it was the spring of hope, it was the winter of despair. [*Question*: In this opening sentence of *A Tale of Two Cities* was Charles Dickens merely calling attention to the extremisms that existed at the time of the French Revolution? Or was he referring to all times and places? (Futher insight into this question may be had by reading different translations of Luke 2: 14).]

A study of this question might involve some of the unanticipated consequences of modern technology: problems of overpopulation resulting from advances in medicine, the rebellion against nonmeaningful work resulting from efficient ways of mass production, or the air, water, and soil pollution resulting from the substitution of coal or nuclear power for hand labor.

Chapter 9. CHANGING VALUES IN AN EMERGING WORLD COMMUNITY

9.1 Faith for an Emerging World Community
EDITORIAL

A republic of free citizens drawn from all parts of the world requires a redirection of traditional beliefs. It demands a faith that reasonable solutions to new and difficult problems are possible. It requires charity toward fellow humans with different religious backgrounds whose viewpoints, though different, are offered with sincerity. And it is based on the hope that persistent inquiry, open discussion and patient effort will, sooner or later, bring about acceptable solutions to these problems.

Wisdom and understanding come not from the certainty that we have already discovered the truth, but from a profound love of truth, and from a humble awareness of the different paths by which men come to it. "The . . . worship of God is not a rule of safety," said Alfred North Whitehead, "it is an adventure of the spirit, a flight after the unattainable. The death of religion comes with the repression of the high hope of adventure."[1] "Faith," wrote John Dewey, "is the power of intelligence to imagine a future which is the projection of the desirable in the present, and to invent the instrumentalities of its realization is our salvation."[2]

Horace M. Kallen once summarized the democratic faith in two sentences:

> Democracy is the method by which hitherto inflexible and unadjustable infallibilities may adjust to one another and live together as a communion of the different on equal terms. . . . To paraphrase Edwin Markham: other ways of thought and life draw circles which shut the different out, as heretics, rebels and things to flout, but democracy and science are the methods that win, for the circle they draw brings the differences in.[3]

This circle should be broad enough not merely to include viewpoints of people now living but also to include those from the past. The circle should be wide enough not only to bring in differences in *space* (e.g., Orientals as well as Occidentals) but also bring in differences in *time* (e.g., the values most highly cherished by peoples in agricultural, pastoral, and hunting and fishing eras of civilization).

It is sometimes affirmed that in our age of television a child of 12 knows more than his grandfather knew when he was 16. And indeed he does know more — *about some*

---

[1] Alfred North Whitehead, *Science and the Modern World* (New York: Macmillan 1935), Conclusion of Chapter 12. Read also Whitehead's *Adventures in Ideas* (New York: Macmillan, 1944), pp. 125–126.

[2] John Dewey, *Creative Intelligence* (New York: Holt, Rinehart and Winston, 1917), p. 17.

[3] Horace M. Kallen, "Democracy's True Religion," (Pamphlet) (Boston: Beacon, 1951), p. 10.

things. But he knows less about other things. And it is knowledge of these other things which will help to counterbalance the provincialism and narrow-mindedness that is a part of every age and of every culture, including our own. Only on the basis of this wider knowledge will we learn to distinguish cult from culture, greatness from notoriety, and wisdom from knowledge. Only as we escape from the provincialism of our time and place can we learn to differentiate the transitory from the permanent, and thus fashion our lives around the things that matter most.

9.2   Tolerance

E. M. FORSTER

The world is very full of people — appallingly full; it has never been so full before, and they are all tumbling over each other. Most of these people one doesn't know and some of them one doesn't like; doesn't like the colour of their skins, say, or the shapes of their noses, or the way they blow them or don't blow them, or the way they talk, or their smell, or their clothes, or their fondness for jazz or their dislike of jazz, and so on. Well, what is one to do? There are two solutions. One of them is the Nazi solution. If you don't like people, kill them, banish them, segregate them, and then strut up and down proclaiming that you are the salt of the earth. The other way is much less thrilling, but it is on the whole the way of the democracies, and I prefer it. If you don't like people, put up with them as well as you can. Don't try to love them: you can't, you'll only strain yourself. But try to tolerate them. On the basis of that tolerance a civilised future may be built. . . .

Tolerance is not the same as weakness. Putting up with people does not mean giving in to them. This complicates the problem. But the rebuilding of civilisation is bound to be complicated. . . .*

Excerpts from E. M. Forster, *Two Cheers for Democracy* (New York: Harcourt Brace Jovanovich, 1938, 1951), pp. 45–48, 70. Reprinted by permission.

The virtue of tolerance is especially needed today because self-centeredness — which traditional theology calls the sin of pride — appears most conspicuously in group pride (tribalism, nationalism, jungoism, racism, cultism) as well as the pride of individuals.

In today's world, "community" means more than fellowship in a family, a tribe, a city-state or a nation. We are now living in a world community whose components are no longer individuals only, but individuals variously fashioned in terms of an extreme diversity of races, religions, nations and cultures. Morality can no longer be confined to a consideration of ways in which individuals become less self-centered and gain in social awareness and group loyalty. Today's problem also includes the question: How can the various *group* loyalties be reduced so that worldly-mindedness may increase? How can we move from ethnocentrism to world-mindedness? As the international community becomes increasingly important, tolerance would seem to be a virture which deserves greater emphasis.

---

*EDITOR'S NOTE   Compare:

Tolerance is not a negative value; it must grow out of an active respect for others. It is not enough in science to agree that other men are entitled to their opinions; we must believe that the opinions of others are interesting in themselves, and deserve our attention and respect even when we think them wrong. And in science, we often think that other men are wrong, but we never think that they are therefore wicked. By contrast, all absolute doctrines think (as the Inquisition did) that those who are wrong are deliberately and wickedly wrong, and may be subjected to any suffering to correct them. — Jacob Bronowski, *A Sense of the Future: Essays in Natural Philosophy*, (Cambridge, MA. and London, Eng.: MIT Press, 1972), pp. 21, 258.

[I most heartily agree that] Love is a great force in private life; it is indeed the greatest of all things: but love in public affairs does not work. It has been tried again and again: by the Christian civilisations of the Middle Ages, and also by the French Revolution, a secular movement which reasserted the Brotherhood of Man. And it has always failed. The idea that nations should love one another, or that business concerns or marketing boards should love one another, or that a man in Portugal should love a man in Peru of whom he has never heard — it is absurd, unreal, dangerous. It leads us into perilous and vague sentimentalism. "Love is what is needed," we chant, and then sit back and the world goes on as before. The fact is we can only love what we know personally. And we cannot know much. In public affairs, in the rebuilding of civilisation, something much less dramatic and emotional is needed, namely, tolerance. Tolerance is a very dull virtue. It is boring. Unlike love, it has always had a bad press. It is negative. It merely means putting up with people, being able to stand things. No one has ever written an ode to tolerance, or raised a statue to her. Yet this is the quality [most needed in today's complex world] . . .

So Two Cheers for Democracy: one because it admits variety and two because it permits criticism. Two cheers are quite enough: there is no occasion to give three. Only Love the Beloved Republic deserves that.*

---

*EDITOR'S NOTE   The following poem, author unknown, seems to fit here:

I dreamt death came the other night
And heaven's gates swung wide.
With kindly grace an angel came
And ushered me inside.

And there to my astonishment
Stood folks I'd known on earth,
Some I had judged as quite unfit
Or of but little worth.

Indignant words rose to my lips!
But never were set free —
For every face showed stunned surprise:
No one expected *me*!

9.3   The Mass Mind
JOYCE CARY

Every age, they say, has its special bit of nonsense. The eighteenth century had its noble savage, and the nineteenth, its automatic progress. Now we have this modern nonsense about the "mass man." We are all told constantly that people are becoming more and more standardized. That mass education, mass amusements, mass production, ready-made clothes, and a popular press are destroying all individuality —

From Joyce Cary, "The Mass Mind," Copyright Curtis Brown, Ltd. By permission.
Reprinted in *Man in the Expository Mode*, Book Six, pp. 105–110, edited by Sarah Solotaroff (Evanston, Ill.: McDougall, Littell, 1970).

turning civilization into a nice, warmed, sterilized orphan asylum where all the little lost souls wear the same uniforms, eat the same meals, think the same thoughts, and play the same games. . . .

I was convinced of all this myself till I went to administer the affairs of a primitive tribe in Africa. There I found that the tribal mind was much more truly a mass mind than anything I had known in Europe. The nearest approximation to it was among illiterate peasantry in remote country districts. Tribesmen and primitive peasants are intensely narrow and conservative. Their very simple ideas and reactions guide them in a mysterious and dangerous world.

I found that young chiefs with enterprise and ambition were keen to learn about the world outside the tribe. If they got away from it, they tended to put on European dress. To them, European dress was not a mark of mass mind, but of the free and independent mind. . . .

Education, contact with other peoples, breaks up tribal uniformity of thought and custom, brings in new ideas. That is, it makes for difference. The celebrated eccentrics of former centuries were either lunatics — or educated men.

New ideas also make for conflict. Old African chiefs hated roads and railways: they said they brought in strangers who corrupted the young people with new ideas and made them rebellious. They were quite right. It is far easier to rule a primitive tribe than a modern democracy where every individual is ready to criticize the government, where everyone has his own ideas about politics and religion, and where dozens of societies, unions, religious sects claim independence and support ambitious leaders who are ready to fight at any time for their "rights." . . .

You do not need traffic police where there is no wheeled traffic. You do not need postal bylaws where no one knows how to write. But the modern state, simply because of the independence of its citizens, the complication of their demands, needs a huge machine of law and police. This is not a proof of the mass mind but the exact oppposite — of a growing number of people who think and act for themselves, and, rightly or wrongly, are ready to defy the old simple rules founded on custom. . . .

Thus, the modern state has lost its mass mind in getting education. But, you will say, this education destroys the primitive mass mind only to replace it with a number of mob minds: in the crowds which queue for the films or a match, read the same newspapers, and shout for the same spellbinders. Mass education is driving out the sound, traditional culture to bring in a lot of half-baked slogans. It produces the shallow brain only to be distracted from serious reflection.

But these "mobs" have no resemblance to those of the tribal world where every individual does the same thing at the same time — hunts, dances, drinks in the mass. Even if he had the will to do anything else, it would not be there to do. The modern individual has an immense choice of occupation and amusement. So that the "mass" of sight-seers at any show place today is actually composed of individuals who have freely chosen to join that crowd and will join a different one tomorrow. What looks like a proof of the mob mind is really evidence of spreading interests among the people and a variety of occupations. . . .

The West is not producing a mass mind, but a variety of strong minds with the richest sense of adventure and will for discovery. The East is not succeeding in obtaining a mass mind either — it is going in the opposite direction. Merely by process of education, it is producing every year people who can at least think a little more freely than illiterate peasants, who are very likely therefore to think critical thoughts, however much they may hide them. That is why the task of the dictatorship becomes constantly more difficult, why it is obliged to stiffen its grip, to hire more police, to bribe more spies, and to purge its own party, every year or so, of "deviators."

What I suggest is that no kind of education, however narrow, can produce the mass mind. The reason is that minds are creative, that thoughts wander by themselves and cannot be controlled by the cleverest police. All education is free in this sense; it cannot be shut up within walls. To teach people to think, if only to make them more useful as soldiers and mechanics, is to open all thoughts to them — a whole world of new ideas. And though the dictator may wish to think of them as a proletariat they have already begun to leave the proletariat.

9.4   Two Types of Identity: Defensive and Transcendent
HOWARD F. STEIN

This essay is . . . a discussion of two types of identity: the *gnostic* [or *defensive*] and the *transcendent*. The former requires closure, absolutism, completeness, the overcoming of individuality and separateness; its goal is perfection and purity. Transcendence, on the other hand, values the endless possibilities conceivable through impurity, and values the continuous process of growth and development as opposed to the stasis promised by perfection.

On the surface, for the new gnostic identities, the answer to the question "who am I?" is uncomplicated. For instance, white ethnics may focus on Catholicism fused with central southeast European ancestry; blacks may emphasize race, African origins, "soul" (which, incidentally, the white ethnics have "catholicized" while adopting it for themselves); American Jews now have expanded their religious identity to include an ethnonationalism, in defense of a peoplehood and the state of Israel; the American youth culture stresses age and the "generation gap," repudiating parental values; Christian neofundamentalists reject modernity and seek a return to the faith of biblical literalism and infallibility. Ignoring the accumulated wisdom that indicates that the dynamics of identity formation is a complex matter, the advocates of the new identities simplify it for their own needs. Identity becomes a matter of either/or. There is no middle ground. One is either a convert or an adversary. The advocates do not stop there: they reinterpret the entire process of development to corroborate their own views and justify their own resolutions. They propose, systematize, and proselytize a new normative psychology, remaking "man" and human development in their own image. *Separatist* psychologies provide the rationalization for *separatist* identi-

Brief excerpts by Howard F. Stein (Meharry Medical College), from "Identity and Transcendence." Reprinted from *School Review* 85: 349–375, May 1977, by permission of The University of Chicago Press. (Footnote references are omitted.)

ties, withdrawing from universalism: thus the burgeoning of black psychology, American Indian psychology, white ethnic psychology, neofundamentalist psychology (as opposed to Darwinian). And of course, "American" psychology is nothing but Judeo-WASP psychology! . . .

DEFENSIVE IDENTITY

This quest for identity is essentially defensive. What one is "for" is defined in terms of what one is "against." Any assertion of "who I am" is simultaneously accompanied by an insistence on "who I am not." The boundaries must be clearly demarcated to insider and outsider alike. There is a dread of identity, a profound insecurity, however rationalized, that forces one to withdraw from openness, so that exclusiveness and parochialism are thereafter glorified and sentimentalized. Out of fear of deep relationships, one withdraws from communal concern to self-preoccupation. . . .

Personal identity thus becomes rigidified. Likewise, group identity becomes an impenetrable, timeless collective in which one finds refuge and respite. Because one dreads what the flow of time may portend, one invests in a frenetic immediacy or in a bucolic past, or both. A myth of the past gives some relief from the dread of the future. A dichotomy of sacred past and profane present (and immediate past) proliferates: rural versus urban, religious versus secular, Catholic ethnic versus Protestant Anglo-, simple versus complex, pure and organic versus impure and artificial, order versus permissiveness, quietude versus activism, status quo versus change, American nativist or populist versus the northeastern WASP-Jewish "establishment" — yet another expression of self-definition by opposition — . . . [such "either me or you" attitudes] generate the further need to shore up the battlements. . . .

While genuine self-actualization implies the capacity for close interpersonal relations and commitment, pseudo self-actualization is impelled by dread of any enduring relationship and community. . . . [The *defensive* person or group emphasizes] a localistic self-interest and self-detemination, whether by an individual or by a collectivity of individuals who perceive themselves to have a common interest. As the slogans go, "I look out for Number One" (i.e., myself); "Do your own thing"; "I tell it like it is"; "I call it like I see it." There is no reaching out toward otherness: quite the opposite — the fear of the strange and different and the insistence on sameness and conformity. The bond of the community that expresses the new identities is that of fear, and it is this amorphous fear that brings together individuals to protect one another. The illusion of community is sustained by threat. . . . Genuine community, on the other hand, does not need an external force to produce internal cohesion. Personality and community are mirrors of one another. . . .

Because the boundaries that separate and distinguish individuals and groups are inherently vague and permeable, highly visible, public symbols and rituals of identification come to serve as emblems or markers of "who I am" and "who I am not." An insistence on "pluralism," "corporate identity," "the right to be different," and the like absolutizes from within what is to be respected by those outside. The very creativity, self-actualization, and diversity that adherents to the new identities idealize they cannot allow to be realized, by themselves or others. The insistence on and the perpetuation of difference itself, not the process of personal growth whose outcome is uncertain, is the operant goal, although the process of separation and contrast is rationalized as "becoming oneself." One is not different simply as a consequence of creativity; one actively creates difference. While universalizing an ethic of freedom and self-determination in the abstract, the new identities in concrete situations retain these prerogatives only for themselves. . . . Not openness and mutuality but manipulation, grim mistrust, explosive rage, self-preoccupation, the need to inflict hurt — these are what are "encountered" in the new identities. Far from being a matter of inwardness and private introspection, the new identities are abrasively public, seeking not only public exposure but also the exposure and capitulation of the accused. Other-directed to the core, they must engage in comparison to sustain their sense of superiority. . . .

TRANSCENDENT IDENTITY

[In contrast to such *defensive* identity, the identity of *transcendence* finds freedom and self-actualization in the type of social concern] which Heinz Anshacher defines as "an interest in the interest of others." . . . Genuine freedom respects diversity but does not need to idolize difference and insist on a limited range of legitimate variability. . . .

[To outgrow the *defensive* types of immaturity, we must realize that] to transcend implies the ability to leave behind, to outgrow, without the need to flee; the ability to stay without the need to dig in; the ability to be independent yet interdependent, without the mutual suffocation of dependency. To transcend is not to reach, to attain, but to move toward. It is within the concreteness of the finite that the infinite is intimated and becomes present.

Transcendence does not require the ever-watchful eye of deadly seriousness. It thrives — indeed, is sustained — on play, on surprise (recall Friedrich Schiller's remark that man is at his most human when he is at play).* Transcendence combines attachment *and* detachment, embracement *and* renunciation. . . .

The individual who transcends is not narrowly adjusted or overadapted to his or her cultural environment but continuously synthesizes, incorporates, revises, and creatively adapts.

[The relation of an individual to the culture of which he is a part was stated in 1924 by the anthropologist Edwin Sapir:]

> To say that individual culture must needs grow organically out of the rich soil of a communal is far from saying that it must be forever tied to that culture by the leading strings of its own childhood. Once the individual self has grown strong enough to travel in the path

---

*EDITOR'S NOTE   The concluding portion of Chapter 7, dealing with humor, is intended to illustrate this type of transcendent identity.

---

most clearly illuminated by its own light, it not only can but should discard much of the scaffold by which it has made its ascent.

A genuine cultural relativism can only be built from the categorical imperative of universalism whose highest affirmation is the complementarity of selfhood and otherness. Likewise, a genuine pluralism does not attempt (or need) to clearly segment and classify individuals or groups but welcomes the necessary *impurity* of open-ended identity. For the individual capable of genuine autonomy and interdependence (which presuppose one another), the question is more important than the answer, the method more important than the result, the process more important than the conclusion or the product. Life is always Becoming.

9.5 Progress in Religion
MARK TWAIN

During many ages there were witches. The Bible said so. The Bible commanded that they should not be allowed to live. Therefore, the Church, after doing its duty in but a lazy and indolent way for 800 years, gathered up its halters, thumbscrews, and firebrands, and set about its holy work in earnest. She worked hard at it night and day during nine centuries and imprisoned, tortured, hanged, and burned whole hordes and armies of witches, and washed the Christian world clean with their foul blood.

Then it was discovered that there was no such thing as witches, and never had been. One does not know whether to laugh or to cry. Who discovered that there was no such thing as a witch — the priest, the parson? No, these never discover anything. At Salem, the parson clung pathetically to his witch text after the laity had abandoned it in remorse and tears for the cruelties it had persuaded them to do. The parson wanted more blood, more shame, more brutalities; it was the unconsecrated laity that stayed his hand. . . .

[Again, for over a thousand years] the Roman Church has owned slaves, bought and sold slaves, authorized and encouraged her children to trade in them. Long after some Christian peoples had freed their slaves the Church still held on to hers. If any could know, to absolute certainty, that all this was right, and according to God's will and desire, surely it was she since she was God's specially appointed representative in the earth and sole authorized and infallible expounder of his Bible. There were the texts; there was no mistaking their meaning; she was right, she was doing in all this thing what the Bible had mapped out for her to do. So unassailable was her position that in all the centuries she had no word to say against human slavery. . . . [Then in] England an illegitimate Christian rose against slavery. It is curious that when a Christian rises against a rooted wrong at all, he is usually an illegitimate Christian, member of some despised and bastard sect. . . .

Excerpts from "The Human Condition . . . Bible Teaching and Religious Practice," written originally in 1890 by Mark Twain (Samuel L. Clemens, 1835–1910), and reprinted in *A Pen Warmed-up in Hell: Mark Twain in Protest* (pp 138–143), edited by Frederick Anderson, (Copyright © 1972 by Mark Twain Company. Reprinted by permission of Harper & Row, Publishers, Inc.

Yet now at least, in our immediate day [1888], we hear a Pope saying slave trading is wrong, and see him sending an expedition to Africa to stop it. The text remains; it is the practice that has changed. Why? Because the world has corrected the Bible. The Church never corrects it; and also never fails to drop in at the tail of the procession —and take the credit of the correction. As she will presently do in this instance. . . .

Is it not well worthy of note that of all the multitude of texts through which man has driven his annihilating pen he has never once made the mistake of obliterating a good and useful one? It does certainly seem to suggest that if man continues in the direction of enlightenment, his religious practice may, in the end, attain some semblance of human decency.*

---

*EDITOR'S NOTE   Not only in theology, but in other fields as well, the most innovative and revolutionary ideas quite often come from people with little or no "education" in traditional ways of thought. In his lecture "The Conflict of Science and Society," the science historian C. H. Darlington wrote:

> It is no accident that bacteria were first understood by a canal engineer, that oxygen was first isolated by a Unitarian minister, that the theory of infection was established by a chemist, the theory of heredity by a monastic schoolteacher, and the theory of evolution by a man who was unfitted to be a university instructor in either botany or zoology. . . . We need a Ministry of Disturbance, a regulated source of annoyance; a destroyer of routine; an underminer of complacency.

Read also "An Immoral Morality," by Philip S. Kaufman, O.S.B., *Commonweal* 107: 493–497, September 7, 1980.

9.6   Absolute Truth — Seen in Changing Perspectives
ADIR COHEN (MARTIN BUBER)

Buber sounds the alert against the doctrine of the relativity of truth. This doctrine proclaims that no actual truth exists for man, but that all truths are contingent on the social circumstances from which they derive. Every man is subject to a profusion of external and internal conditioning circumstances, and it is these that determine what he believes to be the truth and what he designates as such. Although Buber does not deny the fact of men's dependence on the conditions of their social class, he argues that men's nature is not identical with this dependence. In a number of respects, the boundaries of human nature extend beyond the limits set by man's conditioning circumstances. There exists in man's soul an element that is original to him and personal, and not merely the consequence of society's influence. This aspect of man's soul sometimes strikes out toward absolute and unconditioned truth. Even at such times, man cannot free himself from his dependency on the conditions that determine his fate. Yet, for all that, a change does occur: Some small particle of independence imbeds itself in the matrix of man's contingent existence.

Brief excerpts from Adir Cohen (University of Haifa, Israel), "The Question of Values and Value Education in the Philosophy of Martin Buber," *Teachers College Record* 80: 743-770, at 707-708, May 1979. (Footnote references are omitted). By permission.
   Read also *The Road of Science and the Ways of God*, by Stanley L. Jaki, Chicago: The University of Chicago Press, 1978.

Buber remonstrates against the alienation of our era from this fundamental fact of our existence. Because of our skepticism concerning the possibility of absolute truth, we impose the principle of utility on the concept of truth, which in turn acquires a relative character. Rather than pursue absolute truth, we bestow the title of truth on whatever serves our own best advantage.

Buber asks whether it is in our power to acquire truth. He does not pretend that the absolute is within one's grasp and there for the taking; but he does believe that the quest for truth and the belief in truth's existence have the effect of producing in man's soul the proper relationship toward truth. This relationship is created by man's breaching the confines of his conditioning, not in order to escape from it — something he can never accomplish — but in order to experience, even in a small way, the condition of noncontingency. The sense of being free from conditioning quickens man's relationship to truth. The soul, in aspiring to truth, takes on authenticity. But whoever believes that all truths are relative and that only what is advantageous is true is likely to alienate truth from himself, and to become himself totally estranged from truth. . . .

Buber alerts us to the dangers of the modern period's pragmatic approach, which brings in its wake the denial of both the value and the reality of the concept of truth, a denial founded on a utilitarian base. He dismisses the attempt — itself nothing more than a delusion — to oppose the hypothesis of man's conditioned status with an axiomatic doctrine upholding man's unconditioned nature. Man must understand the conditioned nature of his thought and, with this understanding for his starting point, he must also bring about the cohesion of the whole of his essential nature that apprehends being. Only in this manner can man forestall the disaster that lies in wait for him. . . .

[The] great danger posed in the modern period [is] the granting of priority to collectivism. This collectivism appropriates to itself the full responsibility the individual ought to assume. The collective takes on the character of an existential first principle to which man is made a corollary and is thus deprived of his personal accountability. In this way an important value is undermined: the value of personal response. In the dialogue between the generations, the multitude cannot take the place of the individual. When such a perversion occurs, truth is exposed to the imminent threat of destruction. As Buber points out, man discovers truth only when he fulfills its claims; human truth entails the responsibility of the individual. In contrast, the collective, which dominates modern times, proclaims the principle of response to group interest — either real or imagined — to be demonstrable and irrefutable truth, against which the individual is powerless either to press the claims of a truth known to himself or to act in the light of his own judgment.

Buber discerns in the appearance of the "man-without-truth" one of the outstanding symptoms of the crisis of our times.

9.7   A New America?

STANLEY E. AHLSTROM

[To better understand contemporary America, we should reexamine the Moral Shock which occurred when the Great Awakening dethroned New England Puritanism nearly two centuries ago.]

Moral shock, the sudden discovery that dry rot has weakened the supporting members of a very comfortable structure of values, is a traumatic experience often followed by religious doubt which then yields, gradually or suddenly, to a new religious and ethical outlook. For a great many Americans the [1968-1978] era was traumatic in just this sense. That is why it may be understood as a Great Awakening even though it was a time of fear and trembling for many Americans. The issues which occasioned all this private and collective consternation were very numerous, and each of them could be subdivided. There were at least five, however, that gained massive public attention, and it is hard to see one as more important than the others.

They can be briefly listed: (1) race and racism, (2) war and imperialism, (3) sex and sexism, (4) exploitation and environmentalism, and (5) government and the misuse of power. Underlying all of these was the fundamental question of Justice, which is the first virtue of any society. . . .

It is an unquestionable fact that the country has in recent years experienced a veritable explosion of new forms of religious organization and expression. . . . [including] evangelical youth movements . . . [which] share many organizational and ideological characteristics of Mr. Moon's much criticized Unification Church. When seen in a full perspective, therefore, the phenomenon of America's new religions becomes so valuable an index of the elements of change in the moral and religious realm that it is worthwhile to attempt a brief summary statement.

1. Extreme diversity of religious belief and of correspondingly distinctive ways of life have from the earliest times been a characteristic feature of the American experience. A growing commitment to libertarian individualism encouraged this tendency even in later centuries even after governmental intervention in the social order had become necessary. Denominational schisms, as well as the founding of sects, cults, and new religions, became prominent aspects of American life.

2. Immigration, migration across the continent, and very diverse forms of rapid social change led to the formation of innumerable large and small subcultures whose life situations and religious traditions varied accordingly. In these myriad contexts charismatic religious leaders could and did attract followings of extremely diverse types.

Brief excerpts from Stanley E. Ahlstrom (Yale University), "Changing Religious Values," *Daedalus* 107: 13–30, Winter 1978. Reprinted by permission of the Academy of Arts and Sciences from *Daedalus*, Winter 1978.

This entire issue of *Daedalus* is devoted to "A New America." Earlier, in his essay, Ahlstrom quotes Jonathan Edwards: "Providence is continually bringing forth things new in the state of the world, very different from what ever was before. . . . And the scheme will not be finished or the design fully accomplished, the great event fully brought to pass, till the end of the world and the last revolution is brought about."

In his article, Stanley E. Ahlstrom characterizes the 1950s as The Placid Era and the 1960s as The Traumatic Era. As for the 1970s, he writes: ". . . amid the shocks and disappointments of the 1970s, the militancy of American dissent waned, but in almost no ways has it led to a rebirth of confidence and hope. . . . [hence] the legacy of the Traumatic Years can be interpreted as at once both momentous and unresolved."

3. The new industrial revolution that followed World War II created still other grounds for religious discontent as older forms of *Gemeinschaft* yielded to more impersonal forms of living together, and these tendencies to alienation accelerated during the 1960s. In the antitechnocratic countercultural ethos that then emerged, neither the moral attitudes nor the traditional theology of the major denominations had much appeal. The religious establishment was apprehended as both conventional and authoritarian.

4. The positive result of mounting dissatisfaction was a widespread and highly variegated turn toward other-minded religious movements according to principles of elective affinity, and usually in ways that if not formally communal were at least responsive to a pervasive desire to share and express a meaningful structure of moral and religious values.

5. Amid the shocks and disappointments of the 1970s the militancy of American dissent waned, but in almost no ways had it lead to a rebirth of confidence or hope. As a result new religions continue to multiply and flourish. American dissent has waned, but there is little or no evidence of a rebirth of confidence, and the future is more uncertain than ever. As a result the new religions continue to subdivide and flourish. As usual their diversity was extreme, ranging from Satanism to disciplined forms of Zen. Most nearly traditional is a noticeable attraction to evangelical groups, which have always encouraged meaningful small-group relationships, and which are themselves in a broad sense countercultural in outlook. By and large, therefore, the new religions tend to exhibit an untraditional tendency: opposition to dogmatism and code morality; a strong disapprobation of the exploitative mentality, pollution of the biosphere, and the wasting of natural resources whether by industry or through the country's endemic gluttony. They tend to feel and express a sense of oneness with the natural world which is conducive to a mystical approach to reality that may verge on pantheism or on the esoteric. A discountenancing of racist and sexist stereotypes and behavior is almost everywhere apparent, as is a strong emphais on warm and authentic personal relationships. When seen as a whole, the new religions in many ways perpetuate the aims and ideals of the older counterculture. They do not, by and large, reinforce the social attitudes engendered by the Puritan ethic. They try to ameliorate the ways in which monolithic institutions and materialistic striving tend to dehumanize the social order. If this analysis is to any considerable degree accurate, therefore, one may say that the new religions in concrete and very intense ways instantiate, or at least suggest, the less intense but nevertheless pervasive and enduring impact of the Traumatic Era on American attitudes and behavior. . . .

If we take a broader view of the years since President John F. Kennedy issued his spirited summons to the nation, the overwhelming fact is that the entire religious realm — moral, spiritual, and attitudinal — has been so fundamentally altered that a negative response to the [question A New America?] is unthinkable. A new and comprehensive agenda of expectations and reform has gradually taken shape. Yet the evaluations and priorities placed on these new goals for the republic are very diverse. For many people, especially those with long memories, John Donne's sense of "all coherence gone" is the dominant reaction. A well-behaved America has passed away, and with it the certitudes that had always shaped the nation's well-being and sense of destiny. For as many others, and especially those who in various ways had supported the movements of protest and reform which made the era memorable, the sense of disorientation is far less deeply felt. For most of them urban decay, high levels of crime, gross inequalities, and malfunctioning institutions are simply constitutive of the American way of life. Rapid social change and shifting mores are the normal conditions of existence. Even among the more thoughtful elements of this latter constituency, however, there is neither exultation nor a feeling of triumph, but rather widespread doubts as to the possibilities for significant institutional change or of any basic shifts of power in the economic order. Thus for this constituency as well as for the other, America has a clouded future. Because such a convergence of views is indeed new for America, the legacy of the Traumatic Years can be interpreted only as at once both momentous and unresolved.

9.8   A Collection of Ingredients for Transition into the '80s
HARLAN CLEVELAND

I will take my text from some unconscious philosophy that came out of the nuclear near-accident at Three Mile Island.

A crisis illuminates the stage of public and international affairs, and often produces revealing comments by which officials and citizens knife through to the heart of a great complexity and make it suddenly clear.

There was the officer in Vietnam who said that we have to destroy this town in order to save it. And there was the technician at Three Mile Island who was asked whether a worker might not be able to fix a stuck valve inside the radioactive plant, and replied: "In theory he can, but in practice he can't." He wasn't trying to be funny, but his words were captured in the New Yorker — and will doubtless be immortalized in Bartlett's Familiar Quotations some day.

In theory we can, but in practice we can't. For a nation of pioneers, of doers, conquerors of a continent and of outer space, this learning has come hard. And as we've learned what we can't do with traditional forms of power, some Americans are talking nonsense about a decline in our power to do anything.

My thesis is the opposite: Our power to affect events is greater than ever — but we have to get our heads on straight about the nature of the events to be affected and the nature of our power to affect them. Both are already in rapid transition.

So let's look at the transition we already are in, from the '70s to the '80s. It comprises, of course, a variety of changes in beliefs, loyalties, fears, aspirations, doctrines and assumptions about personal and national futures. These changes are, I think, broadly consistent with each other. There isn't yet a generally accepted name to characterize the period we are in transition to — for my taste, "post-industrial" is too retrospective a tag for so different and exciting a future, and too economic a name for a period in which the analysis of political, cultural and psychological dynamics will be at least as important as economic analysis to an understanding of what is going on.

The transition, I think, consists mostly of changing concepts of security, changing concepts of growth and changing concepts of equality (or "fairness").

I suggest to you a possibly illuminating exercise. Each of you might independently set down what you think are the most significant elements of the transition we are in — then compare your lists and see if you can collectively produce a truly comprehensive map of the transition.

Here are some examples. I think we are clearly proceeding (not without plenty of friction and conflict):

- From a balance of power based on certainty to a balance of power that depends for its stability on uncertainty.
- From concepts of security as military defense to concepts of security as including oil, environmental risks, nuclear proliferation, population growth, inflation, unsafe streets and Islamic revolutions.
- From the "inner logic" of technological development and the "invisible hand" of the market to social direction-setting for new technological developments and political bargaining as a dominant force in the marketplace.
- From an ethic of quantitative growth (GNP) to an ethic of stability, quality and control of one's own destiny.
- From more children to fewer children per family — with all that this enormous change implies.
- From preoccupation with physical limits to growth to a new emphasis on recycling of nonrenewable resources, on biological resources (because they're renewable), and on information as an expandable resource.

We are also proceeding, it seems:

- From concepts of noblesse oblige, charity and government largesse to concepts of rights and entitlements.
- From the New Deal — government as savior — to perceptions that government is the problem, and effective demands for "limits to government."
- From colonial rule and industrial leadership to a global fairness revolution.
- From local and national technologies to inherently global technologies (for weather observation, military reconnaissance, telecommunications, data processing, remote sensing, orbital industries, etc.) and as a result:
- From concepts of national ownership, sovereignty and citizenship to ideas like the ocean commons, international monitoring of environmental risks and "the common heritage of mankind."

That's only a start. Each of you can make your own list from your own experience and study. But for our present purposes my point is this:

If you chart the direction of these conceptual changes, you find a common characteristic: Our concepts are all widening out to include factors that used to be regarded as "externalities" — the economist's fancy word for subjects that don't fit into a traditional discipline or profession or analytical system, yet seem to be disturbingly relevant all the same. . . .

We applauded a goal of national energy independence when the problem was the management of international energy interdependence. We produced new gadgets and only then inquired about their consequences. We built highways and discovered only later their effect on urban living. . . .

We plunged into the use of nuclear power for electricity without asking the hard questions about the back end of the nuclear fuel-cycle — about safety, about waste, about proliferation. We pursued growth without asking "growth for what?" and "growth for whom?" We were persuaded by narrow-gauge, straight-line extrapolations that we were running out of resources, when we were mostly running out of imagination. . . .

We are coming to realize that whenever we make avoidable trouble for ourselves, Abe Lincoln and Walt Kelly were right in fingering the enemy as us. We — you and I, not merely the other guys — find it seductively comforting to tunnel our vision, focus too sharply on one issue at a time, neglect to ask the questions that illuminate the ways in which, as the study of ecology has now taught us, everything is related to everything else.

9.9   A Potpourri of Humanist and Ecumenist Thinking

Although our intellectual, moral, religious, and cultural traditions go back thousands of years, we in the twentieth century must refashion our traditional beliefs from the viewpoint of our modern post-Reformation, post-Enlightenment, post-Newtonian, post-Darwinian, post-Marxist, post-Freudian, post-Vatican II, post-. . . . world. Since the modern communities are united through political and economic organizations, as well as religious ones, the following statements reflect interpretations of ancient values from modern viewpoints. They may be considered to be both theological and scientific, both religious and secular.

(A)   The search for personal integrity involves the practical will, the rational mind and the aesthetic feelings. We lose integrity when any one of these facets of our nature is over-emphasized so as to exclude the other two. Hence if the religious mystic's "oneness-with-God" becomes an end-in-itself, it may easily degenerate into indiscriminate emotion, a will-o'-the-wisp type of mystery-mongering, destroying moral and intellectual discernment in favor of irresponsibility, irrationalism, and obscurantism.

I cannot accept any definition which identifies mysticism with excited or hysterical emotionalism, with sublimated eroticism, with visions and revelations, with supernatural (dualistically opposed to natural) activities, nor, on the philosophical side, with irrationalism.[1]

---

[1] Adapted from W. R. Inge, *Mysticism in Religion* (University of Chicago Press, 1948), p. 154. In *Christian Mysticism* (London, 1899, New York, 1956, p. 299). W. R. Inge asks us to abandon ". . . the mischievous doctrine that the spiritual eye can see only when the eye of sense is closed." [Read also *Albert Schweitzer: An Anthology*, edited by C.R. Joy, (Boston: Beacon Press, 1947), pp. 225-234.]

(B)   The statement "God exists" means that man is always more than man. It means that wherever people are, something new happens. It means that man is alive because he contains within himself a principle which somehow transcends his present self and summons him to surpass himself through earnest and creative endeavor. Hence the statement "There is a God" does not deal with a being having a supposed existence independently of man. Man may question the being of a planet or make a statement that stars exist. But since God has entered into the very definition of man as man, "belief in God" is nothing more than an assertion of self-confidence, based on historical examples of prophets and saints whose lives provide the Good News which inspires our own lives with Hope and with Meaning.

Belief in God demands the abandonment of idolatry: it means abandonment of egocentrism and ethnocentricism, that is, the forsaking of the all-too-human tendency to make an absolute of the present state of his own self, his own church, his own race or his own culture. Belief in God, therefore, demands that religious leaders, no less than secular leaders, should openly declare that all human life, including that of ecclesiastical institutions, is in need of unremitting reform and of unceasing criticism.

It follows that when religious persons ask "Do Heaven and Hell really exist?" they are not really seeking information about another world. They are simply asking "Is it reasonable for us to hope for social concord and for human community (Heaven) or must we abandon all hope and give way to despair and alienation (Hell)?"[2]

(C)   [A study of the great thinkers of the past should better enable us ". . . to produce that happy blend, thanks to which reason could be harnessed to facts and religion to action."[3]

(D)   Interpreting "God" to signify a cosmic basis for hope, Jurgen Moltmann has summarized the Judeo-Christian tradition as follows:

> Human life must be risked if it would be won. It must expend itself if it would gain firmness and future. . . . The social institutions, roles and functions are means on the way to this self-expending. They have therefore to be shaped creatively by love, in order that men may live together in them more justly, more humanely, more peacefully, and in mutual recognition of their human dignity and freedom. . . . Thus self-expenditure in this world, day-to-day love in hope, becomes possible and becomes human within that horizon of expectation which transcends this world. This world is not the heaven of self-realization, as it was said to be in idealism. This world is not the hell of self-estrangement, as it is said to be in romanticist and existentialist writing. The world is not yet finished, but is understood as engaged in a history. It is therefore the world of possibilities, the world in which we can serve the future, promised truth and righteousness and peace. This is an age of diaspora, of sowing in hope, of self-surrender

---

[2] Freely adapted from Gregory Baum (O.S.P., Professor of Theology at St. Michael's College in the University of Toronto, and editor of *The Humanist*), *Man Becoming: God in Secular Experience* (New York: Herder and Herder, 1970), pp. 100, 178, 185–186, 197, 236–238.

[3] Teilhard de Chardin, *The Phenomenon of Man* (New York: Harper & Row, 1959), p. 210.

and sacrifice, for it is an age which stands within the horizon of a new future. Thus self-expenditure in this world, day-to-day love in hope, becomes possible and becomes human within that horizon of expectation which transcends this world.[4]

(E)   The God of orthodox churches has usually been pictured as one most at home in the past, as relating to the present only through the churches. . . .

Only if we think of God as the power of the future can hope be directed towards him, for it is the power of the future that can contradict the negativities of the present and free man to overcome them. God as the power of the future is not only the power to determine the future of our present, but determined the future of all past times on their way to becoming present. . . .

The futurity of God does not altogether exclude the notion of his eternity; but it transforms it. For God is to be thought of as the future of every past, the future of every present . . . [and as the object of hope which transcends the world and which inspires both personal excellence and social justice.][5]

(F)   O Lord it is easy to dwell with You! So easy to believe in You! When Spirit clouds over and I, crushed, am made dumb, When even the smartest people know not what tomorrow will bring You bestow the clear assurance of being Vigilantly keeping the channels of Goodness unclogged. Surpassing thus the summit of earthly glory I behold the Way, which alone I never could have found Wondrous Way, opposite to despair, Whence myself shall become the reflection of Your world. What need have I to speak what You alone shall reveal to me, and if I find not the time to carry it through, It means You've chosen others for the task.[6]

(G)   Catholicism and Protestantism are both obsolescent phases in the evolution of the Christian religion. . . . [However:] No Christian should be a pessimist, for Christianity is a system of radical optimism. — Bishop William R. Inge (1860-1954)

(H)   . . . to the Christian the Jew is the incomprehensibly obdurate man, who declines to see what has happened; and to the Jew the Christian is the incomprehensibly daring man, who affirms in an unredeemed world that its redemption has been accomplished. This is a gulf which no human power can bridge. But it does not prevent . . . [the two groups from] working together with tolerance and understanding. For the divine on earth is fulfilled not within man but between

[4] Jurgen Moltmann, *Theology of Hope* (London: SCM Press, 1967), pp. 337-338.

[5] Carl E. Brasten, in the magazine *Theology Today* (Princeton Theological Seminary), 24: 208-226, July 1967.

[6] "Prayer," by Alexander I. Solzhenitsyn, translated from the Croatian by Hilda Prpic. Reprinted by permission from *The Christian Science Monitor* (February 15, 1974, p. 1). © 1974 The Christian Science Publishing Society. All rights reserved.
Solzhenitsyn won the Nobel prize in literature in 1970.

man and man, and . . . though it does not have its beginning in the life of individual man, it is consummated only in the life of true community. — Martin Buber in *The Way of Response* (1966), pp. 131, 149, 162. [*Note*: Humanists would interpret such statements to imply that the secular may, in some cases at least, be more sacred than the ecclesiastical.]

(I)   . . . there are infinite other creatures besides man on . . . this earth which no considerate man can think were made only for man, and have no other use. For my part, I cannot believe that all the things in the world were made so for man, [and] that they have no other use. . . . Nature's children all divide her care. —John Ray (1601), Joseph Wood Krutch (1961).

(J)   *Quality of Life* Survival alone is not enough. If life is inhumane, people are not living but merely existing. At some level of minimal subsistence, the desirability of living can legitimately be questioned. If we intend to provide conditions that promote population growth, it is incumbent upon us to insure that the living conditions of those we "invite" to join us are at least adequate. We must . . . look beyond man's physiological needs to his cultural and social needs for living space, recreational space, comforts, and amenities. One does not normally invite guests without taking precautions to see that they are comfortable and well provided for. An alternative, of course, is to cease extending so many "invitations." — Ronald Abler et al (1975)

(K)   [The American] constitutional guarantee of freedom of religion from govern-mental control or support. . . . [is intended] to help create a society in which political and legal values on the one hand and religious values on the other freely interact, so that law will not degenerate into legalism but will serve its fundamen-tal goals of justice, mercy, and good faith, and religion will not degenerate into a private religiosity or pietism but will maintain its social responsibility. — Harold J. Berman, in *Worldview* 22: 46-52, September 1979)

(L)   Year after year we are becoming better equipped to accomplish what we are striving for. But what are we striving for? — Bertrand de Jouvenal

(M)   NOVUS ORDO SECLORUM: A New Order of the Ages — Motto on the United States Great Seal. The motto also appears on $1 bills.

9.10 Justice, Charity — and Ecology
EDITORIAL

The concluding selections of this final chapter raise this question: Are Justice, Charity, and other moral virtues concerned exclusively with *man*; or are they necessarily also concerned with *man and nature*?

This question has a long history. The very first chapter of the Bible contains this sentence: "And God said, Let us make man in our image, after our likeness; and let men have dominion over the fish of the sea, and over the fowl of the air, and over the cattle, and over all the earth, and over every creeping thing that creepeth upon the earth." (Genesis 1:26).

But does "dominion over" mean "exploitation of"? We think not. In today's world, justice calls for fair and charitable treatment of all people on earth. Even more. In our post-Darwinian era, we are coming to realize more and more clearly that the welfare of man is intimately bound up with the welfare of his ecological environment. Ever-increasing human populations demand that we extend justice and charity, not merely to the poor and the downtrodden within our own tribe or nation and not merely to peoples of the Third World. We must extend our concern to other species of plants and animals as well.

Consider a few examples of ecological injustice. In 1776, when the United States became a nation, only about 500 million people lived on earth, and most of the world's land was occupied by wildlife in forests (or plains) that surrounded the farms and cities of man. But today, there are dozens of endangered species whose only hope of survival is to live in zoos — zoos in or near big cities. Also, during the past century, the world's natural timber, gas, oil, silver, copper, and other natural resources have been exploited, and sometimes depleted. Meanwhile, human population continues to increase — in *quantity* if not in *quality*. If the population in 1979 (nearly 4 billion people) had been kept to its 1950 level (about 2.6 billion), every man, woman, and child throughout the world could be enjoying as much food as the upper and middle classes of the wealthy nations now enjoy. A first priority, then, is that the number of mouths to be fed and the number of persons to be clothed and sheltered must be kept within reasonable bounds. A second priority is that large extents of parks, forests, and unpopulated areas must be reserved for wildlife, so there is a reasonable balance between human and nonhuman forms of life. A humane life requires contact with field and stream, and not merely with city pavements.

To recognize that man is an intimate part of "the web of nature" is not to deny that man is near the top of "the great chain of being." Indeed, it is only by the use of his divine gifts of reason and foresight that man can find alternatives to what otherwise will be necessities — famine, disease, wars, starvation. Even as a just king in Plato's ideal society is a steward (agent, manager, provider, trustee), not only for himself but for all the members of his kingdom, so, in our age of ecology, we must learn to think of justice, not merely for the downtrodden and oppressed *peoples* of the world, but also for the other species of animals and plants which perform vital roles in that great web of nature to which we all belong.

In the following selection, observe that the native American Indians agreed to "sell" their lands to the white man only on certain conditions, namely: "The white man must treat the beasts of this land as his brothers. . . . [and must] love this earth as the newborn loves its mother's heartbeat. . . . Care for it as we've cared for it . . . [and] Hold in your mind the memory of the land as it [was] when you [took] it."

9.11 The Challenge of Chief Seattle

. . . The Great Chief in Washington sends word that he wishes to buy our land. How can you buy or sell the sky, the warmth of the land? The idea is strange to us. If we do not own the freshness of the air and the sparkle of the water, how can you buy them?

Every part of this earth is sacred to my people. Every shining pine needle, every sandy shore, every mist in the dark woods, every clearing, and humming insect is holy in the memory and experience of my people. . . .

The great Chief sends word he will reserve us a place so that we can live comfortably to ourselves. He will be our father and we will be his children.

So we will consider your offer to buy our land. But it will not be easy. For this land is sacred to us.

This shining water that moves in the streams and rivers is not just water but the blood of our ancestors. If we sell you land, you must remember that it is sacred, and you must teach your children that it is sacred, and that each ghostly reflection in the clear water of the lakes tells of events and memories in the life of my people. The water's murmur is the voice of my father's father.

The rivers are our brothers, they quench our thirst. The rivers carry our canoes, and feed our children. If we sell you our land, you must remember, and teach your children, that the rivers are our brothers, and yours, and you must henceforth give the rivers the kindness you would give any brother. . . .

The air is precious to the red man, for all things share the same breath — the beast, the tree, the man, they all share the same breath. The white man does not seem to notice the air he breathes. Like a man dying for many days, he is numb to the stench. But if we sell you our land, you must remember that the air is precious to us, that the air shares its spirit with all life it supports. The wind that gave our grandfather his first breath also receives his last sigh. And the wind must also give our children the spirit of life. And if we sell you our land, you must keep it apart and sacred, as a place where even the white man can go to taste the wind that is sweetened by the meadow's flowers.

So we will consider your offer to buy our land. If we decide to accept, I will make one condition: The white man must treat the beasts of this land as his brothers. I have seen a thousand rotting buffalo on the prairie, left by the white man who shot them from a passing train. I am a savage and I do not understand how the smoking iron horse can be more important than the buffalo that we kill only to stay alive.

What is man without the beasts? If all the beasts were gone, men would die from a

Prepared from various sources for the *Montana Outdoors Magazine*, this article was reprinted in *The Minnesota Volunteer* 1: 3-12, November-December, 1976. It is used here by permission of both magazines.

Here is the setting of Chief Seattle's address: In December of 1853 Issac Stevens arrived at Puget Sound (where Seattle is located) as governor of the Washington Territory. He had been commissioned by President Franklin Pierce to persuade the Indians to sell two million acres for $150,000 and then to move off the land. Chief Seattle had wanted the Indians to share this land with the settlers, because sharing had been his way of life. He and his fellow Indians had taught the white settlers how to build lodges of cedar wood and how to cultivate foods native to the region. In gratitude, the settlers named their town for him —Seattle. But now Chief Seattle realized that more bloodshed would surely befall his people if he did not comply with the white man's wishes. This article reconstructs what he said.

great loneliness of spirit. For whatever happens to the beasts, soon happens to man. All things are connected.

You must teach your children that the ground beneath their feet is the ashes of our grandfathers. So that they will respect the land, tell your children that the earth is rich with the lives of our kin. Teach your children what we have taught our children, that the earth is our mother. Whatever befalls the earth befalls the sons of the earth. If men spit upon the ground, they spit upon themselves.

The earth does not belong to man; man belongs to the earth. All things are connected like the blood which unites one family.

Man did not weave the web of life; he is merely a strand in it. Whatever he does to the web, he does to himself. . . .

However, your proposition seems a just one, and I think that my people will accept it and will retire to the reservation you offer them. There we will dwell apart in peace, for the words of the Great White Chief seem to be the voice of Nature, speaking to my people out of the thick darkness that is fast gathering round them like a dense fog floating inward from a midnight sea.

Our children have seen their fathers humbled in defeat. Our warriors have felt shame, and after defeat they turn their days in idleness and contaminate their bodies with sweet foods and strong drink.

It matters little where we pass the remnant of our days. They are not many. The Indian's night promises to be dark. . . . But why should I mourn the passing of my people? Tribes are made of men, nothing more. Men come and go, like the waves of the sea.

Even the white man, whose God walks and talks with him as a friend to friend, cannot be exempt from the common destiny. We may be brothers after all; we shall see. One thing we know, which the white man may one day discover — our God is the same God. You may think now that you own Him as you wish to own our land; but you cannot. He is the God of man, and His compassion is equal for the red man and the white. This earth is precious to Him, and to harm the earth is to heap contempt on its Creator. The whites too shall pass; perhaps sooner than all other tribes. Continue to contaminate your bed, and you will one night suffocate in your own waste. . . .

[My people] love this earth as the newborn loves its mother's heartbeat. So if we sell you our land, love it as we've loved it. Care for it as we've cared for it. Hold in your mind the memory of the land as it is when you take it. And with all your strength, with all your mind, with all your heart, preserve it for your children, and love it . . . as God loves us all.

9.12   A Declaration of Interdependence
HENRY STEELE COMMAGER

When in the course of history the threat of extinction confronts mankind, it is necessary for the people of the United States to declare their interdependence with the people of all nations and to embrace those principles and build those institutions which will enable mankind to survive and civilization to flourish.

Two centuries ago our forefathers brought forth a new nation; now we must join with others to bring forth a new world order. On this historic occasion, it is proper that the American people should reaffirm those principles on which the United States of America was founded, acknowledge the new crises which confront them, accept the new obligations which history imposes upon them, and set forth the causes which impel them to affirm before all peoples their commitment to a Declaration of Interdependence.

We hold these truths to be self-evident: That all men are created equal; that the inequalities and injustices which afflict so much of the human race are the product of history and society, not of God or nature; that people everywhere are entitled to the blessings of life and liberty, peace and security, and the realization of their full potential; that they have an inescapable moral obligation to preserve those rights for posterity; and that to achieve these ends, all the peoples and nations of the globe should acknowledge their interdependence and join together to dedicate their minds and their hearts to the solution of those problems which threaten their survival.

To establish a new world order of compassion, peace, justice, and security, it is essential that mankind free itself from the limitations of national prejudice and acknowledge that the forces that unite it are incomparably deeper than those that divide it — that all people are part of one global community, dependent on one body of resources, bound together by the ties of a common humanity, and associated in a common adventure on the planet Earth.

Let us then join together to vindicate and realize this great truth that mankind is one and, as one, will nobly save or irreparably lose the heritage of thousands of years of civilization. And let us set forth the principles which should animate and inspire us if our civilization is to survive.

We affirm that the resources of the globe are finite, not infinite; that they are the heritage of no one nation or generation, but of all peoples and of posterity; and that our deepest obligation is to transmit to that posterity a planet richer in material bounty, in beauty, and in delight than we found it. Narrow notions of national sovereignty must not be permitted to curtail that obligation.

We affirm that the exploitation of the poor by the rich and of the weak by the strong violates our common humanity and denies to large segments of society the blessings

This statement was prepared for the World Affairs Council in Philadelphia for its 1976-1989 Bicentennial Era programs.

Author of numerous books on American history, and for many years professor at Columbia and at Amherst, Henry Steele Commager was commissioned to formulate this declaration. It appeared in *Today's Education* 65: 86–87, March-April 1976. By permission of the author and NEA.

Read also *On the Creation of a Just World Order: Preferred Worlds for the 1900's*, edited by Saul H. Mendiovitz, New York: The Free Press, 1975.

of life, liberty, and happiness. We recognize a moral obligation to strive for a more prudent and more equitable sharing of the resources of the earth in order to ameliorate poverty, hunger, and disease.

We affirm that the resources of nature are sufficient to nourish and sustain all the present inhabitants of the globe and that there is an obligation on every society to distribute those resources equitably, along with a corollary obligation on every society to assure that its population does not place upon nature a burden heavier than it can bear.

We affirm our responsibility to help create conditions which will make for peace and security and to build more effective machinery for keeping peace among the nations. Because the insensate accumulation of nuclear, chemical, and biological weapons threatens the survival of mankind, we call for the immediate reduction and eventual elimination of these weapons under international supervision. We deplore the reliance on force to settle disputes between nation states and between rival groups within such states.

We affirm that the oceans are the common property of mankind, whose dependence on their incomparable resources of nourishment and strength will, in the next century, become crucial for human survival, and that their exploitation should be so regulated as to serve the interests of the entire globe and of future generations.

We affirm that pollution flows with the waters and flies with the winds; that it recognizes no boundary lines and penetrates all defenses; that it works irreparable damage alike to nature and to mankind — threatening with extinction the life of the seas, the flora and fauna of the earth, and the health of the people in cities and the countryside alike — and that it can be adequately controlled through international cooperation.

We affirm that the exploration and utilization of outer space is a matter equally important to all the nations of the globe and that no nation can be permitted to exploit or develop the potentialities of the planetary system exclusively for its own benefit.

We affirm that the economy of all nations is a seamless web and that no one nation can any longer effectively maintain its processes of production and monetary system without reorganizing the necessity for collaborative regulation by international authorities.

We affirm that, in a civilized society, the institutions of science and the arts are never at war, and we call upon all nations to exempt these institutions from the claims of chauvinistic nationalism and to foster that great community of learning and creativity whose benign function it is to advance civilization and to further the health and happiness of mankind.

We affirm that a world without law is a world without order, and we call upon all nations to strengthen and sustain the United Nations and its specialized agencies and other institutions of world order and to broaden the jurisdiction of the World Court in order that these may preside over a reign of law which will not only end wars but will end as well the mindless violence that terrorizes our society even in times of peace.

We can no longer afford to make little plans, allow ourselves to be the captives of events and forces over which we have no control, or consult our fears rather than our hopes. We call upon the American people, on the threshold of the third century of our national existence, to display once again that boldness, enterprise, magnanimity, and vision which enabled the founders of our Republic to bring forth a new nation and inaugurate a new era in human history. The fate of humanity hangs in the balance. Throughout the globe, hearts and hopes wait upon us. We summon all mankind to unite to meet the great challenge.*

---

*EDITOR'S NOTE   Zbigniew Brzezinski opens his book *Between Two Ages* (1970) with these words:

> The paradox of our time is that humanity is becoming simultaneously more unified and more fragmented. This is the principal thrust of contemporary change. Time and space have become so compressed that global politics manifest a tendency toward larger, more interwoven forms of cooperation, as well as toward the dissolution of established and ideological loyalties. Humanity is becoming more integral and intimate even as the differences in the condition of the separate societies are widening. Under these circumstances, proximity, instead of promoting unity, gives rise to tension prompted by a new sense of global congestion.

A former United States Commissioner of Education put it this way:

> . . . the most urgent task of our democratic society is to invigorate the claims of community while protecting with full vigor the dignity and origins of each individual. — Ernest L. Boyer and Martin Kaplan; "Educating for Survival: A Call for a Core Curriculum," *Change* 9: 22-29, March 1977.

9.13   E Pluribus Unum: A Motto and a Model for World Community
CONCLUDING EDITORIAL

The American Democratic Faith, wrote Ralph Henry Gabriel in 1940, "is a system of checks and balances in the realm of ideas. It asserts the possibility of a balance between liberty and authority, between the self-expression of the free individual and the necessary coercion of the organized group. The democratic faith is, then, in essence, a philosophy of the mean."

The Paradox of Authority is also known as "Plato's paradox" because Plato gave much attention to the question "Who should rule?" (answer: the philosopher-king, the enlightened monarch); but Plato gave little attention to an equally important question, "How may those who rule be restrained?" The paradox is this: If those who rule have complete power, they also have power to censor the speech, writing, and protests of dissident groups. But when such a situation prevails, it is impossible to know whether those who occupy the seats of power are in fact "philosopher-kings" (working for the best interests of all) or whether they have not degenerated into "vicious tyrants" (using power to enhance their selfish interests). If history teaches us anything at all, it surely verifies Lord Acton's maxim that "Power tends to corrupt, and absolute power corrupts absolutely."

The Paradox of Freedom results from the fact that, in any large group of people, there will be some who are immoderate in their desires and overaggressive in their quest for wealth and power. Liberty, if carried to excess, leads to its own destruction; for it then permits the enemies of liberty to gain absolute power, and allows the power-mongers to weaken and to destroy the tolerant. The tolerant by nature tend to be humble and self-effacing. The intolerant tend to be active and aggressive. Hence a society that permits the intolerant and the aggressive to behave without restraint will be allowing such groups to usurp the rights of the less aggressive members of society. Therefore, in order to provide justice for all and to extend its protection to all citizens, the state must actively intervene.

The Method of Democracy. To prevent those in power from becoming tyrannical, democracy guarantees two fundamental liberties. First, the rulers themselves must be subject to replacement according to the changing attitudes of the people who elect them. Second, there must be genuine freedom for attitudes to change by allowing lone thinkers and minority groups to challenge prevailing beliefs. For a democratic society to remain stable, minority groups must never be compelled to feel that they are *fixed and permanent* minorities. Unless all groups have freedom to speak and to organize, majority rule will degenerate into tyranny, and enlightenment will give way to rule by force and prejudice. The whole strength of reason, and of government based on reason, depends on the condition that reason can be set right when it is wrong — that people hear all sides of an issue. Only thus can democracy embody its motto *E pluribus unum* — out of many, one. Only on that basis can any society be called "free."

Our Constitutional System: A Peaceful Way of Maintaining Equity.

All seven editions of *Crucial Issues in Education* rest on the belief — perhaps we should say, rest on the *faith* — that the United States constitutional system provides a framework within which revolutionary changes can occur without serious bloodshed. It is a faith well stated by Chief Justice Charles Evans Hughes on March 4, 1939:

> The most significant fact in connection with this anniversary is that after 150 years, notwithstanding expansion of territory, enormous increase in population and profound economic changes, despite direct attack and subversive influences, there is every indication that the vastly preponderant sentiment of the American people is that our form of government shall be preserved. . . .
>
> If we owe to the wisdom and restraint of the [Founding Constitutional] fathers a system of government which has thus far stood the test [of nearly two centuries of revolutionary change] we all recognize that it is only by wisdom and restraint in our own day that we can make that system last.* If today we find ground for confidence that our institutions which have made for liberty and strength will be maintained, it will not be due to abundance of physical resources or to productive capacity, but because these are at the command of a people who still cherish the principles which underlie our system and because of the general appreciation of what is essentially sound in our government structure. . . .

---

*EDITOR'S NOTE   Here is a 1980 protest against current lack of wisdom and restraint:

> I believe that, in the name of "regulation," something powerful has developed in Washington, almost an invisible government, that is a haphazard, almost ominous development. The regulatory arm of government, whether it be an independent agency or a regulatory division within an agency such as HEW, has few ground rules that govern "regulation." It tends to be an authority without precise restraint and with little appeal mechanism available. — Ernest L. Bower, in *Educational Record* 61: 5-9, Winter 1980. Ernest L. Bower, President of the Carnegie Foundation for the Advancement of Teaching since 1978, was United States Commissioner of Education from 1946 to 1978, and Chancellor of the State University of New York from 1969 to 1976.

These ideas are spelled out in greater detail by Tyll van Geel in *School Review* 85: 584-626, August 1978. (Reread Selection 2.4)

[In] the great enterprise of making democracy workable we are all partners: one member of our body politic cannot say to another — "I have no need of thee." We work in successful cooperation by being true . . . to the spirit which pervades our institutions — exalting the processes of reason, seeking through the very limitations of power the promotion of the wise use of power, and finding the ultimate security of life, liberty, and the pursuit of happiness, and the promise of continued stability and rational progress, in the good sense of the American people.[1]

[1] Address by Chief Justice Charles Evans Hughes at a joint session of the Executive, Legislative, and Judicial Branches of our government commemorating the 150th birthday of our nation. Cited in Merlo J. Pusey, *Charles Evans Hughes* [New York: Macmillan, 1951 (two volumes)]. Vol. 2, pp. 783–784.

9.14   Reason and Humanity: Two Universal Values
CARL BECKER

To have faith in the dignity and worth of the individual man as an end in himself, to believe that it is better to be governed by persuasion than by coercion, to believe that fraternal good will is more worthy than a selfish and contentious spirit, to believe that in the long run all values are inseparable from the love of truth and the disinterested search for it, to believe that knowledge and the power it confers should be used to promote the welfare and happiness of all men rather than to serve the interests of those individuals and classes whom fortune and intelligence endow with temporary advantage — these are the values which are affirmed by the traditional democratic ideology. But they are older and more universal than democracy and do not depend upon it. They have a life of their own apart from any particular social system or type of civilization. They are the values which, since the time of Buddha and Confucius, Solomon and Zoroaster, Plato and Aristotle, Socrates and Jesus, men have commonly employed to measure the advance of the decline of civilization, the values they have celebrated in the saints and sages whom they have agreed to canonize. They are the values that readily lend themselves to rational justification, yet need no justification. No one ever yet found it necessary to justify a humane and friendly act by saying that it was really a form of brutality and oppression; but the resort to coercion in civil government, in war and revolution, in the exploitation of the poor as the liquidation of the rich, has always to be justified by saying that the apparent evil is an indirect means of achieving the greater or the ultimate good. Even the Hitlers and the Stalins, in order to win the support of their own people, [found] it necessary to do lip service to the humane values, thus paying the customary tribute to hypocrisy which virtue exacts from vice.

Whatever the limitations of reason may be, it is folly to renounce it, since it is the only guide we have — the only available means of enlarging the realm of scientific knowledge, the only means of discriminating the social value of the various uses to which such knowledge may be put. Whatever the limitations of reason may be, they are not so great that the civilized man cannot recognize the existence and the necessity of naked force and coercion in an imperfect social world, without attributing to them the creation of those humane and rational values which by their very nature affirm that naked force and coercion are at best necessary evils.

The case for democracy is that it accepts the rational and humane values as ends, and proposes as the means of realizing them the minimum of coercion and the maximum of voluntary assent.*

---

*EDITOR'S NOTE   This enlightenment ideal which Professor Becker reaffirmed in 1940 was eloquently stated by John Stuart Mill in his 1859 essay *On Liberty of Thought and Discussion*. Mill argued as follows:

There is the greatest differences between presuming an opinion to be true, because, with every opportunity for contesting it, it has not been refuted, and assuming its truth for the purpose of not permitting its refutation. Complete liberty of contradicting and disproving our opinion is the very condition which justifies us in assuming its truth for purposes of action; and on no other terms can a being with human faculties have any rational assurance of being right. Opinions which someone seeks to silence:

1. May be true. To deny this is to assume our own infallibility:
2. May contain a portion of truth needed to perfect the accepted (but not wholly sound) position:
3. May stimulate thought, may change prejudices into rationally based beliefs, and may replace formal professions, which are inefficacious for good, with heartfelt convictions.

Whether by Erasmus in the sixteenth century, Locke in the seventeenth, Voltaire in the eighteenth, Mill in the nineteenth, or Becker in the twentieth, the liberal spirit is characterized by an openness of mind, a passion for truth wherever it may lead, and an insistence on the free and unrestricted communication and criticism of ideas and institutions.

Consider also the following 1980 statement by Diana Ravitch:

Politically, we expect schools to teach the superiority of our system of government, not simply because it is ours, but because it is committed to freedom, democracy, and justice. We want children to appreciate the meaning of the Constitution and the Bill of Rights and to comprehend their own rules as citizens in a self-governing society. Children can learn to love the rights and freedoms we hold dear, such as freedom of the press, freedom of religion, freedom of speech, and universal suffrage, only by learning how difficult it has been to secure them over the centuries, and how few are the societies where such rights and freedoms have been enjoyed, either now or in the past. It is not necessary to indoctrinate children in order to teach them the ideals and principles of a free society; they may be taught by debate, by challenge, and by a critical "problems of democracy" approach — the very opposite of indoctrination — because of our belief that these values are so compelling that they can survive critical analysis and prevail in the free market place of ideas. If students learn to value the principles of a free and democratic political system, they will be well prepared both to defend and to criticize, when necessary, the institutions of our society.

Teaching students the rights and responsibilities of citizenship in a free society is one of the most important tasks of the schools. . . ." —Diana Ravitch (Teachers College, Columbia University) "Educational Policies That Frustrate Character Development," *Character: A Periodical About the Public and Private Policies Shaping American Youth*, Vol. 1, No. 7, July 1980 pp. 1-4. (Compare Selection 2.3.)

Consider, finally, the following statement, by Theodore M. Greene in 1954:

Only those teachers are worthy of their calling, or vocation, who have a profound respect not only for truth, in all its inexhaustible breadth and depth, but for the equally unfathomable personalities of their students and of all men everywhere. This respect is, in moments of heightened awareness, so tinged with awe as to be very close to authentic religious reverence.

9.15   Quotations for Further Thought and Discussion

(A) The educated man appreciates both the capabilities and the limitations of the mind in the universal scheme of things. Recognizing his powers, he develops dignity, integrity, and responsibility. Realizing his limitations, he cultivates tolerance, humility and reverence.

The unknowable, the incomprehensible, the insoluble is not merely in the heavens; it is close to us. We experience its effect in our daily lives. Inability to cope with it causes fear, superstition, frustration, suspicion, crime and war. The education of the future, therefore, must deal with man's attitude toward the unknowable as well as his treatment of the knowable. It must put in finer balance reason and faith. It must place in truer perspective the material and the spiritual.

— George W. Gobel (Professor of Law, University of Illinois), cited in *AAUP Bulletin* 42: 256-267, Summer 1956.

(B) More profoundly characteristic of the religious mood than any kind of special knowledge, devotion, or service . . . is a response to the awesome and mysterious in life and the world. . . . [Without such a response] religion seems to me to lose its differentiating quality and to become identical with morality, differing from it, if at all, in emotional tone. In theistic religion and in religious mysticism the response is not so much to the awesome mystery itself as to the Being behind the mystery, even though what this Being is may only be stable in symbols or not at all. In nontheistic religion . . . the response is to the mystery as mystery. The difference between these attitudes is deeply significant, but there is at the same time a relationship between them which justifies the application of the term religious to both. . . .

We need to keep a window open to the uncharted.

A conscious awareness of this mystery does healing work on the inward man. It is the healing work of acknowledged ignorance in the revered presence of that which eludes comprehension — the incomprehensible in each other, in the life we are called upon to live, in the great cosmic setting that reaches from our feet to the infinities.

— Max Carl Otto, "Scientific Humanism," *Antioch Review*, Winter 1943, pp. 530-45 at 541-542, reprinted in *Science and the Moral Life*, by M. C. Otto (New York: New American Library, 1949), p. 165.

(C) [We maintain, in the words of Bertrand Russell, that] education should be guided by "the spirit of reverence" for "something sacred, indefinable, unlimited, something individual and strangely precious, the growing principle of life, an embodied fragment of the dumb striving of the world." . . . Pursuing this life of thinking, the goal of education should be to provide the soil and the freedom required for the growth of this creative impulse: to provide, in other words, a complex and challenging environment that the child can imaginatively explore and, in this way, quicken his intrinsic creative impulse and so enrich his life in ways that may be quite varied and unique. . . . [The] purpose of education, from this point of view, cannot be to control the child's growth to a specific predetermined end, because any such end must be established by arbitrary authoritarian means; rather the purpose of education must be to permit the growing principle of life to take its own individual course, and to facilitate this process by sympathy, encouragement, and challenge, and by developing a rich and differentiated context and environment.

— Noam Chomsky, "Toward a Humanistic Conception of Education" in *Work, Technology, and Education*, edited by Walter Feinberg and Henry Rosemont, Jr. (Urbana: University of Illinois Press, 1975), p. 205.

(D)   Matthew Arnold recognized that "men of culture are the true apostles of equality." In *Culture and Anarchy*, Arnold stated that

> plenty of people will try to indoctrinate the masses with . . . the creed of their own profession or party . . . but culture works differently . . . It seeks to do away with classes; to make the best that has been thought and known in the world current everywhere; to make all men live in an atmosphere of sweetness and light.

However awkward Arnold's language to the modern ear, recognition of those characteristics and dreams that all men share remains the most solid foundations for correcting social inequities.

— John C. Sawhill, in *Harper's* 256: 35-39, February 1979.

(E)   *A Sheaf of Golden Rules*[1]
   (1) *Hinduism*. Men gifted with intelligence and purified souls should always treat others as they themselves wish to be treated.
   (2) *Buddhism*. In five ways should a clansman minister to his friends and familiars: by generosity, courtesy, and benevolence, by treating them as he treats himself, and by being as good as his word.
   (3) *Confucianism*. What you do not want done to yourself, do not do to others.
   (4) *Taoism*. Regard your neighbor's gain as your own gain, and regard your neighbor's loss as your own loss.
   (5) *Tenrikyo Shinto*. Irrespective of their nationality, language, manner, and culture, men should give mutual aid, and enjoy reciprocal, peaceful pleasure, by showing in their conduct that they are brethren.
   (6) *The Hebrew Faith*. Thou shalt love thy neighbor as thyself.
   (7) *Christianity*. All things whatsoever ye would that men should do to you, do ye even to them: for this is the law and the prophets.
   (8) *Islam*. No one of you is a believer until he loves for his brother what he loves for himself.
   (9) *Communism*. From each according to his abilities; to each according to his needs. — J. B. Proudhon, Karl Marx.
   (10) *A Modified Version* (of the golden rule). Do not do unto others as you would that they should do to you. Their tastes may not be the same. — George Bernard Shaw.
   (11) *Native American Indian*. Treat the birds and the beasts as your friends and brothers. Love this earth as the newborn loves its mother's breast.
   (12) *A Contemporary Version* (of the golden rule). We live by the golden rule. The one who has the gold makes the rule.

(F)   Compare also the concluding lines of Shelley's *Prometheus Unbound* (1919):

> To suffer woes which hope thinks infinite,
> To forgive wrongs darker than death or night,
> To defy power which seems omnipotent,
> To love and bear to hope till hope creates
> From its wreck the thing it contemplates.
>   . . . to be
> Good, great and joyous, beautiful and free,
> This is alone life, joy, empire and victory.

[1] The first eight of these rules, together with their original sources, are from "A Sheaf of Golden Rules from Twelve Religions," in R. E. Hoople, R. F. Tyler, and W. P. Tolley (eds.), *Preface to Philosphy: Book of Readings* (New York: Macmillan, 1947), pp. 309–311. (Slightly adapted.)

NAME INDEX

This index lists the names of authors who have been quoted or paraphrased and authors whose books or magazine articles are recommended for supplementary reading. Since nearly all selections in this anthology have been greatly shortened from the original writings, *Crucial Issues in Education* may be viewed as a structured, annotated bibliography of some important writings relevant to today's educational problems.

SUBJECT INDEX

This *Subject Index* should help the reader to recognize the many diverse topics dealt with in this anthology, and to be aware of cross references and related ideas which might otherwise go unnoticed.

Academic excellence,
    need for, 35–40, 50–53, 115–117
    overemphasis on, 40–45, 201–229
    racial and ethnic equality, and, 100–137
    television's challenge to, 4–11
    See also Excellence
Accountability,
    of school administrators, 31–34
    of students, 25–29, 50–53
    See also Measurement
Affirmative action, 105, 112–115
Aggressiveness and altruism, 73–76, 85–97
    See also Self-actualization
Alienation,
    of students, 25–35, 40–65, 171(A)
    of teachers, 62–65
    of workers and unemployed, 187–191
Alternative school programs, 54–56, 122–124
American Indians,
    changing values of, 127–129
    past traditions of, 284–285
    perennial values of, 284–285
    recent history of, 127–128
Americanism, meanings of, 1, 99, 108–111, 124–126, 199
    See also Citizenship; Equality; Fraternity; Liberty; National unity
Art,
    and racial integration, 117–122
    as an aid to creative, critical thinking, 209–211
Assimilation and pluralism, 101–137
Authority,
    and cultural pluralism, 103–105
    and freedom, 66–97
    and religious pluralism, 230–293
    in the classroom, 25–65, 164–170
    of school principals, 31–34, 103–108
    paradox of, 288

Basics,
    and competency, 35–42
    varied meanings of, 17–20, 23, 29–30, 62–63, 214–217, 226–229, 242–264
    why some children fail to master, 38–65, 201–203, 218
Bible, study of in public schools, 244–248
Bilingual education, 129–135
Bureaucracy, dangers of, 31–34, 50, 272–273
Busing, pros and cons on, 112–115

Career education, 106, 173–198,
    and liberal education, 181–182, 260–262
    language as an essential part of, 184–186
    pros and cons on, 176–180
Catechisms for slaves and for workers, 190–191
Catholic teachings, changes in, 241–243, 272–273
Children's minds, 141–144, 260
    See also Context and perspective in thought and language; Language; Myths
Church and state, separation of,
    the American tradition of, 230–248, 279–182
Citizenship,
    definition of, 64, 135
    new dimensions of, 108–111, 133–135, 206–209, 226–229, 231–239, 262–264
Civilization,
    expanding meanings of, 66–97, 108–111, 133–135, 227–229, 262–293
    religious ideals for, 115–117, 264, 279–282, 291–293
    truth as central to, 82–83, 90–97, 226–229, 263–264, 290–291
Classroom management, 25–65, 102–108
Cognition,